Organisational Behaviour

Theory and Practice

G. A. Cole BA MA MIPD MIMgt

Research Fellow,
University of Sussex Institute of Education

Gerald Cole has worked in a wide variety of organisations — large and small, public and private, and voluntary as well as for profit. He has been a lecturer and researcher in management subjects for many years. His other books for DP Publications include Personnel Management: Theory & Practice, Strategic Management and Management Theory and Practice. He is a non-executive director of four small/medium sized companies and is an external examiner for DMS & CMS courses at Middlesex University. He is an active member of the Society of Authors. His current research includes investigating the processes by which people learn at work.

DP Publications Ltd
Aldine Place
London W12 8AW
1995

Acknowledgements

Sutton Coldfield
College of F.E
LIBRARY.

Acc. No.

№ 6 3 2 0 7

Class. No.

658·3

I am grateful to my younger son Giles, for his help with the proof-reading and completion of the index.

Most of the information for the case studies came from the public domain, but the following individuals contributed to my summaries:

Michael Green,
Transitional Space Management Consultants

Annette Hutchinson,
Employee Development Strategy Manager, Royal Mail.

A CIP catalogue record for this book can be obtained from the British Library

ISBN 1 85805 135 5

Copyright G.A. Cole © 1995

All rights reserved

No part of this publication may be reproduced, stored in a retrieval system, or transmitted in any form or by any means, electronic, mechanical, photo-copying, recording, or otherwise, without the prior permission of the copy-right owner except in accordance with the provisions of the Copyright, Designs and Patents Act 1988 or under the terms of a licence issued by The Copyright Licensing Agency Ltd, 90 Tottenham Court Road, London W1P 9HE. Applicants for the copyright owner's permission to reproduce any part of the publication should be addressed to the publisher.

Typeset by:

KAI Typesetters, Nottingham

Printed in Great Britain by:

BPCC, Aylesbury

Contents

Preface

Aim of the book

1. The aim of the book is to provide readers with a clear, concise and comprehensive introduction to the theory and practice of behaviour in organisations. The book is set out in three main parts as follows: 1. Knowledge Base, 2. Workbook, 3. Case-studies. The knowledge base of the subject-area is mapped out in the nineteen chapters which form Part One of the book, which examines the theory and practice of Organisational Behaviour. Part Two is a Workbook Section designed to provide opportunities for active reflection on the knowledge base, and for addressing selected issues of Organisational Behaviour. Part Three is devoted to a selection of short case-studies in Organisational Behaviour, taken from a range of different organisations.

2. The book is aimed particularly at the requirements of BA (Business Studies) courses in Organisational Behaviour, but is also likely be suitable for students studying the topic as an element of a postgraduate course in Management or Business Studies, including the Diploma in Management Studies and the introductory stages of an MBA course. The book should also be useful to those taking the relevant examinations of leading accountancy and other professional courses.

The need

3. Students of a subject like Organisational Behaviour, which draws upon several of the social sciences, are likely to be helped by a textbook that both gives adequate coverage of the subject-matter and maps it out in an accessible manner. A subject map can reduce the rather diffuse geography of Organisational Behaviour into a form that simplifies the terrain and brings key parts of it into much sharper focus. Such a representation enables readers to see both the overall landscape and, more importantly, the relationship between the different key features.

4. The book opens by discussing the concept of Organisational Behaviour and aims to set it in the context of work organisations. Part One develops the principal concept and shows how it is applied in work organisations. Problems and issues arising from attempts to adopt, and adapt, the concept are noted and commented on throughout the text. Behaviour in small and medium-sized enterprises and not-for-profit organisations is considered, as well as in large commercial and public-sector organisations. The idea throughout the book is to facilitate students' efforts to match their reading

to their lecture topics, and to provide lecturers with reference and exercise material to support classroom activity. As befits a book designed to map out the ground of a subject, ample use is made of diagrams to illustrate basic concepts, and thus facilitate learning.

Approach and layout

5.   The book aims to cover all the key features of Organisational Behaviour, and to set out the basis of the subject in a clear, concise and easily-digestible form. Where in-depth treatment of a particular topic may be called for, students are pointed towards relevant texts by leading theorists and researchers in Organisational Behaviour. Ample references to these are provided on a chapter-by-chapter basis, and in the final bibliography. In any case students should, ideally, be reading their professional journals and quality newspapers for further evidence of Organisational Behaviour in practice. Most chapters conclude with a range of questions designed to stimulate thought and discussion about what has just been read.

6.   The subject-matter in Part One has been set out in eighteen chapters, which focus on key aspects of Organisational Behaviour. The chapters are clustered under a number of sub-headings designed to clarify understanding of the subject. The sub-headings are as follows:

   ☐   Introduction — definitions; the theoretical background; the place of Organisational Behaviour in the management of work organisations.

   ☐   Organisational Structuring — organisation structures; the impact of technology; designing effective organisations.

   ☐   Individuals in Organisations — personality and other differences; individuals' perceptions, values and attitudes; motivation, job satisfaction and performance; individual learning in organisations.

   ☐   Groups at Work — group behaviour and communication; decision-making in groups; leadership issues; stress and conflict in organisations; organisation culture.

   ☐   Organisational Change — models of change; Organisational development; human resource management and organisational change.

   ☐   Organisational Behaviour in Context — international aspects of Organisational Behaviour; Organisational Behaviour and strategic management.

7.   Part Two of the book is a workbook devoted to mini-cases, scenarios and exercise questions focusing on important issues of Organisational Behaviour. A lecturers' supplement providing further ideas and comments on selected questions will be supplied as an aid to the staff concerned. The order in which the questions are presented follows the development of the

material in Part One. Compared with the discussion questions set at the end of each chapter, those that make up the Workbook tend to be more application-oriented, ie they are as much concerned with assessing the *consequences* of organisational behaviour as with enabling students to demonstrate their understanding of the underlying theories.

8.   Part Three serves to extend the knowledge base of Part One by recognising that students need to see how organisational behaviour turns out in real situations. To meet this need, a number of case-studies drawn from actual experience have been described. These cover a range of different organisations, thus providing several different contexts for thinking about organisational behaviour — large and small organisations, industrial/ commercial enterprises, public sector organisations, as well as not-for-profit organisations.

9.   A Glossary has been included at the beginning of the book in order to clear a way through the inevitable jargon that surrounds much of the subject-area. It aims to provide a ready checklist of key terms and phrases, expressed in a nutshell, which should be useful to home and overseas readers alike.

Use of the book

10.   Ideally, students should first read and digest the opening chapter of the book in order to begin to get the feel of the subject matter, and to locate it in the general activity called 'management'. Thereafter, they should read those chapters, or clusters, which are appropriate to the topics being covered by their lecturers. The sequencing of the chapters is not unlike that adopted by other books on this subject. However, students are advised to work through their reading in the clusters of relevant chapters that appear under each sub-grouping.

11.   Since different courses have different proportions of time allocated between formal lectures and self-study, students should use their own judgement as to how they should best tackle their reading. The fact that the knowledge base is set out in clusters of relatively short chapters should make it easy to 'pick and mix', as appropriate.

12.   The exercises in Part Two can mostly be handled on an individual basis, but some lend themselves especially to group work. All should provide the basis for encouraging reflection on, and understanding of, Organisational Behaviour. The case-studies in Part Three are linked to one or more appropriate chapters in Part One, but can be read quite independently. The ideal is to achieve a partnership between all three parts of the book, enabling students to follow up their reading and lecture-notes by examining relevant case-studies, and working on key questions and problems.

13. For students who wish to go deeper into a topic, guidance is given on further reading. In any case, all references to theorists and practitioners who have contributed to ideas about Organisational Behaviour are clearly acknowledged and referenced.

Lecturers' Supplement

14. A lecturers' supplement is provided free of charge to lecturers adopting the book as a course text. Application should be made, on departmental headed notepaper, to the publishers.

Readers' Suggestions and Comments

15. Every textbook represents a compromise between sufficient coverage, adequate depth, and overall clarity of presentation, particularly in an eclectic subject such as Organisational Behaviour. Where the balance can be improved, readers' comments will always be welcome.

Gerald Cole

Sussex, England

August 1995

Glossary

This glossary of Organisational Behaviour Terms is intended to provide a brief description of a number of key terms used in Organisational Behaviour. In some cases fuller definitions are given in the relevant chapter.

Added value. Measure of productivity expressed in financial terms and which indicates the effect of the workforce on sales revenue, usually expressed as the total value of sales less the cost of purchases (of goods and services).

Assertiveness. Behaviour in which the individual states his needs and wishes in a way that does not overrule the rights of others to express their needs and wants, and in contrast to *aggressive behaviour*, which ignores or dismisses the rights of others.

Attitude. A predisposition in an individual to make certain kinds of judgements about external events and other people's behaviour, usually based on deeply-held personal values.

Authority. This refers to the formal power to act conferred on an individual to enable him to fulfil his responsibilities. It is usually fairly well-defined in order to limit the powers available to the individual.

Body language. Non-verbal indications of behaviour, usually involving body movements and gestures, sometimes made deliberately but more often sub-consciously.

Bureaucracy. A term used by Max Weber to describe what he called 'rational-legal' authority, in which an individual's power arises from the nature of his position as prescribed by the organisation's rules and procedures. Can be contrasted with:
1) *traditional authority*, in which power arises from customary practices usually based on clear family or tribal connections, and
2) *charismatic authority*, which arises principally from the force of an individual's personality.

Change Agent. An external person, usually a behavioural scientist, who acts as a facilitator or catalyst in the process of change in an organisation, and who provides key analytical skills designed to give the client organisation's members an insight into what is going on in terms of people's reactions to change in themselves, their colleagues and their environment.

Classical Management Theory. A body of theory about managing organisations which claims to provide universal principles on which good practice can be modelled.

Committee. A formally-established group for the purposes of *decision-making*, incorporating explicit roles (eg Chairman, Secretary) and rules of procedure (agenda, minutes, voting).

Competence. Refers to a person's ability to perform a task to an externally-agreed standard, whether set by the organisation or some third party. Competences are derived from key job roles and are usually described in terms of their context (eg a 'range statement') and specified performance criteria.

Competition. A situation in which two or more individuals or groups are seeking to pursue the same or similar goals in the same environment. Sometimes refers to other organisations, especially in the commercial sector, which are aiming at the same or similar markets. In both cases the competing individuals or groups are intending to achieve their goals at the expense of the other (s).

Conflict. A condition that arises when two or more individuals or groups perceive their own interests as being challenged by the other(s), and where strong feelings can be aroused. Conflict can be dealt with in several different ways leading to one of the following outcomes: win-lose, compromise or lose-lose.

Counselling. A skilled activity in which the counsellor helps the 'client' to understand their problems, take responsibility for them and develop ways of overcoming them using their own inner resources.

Culture (Organisation). The essential collection of shared values which provide both explicit and implicit signposts to preferred behaviour in the organisation.

Decision. A commitment to a particular course of action, sometimes taken unilaterally but usually following discussion and negotiation with others.

Deductive learning. Refers to learning in which new ideas or concepts are tested out in practice and conclusions drawn from the results. Sometimes referred to as 'Rule-Eg'.

Empathy. Refers essentially to a person's ability to see a situation from the point of view of another, and letting them know it. It does not imply agreement with the other, but merely non-judgmental acceptance of the latter's viewpoint.

Empowerment. A term used to describe various degrees of delegation in organisations, but usually where there is a genuine attempt to grant increased *authority* and *responsibility* to people at every level.

Environment. Usually refers to the external context in which an organisation operates, including the activities of stakeholders and other external sources of change, but can also be used to refer to internal conditions within an organisation, such as management styles, employee attitudes, technical environment and financial situation. External environments can be stable or dynamic and simple or complex.

Group, formal. A number of people brought together in some fairly well defined roles and inter-relationships by the management of an organisation. Such groups are formally recognised within the organisation, are given appropriate resources, and usually possess a degree of authority.

Group, informal. This is a group which is not formally recognised by the management of an organisation, but which has been formed by a group of employees for their own purposes, and has the power to work against organisational goals as well as to collaborate with them. Informal groups are usually less permanent than formal groups.

Group think. A term used to describe a situation within a group where group norms and group decisions become the exclusive focus of attention, and where individual opinions or disagreements are suppressed.

Hawthorne effect. Term used to describe changes in productivity and motivation arising primarily from the attention given by management to the employees concerned, rather than by any other changes in employment conditions, such as bonuses and hours of work.

Hygiene factor. According to Herzberg, this is an element of work motivation which arises from the environment or context of the individual's job, such as status and incentive payments, in contrast to *Motivators*, which arise from the person's experience of the job, such as achievement and intrinsic job interest. Hygiene factors do not trigger motivated behaviour, but can cause individuals to become de-motivated.

Inductive learning. Learning manifested in the ability to form concepts or make generalisations as a result of observing or experiencing external events. Sometimes referred to as 'Eg-Rule'.

Job. The name given to a particular set of tasks allocated to a particular individual or position, for which the job-holder will be held accountable. The arrangement or revision of tasks allocated to a job is called *job design*.

Job enrichment. Usually refers to the enhancement of a job by the addition of motivating factors, such as job interest and responsibility. Is different in kind from job enlargement, which is essentially the addition of extra tasks to an existing job.

Leadership. A process within groups in which one person, either by virtue of position or personality or both, obtains sufficient commitment of the other members to facilitate the achievement of group goals.

Leadership style. A term used to describe the manner in which a person exercises leadership, especially in relation to their treatment of people and tasks.

Learning. A process by which individuals acquire knowledge, understanding, skills and values, and usually described in terms of demonstrable behaviour (ie evidence of learning). Often described as *deductive learning* or *inductive learning* (see above).

Mechanistic organisations. Refers to organisations which are not only highly-structured but whose processes are seen as serving the structure. Thus the operation of the organisation is seen as a machine process which sustains the balance between the different parts. In this situation people's needs are seen as secondary to the needs of the structure. Contrasts with *organic structures* (see below).

Motivation. The processes, both instinctive and rational, which occur in an individual when seeking to satisfy perceived needs and wants.

Motivators. These are factors arising from a person's experience of a job, such as achievement and intrinsic job interest, and which cause that person to become motivated to put effort into the job. Motivators usually have a positive effect on a person's drive, unlike *hygiene factors* (see above).

Norms. Essentially collective values, usually manifested in the form of (1) explicit rules, laws and codes of practice, and (2) implicit group attitudes or culture.

Organic organisations. Refers to organisations which are designed so as to reflect the dynamism of all the relationships between people, tasks, technology and environment. Organic organisations achieve a degree of flexibility that does not exist in *mechanistic organisations* (see above).

Organisation behaviour. A reference to the study of the way individuals and groups behave at work, including the analysis of the interrelationships between individuals and groups, their interaction with their environments and the conduct of change.

Organisation development. A long-range, or strategic, approach to change involving the whole organisation, or a major part of it, and aimed at improving organisational processes and cultural development as a major contribution to the organisation's mission and goals.

Organisation structure. A term used to describe the intangible network of relationships between jobs, job-holders, roles and organisational groupings by which organisations achieve sufficient differentiation and coordination of human effort to meet their strategic goals.

Perception. Usually refers to a person's distinctive understanding of a situation, which may or may not reflect the objective truth of the situation. Is considerably influenced by such factors as intelligence, awareness of facts, and past experience.

Personality. The unique pattern of attitudes, predispositions and behaviour possessed by an individual. Research has attempted to identify common patterns and thus produce personality types (eg outgoing patterns versus inward-looking behaviours).

Policy. A statement of the manner in which work activities are to be pursued, thus contributing to the development and implementation of a set of dominant values in an organisation (ie its *culture*).

Power. The ability to achieve results through people's acquiescence, whether encouraged by the organisation or not. Can be distinguished from *responsibility* and *authority* (see separate entries).

Psychometric tests. Tests applied to human beings in order to attempt to measure individual performance, usually by comparison with others on the basis of objective and standardised questions. Usually discussed in terms of individual aptitudes, abilities and personality.

Responsibility. This refers to an individual's formal accountability to a superior in the organisation. Unlike tasks it cannot be delegated to another, as it is personal to the job-holder.

Role. Essentially the expectations that the individual and the members of his role-set have about the nature of the job and the way it is to be carried out.

Role-set. All those jobs/roles that directly impinge on the job-holder's own job/role to form a small job/role network in which context the job-holder undertakes his work and plays out his role.

Scientific management. A phrase coined by F.W.Taylor to sum up his analytical and rational methods of measuring work and the subsequent design of work to produce the most efficient way of working in the circumstances.

Socio-technical system. A term used to describe work systems which combine the demands of technology and production requirements with the interpersonal needs of people as individuals and in groups.

Strategy. Essentially a long-range plan for an organisation comprising a statement of mission and goals, company policies and resourcing provisions, which provides the organisation's employees with direction, guidance and support in the conduct of the organisation's affairs.

Stress. Refers to the bodily changes that can take place when the external pressures on an individual reach an intolerable pitch causing weakened job performance and ill-health. The level of stress depends on several factors, especially the individual's personality and perceptions of his ability to cope with the external pressures.

Synergy. A term used to describe the extent to which the deployment of a range of resources produces results in excess of the sum of the resources invested. Often referred to as the '2+2= 5 effect'.

Systems, open. Usually refers to an entity (eg an organisation) which takes in inputs from its environment, processes them by means of human efforts, the application of finance and the use of technology, in order to produce outputs in the form of goods and services. A key feature of an open system is that it interacts with its environment, and thus a crucial aspect of the processing activities is to generate feedback on results.

Theory Z. An expression coined by Ouchi to describe a process of organisation, modelled on Japanese practices, that encourages management to focus on the coordination of people's efforts rather than technological requirements in the pursuit of enhanced productivity.

Work organisation. A group or groups of employees assembled in a structured and relatively permanent way in order to achieve group goals and objectives by a collaborative effort.

Work design. Refers to the analysis and subsequent re-structuring of the activities in which people engage in a work situation. Work design is manifested in the clustering of such activities into jobs, which themselves are designed to achieve change and/or effectiveness in the pursuit of organisational goals.

Part one

The knowledge base of Organisational Behaviour

Introduction

The single chapter (Chapter 1) in this opening section maps out the subject-area of Organisational Behaviour, provides a working definition of a work organisation, and outlines some of the issues linking organisational behaviour with management theory.

1 The scope of organisational behaviour

Introduction

I. The point of this opening chapter is to sketch out the broad scope of Organisational Behaviour, identify a small number of key concepts, and then relate the subject to the world of management and business. Organisational Behaviour is not a homogeneous subject, but the result of a mingling of other disciplines such as psychology, sociology, politics, philosophy and economics. The fact that a subject called Organisational Behaviour exists in Business and Management courses is due to the need of those charged with managing people and systems at work to inform their thinking as they address the underlying social and behavioural issues that confront them.

Organisational behaviour

2. As noted below, organisations are social structures. That is to say they are composed of those highly complex, and frequently unpredictable, beings known as 'humans'. Organisations are often referred to as if they had a life of their own (they are reified), because this makes it easier to describe behaviour within groups. However, organisations, as such, cannot behave independently of the human beings that form them. Nevertheless, a great deal of management time is devoted to encouraging people to believe that the organisation (eg the team, the company, the department) is a separate entity, because that allows managers to develop loyalties, common viewpoints and synergy under the name of 'team-spirit' and 'our culture'. The reality is, however, that an organisation is never exactly the same phenomenon from one moment to the next. This is entirely because it is composed of individuals, each of whose physical, emotional and intellectual states can fluctuate from hour to hour. It is often remarkable, for example, how a team-sport can spotlight the changes in the attitude and performance of a team that is losing a match, but suddenly scores a goal, or captures a wicket, and from then on is transformed into a match-winning combination.

3. What then is 'Organisational Behaviour', if that is not a contradiction in terms? For the purposes of this chapter, the following working definition is proposed:

> *Organisational Behaviour is a term applied to the systematic study of the behaviour of individuals within work groups, including an analysis of the nature of groups, the development of structures between and within groups, and the process of implementing change. The rationale of Organisation Behaviour is to predict and/ or control individual and group behaviour in the pursuit of management goals, which may or may not be shared throughout the organisation.*

This definition indicates that the principal issues addressed by Organisational Behaviour are:

1. individual behaviour and performance at work

2. the nature and working of people in groups

3. the nature of social structures and organisation design at work

4. the processes involved in adapting behaviour to meet changing conditions. These issues are dealt with in the context of work organisations and the goals that have been set for them by their leaders.

4. The subject-matter of Organisational Behaviour is complex. There are several reasons for this. Firstly, there is the eclectic nature of Organisational Behaviour. The fact that it is composed of a blending of various social sciences makes it a useful quarry from which practising managers can extract much relevant information and guidance. However, that also makes it less easy to describe the core of a subject, whose principal components are made up of a wide range of other topics of study, including the following:

Psychology	*Sociology*	*Politics*	*Philosophy*	*Economics*
* personality studies	* study of groups	* power	* ideologies	* use of
* motivation	* organisation structures		* views about	resources
* perception	* social structures	* authority	the nature of	* scarcity
* individual needs	* gender issues	* leadership	mankind	* costs
* learning	* culture	* conflict	* competition	
* stress	* systems theory	* cooperation		
* individual decision-making	* organisational change			

5. Secondly, there is the problem of defining what is an 'organisation'. For, as Morgan (1986)[1] states in his illuminating critique of organisations as metaphors,

' ...organisations are complex and paradoxical phenomena that can be understood in many ways. Many of our taken-for-granted ideas about organisations are metaphorical.....For example, we frequently talk about organisations as if they were machines....'.

It is precisely because the concept of 'organisation' is so difficult to understand that we prefer to describe organisations variously as machines, organisms, networks, cultures and similar metaphors. As will be seen, as the reader progresses through the book, all these components, and more, will be addressed in the context of work organisations. Having just provided a working definition of Organisational Behaviour, it would make sense to address the question of what is an 'organisation'?

Organisation defined

6. It is important to attempt some working definition of 'an organisation', so that we have a basic concept on which to base any discussion of 'Organisational Behaviour'. Whatever an 'organisation' is, it is certainly a means to an end rather than an end in itself. As mentioned above (para 2) an organisation is always to some extent in a state of flux due to the ever-changing dynamics of individuals and groups. Nevertheless, when a group of people come together in some common enterprise they organise themselves, whether implicity or explicitly, to achieve the reason or purpose that has brought them together. It is likely that the latter is an enterprise that cannot be undertaken satisfactorily by an individual acting alone. The most commonly experienced forms of organisation known to us will usually include the following:

Family groups	Sports teams	Schools
Club committees	Work groups	Churches

We might also refer to animal organisations such as ant colonies, wolf-packs and bee-hives, as well as acknowledging the organisation evident in the physical make-up of all forms of life, including the human body.

7. Where does all this us lead in terms of reaching a working definition? We could just restrict ourselves to a very basic definition of organisations as follows:

> *An organisation exists when two or more persons agree to collaborate over a period of time in order to achieve certain common goals.*

Such a basic definition encompasses practically any level of social unit from the nuclear family upwards. It does, however, exclude the use of the word 'organisation' as applied to physical organisms, such as the human body, where the term is used to describe the physical layout or mechanics of the entity. Thus the kind of organisation which is the subject of this book is specifically concerned with *social* units, and the *human* behaviour and devices drawn up by people from time to time to enable their activities to be coordinated and measured.

8. However, in the world of business and management we are concerned with work organisations, where people are paid for their contribution to the organisation's activities, and are expected to conform to a range of rules and other performance standards. Organisations in these circumstances are usually structured in a formal way, which both recognises individual responsibilities and yet circumscribes them at the same time. The more junior the position held in the organisation, the more restricted is the scope for decision-making. More senior positions are allocated greater freedom of discretion. This difference of treatment between higher-level and lower-level job-holders points up one of the key differences in approaches to organisation theory. There are theories that insist that people must be controlled and 'organised' if work organisations are to achieve their objectives efficiently; there are other theories, which suggest that individuals perform better if allowed freedom and responsibility, and therefore should be subject to fewer controls. These contrasting theories will be examined in subsequent chapters (see especially Chapters 2 and 7).

9. Clearly there is an underlying logic at work in 'an organisation', be it implicit or more-or-less conscious and rational. It also seems that organisational forms (pairs, trios, teams, head offices and world-wide operations etc) are the result of perceived needs on the part of the members of groups and their leaders. There is also a strong tendency for organisations to develop a *structure* as a means of allocating tasks and responsibilities. In work organisations, in particular, the senior management are usually charged with designing and/or adapting the organisation structure to meet changing requirements. Thus it is acknowledged that the life and working of an organisation will be influenced by changes in both the internal environment (eg by the introduction of new technology) and the external environment (eg by changing tastes and fashions among consumers). As work organisations mature over time, they develop particular patterns of behaviour, or 'house-styles'. These patterns have been the focus of much study by researchers, and have come to be called the 'culture' of organisations. In the 1980's and 90's culture has been seen as of critical importance to firms wishing to gain competitive advantage and 'success' in their marketplace (eg see Goldsmith & Clutterbuck (1984)[2]. Key aspects of culture are discussed in Chapter 13.

10. It is now possible to propose a somewhat fuller definition of an organisation, in the context of work, as follows:

> *A work organisation consists of a group (large or small) or groups of people who collaborate in a structured and relatively permanent way in order to achieve one or*

more goals which they share in common, and which they could not achieve by acting on their own. Such an organisation is structured in a manner which formally recognises, and places, the tasks and roles that individuals are expected to fulfil. The operation of work organisations implies a considerable degree of control over individual members, especially those most junior in the task structure. The predominant values and standards of the members of an organisation develop over time to form an organisation culture, which is a preferred way of doing things. The particular form and culture adopted by an organisation is considerably affected by technological and environmental factors.

11. The above definition will be used as a platform for much of what follows in the book. It is intended as a guide to the underlying concept of 'organisation' that Organisational Behaviour employs, implicitly and explicitly, in its dominant theories. Later it will be possible to revisit this working definition in the light of the content of later chapters. By way of comparison at this stage, Pugh's (1990)[3] definition of what he calls 'Organisation Theory' can usefully be recalled. His rather matter-of-fact definition is set out as follows:

> '.....organisation theory can be defined as the study of the structure, functioning and performance of organisations, and the behaviour of groups and individuals within them.'

In introducing his very useful set of selected readings on Organisational Theory, Pugh is covering the ground we refer to here as Organisational Behaviour, and he too emphasises the eclectic nature of the subject.

Organisational behaviour and management theory

12. In addition to the disciplines referred to in paragraphs 1 & 4 above, the study of Organisational Behaviour also encompasses what might be called Management Theory. This is a loosely-knit body of knowledge about the behaviour of people in work organisations, which aims, in particular, to explain behaviour in terms of the achievement of work goals. Management Theory is especially concerned with issues of goal-setting, resource-deployment, employee motivation, team-work, leadership, control and coordination, and performance measurement. Like Organisational Behaviour, it is an eclectic subject, which draws on the social sciences for most of its material. As a field of study in its own right, Management Theory has developed over the course of the last hundred years. The stimulus has been provided mainly by the onset of mass production in industry, the development of large-scale organisations serving economic ends, and the phenomenon of business competition. Interest in management has also been stimulated by the pressures for greater efficiency and productivity in the public as well as the private sector. Over the years, the subject of management has been approached from a number of different perspec-

tives, each identifying problematic issues and, usually, proposing a range of possible solutions.

13. Today it is possible to allocate the principal exponents of these perspectives into a number of groupings as follows:

a. Classical theorists

Perspective	Typical Issues	Exponents	Dates
'Scientific', ie rational design and operation of organisations	Structure of organisations Division of labour Authority levels Spans of control 'Scientific' management	Henri Fayol F.W.Taylor L.F.Urwick Max Weber	1880's to 1940's

b. Human Relations theorists

Perspective	Typical Issues	Exponents	Dates
'Social', ie attention to people's social needs at work	Group identity Workers as members of a group Importance of informal groups	Elton Mayo Roethlisbeger & Dickson	1927-36

c. Social Psychological School

Perspective	Typical Issues	Exponents	Dates
Individual needs and motivation Individual needs	Acknowledgement of individual contribution F.Herzberg Personal motivators Self-actualisation Achievement Individual independence Supportive relationships	Abraham Maslow Douglas McGregor R. Likert C. Argyris D. McClelland	1950's 1960's

d. Leadership theorists

Perspective	Typical Issues	Exponents	Dates
Leadership qualities and style	Nature of the qualities Leadership styles	D. McGregor Tannenbaum/ Schmidt C.Argyris Blake/ Mouton	1950's- 1960's
	Situational/ functional aspects of leadership Contingency approach	F.E Fiedler Victor Vroom John Adair W.Reddin	1960's - 1970's

e. Systems theorists

Perspective	Typical Issues	Exponents	Dates
People in systems (social and technical)	Link between social needs and technical requirements Organismic nature of groups	Trist/ Emery Burns/Stalker	1950's - 1960's

f. Contingency theorists

Perspective	Typical Issues	Exponents	Dates
Structure/ design depends on situation	No 'best' structure Production environment affects structure	Joan Woodward	1950's
	External environment affects choice	Lawrence & Lorsch	1960's
	Organisational size, history etc affects structure	Pugh et al	1960's
	Contingency factors including power affect structure	Mintzberg	1970s-1980's

In addition to the above, which have been well-researched and written-up, there is a more recent group of researchers whose focus has been on successful, or 'excellent', businesses. Here the emphasis is on trying to establish which are the key ingredients of successful firms in the highly competitive private sector. These I have called the 'Quality Management' theorists, since their findings suggest that successful management is primarily founded on (a) meeting customers' needs for a number of key aspects of product and service, which together make up their notion of 'quality', and (b) providing good value for the customer (see Cole,1994)[4.]

g. Quality management theorists

Perspective	Typical Issues	Exponents	Dates
Providing customer with quality and value	Nature of 'quality' Total quality approach Nature of 'value' Price versus quality	W. Edwards Deming J. Juran M. E. Porter	1970's - 1980's

14. The concepts and issues just referred to can be compared with the components of Organisational Behaviour outlined in paragraph 4 above, and not surprisingly there is a great deal of congruence between them. The difference in emphasis between Organisational Behaviour and Management Theory is principally that the former is concerned with examining the behaviour of people at all levels in groups, whilst the latter is more focused on the control of people's behaviour by their managers in the pursuit of organisational goals. Since, for Business Studies students, the subject of Organisational Behaviour is intended to shed light on human behaviour in

work situations, the overlap between that subject and wider Business and Management issues is entirely beneficial and reinforcing.

The structure of the remaining chapters in this book

15. This opening chapter has set out some of the important general issues relating to Organisational behaviour, its key components, and their relationship to general Management Theory. Now the logic behind the rest of this book can be explained as follows:

    a. organisations are composed of, and designed for, people

    b. work organisations, in particular, are designed around social structures of one kind or another

    c. these social structures are designed to facilitate the achievement of common goals (the provision of goods and services)

    d. structures are designed around tasks (responsibilities), physical and technological factors, individual needs and skills, and the overall value-system, or culture, of the groups concerned

    e. leadership is a vital issue in groups and organisational structures

    f. organisations do not exist in a vacuum, but are responsive to, and impact on, their external environment

    g. organisations are subject to changing conditions, both internal and external

    h. the behaviour of people in organisations is a vital factor in strategic management.

16. The next three chapters examine aspects of organisational design. These provide a background picture of the organisation *structures* within which people have to work. The following four chapters deal with the nature and role of *individuals* within organisations. Then Chapters 9 to 13 examine various aspects of *group behaviour* at work, including *decision-making and leadership* issues as well as the phenomenon of organisation *culture*. Chapters 14-16 consider the problem of *organisational change*, Chapter 17 examines issues of Work Design, and the final two chapters place the issues of Organisational Behaviour into a wider *international and strategic context*.

17. The Workbook (Part Two) is intended to be utilised as readers work through the various chapters. In addition to the general discussion questions at the end of each chapter in Part One, there are numerous additional questions, scenarios and exercises on a chapter-by-chapter basis in the Workbook section. Some of the additional items are supplied with outline answers or further material for bona fide lecturers only.

18. The final part of the book — Part Three contains a number of short case-studies relevant to various aspects of Organisational Behaviour. The cases are drawn from real situations in real organisations.

References

1. Morgan, G. (1986), *Images of Organisation*, Sage.
2. Goldsmith, W. & Clutterbuck, D. (1984), *The Winning Streak*, Penguin Books
3. Pugh, D.S. (ed) (1990), *Organisation Theory – Selected Readings (3rd edn)*, Penguin
4. Cole, G.A. (1994) *Strategic Management – Theory and Practice*, D P Publications

Questions for reflection/discussion

1. What are the main organisational issues addressed by the subject of Organisational Behaviour?

2. How far is it possible to argue that an organisation is an entity in its own right? What does your answer tell you about the nature of 'organisations'?

3. To what extent are there differences in subject-matter between Organisational Behaviour and Management Theory? What particular topics or issues distinguish them?

Organisational structuring

This section contains three chapters that examine key aspects of organisation structures. Chapter 2 looks at some basic issues in organisation structuring, including references to the useful work of Henry Mintzberg, and describes the ideas of important contributors to 'classical organisation structure', 'scientific management' and bureaucracy. Chapter 3 considers a number of issues in contingency approaches to structuring, provides examples of a range of common structures to be found in present-day organisations, outlines some of the main characteristics of organisations as open systems and reviews the effect of the external environment on organisational structures. Chapter 4 moves away from a consideration of the structural and functional aspects of organisations to examine the human aspects of organisations starting with a review of the famous Hawthorne Experiments and briefly touching on aspects of motivation, job satisfaction and management style at work.

2 Organisational structures I – basic issues and classical responses

Introduction

1. The mechanics of how people organise themselves when in groups has been a topic of great interest to theorists and practitioners alike. The theorists can be broadly placed in two groups — one group approaching the study of organisations from a sociological viewpoint (eg Weber, Morgan), and the other taking a managerial perspective (eg Mintzberg, Pugh, Handy). Our interest here is more in the managerial and business perspective, and this bias will be evident in what follows in the next three chapters.

2. The structures developed for work organisations, their nature, and the reasons why they are, or should be, adapted to increase their effectiveness have a considerable bearing on the subject of Organisational Behaviour. This chapter looks at such structures, considers the issues they raise for the management of organisations (ie people in groups), and summarises the most important models of organisation that have been put forward by theorists and practitioners.

3. What is an organisation structure? Mintzberg (1979)[1] puts it as follows:

   ' The structure of an organisation can be defined simply as the sum total of the ways in which it divides its labour into distinct tasks and then achieves coordination between them.'

Although Mintzberg refers to the organisation as 'it', he is describing structure in organic terms. The fact is that we tend to talk about organisation structures as if we could actually see them, and draw up organisation charts to prove to ourselves that a structure of a particular design exists. However, what we are doing, in effect, when referring to such charts is simplifying what is, in reality, a highly complex set of interrelationships between tasks, responsibilities, authority levels and individual job-

holders. For our purposes here we can adopt the following working definition of organisation structure:

> *An organisation structure is an intangible web of relationships between
> people, their shared purposes and the tasks they set themselves to achieve
> those purposes. The prime purpose of structure is to achieve an effective
> balance between the division of tasks and responsibilities on the one hand,
> and the need to coordinate individuals' efforts and roles on the other. The
> understanding that members of an organisation acquire about their own
> 'structure' may be as much based on unwritten evidence and informal
> arrangements as on any formal statements of rules, procedures and role
> descriptions.*

As will be seen shortly, there are many organisations (especially large
ones) that go to great lengths to prescribe their organisation structures.
There are countless others that have informal arrangements, where the
sense of structure is tacit and flexible. And, it is important to note, most
work organisations embrace a range of structures within their boundaries.

4. What is the purpose of an organisation structure, whether explicit and
formal or tacit and sensed? At the very least an organisation structure is
acknowledging a group's need to allocate tasks and responsibilities
between the members; it may also identify and clarify particular roles and
levels of responsibility; secondly, it is a recognition of the need to coordinate activities and roles once they have been allocated; it is also an attempt
to facilitate and regulate (a) the flow of information in the group and (b)
the decision-making processes; and, finally, it is likely to serve in some
measure as a means of resolving differences or problems between
members.

Fundamental issues of structure in organisations

5. As just mentioned in the previous paragraph, organisation structures are
brought about in order to (a) allocate work and authority on the one hand,
and (b) to coordinate and control activities on the other. They may also be
designed in response to other pressures, such as changing commercial,
social and labour environments, and the need to incorporate new technology (see next chapter). The allocation of work and authority is an aspect
of the division of labour, or the differentiation of work activities. This calls
for a breakdown of tasks and responsibilities, ie an essentially *disintegrating*
function. The coordination of activities and the linking of authority
centres, by comparison, is an essentially *integrating* function. Thus every
structure represents an attempt to deal with two conflicting forces of disintegration and integration. What this structure of relationships (see para 3
above) aims to provide is a framework that can contain the pressures
exerted by these two opposing forces. As will be seen later, some groups
prefer to work with clearly-defined boundaries, which emphasise differentiation and provide the security of a rigid structure of relationships. Others

prefer to organise themselves along more tacit lines, with flexible relationship boundaries between tasks, job-holders and the exercise of authority. Mintzberg (1979[1],1983)[2], by comparison, treads something of a middle path in his vision of the five basic parts of organisations, which link together to form a kind of semi-organic structure (see Fig. 2.1).

6.   Mintzberg's ideas, which will be referred to again later, are based on the concept of an organisation in five segments — a *strategic apex* comprising the chief executive and directors; then, proceeding down the operational line, a *'middle line'* of operational management, followed by the *'operating core'* of those directly involved in supplying the firm's goods and services; on either side of the operational line (traditionally called 'the line' in classical thinking)) are (i) the *'technostructure'* comprising functional specialists and advisors, and (ii) the *'support staff'*, who provide corporate services (and who in classical terms would be seen as 'staff' employees).

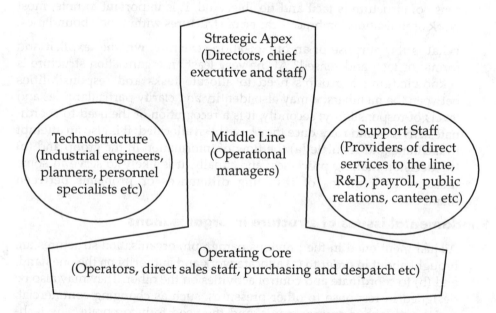

Figure 2.1.   *The basic parts of organisations - adapted from Mintzberg (1979)*

7.   Given the underlying tension that exists in every organisation between the forces of disintegration and those of integration, what are the fundamental issues that have to be faced by those designing, or re-designing, an organisation structure? The most important issues are shown in the following Table (Figure 2.2), which sets them out in summarised form. Basically, the issues have to be addressed in terms of the principal alternatives that are available to deal with them. In reviewing the alternatives, the sort of questions that might arise include the following:

1. How far do our operations require a high or low degree of task differentiation?

2. To what extent do we (the senior management) want to keep tight control?

3. Do we see the organisation structure primarily in mechanistic or organic terms?

4. Should authority (eg to commit resources) be reserved to the centre or devolved?

5. To what extent should jobs and tasks be closely defined and prescribed?

6. As a general rule, how many people should one manager or supervisor be in charge of at any one time?

7. How best can we deal with communication flows and decision processes *across* the organisation?

8. What factors in our external environment have to be considered?

8. Such questions have to be asked against the background of the organisation's internal and external environments. Therefore contextual matters such as the complexity of operations, the state of the technology currently employed, the employee recruitment and training situation, and the degree of stability, or turbulence, in the external environment all have to be taken into account. The prime issues to be addressed together with their principal alternatives are as in Fig.2.2.

Although the above alternatives are expressed in polar terms, there are clearly any number of choices along each scale, which should be seen as a continuum rather than as a stark choice between extremes. In tackling the above issues, a number of key internal variables need to be taken into consideration, as well as the external environment. These are discussed in the next few paragraphs.

Issue	Options/ Alternative Structural Forms	
1 Specialisation/ Differentiation	High requirement	Low requirement
2 Coordination/ Integration	Tight control/ closely-knit	Loose control/ loosely-knit
3 General approach	Highly-prescriptive/ 'mechanistic'	Flexible/ 'organic'
4 Allocation of authority	Widely dispersed/ decentralised	Centralised
5 Standardisation of work/ tasks	Tightly specified	Loosely specified
6 Formalisation (of roles)	Prescriptive/ detailed	Discretionary/ flexible
7 Authority levels/ hierarchy	Many levels/ Tall structure	Few levels/ Flat structure
8 Unit size	Large	Small
9 Span of control	Large numbers supervised directly Wide structure	Small numbers supervised directly Narrow structure
10 Locus of decision-making	Head office/ centralised	Operating Units/ decentralised

Figure 2.2   *Fundamental Issues of Organisation Structure*

Major variables in organisation structures

9.   In establishing a structure to facilitate their activities (ie responding to the issues raised above), the members of an organisation will be confronted by, and seek to resolve, the often conflicting demands between a number of important variables. These basically are as follows :

  1   **Purpose/ Goals** (ie the fundamental aims and goals of the group)

  2   **People** (ie those who make up the organisation)

  3   **Tasks** (ie those basic activities that are required to achieve organisational aims and goals)

  4   **Technology** (ie the technical aspects of the internal environment)

  5   **External Environment** (ie the external market, technological and social conditions affecting the organisation's activities)

In diagrammatic form these key variables can be set out as follows (Fig. 2.3):

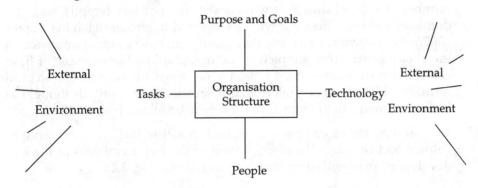

Figure 2.3   *Major variables in establishing organisation structure - I*

10.   As when undertaking any enterprise, the designing of a suitable structure for a group must begin with some idea of what the organisation is there for, and where it intends to go. In other words, the *prime purpose* or raison d'etre of a group of people plays a key role in enabling the members to decide what kind of structure they need. In making this decision the group must usually take account of their *external environment,* ie the market or client groups they are intending to reach, the technological, economic, legal and political background, and the nature of that environment in terms of change or stability. The next step is likely to be to identify the *key tasks* that must be accomplished if the group is to succeed in its purpose. This leads on to a consideration of the *skills* and *talents* of the existing members and the identification of any gaps in their portfolio of skills and know-how, which may be filled by the employment of newcomers or by training the present group. Lastly, the question of *technology* will have to be addressed. What production systems are already in operation, or planned? What equipment will be necessary? How well can existing staff cope with new technology? Each of these variables is affected to a lesser or greater extent by its companions, and in practice the thinking processes involved in designing a structure would not be nearly so tidy as the diagram suggests. Nevertheless, the five variables identified will have to be juggled at one time or another if an effective structure is to emerge. Given the dynamic nature of 'organisations', it is always likely that there will be pressures to adapt the structure in one or more parts of the organisation, if not overall. Thus structuring and re-structuring is a continual process in the life of many work organisations.

11.   There is one other important variable, which may now be added to our list — organisational values, or what is commonly called *'culture'.* Whilst, of course the values and attitudes of the founders of an organisation will play a part in the way that organisation is structured, it is only as all the

members of an organisation contribute to the value-system that a more rooted culture emerges. In fact, as organisations grow, they may develop a number of sub-cultures that will coexist more or less happily with the dominant culture. This topic will be examined in greater detail in Chapter 13. For the present we can note that culture can have a strong influence on the choice of structure adopted by an organisation. For example, if tight control over decision-making is seen to be important, then an hierarchical formation is likely to be preferred. If delegation of authority is thought to be crucial, then a flatter structure is likely to be selected.

12. We can now revise our basic structural model to include a reference to culture, and complete the identification of the major variables at work in developing an organisation structure, as follows (Fig. 2.4):

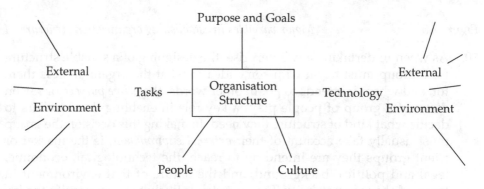

Figure 2.4   *Major Variables in Establishing Organisation Structure - II*

In using the above model, it is important to bear in mind that it can only offer a simplification of the nature of the processes involved in creating an organisation structure. It cannot, for example, indicate the weight that each factor might carry in any one situation, nor can it illustrate the 'chemistry' involved in the interaction of one factor with the others. What it does show is the basic factors involved, and this is important because it enables us to analyse the concepts of organisation, and organisation structure, as a step towards understanding what they signify. Finally, it must be pointed out that any emergent structure that develops will itself exert some influence on the other factors in the model. Thus the whole process of organisational interaction is a dynamic process, in which change and adaptation in one part of the model will have a knock-on effect somewhere else in a more-or-less restless cycle of change.

Basic organisational types

13. Given that all organisations have some degree of structure, the variations between them boil down to their relative complexity/ simplicity, or, as Morgan (1986)[3] would prefer to put it, it depends on the kind of metaphor

we have in mind. His fascinating description of images of organisation encompasses the following different metaphors (ie where an organisation is described in terms of something else). Organisations, according to Morgan, can be seen as:

> **Machines** — the mechanistic or classical view
>
> **Organisms** — the organic view
>
> **Brains** — the cybernetic view
>
> **Cultures** — a product of their dominant values
>
> **Political Systems** — concerned with the distribution of power
>
> **Psychic Prisons** — sources of stress for individuals
>
> **Flux and Transformation** — constantly changing organisms
>
> **Instruments of Domination** — a means of exerting power, however legitimate

Morgan takes the view that whilst our use of metaphors enables us to manage our thinking about organisations, it does so in a way that is too restrictive. Once we have selected our metaphor we tend to see organisations only in terms of that particular metaphor. His solution is to think about organisations in a broader way, which he calls 'imaginization' or the ability to symbolise the links between images and action.

14. Of the various metaphors identified by Morgan, the first — the mechanistic view — has held sway for many years. The spread of bureaucracy (see below) as the most widely-practised form of administrative organisation is a major example. The Classical theorists of management firmly believed that not only was structure the most important variable in organisations, but that structures were capable of being devised rationally and should be implemented as if they were machines. Thus organisations were seen in terms of (a) the efficiency of the linking of their various parts, and of (b) their predictability as phenomena to be managed. As Morgan puts it

> 'The whole thrust of classical management theory and its modern application is to suggest that organisations can or should be rational systems that operate in as efficient a manner as possible.'

All this is a far cry from the viewpoint that expresses the organisation in terms of a set of inter-relationships (as in paragraph 3 above).

15. It was not for nothing, therefore, that several of the earliest classical theorists (eg FW Taylor, the Gilbreths and Henry Gantt) earned the name of 'scientific managers', for their promotion of efficiency in job and work design. Others (eg Henri Fayol and LF Urwick) concentrated on the effi-

ciency of management based on classical 'principles'. At about the same time that the classical management theorists were promoting their ideas, a German sociologist, Max Weber, was studying authority systems in organisations and concluding that authority deriving from the office of the job-holder was a key reason for the acceptance of authority in many organisations. He gave this form of rational-legal authority the name 'bureaucracy'. What were the principal ideas and findings of these classical theorists? We turn first to the classical management theorists Fayol and Urwick, as examples of efforts to introduce rationality and efficiency into the management of organisations.

Classical theorists — the search for universal principles

16. The classical theorists were practising managers who developed theories about the management of people in organisations based on their own experience of work. Their principal concerns were with such concepts as the division of labour, span of control, hierarchy of authority, and efficiency through work design. Their ultimate aim was to develop a set of universal principles of management, or organisation, that would apply to an organisation regardless of context. The greatest pioneers of such theories were the American engineer and industrialist, F.W.Taylor (1856-1915), whose contribution will be considered shortly, and the Frenchman, Henri Fayol, mining engineer and entrepreneur (1841-1925). They were followed by such names as Frank and Lilian Gilbreth, Henry Gantt, and L.F Urwick.

17. First we consider the contribution to classical principles of Henri Fayol, who in his lifetime was a very successful businessman in his own right. He trained as a mining engineer and subsequently worked for the same company all his working life, becoming managing director at the age of 47 and only retiring from the board after his 77th birthday. The publication in 1916 of his seminal work 'Administration industrielle et generale' brought to light the distillation of a lifetime's experience of management. His ideas and 'principles of management' were translated into English and published under the title 'General and Industrial Management' in 1949[4]. The foreword to the English edition was made by a post-war disciple of Fayol's, the management consultant Lyndall F. Urwick (see below). In reviewing what he considered to be the key activities of any industrial undertaking, Fayol described six such activities, five of which were commonly known at the time (technical, commercial, financial, security and accounting activities) and one ('managerial' activities) which was less understood and which he proceeded to expand on. To manage, argued Fayol, meant 'to forecast and plan, to organise, to command, to coordinate and to control.' He developed a list of 'principles of management' which he claimed worked well for him, and these are summarised as follows (Fig. 2.5):

1.	Division of work	Reduces the span of attention or effort for any one person or group. Enables practice and familiarity to be developed.
2.	Authority	This is the right to give orders. It should be seen in the context of responsibility.
3.	Discipline	This includes the outward marks of respect for authority in accordance with agreements between the firm and its employees.
4.	Unity of command	Each person should have only one superior at any one time.
5.	Unity of direction	One head and one plan for any group of activities with thesame objective.
6.	Subordination of individual interest to the general interest	The interests of one individual or group should not be allowed to override the general good. It is recognised that this is a difficult area for management.
7.	Remuneration	Pay should be fair to both the employee and the firm.
8.	Centralisation	This is always present to some degree, depending on the size of company and the quality of its managers.
9.	Scalar chain	This is the line of authority from top to bottom.
10.	Order	There should be a place for everything, and everything in itsplace. The right man in the right place too.
11.	Equity	This is a combination of kindliness and justice towards employees.
12.	Stability of tenure of personnel	Employees should be given time to settle into their jobs. This may require a lengthy period in the case of managers.
13.	Initiative	Within the limits of of authority and discipline, all levels of staff should be encouraged to show initiative.
14.	Esprit de corps	Harmony is a great strength to an organisation, and so team work should be encouraged.

Figure 2.5   *Fayol's principles of management*

18. Fayol's 'principles' illustrate the classical interest in structure and order in organisations. The assumptions behind the list include the necessity of an ordered and coherent structure of relationships, the right of managers to

'manage', and an acknowledgement of the need to treat employees fairly and respectfully. Much of what he outlines above applies to the kind of formal organisational type that we call bureaucracy. Many of the principles have subsequently been adopted by managers in all kinds of organisations, and have come to be regarded as 'good practice'. However, taken as a whole, the principles apply less easily in modern conditions, where rapid change makes formal structures less effective, and where paternalistic management styles are unsuited to the sense of independence of present-day employees, and to the need for individuals to accept greater responsibility for their own work in less-hierarchical organisations.

19. Lyndall F Urwick was a disciple of Fayol's, and enthusiastically propounded the view that the development of management principles could be widely applied and would lead to success in management (which at that time he termed 'administration'). In 1952, Urwick[5] published a consolidated list of 10 principles, which are an excellent example of classical management thinking. The list is as in Fig. 2.6.

20. As a statement of the elements of classical organisation theory, Urwick's list could hardly be bettered, focusing as it does on structural issues and organisational mechanisms. If the present business world were one in which stability ruled in the external environment, and in which people at work were submissive to their superiors, then Urwick's principles would stand a reasonable chance of being widely applied by managements. However, the truth is that such principles are too neat and formalised for modern conditions in most western nations, where rapidly changing external conditions require flexibility of approach, and where employee attitudes favour greater personal discretion rather than less, and where managers have to earn the respect of their team-members rather than expect it as of right. This is not to say that certain principles could not be, or are not, capable of being implemented in modern organisations. For example, the Principle of the Objective is assumed in much of what is contained in firms' mission statements and the efforts that firms make to develop a unified culture based on that mission. Similarly, there is considerable agreement about the commonsense nature of the span of control and the notion of coordination. Nevertheless, such concepts can hardly be applied as universal principles as intended by Urwick. In some circumstances they may be appropriate, but in others they will undoubtedly be inappropriate. What is required today demands more of a contingency approach (see Chap.3), in which the structure is adapted in response to the demands of the other factors in organisations as indicated in Figure 2.3 above.

1. The Principle of the Objective	The overall purpose, or objective, of the organisation is its raison d'etre.
2. The Principle of Specialisation	One function only per group
3. The Principle of Coordination	The process of organising is primarily to ensure coordination of effort.
4. The Principle of Authority	Every group should have a supreme authority, and there should be a clear line of authority over others
5. The Principle of Responsibility	A superior is absolutely accountable for the acts of his subordinates.
6. The Principle of Definition	Jobs, duties and relationships should be clearly defined
7. The Principle of Correspondence	Authority should be commensurate with responsibility
8. The Span of Control	Noone should be responsible for the work of more than five or six subordinates whose work is interlocked.
9. The Principle of Balance	The various units of the organisation should be kept in balance.
10. The Principle of Continuity	The structure should provide for the continuation of activities.

Figure 2.6 　　　　　　　　*Urwick's principles of administration (Management)*

F.W. Taylor and the scientific managers

21. Frederick Winslow Taylor served an apprenticeship in engineering before moving to the Midvale Steel Company in Pennsylvania where in the course of eleven years he reached the position of shop superintendent and acquired his basic ideas about 'scientific management'. When, in 1889, he left Midvale for the Bethlehem Steel Company, he had his first opportunities for putting his ideas on efficiency to the test. The results he achieved were outstanding in terms of increased worker productivity. After three years of following 'scientific' principles at the Bethlehem Works, Taylor was able to show that, over that period, handling costs per ton had been reduced by half, labour productivity had increased to the extent that 140 men were finally producing as much output as over 400 previously, and labourers' pay had risen to an average of 60% more than their fellow-workers in neighbouring firms.

22. The main thrust of Taylor's enthusiasm and determination was directed at the efficiency of working methods, especially by means of time and motion

study. His experience as worker as well as in management had convinced him that the average worker put in a minimal amount of effort into work, a tendency he described as 'soldiering'. He distinguished two types of soldiering — (a) *natural* soldiering, which referred to an individual's natural tendency to take the easy route, and *systematic* soldiering, which was the deliberate and organised restriction of the work-rate by employees. Taylor concluded that the reasons for soldiering were basically threefold:

1. Fear of unemployment (for which he had considerable sympathy)
2. Response to fluctuations in earnings (as a result of management's arbitrary systems both of day-rates and piece-rates)
3. The management's 'rule-of-thumb' approach to work organisation, which basically allowed the workers to decide working methods

23. Taylor's response to this situation was to introduce what he recognised would be a revolutionary new method — for management and workers alike — ie scientific management! This would aim to increase wages but reduce labour costs through vastly improved productivity. Given the background of massive unemployment, and the hiring and firing of workers that was common practice at the time, Taylor's aims must have seemed utopian to his contemporaries. He was firmly convinced, however, that (a) workers need not spin out work in order to ensure that they would remain in employment, (b) managers could measure work more accurately and yet fairly, and (c) greater effort by workers could lead to higher wages on a more or less permanent basis. Finally, he was convinced that if a breakthrough could be achieved in the first three convictions, then the result would be beneficial to everyone.

24. The 'scientific' approach required *management* to take the following steps:
1. Develop a science (ie study) for each operation to replace rule-of-thumb
2. Determine accurately from the study the correct time and method for each job
3. Set up a suitable organisation to take all responsibility from the workers except for that of actual job performance
4. Select and train the workers (with the implication that lazy, ineffective or uncooperative workers would be sacked)
5. Accept the fact that management itself must be governed by the science developed for each operation, and must surrender its arbitrary power over the workers (ie once work was measured and rates set, they must abide by the outcomes)

What Taylor was attempting to implement was a pioneering form of productivity improvement based on work study linked to rates of pay. The practice at the time was to pay individual workers either on a day rate, which was earned by every member of a gang, regardless of how hard or little he worked, or on a 'guesstimated' piece-rate. In either case if earnings increased beyond management's targets, then the management would arbitrarily reduce the rates per day or per piece!

25. Taylor's view was that it was up to the management to measure the work properly in the first place, then set an appropriate rate, and pay whatever the workers were able to earn as a result of their labours. Thus efficient workers would be adequately rewarded for their productivity. In a paper to the American Society of Mechanical Engineers in 1903, Taylor[6] described his approach at the Bethlehem Works

> 'Before undertaking the management of these men [gangs of yard labourers], the writer [Taylor] was informed that they were steady workers, but slow and phlegmatic, and that nothing would induce them to work fast. The first step was to place an intelligent college-educated man in charge of progress....He ...was soon taught the art of determining how much work a first-class man can do in a day. This was done by timing with a stop-watch a first-class man while he was working fast...(and) to divide the man's work into its elements and to time each element separately. The man selected from one of these gangs.....was called upon to load on piece work from forty-five to forty eight tons (2,240 lbs) each day. *[NB The average at the time was between 12 and 13 tons per man]* He regarded this task as an entirely fair one, and earned on an average....60 percent more than he had been paid by the day.'

26. There was considerable opposition to Taylor's project, but as the labourer concerned continued to earn the high rate, so

> '...this object lesson gradually wore out the concerted opposition, which ceased rather suddenly after about two months.'

It is important to recognise that Taylor was not promoting slave-driving, and his rates were established on what a worker could achieve over a sustained period of time. Unfortunately, most managers at the time lacked Taylor's expertise in work measurement, and thus still found themselves in the position of having to reduce rates in order to compensate for the loose timing of jobs.

27. The part that *workers* were expected to play in the 'scientific' approach was as follows:

1. They were to cease worrying about the division of the fruits of production as between wages and profits

2. They would share in the increased prosperity of the firm by working in the 'correct' way and receiving wage increases of between 30 -100%

3. They must give up their soldiering and cooperate with management to develop the science

4. They must accept that the management would now be responsible, within the framework of the scientific approach, for determining what was to be done, and how

5. Agree to be trained in the new methods

28. Today the above exhortations seem rather naive, but at the time Taylor was convinced that workers would be attracted by the rewards and the improved regularity of pay which he believed would come about from the adoption of scientific management. He believed that individuals would come to see the greater importance of contributing to a larger cake, in which all would share, rather than arguing about dividing an existing, and probably smaller, cake. For him the sheer reasonableness of scientific management meant that work and pay could be measured scientifically, and therefore there would be no place either for the restrictive influence of trade unions, or for arbitrary behaviour by management. The science itself would be able to provide both the necessary rewards and the fairness of their distribution.

29. Contemporaries of Taylor argued that the scientific approach reduced workers to the status of automatons, but his response was to assert that individuals wanted clarity of task and standards. History has shown that whilst scientific management has produced a range of benefits for shop floor practices, especially in the area of work measurement and method study (see below), the cost has been considerable — overspecialisation leading to narrow tasks and restrictive employee attitudes, arguments and disputes over piece-rates, and the production of a brand of employees with task-specific and often low-level skills. Add to this the boredom and frustration experienced at work by countless workers, and the counterbalancing need to introduce job enrichment and similar techniques, and the balance sheet for scientific management does not look too healthy! Unfortunately, the underlying rationale of the 'scientific' approach has not proven attractive enough to overcome the restrictions on task discretion experienced by the workers. Nor has the level of mutual trust between management and worker been sufficiently high, except in a few cases. Taylor's success at the Bethlehem Works was due in no small measure to his own perseverance and single-mindedness, together with the moral willingness to accept almost total unpopularity over a period of some three years. Managers in other firms neither had the resilience to see their plans through in the face of concerted opposition, nor could they gain a sufficient degree of enthusiasm and commitment from either workers or other managers.

The Gilbreths — the 'One best way'

30. Frank and Lilian Gilbreth were younger contemporaries of Taylor. They were especially keen on the idea of scientific management and its application outside the factory floor. Following discussions with Taylor they

carried out experiments with bricklayers, and found that by analysing, and subsequently redesigning the working methods of typical bricklayers, they could reduce the number of movements required to lay bricks from 18 per brick to 5. The Gilbreths (1911)[7] became convinced that it was possible to find the 'one best way' to perform any manual task. This involved studying the work and its component tasks, discovering the most efficient way of working, and then laying down systematic rules and procedures for their achievement. The results were that employees were not only able to be paid rates well in excess of competitors, but were also freed from much of the effort and fatigue involved previously in the same work.

31.   The Gilbreths took the view that what they called the Science of Management consisted of applying measurement to management and abiding by the results. They completely separated the planning of work from its execution. Once work had been planned by the management, the employees had no discretion over how it was done. The sheer detail of the Gilbreths approach to work measurement was remarkable. They invented a system for identifying different movements involved in manual tasks, such as searching, finding, selecting, grasping and holding. The basic elements of the system (ie the individual motions) were given the name 'Therbligs' (Gilbreths spelt backwards!). They are still used today as the basis for Method Study symbols. The Gilbreths also invented the flow process chart, which enabled whole processes, or operations, to be analysed. These charts also incorporated symbols, in this case five, covering the principal elements of any process — inspection, storage, operation, transportation and delay.

Henry Gantt

32.   Henry Gantt was a colleague of Taylor's at the Bethlehem Works. Although accepting much of the wisdom of scientific management, Gantt felt that insufficient attention was paid to the worker's needs, especially where piece-rates were in operation. He devised a payment system for piece-rates, which not only encouraged the most effective workers, but which avoided *penalising* the less effective and thus discouraging them. His system brought about numerous improvements in shop-floor efficiency as well as enhancing employee morale. Taylor's view was that

> 'Mr. Gantt's system is especially useful during the difficult and delicate period of transition from the slow pace of ordinary day work to the high speed which is the leading characteristic of good management.'

Unlike the Gilbreths, Gantt did not believe in the 'one best way', but took a contingency view (ie what is the best way in the present circumstances). Like the Gilbreths, he did produce some useful ways of charting the progress of work, and variations of his charts are in use today.

The legacy of scientific management

33. The principal benefit deriving from scientific management was that it stimulated interest in the measurement of tasks and processes, which was of considerable use in designing plant and revising working methods. It thus provided the basis for Work Study and other quantitative techniques at work, and gave rise to a whole new specialism — industrial engineering — which for thirty years or more was the dominant force in improving industrial efficiency in the United States and Europe. Its fruition in modern times is realised in such approaches as Total Quality Management. Scientific management also helped management and workers to understand that greater efficiency leading to higher output with lower labour costs could bring benefits to both sides. In particular, Taylor's arguments that greater efficiency need not lead to reductions in demand for labour, and hence to more unemployment, but to *increased* job opportunities, gradually dawned on subsequent policy-makers in following decades. Japanese industrial concerns in the years following World War II rebuilt their industrial might in no small measure on the strength of their adoption of many scientific management ideas.

34. Elsewhere, however, the legacy of *disadvantages* that scientific management has left is substantial, including the fragmentation and de-skilling of jobs at the production level, the encouragement of a *'carrot-and-stick'* approach to employee motivation, and the separation of the workforce from the planning of their work (ie the opposite to what firms are trying to achieve through the use of devices such as Quality Circles). On balance, the scientific approach has provided a basis for improving productivity through improved understanding of work processes, but at the cost of alienating the production workforce from the goals of their managements. Like many other management concepts, 'scientific management' can only be applied selectively, in given situations, to achieve specific ends.

Weber and the concept of bureaucracy

35. Weber (1864-1920) spanned the same period approximately as Fayol, Taylor and the Gilbreths. Unlike the scientific managers mentioned above, Weber was a social scientist — an academic — with an interest in organisations, especially the study of how authority was handled. He did not see it as his role to promote one system, or model, of organisation against another, but rather to analyse organisations, especially in relation to the question of authority, with the object of attempting an explanation of his findings. In his analysis, Weber (1947)[8] identified three basic types of legitimate authority — *traditional*, *charismatic* and *rational-legal*. Legitimate authority in this sense means authority which has (a) come to be accepted by those over whom it is exercised, and (b) which is seen as requiring their obedience. It is important to distinguish 'authority' from 'power'. The

latter implies having the ability to exert dominance over others, whether they like it or not. Authority, by comparison, implies a degree of acceptance of the exercise of power by those over whom it is administered. Thus, under authority, power can be wielded in a way that is generally acceptable to followers.

36. Weber's three types of authority can be summarised as follows:

   1 *Traditional Authority.* This is authority based on tradition and custom. Thus hereditary rulers are accepted by those they govern on the basis of their birth, rather than on personal merit, or by election, for example.

   2 *Charismatic Authority.* This is authority based on the personal qualities of the leader. Charismatic leaders win the confidence of their followers by sheer personality as much as by other factors.

   3 *Rational-legal Authority.* This is authority derived from the formal office, or position, of the job-holder, as bounded by the rules and procedures of the organisation. This type of authority predominates in the structural form which Weber termed 'bureaucracy'.

37. Weber's work was not published in English translation until 1947, when his book 'The Theory of Social and Economic Organisation' appeared. 'Bureaucracy' described a particular form of organisation structure based on the acceptance of authority arising from the office (ie 'bureau') of the job-holder, as bounded by a set of rules and procedures. Bureaucracy, according to Weber, is an organisation having the following main features:

---

1. A continuous (ie not just *ad hoc*) organisation of functions bounded by rules

2. Specified spheres of competence (ie specialisation of jobs, limited allocation of authority, and rules governing the exercise of that authority

3. An hierarchy of offices (ie jobs), where jobs at one level are subject to the authority of jobs at the next highest level

4. All appointments are made on the basis of technical competence (ie ability to do the job)

5. The officials of the organisation are separated from its ownership

6. Offices exist in their own right, and job-holders have no rights to a particular office

7. Rules, decisions and actions are made explicit, and recorded in writing

---

38. Bureaucracy, in these terms, cannot result in the arbitrary exercise of power, for it is a legitimate form of authority, founded on the competence and expertise of the post-holder, and subject to checks and balances in the form of published rules and procedures. Weber himself regarded bureaucracy as a most efficient form of organisation for dealing with complex activities. March & Simon (1993)[9] comment that

> '....Weber goes beyond the 'machine' model in significant ways....But, in general, Weber perceives bureaucracy as an adaptive device for using specialised skill, and he is not exceptionally attentive to the character of the human organism.'

Morgan (1986) takes a somewhat different view of Weber's own attitude towards bureaucracy in commenting

> 'Weber... saw that the bureaucratic approach had the potential to routinise and mechanise almost every aspect of human life, eroding the human spirit......he also recognised that it could have grave political consequences in undermining the potential for more democratic forms of organisation...his writings on bureaucracy are thus pervaded by a great scepticism...'.

39. Sofer (1972)[10], writing more than 20 years ago, commented that

> 'Most commentators feel that the scale of the modern state and the vastness of the services it offers make this [ie bureaucracy] form of 'expert' administration inevitable, or at any rate difficult to avoid, in government.....This form of administration provides reassurance for the electorate that technical considerations of efficiency guide the decisions made by their representatives, that the persons carrying out the decisions are appointed on the basis of their competence, and that the policies decided on will be administered without favouritism or discrimination between individuals.'

Sofer's comments sum up the predominant view of those who see bureaucracy as important — even essential — for the exercise of impartiality in public organisations. However, the hierarchical structure and other features of bureaucracy have been adopted by countless other types of organisations outside the public administration sector, eg large businesses, not-for-profit organisations and charities. Why has this come about?

40. The two greatest factors contributing to the growth of bureaucracy are *size* and *complexity of operations*. Growth in size leads to greater specialisation of jobs with associated requirements for ordering and re-ordering the boundaries between jobs, and for regulating the relationships between them, including defining the authority of some jobs over others. Size inevitably leads to issues of control and coordination, and bureaucratic structures are well-placed to meet these. Complexity often accompanies sheer size of operation, but may also be a factor in small-scale operations. Here the interlocking of one job with another is crucial, as is the network of deci-

sion-making required in complex work. A well-organised structure capable of meeting the organisation's objectives is likely to be supplied in bureaucracy. One other major factor in the growth of bureaucracy is accountability. When sheer size of operations, in particular, means that taxpayers, owners and others with a vested interest in the results of the organisation's activities, cannot possibly exercise direct control themselves, then it is important to know that the actions taken in the name of the organisation are done skilfully, professionally and in good faith. Thus, the accountability of those in authority to those with an interest in the organisation can be reasonably assured through a bureaucratic form of decision-making and control.

The dysfunctions of bureaucracy

41. However, like many other human endeavours, bureaucratic structures can have their weaknesses, or what have been described (Gouldner,1955)[11] as dysfunctions. In his research, Gouldner studied the effects of introducing bureaucracy into an organisation which had been operated on informal lines with an easy-going management style. The new approach resulted in a *reduction* in output and efficiency, accompanied by employee resentment at the changes. The detailed findings from Gouldner's studies led to his distinguishing three different patterns of bureaucracy as follows:

    1   *Mock Bureaucracy.* This described a situation where bureaucratic rules and procedures had been imposed on a group from external sources (eg a head office), and where they were either ignored or merely given lip-service. In this situation the group developed their own informal rules and procedures, whilst apparently giving acknowledgement to the formal procedures as laid down.

    2   *Representative Bureaucracy.* This described a situation where the employees and their management both accepted the rules and procedures as in their mutual interest.

    3   *Punishment-centred Bureaucracy.* This described a worst-case scenario in which either the management or the employees attempted to impose their rules on each other, and where failure to observe the rules was seen as grounds for imposing sanctions against the other side. In this situation each side considered its rules as legitimate, and there was no common ground between them.

42. In contrast to Weber's thinking on bureaucracy, which was dominated by his sense of how rational it was, Gouldner showed that human feelings and opinions also needed to be taken into account, if bureaucracy was to be introduced successfully. Weber, in his analysis of bureaucracy, focused on its structural aspects (hierarchy, spheres of competence etc) and on its management of expertise (eg appointment procedures). Gouldner, by comparison, emphasised the behavioural aspects of bureaucracy. He

noticed, for example, that rules generated not just anticipated responses (eg obedience), but also unanticipated responses, such as minimal acceptance. He recognised that in any one organisation there could be a reaction to rules and procedures along any of the three forms of bureaucracy mentioned in the previous paragraph.

43. Since Weber's analysis, it seems that subsequent researchers have concluded that although the rational and efficiency aspects of bureaucracy are a great strength, they cannot be embedded successfully in an organisation without the mutual consent of the management and employees. In a punishment-centred form, or what Morgan (1986) sees as 'social domination', the potential for conflict within the organisation is greatly increased. Morgan sees the value of viewing organisations as instruments of domination as

> '...these perspectives....show how even the most rational and democratic forms of organisation can result in modes of domination where certain people acquire and sustain a commanding influence over others, often through subtle processes of socialisation and belief.'

Thus, even when a bureaucratic system has been established and found acceptance to all the parties, it seems that the need to ensure that the leadership manage by consent will always be present. Even leaders who at first have shown their good faith towards their followers may be tempted to hang on to power or further their own interests, when they should be prepared to step aside for the common good. One of the reasons behind the appointment of non-executive directors to a board is that they should act as guardians of the corporate conscience, and help to ensure that their executive colleagues always act in good faith on behalf of the company.

References

1. Mintzberg, H. (1979) *The Structuring of Organisations*, Prentice Hall

2. Mintzberg, H. (1983) *Structure in Fives*, Prentice Hall

3. Morgan, G, (1986) *Images of Organisation*, Sage Publications

4. Fayol, H. (1949) *General and Industrial Management*, Pitman

5. Urwick, L. (1952) *The Elements of Administration*, Pitman

6. Taylor, F.W. (1947) *Scientific Management*, Harper & Row
   (NB This volume contains 'Shop Management' (1903) and 'The Principles of Scientific Management' (1911) as well as Taylor's Testimony Before the Special House Committee, U.S. House of Representatives (1912).

7. Gilbreth, Frank (1911) *Motion Study*, van Nostrand

8. Weber, M. (1947) *The Theory of Social and Economic Organisation*, Free Press

9. March, J. & Simon, H. (1993) *Organisations* (2nd edn), Blackwell

10. Sofer, C. (1972), *Organisations in Theory and Practice*, Heinemann

11. Gouldner, A. (1955) *Patterns of Industrial Democracy*, Routledge & Kegan Paul

Questions for reflection/discussion

1. To what extent can it be claimed that organisation charts have little to do with reality?

2. What are the core issues that designers of organisational structures have to face?

3. Given the potential for *disintegration* that exists in organisations, how far can coordination and cooperation be influenced by the choice of structure?

4. What, in today's conditions, appear to be the greatest limitations of the classical organisation theories?

5. To what extent have the ideas of F.W.Taylor failed to gain acceptance because of weak management styles rather than because of technical weaknesses in his theories?

6. How far does sheer size of operation mean that a bureaucratic structure is inevitable?

7. To what extent do you agree that *any* form of rational-legal authority can be used both to dominate others and ensure a lengthy stay in power?

3 Organisation structures II — contingency and other approaches

Introduction

1. In the previous chapter we outlined several of the key issues facing the designers of organisations, and described the contributions of leading theorists of classical organisation, including the theorists of bureaucracy. In this chapter we examine the ideas of other individuals who have contributed to our understanding of organisations, but who have taken a contingent, or circumstantial, view of organisation structures. These later theorists have suggested that there is no ideal organisation structure per se, but only one that is suited to particular organisational circumstances and conditions. Some have proposed a systems view of organisations, in which social and technological aspects of organisation interact with the external environment to produce a system that is capable of receiving inputs from the environment, processing them, and then returning outputs to the environment in the form of goods and services. What all these theorists have in common is a respect for the inter-relatedness of the key variables referred to in Figures 2.3 and 2.4 in the previous chapter, especially the relationships between *structure, objectives, tasks, people, technology* and *environment*.

2. In this chapter we will examine the work of several important contributors to systems and contingency theories of organisations. These contributors and their principal approaches are summarised below by way of introduction (Fig. 3.1).

Woodward and colleagues

3. Joan Woodward and colleagues at the South east Essex Technical College carried out a seminal piece of research between 1953 and 1957, which began as enquiry into the relationship between (classical) management principles and business success, and was soon transformed into a study of the relationship between company objectives, techniques of production and organisation structure. In her introduction to the first published report of the research (1958)[1], Woodward noted that

Contributor	Issues confronted	Principal approach
Joan Woodward	Impact of production demands and technology on organisation structure	Survey of 100 manufacturing firms in S. Essex to chart history, objectives, processes, methods, organisation structure etc. Ten categories of production systems identified
T. Burns and J. Stalker	Adaptation to changes in in firms technical and commercial situations.	Categorisation of two ideal types of structure – (a) mechanistic, and (b) organic.
J. Lawrence and J. Lorsch	The tension between need to differentiate tasks and need to coordinate tasks/people. The effect of the external environment on states of differentiation and integration.	Study of relationship between structure and environment in six plastics firms. Comparison between the plastics firms and four other firms, representing differing environments.
Trist and Bamforth	Interrelationship between social and technical aspects of work.	Concept of organisation as a 'socio-technical' system.
D. Pugh and Aston school	Relationship between structure and seven major organisational variables (ownership, size etc)	Surveys of variety of organisations employing more than 150 staff, interviews with CEOs.
H. Mintzberg	Resolving the conflict between specialisation and coordination Proposing a new model of organisation based on five structural configurations.	Synthesis of the literature.

Figure 3.1   *Systems and contingency theorists*

'When...the firms were grouped according to similarity of objectives and techniques of production, and classified in order of the technical complexity of their production systems, each production system was found to be associated with a characteristic pattern of organisation. It appeared that technical methods were the most important factor in determining organisation structure and in setting the tone of human relationships inside the firms.'

In view of the content of the theories of organisation referred to in the previous chapter, which, it must be said, were very much in favour in the 1950s, it is interesting to note Woodward's additional comment that

> ' The widely accepted assumption that there are principles of management valid for all types of production systems seemed very doubtful...'.

4. Woodward's research was based initially on a survey of 100 firms each employing more than 100 employees, and all in manufacturing. Her team visited each firm to obtain information on the following:

□ History, background and objectives

□ Manufacturing processes and methods

□ Organisation charts

□ Analysis of costs under wages, materials and overheads

□ Analysis of labour structure, including span of control

□ Organisation and operation of sales, R& D, personnel, inspection, maintenance, and purchasing departments

□ Production control and planning procedures

□ Cost or budgetary control procedures

□ Management and supervisor recruitment, training and qualifications

□ Yardsticks of efficiency (profitability, market standing, reputation etc)

5. The results of the survey showed that the firms were organised and run in widely different ways, which did not appear to be related either to size or type of industry. The keys to explaining the differences appeared to lie in two factors — first, the firm's objectives in terms of what market it was aiming to supply. For example, a firm that was in the business of building prototypes of electronic equipment could not employ the same production methodology as a firm engaged in mass-production. Importantly, Woodward concluded that:

> 'the criterion of the appropriateness of an organisational structure must be the extent to which it furthers the objectives of the firm, not...the degree to which it conforms to a prescribed pattern. There can be no one best way of organising a business.'

6. The second, and by far the most decisive, factor was the influence of technology. The firms studied were classified into ten different categories, based on their technical methods. The classification formed a scale of tech-

nical complexity, which the researchers defined in terms of (a) the extent to which the production process was controllable, and (b) the relative predictability of its results. Woodward's classification provided a standard by which all future analysis of manufacturing organisation could be judged. The ten categories were clustered into three principal groupings as follows (Fig. 3.2):

Group I	I	Production of simple units to customers' orders
Small Batch and	II	Production of technically complex units
Unit Production	III	Fabrication of large equipment in stages
	IV	Production of small batches
	V	Production of components in large batches subsequently assembled
Group II	VI	Production of large batches, assembly line type
Large Batch and	VII	Mass production
Mass Production	VIII	Process production combined with the preparation of a product for sale by large-batch or mass-production methods
Group III	IX	Process production of chemicals in batches
Process	X	Continuous flow production of liquids, gases and solid
Production		shapes

Figure 3.2   *Woodward's Classification of Production Systems*

7.   One of the key findings of Woodward's research was that firms using similar technical methods had similar organisation structures. She noted, in particular, that:

> 'different technologies imposed different kinds of demands on individuals and organisations, and that these demands had to be met through an appropriate form of organisation ...'.

Woodward identified the following differences in structural and other organisational factors:

a.   The number of levels of authority in the management hierarchy increased with technical complexity. Thus, there were typically six levels in process production compared with *three* levels in unit production.

b.   The span of control of supervisors was greatest in mass production (typically between 41 and 50 people controlled), compared with 21 - 30 in unit production, and 11 - 20 in process production.

c.   The ratio of managers and supervisory staff to other personnel was smallest in process production and greatest in unit production. Thus, there were more than three times as many managers for the same number of personnel in process firms as in unit production firms.

d. The firms with the greatest technical complexity had the following additional characteristics — lower labour costs, an increase in the ratio of indirect to direct labour, a higher proportion of graduate employees, and a wider span of control for the chief executive.

8. Woodward also found that production groups at both ends of the classification scale had a more flexible organisation, with less clearly-defined duties and responsibilities, compared with the middle groups (large batch and mass production). Other differences were that the amount of written, as opposed to spoken, communication increased up to assembly-line production, but decreased considerably in process production. Specialisation between management functions was found more frequently in large-batch and mass production compared with either unit or process production. The former type employed more specialists and tended to adopt a traditional line and staff pattern. This type also tended to have more labour problems than the other two, primarily because of the pressures exerted on people by the assembly-line system. As Woodward commented

> ' The production system seemed more important in determining the quality of human relations than did the numbers employed.'

9. Following their initial studies, Woodward's team (1965)[2] selected twenty of the original hundred for more detailed investigation. They undertook a closer examination of (1) the manufacturing process and its supporting activities (especially development and marketing), (2) the number and nature of decisions taken in the management hierarchy, (4) the kind of cooperation required between members of the management team, and (5) the kind of control exercised by senior executives. They also made an assessment (6) of the situational demands (the technical situation and the firm's objectives) in each firm. The conclusions they drew about the relationship between manufacturing, development and marketing can be summarised as follows:

a. In *unit-production* firms the manufacturing cycle began with the marketing function. The job of marketing was to sell customers the idea that what they wanted could be produced. Then the product was designed and developed, often to the customer's particular requirements, before being put into production. In such firms the centre-stage was played by development — *'The skill and ingenuity of those responsible for development were the most important factors in ensuring the firm's success.'*

b. In *mass-production* firms the sequence was product development, then production, and finally marketing. Sales staff's job was *'to persuade the customer, not that the firm was capable of producing what he wanted, but that he wanted what the firm was capable of producing.'* In these firms it was production that was the focus of attention with success depending almost entirely on efficiency and cost reduction.

    c.   In *process production* the first stage was also product development, but here the next stage was marketing to test the product before finally undertaking production proper. Here success depended largely *'on the existence of a market waiting to absorb the products........much depended on the efficiency of the marketing organisation.'*

10.   The team's conclusions about management decisions were as follows:

    a.   In *unit production* more decisions had to be made compared with the other two types, but they were usually short-term and equal in importance. There was little distinction between problem-solving decisions and policy (strategy) decisions, for the first usually led to the second. A large proportion of the decisions made had repercussions on the entire manufacturing process, even to the extent of reopening negotiations with the customer if major changes had to be considered.

    b.   In *mass production* policy decisions were fewer but tended to be more important because they committed the firm to longer-term consequences. Problem-solving decisions did not develop so often into policy decisions. The latter often only affected one manufacturing function because of the greater degree of functional specialism. Decisions in this type of firm were generally more predictable than in unit production.

    c.   In *process production* policy decisions were fewer than in the other two types, but tended to have long-term effects (eg three years to build a plant with twenty years required to give an adequate return on investment). Problem-solving decisions were more frequent, and had to be made close to the production point, often in conditions of some urgency. Policy decisions were thus far removed from problem-solving types. Decisions in this type of production tended to have greater rationality about them and this enabled them to be more predictable right throughout the organisation. Decision-making could be delegated with some confidence, since in a given set of circumstances the technical aspects of the problem were likely to govern the range of available choices, which would tend to be handled similarly by the staff concerned, assuming similar training and qualifications. Senior executives were freed to concentrate on decision-making in areas such as human relations where judgement was called for.

11.   On the subject of coordination between members of management, there were a number of differences in behaviour between the three production types. In unit production, for example, it seemed to be necessary for functions to coordinate their activities on a day-to-day basis to the extent that *'In several firms product development was indistinguishable from production*

itself.' In mass-production there was no day-to-day integration of functions, indeed quite the opposite, but there was a need for cooperation in exchanging information. Thus *'Product development staff relied upon information from marketing about the way customers were thinking and from production about manufacturing facilities for the new products.'* In process production the functions also tended to be separated, although there was a close relationship between product development and process development. In this type of production *'...fundamental research on new products was almost entirely self-contained. It was not controlled by existing production facilities or by customers' requirements; indeed in many cases a market had yet to be found.'* However, both process and mass-production types had to devote attention to cooperation and coordination when bringing a new product into large-scale manufacturing.

12.   Woodward's work confirmed that *'variations in organisational requirements between firms are nearly always linked with differences in their techniques of production.'* Having identified a range of production techniques (ie as in Fig. 3.2 above), it was possible, according to Woodward, to predict what a firm's organisation structure was likely to be. She suggested that there was likely to be a centralisation of authority and a coordination of functions in firms engaged in unit production. Mass production firms, by comparison, would tend to adopt extensive specialisation and delegation of authority. Process production would probably combine specialisation between development, marketing and production together with integration within the functions, and generally cooperative decision-making. Woodward concluded that

> 'The most successful firms are....likely to be the 'organisation conscious' firms, in which formal organisation is appropriate to the technical situation......Next would come the less 'organisation conscious' firms, where informal organisation mainly determines the pattern of relationships. The least successful firms are likely to be the 'organisation conscious' firms, where formal organisation is inappropriate and deviates from informal organisation.'

(Note: *formal* organisation is the term applied to the organisational relationships laid down by the management; *informal* organisation refers to the patterns of relationships developed by employees, which may or may not coincide with the formal pattern. This point will be discussed later in Chapters 4 and 9).

Burns and Stalker's contribution

13.   Another important piece of British research in the 1950's was carried out by Tom Burns and G.M.Stalker (1961)[3]. In this case the researchers studied firstly a small group of electronics firms in Scotland, and then a similar group in England, with the intention of discovering how these firms responded to change in their technical and commercial situations ie how

they managed innovation. As a result of their research, Burns and Stalker contributed two important concepts to the world of organisational behaviour — *'mechanistic'* and *'organic' systems of management*. 'Mechanistic systems were seen as appropriate for conditions of stability and had the following characteristics:

---

a. specialised differentiation of tasks

b. precise definitions of rights, obligations and technical methods of roles

c. an hierarchical structure

d. a preference for vertical interaction between members

e. a tendency for operations and work behaviour to be dominated by superiors

f. insistence on loyalty to the organisation and obedience to superiors

---

In effect, what Burns and Stalker were describing was a typical example of 'classical' organisation principles, or what Weber called 'bureaucracy'. It also has many of the characteristics referred to by Morgan (1986)[4] in his description of organisation as Instruments of Domination.

14. 'Organic' systems were seen as appropriate for conditions of change. Their prime characteristics were:

---

a. tasks less formally defined in terms of methods, duties and powers

b. interaction between individuals develops as much laterally as vertically

c. communication between people of different ranks is lateral and consultative rather than vertical and commanding

d. a network structure of control, authority and communication

e. commitment to organisation objectives seen as more important than loyalty and obedience

f. the top person is not seen as omniscient

The picture presented by organic systems is one of flexibility in command and control, and recognition of individual knowledge, skill and contribution. Job levels are still distinguished, for organic systems, whilst not hierarchical, are nevertheless stratified, but on the basis of seniority of expertise. In such systems it is less easy to distinguish the formal from the informal organisation. There is a greater sense of shared values in organic systems compared with mechanistic systems.

15. For firms operating in generally stable conditions, a mechanistic system of management would be likely to further their overall goals. If, however, internal or external circumstances changed substantially, then an organic approach would be required. If a mechanistic firm stuck to its original management system in changing circumstances, then it would be less likely to achieve its goals. Burns and Stalker did not see the two systems as diametrically opposed to each other. As they noted at the time

> '...the two forms of system represent a polarity not a dichotomy; there are...... intermediate stages between the extremities......Also the relation of one form to the other is elastic, so that a concern oscillating between relative stability and relative change may also oscillate between the two forms. A concern may (and frequently does) operate with a management system which includes both types.'

They were at pains to point out that that they did not regard one system as inherently better than the other, commenting that

> 'The beginning of administrative wisdom is the awareness that there is no one optimum type of management system.'

This latter point has been taken up, tested, and generally confirmed by numerous researchers subsequently. Two such researchers were the Americans, Lawrence and Lorsch, who explicitly used the phrase 'contingency theory' in the publication of their findings shortly after Burns and Stalker's account.

Lawrence and Lorsch

16. Lawrence and Lorsch (1967)[5], both from the Harvard Business School, were interested in the links between organisation structure and environment. They first studied six plastics firms operating in diverse environments, ie where the industry was highly competitive, the product life-cycle fairly short, and where there was considerable new product and process development. Their concern was primarily to assess the impact of environmental conditions on an organisation's ability (a) to divide its tasks (what the researchers called *'differentiation'*), (b) to coordinate its activities (*'integration'*), and (c) to make provision for resolving conflict between the first two. They were thus concerned with one of the primary tensions that exist in work organisations, ie the tension between the need to divide the work, allocate tasks and engage in specialisation on the one hand, and the need for collaboration and coordination between tasks and people on the other.

17. The researchers defined differentiation as more than mere specialisation or division of labour, by including differences in attitude and behaviour on the part of managers. They also defined integration broadly by recognising the quality of the state of collaboration that existed between managers as well as the mechanisms of coordination. Their view was that differentia-

tion and integration were as much achieved through relationships as by mechanistic means —

> '...the organisation must fit not only the demands of the environment, but also the needs of its members.'.

18. The initial study of the six plastics firms was then compared with results obtained from four other firms — two standardised container firms, operating in what was substantially a stable environment, and two firms in the packaged food industry, where the rate of change was regarded as moderate. As a whole their research was notable because of the evidence it provided about the links between the external environment and the structure of an organisation. It was found, for example, that those firms which operated in a highly changing and diverse environment had to adopt a structure that could enable a high degree of differentiation, whilst also providing high levels of integration, usually through cross-functional teams as well as via the management hierarchy. More stable environments called for less differentiation in the structure, but still required high integration, mainly through the management hierarchy. Another important finding was that the major departments within a firm each had to deal with their own particular sub-environments. Thus, R & D and Marketing departments were likely to have to adapt to a relatively diverse and fast-moving environment, whilst production and administration would be more likely to operate within a relatively stable environment. Successful firms enabled differentiation to take place between departments in order to meet the variety of environments faced by them, but also achieved an effective degree of integration between the departments. The result was that many firms did not have one particular structure (eg a highly differentiated, 'mechanistic', structure), but were composed of a mixture of structures, depending on the nature of their environments.

19. Lawrence and Lorsch noted that the more an organisation was differentiated, the more difficult it was to resolve conflict. Higher-performing organisations were found to have developed better ways of resolving conflict than their less-effective competitors. Improved conflict resolution led to states of differentiation and integration that were appropriate for the environment. It was also found that in uncertain environments, the integrating functions were carried out by middle and lower-level management, whereas in stable environments these functions were carried out by top management.

20. The main contribution made by Lawrence and Lorsch to the study of organisational behaviour was to demonstrate the importance of the organisation's environment (including its departmental sub-environments) in determining optimum structure in given circumstances, and to suggest which structural characteristics best match particular kinds of environment. As they themselves concluded

'These findings suggest a contingency theory of organisation which recognises their systemic nature....organisational variables are in a complex inter-relationship with one another and with conditions in the environment......we have found that the state of differentiation in the effective organisation was consistent with the diversity of the parts of the environment, while the state of integration achieved was consistent with the environmental demands for interdependence.......the effective organisation has integrating devices consistent with the diversity of the environment.'

These words of Lawrence and Lorsch prompt the question 'What choices are available to organisations when considering how to differentiate (specialise) and integrate (coordinate)?' It is timely, therefore, to examine some basic structural forms, before going on to consider organisations from the point of view of systems theory.

Basic structural forms

21. In Figure 2.2 in the previous chapter, we listed a number of alternative structural forms. Of those the most common forms ranged between the following:

1. High or low degree of specialisation (differentiation)
2. Tall or flat structure
3. Narrow or wide structure
4. Centralised or decentralised
5. Tight control or loose control

These forms will be considered in turn, commencing with the ways in which organisations may choose to specialise their activities. Since the greatest variety of choices is likely to be experienced in a commercial undertaking, the models which follow apply mainly to business firms. The principal options are between the following:

1. specialisation by function (Figure 3.3)
2. specialisation by product (Figure 3.4)
3. specialisation by geographical location (Figure 3.5)
4. divisionalised structure (Figure 3.6)
5. matrix structure (Figure 3.7)
6. specialisation by customer category (similar to product and divisional structures)

22. By far the commonest method of specialisation is to allocate activities and responsibilities on the basis of common function. Thus, all production matters are unified under a production manager, and all personnel matters

become the prime responsibility of a personnel manager. What functional specialisation does is to give all staff from top to bottom the opportunity to devote their energies to ensuring the success of their own functional group. Whilst this enables the development of experience and the encouragement of expertise, it also carries within it the seeds of conflict between one functional group and another. A feature of functional specialisation is that line relationships (ie where direct authority is exercised over employees) not only derive from the operational management chain but also from the functional management chain. Senior functional managers usually have qualified authority over staff in the line operations, in respect of their functional duties, as well as full authority over their own staff. Mintzberg(1979,1983)[6] refers to this kind of authority in his description of the technostructure. Functional authority does not apply so readily to managers of *service* functions, such as payroll, security etc (or what Mintzberg calls 'support staff'). Functional grouping often provides better career and promotion opportunities than other structural forms, but is less adaptable in meeting the challenge of product diversification or geographical dispersement, for example. A typical *functional structure* is outlined as follows (Figure 3.3):

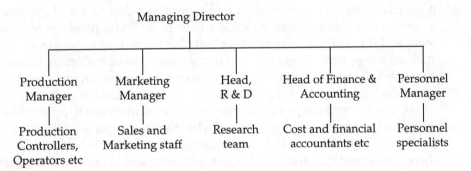

Figure 3.3   *Typical Functional Structure*

23. A common alternative to a functional structure is one based primarily on product/ service range. It is popular with organisations having a wide range of products, such as in pharmaceuticals and in firms providing insurance, pensions and other financial services. As will be noted, there is invariably a functional aspect to structure. In this and others, it is common for certain key functions, such as finance and personnel to be maintained separately from the product groups. An example of a typical *product-based structure*, taken from the pharmaceutical industry, is given below (Fig. 3.4):

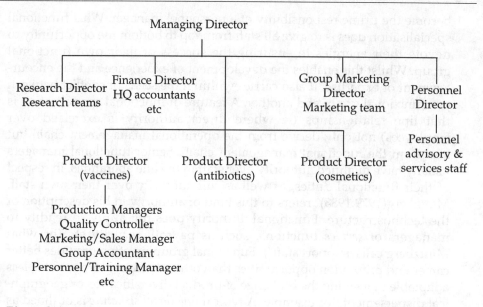

Figure 3.4   *Typical Product-based Structure*

24. A product-based organisation structure implies a decentralised approach to decision-making, which enables a firm to facilitate product-development and diversification by locating both the innovatory pressures and the staff with experience and expertise in the same part of the organisation. It also helps to clarify strategic decisions about future resourcing and sizing of product-groups, since the investment needs and costs of each product-range can be isolated, and the performance of individual products, or groups of products, can be assessed. The disadvantages are that product groups will inevitably be in competition with each other for resources, and therefore central management has to take a clear and firm view as to where it intends to see growth and expansion, and where it intends to maintain the status quo.

25. Specialisation by *geographical location* may be adopted by organisations that have to conduct their affairs on a regional or international basis. This, too, leads to a decentralised form of structure, in which operational matters are dealt with locally, even though strategic activities are handled from the centre. There is thus specialisation through the operating units and integration via the headquarters and functional departments, as exemplified in the transport example shown in Figure 3.5:

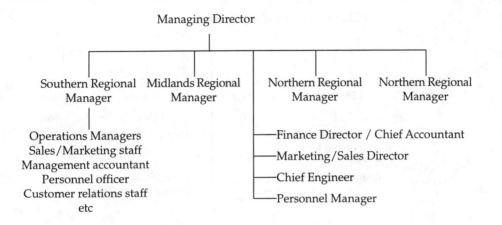

Figure 3.5.   *Geographically-based Structure (transport)*

26. The advantage of such a structure is that it enables regional management teams to exercise considerable discretion in handling their particular region's problems and opportunities — customers may have different service preferences in one part of the country to another; labour relations may be easier in some areas than in others; sheer problems of access may well be different in metropolitan areas compared with rural areas, and costs may well be higher in some areas than in others. The main disadvantage is possible lack of control from the centre, or conversely too *much* control by an over-anxious Managing Director and Board! What is noticeable, as a general rule, is that where there is greater decentralisation there is also a larger span of control for the chief executive. Whilst the Managing Director in a functional structure (Figure 3.3) had only five persons reporting to him, the equivalent role in the product and geographical structures had to cope with between seven and eight direct reports.

27. Given the sheer size and complexity of many modern organisations, some managements have chosen to combine the benefits of some of the above three. One such hybrid is the divisionalised structure (favoured by many of the promoters of excellence). The tendency today is for simultaneously achieving 'loose-tight' properties of structure. Thus, the creation of divisions that amount to semi-independent companies/ units in their own right enables a loose control to be retained at the centre, at least over everything except overall strategy (establishing mission, deciding major goals, priorities for funding and investment etc), where control is tight. An example of a *divisionalised structure* is given in Figure 3.6:

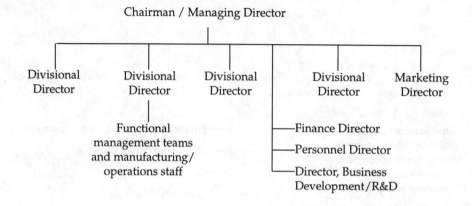

Figure 3.6   *Typical divisionalised structure*

28. The chief executive has a wide span of control under a divisionalised struc-
     ture, but if supported well by both divisional directors and functional
     directors can devote his energies to corporate and strategic issues. In this
     example, the functional directors are likely to be heavily involved in
     setting key standards of performance for divisions. The latter will be likely
     to comprise a full functional team of managers, since they will be acting
     more or less as separate companies with their own customers, operating
     requirements and employee profile.

29. Another structural form — *matrix structure* — has developed in response to
     highly complex organisational requirements in such industries as aero-
     space, civil engineering and space research, where numbers of simulta-
     neous projects need to be steered and coordinated. In these cases, special
     project managers with particular knowledge and expertise are charged
     with steering one or more projects, each with a team of specialist and oper-
     ational personnel. Each project team, however, unlike divisions in the
     example just quoted, does not have the same degree of autonomy over
     issues outside its specific mission, and is therefore subject to functional
     controls by senior functional management (eg on personnel matters,
     quality issues etc). A matrix structure is shown at Figure 3.7.

30. The Project Manager in each case coordinates the work of the project team,
     and has direct contact with the customer or client. The position carries a
     considerable amount of authority to act, but in addition to a direct report
     into the Plant/Site manager, the project manager is also accountable to the
     functional managers in respect of their specialism. Thus, in a matrix organ-
     isation, a project manager usually has more than one boss, and this acts to
     limit discretion. A matrix structure can work effectively for short-term or
     temporary projects, especially when there are several under way at the
     same time. Such a structure, however, is always being pulled in a number
     of different directions, and to be successful requires strong leadership from

all the managers concerned. This form of structure has been described (Handy 1993)[7] as a net.

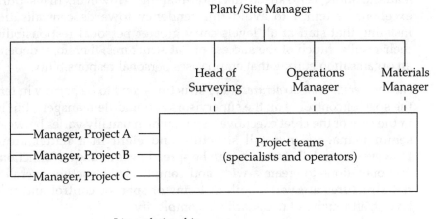

Line relationship

– – – – – – Functional relationship

Figure 3.7   *Matrix structure*

31. A final type of structure is one where specialisation is based on *client/customer groups*, eg retail, wholesale, individual clients etc. As in product, divisional and geographical structures, there is a functional layer of management alongside the heads of the various customer groups, and the chief executive's span of control is likely to be some seven or eight persons. The structure, therefore, looks similar to several of those illustrated above.

32. The list of common structural forms referred to in paragraph 21 above mentioned a number of options available to organisations, viz tall versus flat structures, narrow/wide structures, centralised/decentralised decision-making and authority mechanisms, and tight or loose control mechanisms. These essentially mechanistic considerations are summarised briefly here, before moving on to look at organisations from a systems perspective.

Tall versus flat structure. A tall structure is one with many levels eg seven or more from the chief executive down to the operating staff. A tall structure usually implies a narrow span of control for supervisors and managers and a greater degree of devolved decision-making, but requires many more supervisory and managerial staff. It also leads to longer lines of vertical communication, and possibly to weaker forms of lateral communication between functions and teams. In a tall structure the hierarchy is substantial, and problems of coordination are ever present. In recent years, in the pursuit of excellence, many large corporations have set about reducing their hierarchy in order to produce a flatter structure. The latter contain fewer levels (typically four) between the top and the bottom of the organisation. The result is that there are fewer supervisory and management staff, and wider spans of control for those who remain. This often leads to more centralised decision-making. However, firms pursuing excellence attempt to avoid this tendency towards centralisation by insisting that staff at all levels carry greater personal responsibility for their results. Much of the success of flat structures, therefore, depends on an organisation culture that emphasises personal responsibility.

Narrow versus wide structure. Taller structures tend to be narrow in terms of the span of control of all the supervisors and middle managers, but less so in the case of the chief executive's span, which usually varies between five senior managers in a tall structure and eight in a flatter structure. However, even tall structures can be spread over a range of functions and line operations to create a wide and complicated structure overall. Most flat structures are wide, both in terms of span of control and in sheer layout, although not necessarily in complexity.

33. *Centralised versus decentralised decision-making/ authority.* The extent to which decision-making (including authority to commit the organisation's resources) is centralised depends partly on the size of the operation and partly on the top management's style. The sheer size and complexity of modern organisations means that a considerable amount of day-today decision-making has to be delegated to lower levels of management and supervision. However, even mid-term planning and decision-making has to be devolved in larger organisations, and this is regardless of the shape of the organisation. Of course, some levels of decision-making and authority stem more from the requirements of the work than from the size of the organisation, or the preferences of the top executive. Production responsibilities, for example, are easier to delegate than R&D and investment planning decisions. Where a policy of decentralisation is followed, matters such as financial and personnel practice may also be delegated throughout the organisation. However, in areas such as policy-making and standard-setting, decision-making for all the key functions (production, marketing, R&D, finance, personnel etc) will invariably be reserved to the centre. The principal advantage of decentralised decision-making is that it enables decisions to be shared appropriately throughout the management hierarchy and thus avoids bottlenecks at the strategic apex. The greatest disadvantages are that it can lead to (i) inconsistencies of treatment of customers, and (ii) to conflict internally, if departments take courses of action that are at odds with each other.

Tight or loose control. This refers to the extent of control (monitoring, checking and correcting) exercised by top management over the rest of the organisation. It is mainly a question of the centralisation or decentralisation of decision-making, combined with the number and nature of controls set up by the senior management levels in order to restrain, or contain, the effects of decision-making lower down the management chain. The extent of control depends partly on the chosen structure, and partly on senior management style. In a bureaucratic structure, for example, controls are likely to be widespread and in-built, whereas in an organic structure, controls will include just a few essential items (eg financial reporting), which will be supported by ad hoc controls depending on job requirements. Senior management styles tend to reinforce the chosen structure, thus bureaucratic managers will insist on 'following the rules', whilst managers preferring an organic approach will limit the number of mandatory procedures and encourage flexible, temporary controls as and when expedient. Excellent companies, according to Peters and Waterman (1982)[8], achieve simultaneous 'loose-tight' methods of control. This suggests that the optimum way forward is to insist on rigid adherence to a few vital controls, and then leave the rest of the checking and correcting to local requirements.

Organisations as systems

34. The presentation of the organisation as an open system interacting with its environment was an idea that developed in the decade after the end of World War II, and has been the focus of attention ever since. Put simply, a system is a collection of interrelated parts forming a whole. Typical systems include the solar system, the human body, a computer network and social systems. Systems may be closed or, more usually, open. 'Closed' systems are those which are effectively self-contained and do not interact with their environment. In such systems all processes are recycled, for example as in a space capsule. Most systems, however, are open systems, in which interaction with the environment is crucial to their operation. Such systems typically absorb inputs from their environment, convert them in appropriate ways, and then return their products into the environment. In open systems feedback from the receiving environment is an essential element in the total process, as this enables decisions to be made about subsequent inputs and processes.

35. Organisations can be regarded as open systems (see Fig. 3.8), which absorb inputs in the form of people, materials, finance and information, and process them to produce a variety of goods and services. Complex systems usually have a number of sub-systems operating within them (eg cardiovascular system in the human body). Organisations are no exception, since some degree of differentiation is invariably present, and this usually produces a number of different sub-systems (eg the administrative system, the R&D function, the production system etc). Feedback of results is an important aspect of organisational systems as they endeavour to supply the needs and demands of their users. Morgan (op.cit) suggests that the theorists of organisations as systems have had an enormous impact on the

way we think about organisations, especially by moving us away from the mechanistic vision -

'The idea that organisations are more like organisms has changed all this, guiding our attention toward the more general issues of survival, organisation-environment relations, and organisational effectiveness. Goals, structures and efficiency now become subsidiary to problems of survival and other more 'biological' concerns.'

36. The cycle of events portrayed in Figure 3.8 emphasises the role of feedback in the operation of an open system. Without feedback an organisation would be hard put to decide what inputs (and how many) it required to achieve present or planned outputs. It would also be badly placed to allocate its resources and decide its priorities without feedback from the environment. No wonder that much organisational behaviour is directed towards managing feedback in every function and at every level!

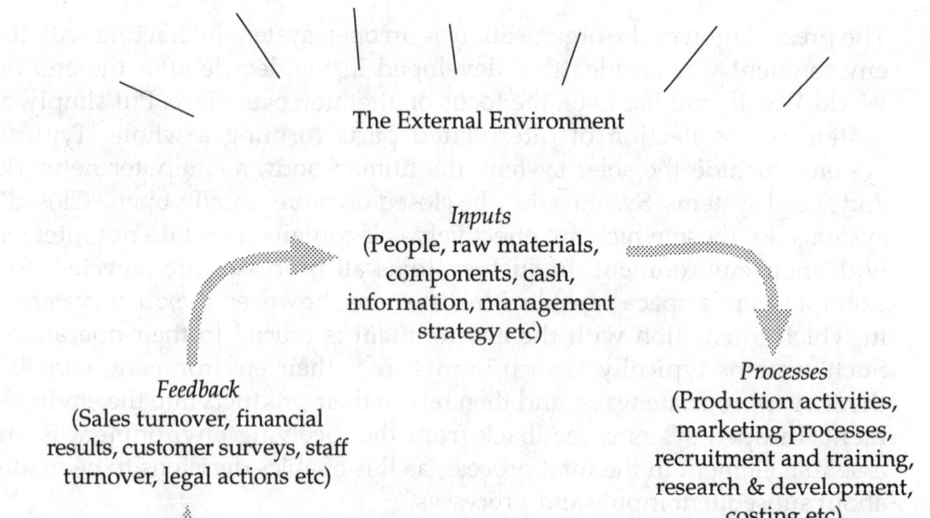

The External Environment

Inputs
(People, raw materials, components, cash, information, management strategy etc)

Processes
(Production activities, marketing processes, recruitment and training, research & development, costing etc)

Feedback
(Sales turnover, financial results, customer surveys, staff turnover, legal actions etc)

Outputs
(Products, services, employment, revenue, profits, taxes, waste etc)

Figure 3.8   *Organisations as open systems*

37. Pioneering work in the area of organisations as open systems was undertaken in the 1940s by Trist and Bamforth[9], two researchers with the London-based Tavistock Institute of Human Relations. Trist and his colleague were interested in the impact of mechanisation on social and

work organisation in coal mines. Prior to mechanisation coal had been extracted by small, closely-knit teams of men working at their own pace in autonomous groups, often completely isolated in the dark. The system they operated was known as the short wall method of coal-getting. The bonds that developed during working hours spilled over into the men's social lives and became part of the fabric of life. At this time there was considerable rivalry between groups, and conflicts between competing groups were frequent, sometimes violent, but always contained.

38. When mechanisation was introduced in the form of coal-cutters and mechanical conveyors, work practices at the coal-face were completely changed. The new system, called the longwall method, required men not in small groups, as before, but in larger groups of 40-50 men plus supervisors. What was being introduced was essentially a mass-production system of coal-getting based on a high degree of job specialisation.

Whereas in the past each small group had undertaken all the jobs required to advance the coal-face, cut the coal, shovel it onto the conveyor and maintain safety, now under the new system most of the primary operations were allocated to a shift (ie all the men at work at a particular 8 — hour period during 24 hours). Thus, the first shift would advance the face, the second shift would cut it, and the third would load it onto the conveyors. What had been an all-round job for each group now became a narrow, specialised, one. The effects were substantial, and mostly negative — the closely-integrated social structure of the small teams was broken down, and this led to increased haggling over pay, inter-shift competition for the best jobs, the seeking of scapegoats in other shifts when things went wrong, and a noticeable increase in absenteeism.

39. The outcomes identified by the researchers led them to the conclusion that effective working required the interdependence of technology and social needs. It was not enough to regard the working environment purely as a technological system into which people must be fitted. Nor was it enough to regard it primarily as a social system. It had to be a combination of the two, and this they called a 'socio-technical system'. So considerable were the difficulties of the longwall method that it was scrapped in favour of a composite method, which went some way towards meeting the social needs of the miners, whilst utilising the benefits of mechanisation. Thus each shift was enabled to carry out all the basic operations (advancing, cutting, conveying), and within the enlarged groups tasks were allocated by the leading members. The payment system was revised so as to incorporate a group bonus. As a result of these changes productivity improved, absenteeism was reduced and accidents were fewer.

40. Whereas Woodward had found that, in a manufacturing context, technology exerted the greatest influence over structure, Trist and Bamforth found that, in the different circumstances of coal-getting, technology was

not the prime determinant. It had to be tempered by a consideration of social needs in the workplace, where it was co-equal with the latter. Thus, technology and social needs were inextricably entwined.

41. In an open system, such as an organisation, the external environment is a crucial element in determining the effectiveness of the system in achieving its goals. Trist again contributed to our knowledge of environments through his work with F.Emery, a colleague at the Tavistock, when in 1965[10] they produced the first classification of environments. This identified four basic types of environment, which were seen as applicable to organisations generally. These four environments were briefly as follows:

1. **Placid, randomised** ie a relatively unchanging and homogeneous environment, whose demands are random
2. **Placid, clustered** ie also relatively unchanging and homogeneous, but where threats and opportunities are clustered around particular aspects of the organisation's life eg market position, scarce employee skills
3. **Disturbed, reactive** ie where competition is intense and may involve hindering tactics
4. **Turbulent field** ie a dynamic and rapidly changing environment, which requires frequent adaptation for survival.

Trist and Emery considered that turbulent environments, in particular, called for a flexible and organic structure in an organisation. Their views may be compared with Mintzberg's analysis of environments in paragraph 55 below.

Pugh and colleagues

42. In the light of the different approaches and alternative structural forms mentioned previously in this chapter, it is timely to examine the work of Professor Derek Pugh and colleagues, originally known as the Aston Group[11], because of their research base at the University of Aston, Birmingham, but who have subsequently expanded into other institutions, principally the London Business School. The original research began some thirty years ago with an investigation into the interrelationship between technology, environment and structure. The research aimed to see what effect an organisation's context had on its structure. Context was analysed under a number of variables such as size, ownership, technology of manufacture, whilst structure was analysed in terms of such variables as specialisation, formalisation, and configuration. The Aston team were aware of the problems of trying to describe organisations in general, and thought

that it would be more constructive to try to generalise about organisational *characteristics*. A key question for the researchers was

> '..to what degree should organisational characteristics such as those above [size, technology etc] be present in different types of companies?' They understood that to answer this question there must be 'accurate comparative measures of centralisation of authority, specialisation of task, standardisation of procedure, and so on, to set beside measurement of size, technology, ownership, business environment and level of performance.'

They then proceeded to devise a number of measures.

43. The six structural variables, or dimensions, of organisation selected initially by the team were as follows:

1.	**Specialisation**	(ie number of specialisms and degree of role specialisation)
2.	**Standardisation**	(ie extent of detailed procedures and roles)
3.	**Formalisation**	(ie extent to which rules, procedures etc are written down)
4.	**Centralisation**	(ie degree of formal authority delegated)
5.	**Configuration**	(ie the shape of the organisation in terms of length of management chain, spans of control, and percentage of specialised/support personnel)
6.	**Flexibility**	(ie amount, speed and rate of change in the organisation)

These variables appeared to represent three major underlying dimensions of organisation structure ,viz

1) *structuring of activities,*

2) *concentration of authority, and*

3) *line control of workflow.*

44. On the basis of the first five of the above dimensions, which the researchers concluded

> '...seem to subsume fairly adequate differences in organisational structure as described in the literature',

a number of organisational structure types were identified, based on clusters of firms with similar characteristics. These types were labelled as shown in Figure 3.9.

Type	Characteristics
1 **Workflow bureaucracy**	Highly structured work activities (production schedules, inspection procedures etc), high percentage of personnel not directly engaged in production (eg planning staff, work study etc) and relatively decentralised. Typically to be found in large-scale manufacturing.
2 **Personnel bureaucracy**	Low structuring of activities, high centralisation of authority, and very standardised employment practices. Typical in local/central government departments, and branch factories of large corporations.
3 **Implicitly structured organisation**	Low both on structure and on centralisation, and held together by 'implicitly transmitted custom'. Typical of small manufacturing concerns with owner-directors.
4 **Full bureaucracy**	Highly structured and centralisewith highly-standardised employment practices. Typically found in public services and nationalised industries.

These four main types were subsequently joined by three other interim types, representing marginal cases where just a small increase in size or technology could move them into the closest primary type. These others were:

Type	Characteristics
5 **Nascent workflow bureaucracy**	Slightly less structured than workflow bureaucracy. Typical of subsidiary units in manufacturing groups.
6 **Pre-workflow bureaucracy**	Also less structured than workflow bureacracy but growth or technological change could lead to full workflow type. Typical of small manufacturing firms.
7 **Nascent full bureaucracy**	Less structured than full bureaucracy, but very little change required to turn into full type.

Figure 3.9   *Organisational structure types (Pugh et al)*

45. The main *contextual* variables employed by Pugh and his team in considering the effect of context on structure were as follows:

1   *Origin and history*   of the organisation

2   *Ownership*   (public, private with many share-holders,
    and control   private with owner-directors etc)

3   *Size*   (in terms of employees, net assets, market position etc)

4   *Charter*   (a term used to describe the purpose/ mission of the organisation)

5   *Technology*   (defined in terms of the degree to which workflow processes were integrated through technology

6   *Location*   (the number of geographically-dispersed sites)

7   *Dependence*   (ie extent to which concern was dependent on one or more stakeholder groups, eg customers, suppliers, owners, trade unions etc)

They also considered *Resources* (human and material) and *Performance* (profitability, productivity, market standing etc). These factors, however, took them into difficult issues, as they discovered, for example that it *'was not possible to investigate the variable "resources" adequately'*.

46.   In constructing a framework of structural and contextual variables, the team aimed to generate a number of possible hypotheses about the relationship between technology and centralisation, and other links between structure and context. In other words, their framework should provide the basis for analysing, and predicting the structure and functioning of organisations, at least in respect of their *'machinery for government not the 'process of government'*. The results of the Aston team contributed primarily to extending knowledge about the range of contextual influences that affect structural choices.

The contribution of Henry Mintzberg

47.   Henry Mintzberg, the Canadian academic, has made a particular study of organisations for more than two decades. In 1979 he produced a lengthy and helpful review and analysis of all the leading research on organisation structures. As a conclusion to this and the previous chapter, a summary of some of Mintzberg's ideas could not be more relevant.

48.   Mintzberg's (1979) ideas about structure, based on his studies of the research literature, are set out in four basic building blocks:

---

1 Three *foundations of organisation,* ie the basic parts, the coordinating mechanisms and the system of flows

2 Nine *design parameters,* ie job specialisation, behaviour formulation, training and indoctrination, unit grouping, unit size, planning and control systems, liaison devices, vertical decentralisation, and horizontal decentralisation

3 Four *contingency factors,* ie age and size, technical system, environment, and power

4 Five *structural configurations,* ie simple structure, machine bureaucracy, professional bureaucracy, divisionalised form, and adhocracy.

The basic parts of the organisation were referred to in Chapter 2 (see Fig. 2.1). These, to recap, were: the strategic apex, the middle line, the operating core, the techno-structure and the support staff. The other fundamental aspects of organisation, and the remaining three building blocks, will be summarised in the following paragraphs, which complete this chapter.

49. Mintzberg concluded that there were five principal coordinating mechanisms that organisations seemed to adopt in operating their structures. These can be summarised as follows:

1. *Mutual adjustment,* which *'achieves the coordination of work by the simple process of informal communication.'* (NB A feature of 'organic' systems)

2. *Direct supervision,* where coordination is achieved by *'having one individual take responsibility for the work of others.'* (NB A feature of the classical management theorists)

3. *Standardisation of work processes,* where coordination is built-in to the various work activities (a) by specifications, set procedures, programmes etc. (NB An essentially 'scientific management' idea)

4. *Standardisation of work outputs,* where coordination is achieved by means of output targets and specifications (NB A feature of Management by Objectives.)

5. *Standardisation of worker skills,* where coordination is achieved by training staff in specified knowledge and skills.

50. Mintzberg concluded that simple organisations could achieve coordination largely through mutual adjustment, but that as an organisation increased in size and with a higher degree of specialisation , then direct supervision is required to facilitate coordination. With increasing complexity of operations, direct supervision is not enough, thus standardisation is required, firstly of work processes, then of outputs, and where neither of these is practicable, then the employees themselves must be standardised through their training.

Mintzberg suggested that organisations mostly achieved coordination by employing several of the five mechanisms.

51. Mintzberg's remaining view of the fundamentals of organisation was to see an organisation as a system of flows — flows of authority, work material, information, and decision processes. The flow of authority, for example, describes the allocation of formal authority throughout the management structure. The work flow refers to the regulated flow of work materials in a production process. In all organisations, and especially in service industries information flows are a central feature of organisational life. These are primarily flows of formal communication, but include important elements of informal methods. And, finally, every organisation is to some extent a system of decision flows.

52. Mintzberg's nine design parameters closely follow those that have been mentioned in these last two chapters. However, one or two further points do need to be made about his list. *Behaviour formalisation* refers to the standardisation of work roles, content and rules. The overall effect is to regulate human behaviour. *Training and indoctrination* concerns (I) the required level of knowledge and skill sought by the organisation (ie obtained by prior training or in-company provision), and (ii) the process by which organisational norms (culture) are acquired by employees (ie what Mintzberg calls 'indoctrination'). The intention is to ensure the internalisation of appropriate behaviours by the workforce. *Liaison devices* are integrating devices ranging from specific liaison positions to task forces/ committees, integrating managers and matrix forms of organisation. *Decentralisation* refers to the extent of devolution of power to make decisions. Devolution down the chain of line authority is called *vertical decentralisation,* and devolution to specialists in the technostructure and support services is called *horizontal decentralisation.*

53. Of the four principal contingency factors adopted by Mintzberg, three have been the subject of earlier references in this chapter, viz age/size, technical system and environment. *Age and size* of organisation affect organisation structure in a number of ways. Older and larger organisations tend to be more formalised than younger and smaller organisations. Organisations tend to change their structure with age and size, but this change is rarely smooth, and when the transition comes it usually creates disruption. Mintzberg describes the *technical system* from two perspectives — firstly, a regulation dimension (ie the technical controls over operators), and secondly, a sophistication dimension (ie the complexity of the technical system). When the technical system is highly regulated, operating work becomes more formalised and the structure becomes bureaucratic. When the technical system is sophisticated, the administrative structure increases, there is an increased dependence on liaison devices and an increased tendency to decentralise authority. The technical system has its greatest impact on the operating core of the organisation.

54. Whereas age, size and technical system are internal factors, *environment* represents the external milieu of the organisation. Mintzberg sees the research liter-

ature as pointing towards four principal characteristics of environments, and these may be compared with those of Trist and Emery (see para. 41 above). The four characteristics are as follows (Figure 3.9):

Characteristic	Range	
1. **Stability**	**Stable** ———————	**Dynamic** (especially in terms of unpredictability)
2. **Complexity**	**Simple** ———————	**Complex** (ie sophisticated)
3. **Market Diversity**	**Integrated** ——————— (eg single product, single customer)	**Diversified** (eg multiple products in global market)
4. **Hostility**	**Munificent** ——————— (ie benevolent)	**Hostile** (eg competitive, unpredictable, and requiring a rapid response)

Figure 3.9   Four principal characteristics of environment (after Mintzberg 1979)

55. In concluding his discussion of environments, Mintzberg noted that

'...it is not the environment per se that counts, but its specific impact on the organisation's ability to cope with it....'.

He suggested that if the four characteristics were put into a matrix with the following axes: Complex-Simple versus Stable-Dynamic, then the following basic types of structure emerge.

Environment	Basic Structure
1. Complex but Stable	Decentralised bureaucratic with emphasis on the standardisation of skills
2. Complex and Dynamic	Decentralised organic with emphasis on mutual adjustment
3. Simple and Stable	Centralised bureaucratic with emphasis on the standardisation of work processes
4. Simple but Dynamic	Centralised organic with emphasis on direct supervision

Figure 3.10   *Environment and structure*

56. The contingency factor of *power* has not been a feature of the work described so far, although Pugh and colleagues touch on it in their reference to 'dependence' (ie interdependence) as a key contextual variable (see para 45 above). Mintzberg sees power as an issue of control by groups and individuals. The attempts to control important decision-making outcomes are exercised, according to Mintzberg, from three main sources: outside groups, such as shareholders, owners, parent organisations and governments; members of the organisation, notably top, middle line and specialist managers; and from social/ cultural norms, that is to say fashions and trends in the external environment. The general effect of the first source is to *'concentrate decision-making power at the top of the organisational hierarchy and to encourage greater than usual reliance on rules and regulations for internal control.'* When these outside groups seek control over the organisation, therefore, the outcome is a structure that is both centralised and formalised, ie bureaucratic. A key word used to justify such control is *'accountability'*, ie the chief executive is accountable to the parent company, the owners, the taxpayer etc. Managers seeking power tend, in the case of top management and senior line managers, to encourage centralisation, but in the technostructure and support parts tend to encourage decentralisation, ie to draw power away from the line. Social and cultural trends outside the organisation may cause firms to adopt an inappropriate structure in their haste to keep up with the Jones's. Overall, Mintzberg concludes that the impact of power as a contingency factor is to

> 'exert significant influence on the design of organisational structure, sometimes encouraging organisations to adopt structures that the contingency factors of age, size, technical system, and environment deem inappropriate.'

57. The conclusion to Mintzberg's efforts to synthesise the research on organisations is the production of a set of clusters, or configurations, that can act as a focal point for the study of organisations. The five configurations that emerge reduce the separate influences of the design parameters, contingency factors and other key organisational features into manageable concepts that can be used to further the study of organisational behaviour. In Mintzberg's own words

> 'In each structural configuration, a different one of the coordinating mechanisms is dominant, a different part of the organisation plays the most important role, and a different type of decentralisation is used.' The five configurations can be summarised as follows:

Configuration	Prime coordinating mechanism	Key part of organisation	Main design parameters	Contingency factors
1. **Simple structure** ('non-structure')	Direct supervision	Strategic apex	Centralisation Organic	Age: young Technical: simple Environment: simple/dynamic
2. **Machine bureaucracy**	Standardisation of work processes	Techno-structure	Behaviour formalisation. Specialisation. Centralisation.	Age: old Size: large Technical: simple/regulated Environment: stable/external control
3. **Professional bureaucracy**	Standardisation of skills	Operating core	Training Horizontal specialisation Decentralisation	Environment: complex Technical: simple, non-regulated
4. **Divisionalised form**	Standardisation of outputs	Middle line	Unit grouping (markets) Performance control	Environment: diversified markets Age: old Size: large Power: middle managers
5. **Adhocracy**	Mutual adjustment	Support staff Operating core	Liason devices Organic Unit grouping (functional/ markets)	Age: young Technical: automated Environment: complex/dynamic

Figure 3.11   *Mintzsberg's Five structural configurations*

58. The application of the five-configuration model developed by Mintzberg enables an organisation's senior management to consider the implications of their choice of configuration, to identify those parts of the organisation that are most likely to be affected by it, and to design the appropriate parameters. They can consider these aspects of organisation design against the contingency factors that typify their organisation.

Conclusion

59. This has been a lengthy chapter. However, it has not mentioned the effect of strategy (ie decisions about the organisation's mission, long-term goals, values and the means for achieving all these). This issue will be examined later in Chapter 17. For the moment it is worth recognising that organisation structures, and the processes by which they are implemented, do not just arise because of the pressure of environmental factors, or even because of the perceived needs of managers to coordinate the activities of their organisation.They arise in part because of consciously-made strategic decisions taken by the top management and implemented through the management chain.

References

1. Woodward, Joan (1958), *Management and Technology*, HMSO
2. Woodward, Joan (1965), *Industrial Organisation - Theory and Practice*, OUP
3. Burns, Tom & Stalker, G.M. (1961), *The Management of Innovation*, Tavistock Publications

4. Morgan, G. (1986), *Images of Organisation*, Sage Publications

5. Lawrence, P. & Lorsch, J. (1967), *Organisation and Environment: Managing Differentiation and Integration*, Harvard Business School

6. Mintzberg, H. (1979), *The Structuring of Organisations - a Synthesis of the Research*, Prentice Hall

    NB The principal contents of this book were republished in summary form as (1983), *Structure in Fives: Designing Effective Organisations*, Prentice Hall

7. Handy, C.(1993), *Understanding Organizations (4th edn)*, Penguin Business

8. Peters, T. & Waterman, R. (1982) *In Search of Excellence : Lessons from America's Best-Run Companies*, Harper and Row

9. Trist, E.L.& Bamforth, K.,Some *Social and Psychological Consequences of the Long-wall Method of Coal-getting, in Human Relations (1951, Vol.3)*

10. Emery, F. & Trist, E., *'The Causal Texture of Organizational Environments', in Human Relations*, 18.

11. Pugh, D.S. & Hickson, D.J. (1976), *Organisational Structure in its Context:* The Aston Programme, Saxon House / Gower Publishing

Questions for reflection/discussion

1. According to Woodward's findings, what is the most likely structure to be found in a process industry? How might this compare with the structure of a unit production firm?

2. How far is it practicable for any firm to incorporate both mechanistic and organic elements into its organisation structure?

3. To what extent do organisational structures represent little more than a reaction to the whims of the external world?

4. What are the implications of a significant increase in the span of control throughout a management hierarchy for (a) the shape of the organisation structure, and (b) the management of day-to-day activities?

5. Why might the directors of a large company decide to organisae themselves along divisional lines rather than along purely functional lines?

6. What is a *'socio-technical system'*, and how could you apply your definition to your place of work, or study?

7. To what extent does an organisation's ability to act as an open system depend on the attitudes and skills of its senior management?

8. How closely does Mintzberg's five-configuration model of organisations compare with the model proposed by Pugh and colleagues? As well as common features, what differences do you note?

4 Organisation structuring: the human aspects

Introduction

1.   In the previous two chapters we have examined some of the key issues involved in designing organisation structures. Although some references were made to the human consequences of alternative structures and mechanisms, the emphasis in those two chapters was firmly on the structural framework itself and its associated working mechanisms. This chapter will look more closely at the human aspects of designing and operating organisations. We begin by summarising the pioneering research into *human* factors at work (the Hawthorne Experiments) conducted by Mayo, Roethlisberger and Dickson in the United States between 1927 and 1936. This research gave the world of organisation and management theory the term 'Human Relations School'. This was an acknowledgement of the importance of examining people's needs in the design and operation of organisation structures.

2.   The well-publicised results of the Hawthorne Experiments led to a widespread interest in the significance of human relations in the workplace. Not only were the social needs of people in groups studied, but also the needs and motives of people as individuals. The main summaries of the leading research findings, and a discussion of their effect on organisational theory, are contained in subsequent chapters (see Chap.7 on motivation, and Chap.11 on leadership. In this chapter we introduce the principal ideas and paradigms of the writers whose work has fallen into the neo-Human relations (or Social Psychological) School. These include Homans (1950), Maslow (1954), Argyris (1957), McGregor (1960), Likert (1961) and Herzberg (1968), McClleland (1961) and Alderfer (1974).

Human relations — the Hawthorne Experiments

3.   The Hawthorne Experiments, as they were called, began in the Western Electric Company's Hawthorne plant in Chicago in 1927, when Professor Elton Mayo of Harvard was invited into the company to give advice

following a surprising development in the company's own researches. The company, which prided itself on its welfare policies, had already begun some studies into the effects of different physical working conditions on its employees. This decision represented a modest step forward from scientific management in that, although the emphasis was on the effects of *physical* conditions on employees, nevertheless the *employee* rather than work itself, and control over work, became the focus of attention. What prompted the Company's call to Mayo was an unforeseen consequence of a study into the effects of different levels of lighting on employee productivity and morale. The surprise element was that the workers in the study increased their productivity whether the lighting was improved or not. Clearly, some other factor was at work. Over the course of the next few years, the Harvard team and the Company investigators, jointly gathered substantial evidence of important *social* factors at work in the factory. They were able to show, for example, that membership of a group was important to individuals, and that relationships with supervisors could have a positive or negative effect on people's attitudes towards their work. More importantly, they discovered that groups had *power*, and especially the power to introduce their own norms and standards into the workplace, thus forming an unofficial organisation alongside the official structure of relationships.

4.   The Hawthorne researches represented the first real attempt to investigate 'the human factor' at work, and thus undertake genuine social research. In so doing, they were able to redirect attention away from the rather instrumental issues of the time, namely productivity, fatigue, absenteeism and industrial accidents, towards a more positive consideration of employee needs and motives at work. Briefly, the researches Roethlisberger & Dickson, 1939)[1] can be summarised as follows:

Stage One (1924-1927). This stage preceded the Harvard team's entry, and led to the surprise finding, for which further explanation was required. The facts were that two groups of employees of comparable work performance were isolated from the other workers and located in a separate part of the plant as part of a study into the effects of lighting on productivity and morale. One group, the control group, received a consistent level of lighting, while the other group, the experimental group, received varying levels of lighting. To the surprise of the Company research team, both groups showed *increased* productivity. Yet more suprisingly, the experimental group's production rate continued to rise even when the lighting was deliberately reduced! This was not what the researchers had expected, and clearly some factor other than purely physical working conditions was influencing the behaviour of the groups. It was at this point that the company decided to call in Mayo and his colleagues.

5. **Stage Two (1927-1929).** This was termed the *Relay Assembly Test Room* stage, and was intended to take a closer look at the effects of differing physical conditions on productivity. There was no intention at this stage to investigate possible *social* phenomena at work in the groups. Once again a group of workers (five women) were separated from the rest, put into a separate room, and set to work at their usual tasks. Over a period of several months a number of changes were deliberately introduced into their work routine — rest pauses were changed several times, as was the timing and length of the lunch break; changes were also made to their payments system. On each occasion the women were consulted about the changes. It was found, again to the researchers' surprise, that whether conditions were improved or worsened, the women's productivity continued to rise! As the experiment continued, however, two of the group began to display antagonistic and uncooperative behaviour towards their work and their supervisors. It was not discovered why they reacted in this way. The two women were spoken to about their behaviour, which did not improve and their productivity slackened. They were, therefore, sent back to the ranks of the other factory workers, and two other women were selected to replace them. By this time the researchers were becoming aware of powerful social forces at work in the group —

    '...two essentially different sorts of changes occurred in the first seven periods of the experiment. There were those changes introduced by the investigators in the form of experimental conditions.......There was another type of change, however, of which the investigators were not so consciously aware. This was manifested in.....a gradual change in social interrelations among the operators themselves, which displayed itself in....new group loyalties and solidarities......(and) .....in a change in the relation between the operators and their supervisors.' (p.58-9)

6. The Test Room experiment continued for a further two years, and its results continued to puzzle the investigators —

    'The general upward trend in output independent of any particular change in rest pauses or shorter working hours was astonishing. The improvement in mental attitude throughout the first two years..... was also perplexing.'

    No less than five interpretations were put forward by way of explanation, mostly suggesting different aspects of working conditions, but one which suggested that the increased output and improved attitude were down to the changes in the method of supervision. This interpretation suggested that *'Social factors were the major circumstance limiting output.'*

7. **Stage Three (1928-1931).** The company had already decided before the ending of the relay assembly group experiments to attempt to find out more about employee- supervisor relations. Since better relations in the Test Room appeared to be one factor in the improved morale of the group, the investigators decided to develop an interview programme designed to

elicit employee attitudes towards supervision and other issues of interest to employees. They accordingly set up a programme, whose first object was to improve supervisor training and performance, and, secondly, to find out about more about employees' attitudes towards such issues as working conditions, supervision and jobs. The interviews were conducted by selected supervisors, who were trained for the work, which at first proceeded by way of structured interviews dominated by the interviewer's agenda. As the programme continued, however, the interviews became more open-ended and employees were encouraged to say what they thought was important to them. Supervisors were interviewed not by other Company staff, but by two Harvard researchers, including Roethlisberger. By the completion of the programme more than 20,000 employees had been interviewed, and a wealth of material gained. Against the economic and social -background of the time, such a programme was strikingly novel, almost revolutionary! What the results showed beyond all doubt was that social relationships at work were of major importance to employees. The Company also recognised that its supervisors must henceforth give much more attention to the task of communicating with their employees.

8. **Stage Four (1931-1932).** Evidence coming from the later stages of the interview programme showed that

    '...early in 1931, the investigators' attention had been called to the fact that social groups in the shop departments were capable of exercising very strong control over the work behaviour of their individual members.....Their reports showed very clearly that they were encountering several related phenomena, the importance of which had escaped them before this time. Chief among these was the restriction of output.....wage incentive systems....had been rendered ineffectual by group pressure for controlled output.....There was evidence of informal leadership on the part of certain persons who took upon themselves the responsibility of seeing that the members of the group clung together and protected themselves from representatives of other groups within the company who could interfere with their affairs.'

    It was felt that a more systematic enquiry was needed, and this led to the establishment of a further set of experiments known as the *Bank Wiring Observation Room* stage.

9. Here a group of fourteen men was separated from the main production area, but employed under the same working conditions as those outside. As this study was intended (a) to focus specifically on *social* issues, and (b) to be given in-depth treatment, the group's behaviour was to be monitored by two investigators — one acting as an observer in the workplace ('in the role of disinterested spectator'), and the other acting as an external interviewer ('to remain an outsider to the group as much as possible.') The

team recognised that the role of observer was a difficult one. He had to establish friendly relations with everyone in the group, and win their confidence, which meant becoming part of the situation he was studying. Yet he had to remain objective and impartial:

'To keep his own feelings and prejudices from coloring the material recorded...'.

Accordingly, a number of rules for the observer were established, eg not to give orders or assume any authority, not to enter into arguments unless forced, and always to maintain confidences. The interviewer's role was to conduct interviews in privacy by appointment with a view to obtaining information about individuals' attitudes, thoughts and feelings. As the research report pointed out

'Their (the workers) active participation in the department, and, to a certain extent, in the larger company structure was subject to direct observation. Their participation in the wider community and their subjective attitudes, beliefs and feelings towards their immediate surroundings in the plant could not, however, be observed.....the best available technique was the personal interview.' (p.390)

10. The working conditions and payment system applying to the group were the standard arrangements. There were, however, two major differences in their situation —

'segregation in a separate room and their knowledge that they were being studied.'

Neither of these two factors appeared to appreciably alter the findings of the study. Both output and attitudes remained substantially the same throughout the period of observation. The only changed feature noticed was that the men were less subdued in the observation room than they had been in their department. The overall result was that the men continued to restrict production in accordance with their own standards. They also developed their own rules of behaviour, and resisted any attempts by their supervisors to intervene. They developed their own, informal, organisation, and demonstrated to the researchers that informal, unofficial, behaviour at the workplace can be as active as formal, officially-condoned behaviour. Thus, the expression 'formal/ informal organisation' was added to the literature of social science.

11. **Final Stage (1936).** The final stage of the Hawthorne Experiments focused on employee relations, and took the form of employee counselling interviews. The gap between this and the previous stage was the result of the worldwide economic slump in the early 1930s. Only when conditions had sufficiently improved did the Company decide to reinstate the interview programme. The resumption of the programme was an indication of the Company's lasting interest in, and commitment to, employee welfare and

development. In this round of interviews, called the 'personnel counselling' programme, employees were encouraged to discuss their work problems with trained personnel specialists. The latter were given a consultancy type role with no line authority, and had to work in cooperation with line supervisors. The latter were responsible for identifying possible candidates for interview and making arrangement for interviewees to be away from their posts for the 80 minutes or so required by the typical interviewer. The major problems addressed by the programme were (1) individual adjustment to the industrial structure, (2) communication and control, and (3) changes in the social structure. As a result of bringing such issues out into the open, the Company was able to reap the benefits of improved employee relations with supervisors and managers, and better individual adjustment at work.

The Hawthorne contribution to organisation studies

12. The Hawthorne Experiments were the first systematic attempt to undertake serious social research into the workplace. They helped to redirect attention away from issues such as fatigue, accidents and response to physical working conditions — all of which treated human beings primarily as *physical* organisms — and towards a consideration of people as intelligent human beings, worthy of the respect of their supervisors and alive to all the possibilities of human interaction at work. In particular, the experiments showed that:

---

1. Workers should not be viewed in isolation from others, but as members of a group

2. Membership of a group, and the status that goes with it, is as important to individuals as monetary incentives or good physical working conditions

3. Informal (unofficial) groups can exercise a strong influence over employees in the workplace

4. Supervisors and managers need to take account of the social and psychological needs of employees in securing their commitment to organisational goals

5. Groups of individuals who are made to feel special will respond in positive ways to organisational demands

6. The results of conducting research in the workplace may not always be what the researchers anticipated, or indeed hoped for!

..... continued

> 7. The pattern of behaviour, where people's positive response to being part of a research project obscures other factors in the work environment, has been called the 'Hawthorne Effect'. This concept has proven to be a major contribution to social science
>
> 8. Paying prime attention to the job or task as a means of raising productivity (ie the scientific management/ industrial engineering approach) is likely to prove counter-productive, unless employees' social needs are sufficiently catered for at the same time.

Human relations after Hawthorne

13. The decade which followed the ending of the Hawthorne Experiments was dominated by a war, which involved all the leading industrial nations of the world. At the end of the war in August 1945, the economies of the Axis Powers (Germany, Italy and Japan) were in ruins, and those of Britain and the Soviet Union severely weakened. Only the United States emerged stronger from the war. Every nation, however, now had to re-direct, if not to re-build its economy, away from military priorities to peaceful concerns, and to do so in a manner which reflected peoples' needs in a post-war society. Would the struggle for efficiency and productivity lead business concerns back to the concepts of scientific management, or to a broader human relations perspective, or to a mixture of the two?

G.C. Homans

14. George Homans (1950)[2] was one of the first theorists to take a closer look at the nature of the influential, informal, groups first identified by the Bank Wiring experiments at Hawthorne. In studying the ability of powerful informal groups to control the behaviour of their members, he identified three key elements in the social system of groups. These were: *activities* (ie the tasks performed by the members), *interactions* (ie between the members), and *sentiments* (ie individual and collective attitudes). Homans saw these key elements as interdependent. That is to say, change in any one of the elements affects the other two. Homans noticed, in particular, that as individuals collaborated over a period of time, they developed common ways of thinking, and thus began to devise their own rules of behaviour for the group as a whole. Individual thinking and behaviour gradually began to be supplanted by group attitudes, which became dominant (ie peer group pressure).

Abraham Maslow

15. Maslow's principal hypothesis was that human beings have common groups of needs, which tend to be satisfied in a more or less hierarchical way. Whilst the theory has been criticised because of its rigidity and partial applicability, it nevertheless helps to identify the crucial sets of needs that are present in every human being. Maslow (1954)[3] concluded that there were five sets of needs, which can be summarised as follows:

1	**Physiological**	Satisfying basic appetites (food, sleep etc), ensuring shelter and acquiring clothing
2	**Safety/Security**	Need to avoid danger and deprivation
3	**Social/Affiliation**	Personal acceptance by others, belonging to a group
4	**Esteem**	Desire for recognition; gaining self-respect
5	**Self-actualisation**	The drive towards self-fulfilment

16. Maslow's initial view was that individuals had to satisfy lower level needs before seeking to satisfy higher levels. Subsequently, however, he modified his assertion (when/where?). His ideas were modified further by Alderfer (1972)[4], who introduced the idea of needs along a continuum rather than in an hierarchy (ERG theory). Alderfer concluded that there were only three sets of needs — *Existence, Relatedness* and *Growth* — and that individuals could move backwards and forwards along the continuum in order to satisfy each set of needs. The Existence needs correspond roughly to Maslow's physiological and security needs, the Relatedness correspond to Maslow's belonging needs, and Growth needs are similar to Maslow's esteem and self-actualisation needs. Alderfer did produce some research evidence in support of his ERG theory, but, whilst noted as interesting by the research world, his results are considered to be inconclusive.

17. Whatever view one takes of the validity of the ideas of Maslow and Alderfer, they can still be useful in an impressionistic way. Taking a historical perspective, for example, it is clear from the Hawthorne case that the 1920's were dominated by attention to physiological and security needs. The organisation of work was regulated so as reduce fatigue, absenteeism and accidents. In some cases, there was also an attempt to introduce security into payments systems (eg Taylor and Gantt). Job security was an issue of which managements were aware, but in the economic conditions of the time, were unable to cater for. What the Hawthorne case demonstrated, in particular, was that social and affiliation needs were very important to individuals, and, significantly, could outweigh monetary (ie security) considerations.

The social psychologists

18. In the post-war years of the 1950s, the focus of attention in the United States began to be redirected towards higher needs, as the search began to find out what motivates people at work. This led to the so-called 'social psychological approach' to management and organisation theory. Most of the theories generated by the leading exponents of this approach have not been proven convincingly under research conditions. However, like most of the social research conducted in the twenty years after the Second World War, the concepts that have been developed have stimulated further investigations, and have been applied in practice by managers in a wide range of organisations. The principal members of the social psychological school were Chris Argyris, Douglas McGregor, Rensis Likert and Frederick Herzberg, whose ideas are summarised briefly below.

C. Argyris

19. As a result of his studies into the effects of management practices on individual behaviour and personal growth at work, Argyris (1957)[5] developed his so-called 'Immaturity-maturity theory' to explain the stages people have to move through in order to become mature human beings. He then examined management practices to see how far they contributed to the process of maturation. One conclusion he came to was that the reason for the apparent laziness of so many workers was not due any innate response (eg Taylor's 'natural soldiering') but because they were being treated as children by the management system. Argyris, like most of the social-psychological theorists, took the individual as the basis for his ideas. The assumption for group behaviour was that, if *individuals* were encouraged to adopt mature forms of behaviour at work, then groups would function more effectively than before.

20. Argyris's theory suggests that an individual moves from immaturity to maturity in a continuous process along seven different dimensions, each of which provides a continuum of immature to mature forms of behaviour. His model has been summarised in Figure 4.1.

    Becoming mature, according to the theory means moving through the scale from passive behaviour to the development of self-awareness and self-control. Argyris argued that, even though factors such as the individual's culture and personality served to limit maturity, nevertheless there is an innate tendency towards mature forms of behaviour.

	Immaturity	*Maturity*
1	Passive behaviour	————> Active behaviour
2	Dependent behaviour	————> Independent behaviour
3	Few ways of behaving	————> Many ways of behaving
4	Erratic and shallow interests	—> Deeper and stronger interests
5	Short-term perspective	————> Long-term perspective
6	Being subordinate	————> Being equal or superior
7	Lack of self-awareness	————> Self-awareness and self-control

Figure 4.1   *Immaturity-Maturity Theory (Argyris)*

21. When comparing the typical hierarchical structure against the above model, Argyris concluded that the former, with its task specialisation, chain of command and other features of formal organisation, positively engendered passivity, dependence and subordination. In other words, he was saying, typical work organisations are designed to keep people immature! The result is that many employees feel frustrated with their work, and try to find informal ways round the system. In one experiment carried out in an electronics firm, Argyris proposed that a group of girls assembling a product under a highly specialised and supervised system should each be given the opportunity to complete the whole job and be responsible for their own inspection. Until then each girl had a very restricted task to perform before handing the job over to someone else. Each task and role had been designed by an industrial engineer. There was a separate inspector to check the goods, and a packer. The whole group was supervised by a foreman. In all, a typical classical (Taylorist) organisation structure! The firm agreed to introduce a system whereby each girl would assemble the whole product, inspect it, pack it, and accept responsibility for it in the event of any complaints. In the first few weeks of the experiment production dropped drastically by more than 70%, then it began to rise, until, by the fifteenth week, it was at an all-time high. Not only did productivity improve, but costs due to errors, wastage and complaints dropped to a mere fraction of their previous level. Clearly, the girls in question were ready for, and eventually capable of, taking responsibility for their work in a constructive and productive manner. Argyris recognised that not all workers are keen to seek greater responsibility and autonomy at work, but he believed that a majority do want these elements in their daily work. This particular belief was taken up by Douglas McGregor, a contemporary of Argyris, in his development of two opposing theories, which he called X and Y.

Douglas McGregor — Theory X and Theory Y

22. What McGregor was trying to achieve in developing Theory X and Theory Y was an explanation of two contrasting sets of assumptions about individuals and their needs at work. Theory X assumptions consider that employees are basically lazy, do not wish to accept responsibility, have little desire for work and want to be directed. These views represent the essence of scientific management thinking — the Taylorist view. As McGregor (1960)[6] himself put it

> '...Theory X is.......a theory which materially influences managerial strategy in a wide sector of American industry today. Moreover, the principles of organisation which comprise the bulk of the literature of management could only have been derived from assumptions such as those of Theory X. Other beliefs about human nature would have led inevitably to quite different organisational principles.' (p.35) In his view, Theory X is '....built on the least common human denominator: the factory 'hand' of the past.......As Chris Argyris has shown.....conventional managerial strategies for.......human resources..... are admirably suited to the capacities and characteristics of the child rather than the adult.'

23. McGregor acknowledged that, in the period between the 1930's and the 1960's, management had adopted a far more humanitarian approach to the treatment of employees. However, these post-Hawthorne improvements had been achieved, according to McGregor, *'without changing the fundamental theory of management.'* What he then proposed was a completely new set of assumptions about people at work — Theory Y — which suggested that people did not inherently dislike work, that they could seek responsibility, and were capable of self-direction. He accepted that these assumptions were not yet validated and would undoubtedly be refined, but reckoned that they would be unlikely to be completely contradicted. When he was writing his influential text 'The Human Side of Enterprise'(1960) , his arguments were directed more at managers than fellow academics, and his 'theories' are best seen in a managerial context rather than an academic one. He was undoubtedly influenced by Maslow's ideas of human needs, and it is easy to see the practices of scientific management and bureaucratic organisations reflected in the lower level needs referred to by Maslow. McGregor, in Theory Y wanted organisations to lift their employees up the Maslow hierarchy so that they could taste recognition and self-fulfilment at work.

24. The principal assumptions contained in the respective theories X and Y have provided a useful guide to managers in identifying their attitudes towards employees, and enabling decisions to be made about new approaches to human resource management. They are probably best viewed as alternative cultural types, indicating the opposite ends of a

continuum of commonly-accepted assumptions about people's motives in the workplace. Briefly the two sets of assumptions are as follows Fig. 4.2):

Theory X	Theory Y
1. Most people find work inherently distasteful	1. Work is as natural as play or rest
2. People therefore need to be coerced, controlled and directed	2. People will exercise self-direction and self-control when committed to objectives
3. The average person prefers to be directed, does not want responsibility, is unambitious and seeks security above all else	3. This commitment is a function of achievement rewards
	4. Under proper conditions people will not only accept but actively seek responsibility
	5. The capacity to exercise imagination, ingenuity and creativity is widespread
	6. The intellectual potential of human beings is being under-utilised in industrial life.

Figure 4.2   The Assumptions of Theory X and Theory Y

Rensis Likert — new patterns of organisation

25. Likert's work at the University of Michigan (USA) focused particularly on the relationship between management behaviour and high production. His research indicated that high-producing managers (and supervisors) not only utilised the tools of classical management in their work (eg work study, budgeting), but also paid attention to the development of supportive relationships in their work-teams. They also encouraged participative practices among the team members (see Chapter 11). Likert (1961)[7] developed his idea into a novel concept of the 'linking pin' form of organisation structure, based on the role of section/ unit leaders in the next highest group as well as in their own team. As Figure 4.3 shows, the linking pin formation still has a predominantly hierarchical look about it, but nevertheless relies more on the interactions between interlocking teams than it does on strictly specialised functions with little lateral communication.

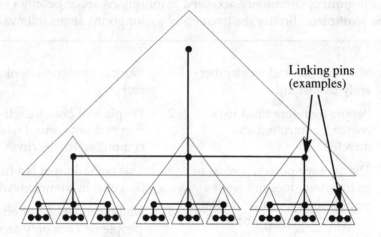

Linking pins
(examples)

Figure 4.3   Linking pin form of structure (Likert)

26. Likert, like McGregor, was interested in the assumptions implicit in organ-isation structures and managerial behaviour (ie leadership style). He iden-tified four approaches (Systems 1-4), which he described as follows:

System 1	**Exploitive-authoritative** approach	Power and direction come from above; threats and punishment employed
System 2	**Benevolent-authoritative** approach	Top-down emphasis, but upwards consultation allowed; rewards available as well as threats
System 3	**Consultative** approach	Power and direction operate after discussion with employees; communication flows up as well as down; some teamwork and employee involvement
System 4	**Participative-group** approach	High participation, lateral as well as vertical communication, various forms of motivation encouraged. The ideal system.

27. Likert found that productivity was mediocre under System 1, fair but costly under System 2, good under System 3, and excellent under System 4. The gist of his argument is that people-orientated systems are far more productive than those which are heavily task-orientated. Like many of his contempo-

raries, Likert was almost too keen to look away from the classical era and its mechanistic, task-orientated ethos, towards an organic, person-orientated approach to managing people. The truth, according to other theorists, probably lies somewhere in between these two alternatives. The issue of management style, or leadership style, is discussed in greater detail in Chapter 11.

Frederick Herzberg and the concept of job satisfaction

28. Herzberg (1959[8], 1968[9]) contributed a number of interesting ideas to the study of employees' attitudes towards their jobs. The original research conducted by Herzberg and colleagues was written up in The Motivation to Work (1959). This described the outcomes of a study in which two hundred engineers and accountants were asked about events at work that had resulted (a) in *a marked improvement in their job satisfaction*, or (b) *had led to a marked reduction in job satisfaction.* The researchers discovered from the interviews that five factors seemed to contribute consistently to respondents' experience of job satisfaction. These were: *achievement, recognition, work itself, responsibility and advancement,* with the last three representing the most lasting sources of satisfaction. By comparison, the factors that caused the greatest dissatisfaction were: *company policy and administration, supervision, salary, interpersonal relations and working conditions.* These dissatisfiers all tended to represent short-term sources of dissatisfaction.

29. On the basis of these findings Herzberg and colleagues constructed a two-factor theory of job satisfaction called *'motivation-hygiene theory'*. The satisfiers mentioned above were called *'motivators'*, since they appeared to be effective in spurring individuals on to superior performance. These motivators all seemed to be associated with what a person does at work (job content, responsibility etc). The dissatisfiers were given the somewhat idiosyncratic name of *'hygiene factors'*, since they appeared to result from issues in the working environment rather from the work itself. Motivators appeared to be associated with needs for growth and self-actualisation (ie Maslow's higher-level needs), whilst hygiene factors appeared to be associated with the need to avoid unpleasantness (ie a safety/ security need). The researchers insisted that the two sets of factors were distinct and separate. Their results suggested that (a) where motivators were not available, people were not necessarily *de-motivated,* but were just not motivated, and (b) where dissatisfiers were improved, this did not lead to satisfaction, but only to a *non-dissatisfied* state.

30. The original research was extended to a number of other groups in a variety of industries with similar results (1968). Nevertheless, fellow theorists have consistently felt unhappy with Herzberg's use of the term 'job satisfaction' in a discussion about motivation. Their main criticisms have been (1) that the concept of 'job satisfaction' has not been sufficiently analysed and clarified, and (2) that Herzberg's theory confuses this concept with that of 'moti-

vation'. Practising managers, however, have found the results very useful in helping them to distinguish between *maintenance* practices (hygiene factors), such as wage and salary administration and improvement of supervision, and *motivational* practices, such as recognising achievement, providing intrinsic job interest etc. Indeed, one of the practical consequences of Herzberg's theory has been the development of programmes to build motivators into jobs — so-called 'job enrichment programmes' (see Chap.15).

31. If we apply the ideas and practices of earlier theories to Herzberg's model, we find that the scientific managers concentrated on the hygiene factors of company policy and administration, incentive payments schemes, and tight supervision. No motivators were given consideration. The Human relations school also focused on hygiene factors, but included interpersonal relationships, both between supervisors and groups, and within groups. A by-product of the Hawthorne Studies was that recognition was available to those in the research groups in that they were separated out from the other employees. In all the experiments except the Bank Wiring Room, the employees involved seemed to respond positively to being in the spotlight (the so-called 'Hawthorne Effect'). By comparison, the social psychologists mentioned earlier in this chapter have all looked to *motivators* as the way to enhance individual and organisation performance (Theory Y etc).

Achievement motivation

32. The need for achievement has been identified as an important motivator at work by D.McClelland (1961)[10]. His team at Harvard University studied some of the *differences* between people, and found that, in the higher levels of need, three factors stood out — the need for achievement (n-Ach), the need for power (n-Pow), and the need for affiliation, or belonging (n-Aff). Individuals showing a high degree of n-Ach were noted as:

   ❑ constantly striving for achievement (ie it was no temporary inclination)
   ❑ seeking tasks in which they could exercise responsibility
   ❑ preferring tasks which, though challenging, were well within their capacity
   ❑ actively seeking feedback on their performance
   ❑ being less concerned with social and affiliation needs.

33. McClelland suggested that the need for achievement is a key human motive, which responds to, and is a product of, personal experience and cultural background rather than inherited characteristics. It can thus be indoctrinated by means of training and other attitude-forming activities. A problem for management development, however, is that stimulating managers to develop a greater appetite for achievement may lead to the formation of excessively task-orientated management styles, which could be counter-productive. In the course of his work on achievement motivation, McClleland utilised a selection test known as the Thematic

Apperception Test (TAT), which had been devised by Henry Murray (1938) several years earlier. This helps to identify the strength of an individual's achievement, affiliation and power requirements by means of his or her responses to a number of pictures, which they are asked to comment on. The strength of the various needs is inferred from the answers.

Human relations and management style

34.	Interest in the human factor at work has led not only to a focus on people in groups, and people as individuals, but also on people as leaders. The theory and practice of organisations after Hawthorne was a mixture of classical perspectives and the newer human relations or social-psychological approaches. By the early 1960's organisational theory was beginning to look rather more closely at the role of leadership in groups, as well as at the motivation of individuals. Issues of process were becoming as important as issues of structure, as theorists and practitioners moved further away from mechanistic models of organisation to more organic concepts. The key relationships at this time were structure, organisational processes, people as individuals, people in groups, leadership and communication (see Fig. 4.4). Implicit in much of the thinking was the need to achieve organisational goals in tandem with individual and group goals. Classical issues such as the drive for efficiency and productivity, the mechanics of incentive payments systems, and the need to regulate the workplace environment had not disappeared, but were receiving a much lower priority. Similarly, the welfare orientation of many post-Hawthorne establishments was giving way to less paternalistic forms of management in the face of respect for individuals and individualism.

35.	The issue of leadership will be considered separately in Chapter 11. However, some comment is necessary at this stage, since (a) the treatment of employees in any organisation is determined considerably by the behaviour of their management, ie by the dominant management style, and (b) the success of management is judged partly by their ability to motivate individuals, or groups, at work. These are fundamental issues for students of organisational behaviour, as well as of much interest to practitioners. What ideas have been thrown up by the research community? The principal paradigms have taken one or two dimensions of the leadership situation and attempted to construct a theory around them. Two such dimensions are (1) a concern for people (ie employee-centred styles), and (2) a concern for the task (task-centred styles). In the case of the Michigan Studies in the 1950's (see Likert,1961), these two dimensions were seen as representing the polar extremes of a continuum. Thus, individual managers were either basically people-orientated or task-orientated.

36.	Other studies (eg Ohio, 1957[11], Blake & Mouton,1964)[12] suggested that the two dimensions were separate, and managers could therefore be measured against each one. They could be measured in terms of the strength of both their preference for people and their preference for task, thus enabling them a combined position to be adopted in relation to (1) the task required of them and (2) their attitude towards their staff. Another paradigm is founded on the notions of authority and delegation, or power-sharing. Here leadership can be scored in terms of an individual's desire to retain authority over subordinates, or to share his or her power with them. Behind all these efforts to describe a useful theory of leadership lies a management concern for maintaining harmonious and productive human relations. In recent times, the drive for excellence and competitive advantage has reduced the spotlight on human (ie employee) relations, and instead put customer relations in the centre-stage position.

Conclusion

37. We conclude this chapter by mapping out the key organisational issues that were the concern of researchers and practitioners in what might be called the 'social psychological period' of organisational behaviour. Earlier, in Figure 2.4 in Chapter 2, we noted the major variables of organisation structure as being (1) purpose and goals, (2) tasks, (3) technology, (4) external environment, (5) people and (6) culture. These last two variables have formed the core of this chapter, and Figure 4.3 indicates the priorities that were assigned to them during the 1960's when interest in the human factor at work was at its peak. One additional variable — (7) organisation processes — is included at this stage. This reflects the interest in communication issues and leadership when considering the human resource dimension of the organisation.

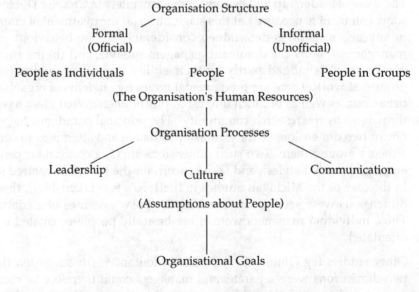

Figure 4.4   *Organisational Priorities in the 1960's*

38. The last three chapters have tried to summarise seven major variables of organisation structure. Having come thus far, we can now move on to consider how organisations can be *designed* so as to accommodate the differing, and sometimes conflicting, demands of all these factors on the overall coherence of the structure. This is the subject of the next chapter.

References

1. Roethlisberger,F.J. & Dickson, W.J. (1939), *Management and the Worker*, Harvard University Press

2. Homans, G.C.(1950), *The Human Group*, Harcourt, Brace & World

3. Maslow, A. (1954),*Motivation and Personality*, Harper & Row

4. Alderfer, C. (1972), *Existence, Relatedness and Growth*, Collier Macmillan

5. Argyris, C. (1957), *Personality and Organisation*, Harper & Row

6. McGregor,D. (1960), *The Human Side of Enterprise*, McGraw-Hill

7. Likert,R. (1961), *New Patterns of Management*, McGraw-Hill

8. Herzberg,F. (1959), *The Motivation to Work (2nd edn)*, John Wiley

9. Herzberg,F. (1968), *Work and the Nature of Man*, Staples Press (GB)

10. McClelland, D. (1961), *The Achieving Society*, Van Nostrand

11. Stogdill, R.M. & Coons, A. (1957), *Leader Behaviour: Its Description and Measurement*, Research Monograph No.88, Ohio State University

12. Blake, Robert & Mouton, Jane (1964), *The Managerial Grid*, Gulf Publishing

Questions for reflection/discussion

1. What impact have the Hawthorne Studies had on the study of organisational theory?

2. How useful is Maslow's hierarchy of needs to the study of the human factor at work? Who has probably gained the most benefit from his ideas - theorists or practitioners? How do you explain your answer?

3. What evidence is there for suggesting that organisations (ie the management) prefer to treat people as immature?

4. What would you say were the dominant issues for Human Relations in the decade of the 1960's? Why do you think these were the key issues at that time?

The individual at work:
physical characteristics,
skills and personality

Individuals in organisations

Having set the scene for the organisational background in the previous three chapters, we can now turn to consider the individuals who make up an organisation and give it life. There are four chapters in this section of the book, which focuses on the following aspects of individual behaviour: personality and individual differences at work (Chapter 5), individual's perceptions — of themselves and their roles in the workplace — (Chapter 6), motivation and job satisfaction (Chapter 7), and individual learning styles (Chapter 8).

5 The individual at work-physical characteristics, skills and personality

Introduction

1. Although we tend to think of organisations in their collective sense, they are, of course, composed of individual human beings. These individuals act out their working lives within the framework of an organisation structure and in the context of a particular organisation culture. Ever since the era of the Hawthorne Experiments in the early part of the century, researchers and practising managers have focused much effort on studying people in small groups and as individuals. They have discovered that differences between individuals are as important as their common features. Subsequent chapters (Chaps 9-13) will look at people in groups, but this and the following three chapters examine key aspects of individuals at work. General issues affecting the application of human resources policies on individuals at work will be considered separately in Chapter 16.

2. An individual at work is perceived by others in three principal ways (see Figure 5.1):

    1. as *a physical person* having gender, age, race and size characteristics;

    2. as *a person with a range of abilities* (intellectual, physical and social);

    3. as *a personality* (ie someone having a particular kind of temperament).

    These three dimensions of being human are outlined in this chapter. Accepting that each person, ultimately, is a unique blend of all three dimensions, it is nevertheless important, from an organisational behaviour perspective, to ask whether it is possible to categorise individuals in some way. Much of the work on the measurement of human performance (psychometrics) is devoted to developing standards of comparison (norms) between individuals. This enables us to describe individuals in terms of broad types, such as similar ability groups and personality types. The value of psychometrics for work organisations is principally as an aid to employee selection and development by improving the chances of allocating people to work, and roles, for which they are best suited.

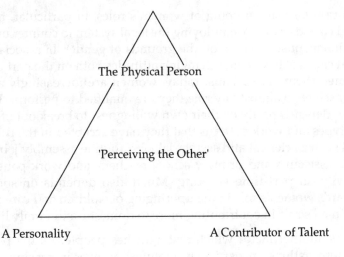

The Physical Person

'Perceiving the Other'

A Personality · A Contributor of Talent

Figure 5.1 · *Our perception of others at work*

Physical Characteristics

3. An individual's sex seems to make very little difference to job performance, except perhaps where brute strength is involved. Studies have shown consistently that there are few differences between men and women in such key areas as problem-solving ability, analytical skills, learning ability and motivation. Whilst men may be less deferential towards authority than women, have higher expectations of success, and may be more aggressive in their behaviour at work, there is likely to be very little practical difference in their behaviour. The one feature of working life where differences are likely is in respect of absenteeism, where women consistently have higher rates than men, due mainly to their primary role in caring for the children of the family.

4. Most of the differences in the way women are perceived at work are due to:

    (1) *stereotyping* (ie assuming that particular groups of people have particular sets of characteristics, which are unchangeable), and (2) *past precedents* in work types and patterns. The stereotyping of women as being only suited to certain, specific, types of work and roles has been a fact of working life in Britain for a hundred years or more, ever since women and children were finally banned from working in near slave-labour conditions in the mines and cotton mills of Northern England. With hindsight it is possible to see that the reaction to those harsh conditions was overly protective, and only in the last decade or so has the underlying paternalism of this situation been addressed (at least, in the Western world).

5. The resultant stereotyping of women's roles, in particular, has been soft-ened considerably by employing the legal system to counter unfair discrim-ination against a person on the grounds of gender. In association with the legal changes have come changing attitudes both on the part of men and of women themselves. Thus, today, women are increasingly able to apply themselves to almost any role they are qualified to perform. Whether they do so depends partly on their own willingness to break out of the mould of job types and work patterns that they have accepted in the past 50 years — jobs such as clerical and secretarial jobs, routine assembly jobs in factories, shop assistants and primary school teachers, and work patterns that rely heavily on part-time working. Much also depends on social attitudes towards women's role in the upbringing of children and care of the elderly, and men's role in contributing more to domestic and family life.

6. *Age* is another factor which distinguishes people. As the populations of Western nations, in particular, manifest an ever-increasing proportion of older citizens, it is likely that work groups will increasingly be composed of older rather than younger employees. This has considerable implications for career development, promotion, labour turnover, absenteeism and motivation. It is likely that career development and promotion for younger employees will slow as higher proportions of older employees remain in the workforce. Turnover is likely to decrease, as older employees become settled in their jobs and locality. Absenteeism is usually lower among longer-serving employees, but this has to be off-set against the likelihood of their being away due to poorer health. The evidence for motivation levels in older people is mixed. Professional employees seem to be generally moti-vated in their work right up to the time of retirement. (reference?) People in other work may be less motivated in their middle years, but may find renewed enthusiasm in their sixties.

7. On the subject of productivity, it might be thought that older employees would be less productive than their younger counterparts, due to slower reaction times, loss of stamina and lower motivation, for example. However, in a recent study in the United States (McEvoy & Cascio, 1989)[1], it was found from an analysis of several other studies that there was no correlation between age and productivity. On the contrary, older employees were just as productive as younger ones. Nevertheless, despite the evidence concerning the work-worthiness of older employees, there has been, and still is, a strong tendency for organisations to seek young persons when recruiting for personnel. This so-called 'ageism' has been challenged recently, and organisations with strong equal opportunities policies have issued guidelines to recruiters warning them of unfair discrimination against potential applicants on grounds of age. The Institute of Personnel Management (now the Institute of Personnel and Development) has also taken a lead in this matter by urging its journal advertisers not to restrict applications for jobs on grounds of age unless absolutely necessary. In step

with its own policy the IPD has produced a Statement on Age in Employment (1991)[2] to

> 'encourage personnel policies and practices which lead to the productive employment of people, irrespective of their age.'

8.   As people from Asia and Africa have increasingly taken up residence in countries that were previously only inhabited by white Europeans, issues of an individual's *racial* characteristics have surfaced in most Western nations. This has led to situations where, as with women, members of ethnic minority groups have been stereotyped in terms of their intelligence levels, work attitudes and general level of motivation. They also have tended to settle for certain specific types of work (eg in public transport, clothing manufacture, food preparation etc). The results of stereotyping have been (1) that minorities have tended to seek refuge in those jobs where they felt secure, thus reinforcing the stereotype, and (2) that individuals trying to break out of the mould have been treated with suspicion, or even downright rejection, both by employers and other employees. In the UK and the European Union, unfair discrimination on grounds of race is illegal, and governments have put considerable effort into persuading employers to embrace the spirit of the law as well as its letter. The ideal aimed for is that, in the workplace, a person shall be selected, or assessed, only on grounds of their ability to perform the job to a satisfactory standard.

9.   Questions of sheer *physical size* do not enter into most selection processes. Only in certain occupations, such as the police and military, is height taken into account. In a few other occupational groups, such as fashion models and aircraft cabin crew, issues of proportions are important (ie height in relation to weight). Some occupations also ban the wearing of spectacles, usually on grounds of safety or credibility (eg models). Nevertheless, like most other human features, size, too, can be the subject of stereotyping and unfair discrimination. Tall individuals (especially men) have been found to be preferred for senior management roles, whilst fat people have been positively ignored for certain roles.

10.   What should count for most in the workplace is the ability *to do the job to a satisfactory level*. All the official guidelines on unfair discrimination at work emphasise the essential justice of appointing, or promoting, employees on the basis of their ability to do the job, which brings us neatly to our second group of characteristics — *human abilities*.

Abilities, aptitudes, skills and talents

11.   To avoid confusion it is worthwhile agreeing some definition of terms here. Abilities in the chapter refer to an individual's capacity to achieve certain levels of behaviour. In this sense, abilities and skills are one and the

87

same dimension of behaviour. *Intellectual abilities* include demonstrable performance with numbers, verbal reasoning, and logical reasoning. *Physical abilities* (often just called skills) include manual dexterity and visual acuity. An understanding of the abilities possessed by job applicants is an important aspect of the selection process. In some cases these can be assumed with some confidence on the basis of individuals' school records, eg certificates of educational achievement in mathematics, English, physics and other relevant subjects. In other cases, it may be possible to infer abilities from what candidates divulge during interview, although that is more a question of assessing an individual's aptitude or talent rather than ability, or skill.

12. *Aptitudes* and *talents* are used here to describe an individual's potential, or pre-disposition towards, certain levels of behaviour. Aptitudes and talents tend to be measured in terms of *potential* achievement in specific types of behaviour (eg an aptitude for numbers, or a predisposition towards social skills etc). Aptitudes and talents are often described as gifts, with the implication that a gift can be utilised or set aside. Important aspects of aptitudes and talents are (1) learning capacity, and (2) individual motivation, topics which are discussed shortly. In the meantime, however, it will be useful to briefly introduce the subject of psychometric testing, ie measuring individual's abilities and aptitudes in a range of intellectual, perceptual and physical dimensions.

Psychometric tests / selection tests

13. To be reasonably certain of a candidate's *current* performance and aptitude levels, many organisations employ experts in psychometric testing to gather information about one or more sets of abilities and aptitudes. Anastasi (1988)[3] describes a psychological test as

   ' ...essentially an objective and standardised measure of a sample of behaviour.'

Thus potential managers in an information technology environment may be tested for their numerical and perceptual abilities, and their ability to reason logically. A sales manager may be tested for numerical ability and verbal reasoning powers. A keyboard operator may be tested for manual dexterity and, possibly, visual acuity skills. Tests are standardised and objective in that (a) they are administered, and scored, in consistent and uniform ways, and (b) the scoring is done according to explicit rules, and not on the basis of the examiner's subjective opinion. Control over tests is achieved principally by restricting their purchase to bona fide users with minimum qualifications, and by ensuring that only qualified staff administer and score them. A key feature of all psychometric tests is that they have to fulfil two principal criteria in use. These are (1) *reliability*, ie tests must provide consistent results when measuring the same characteristics, or factors, on two or more occasions, usually on a test-retest basis; and (2) *validity*, ie they must be able to measure what they claim to measure.

14. The most widely-used and respected tests have been conducted over many years on a substantial number of their target populations. Their results have enabled normative standards (benchmarks) to be issued against which individual results can be compared. Thus, when a percentage of correct answers is given in response to a particular test, this raw score is fairly meaningless until compared with the scores of others who have taken the same test previously. As Anastasi puts it

> 'Like all raw scores, percentage scores can be interpreted only in terms of a clearly-defined and uniform frame of reference.'

Norms may be drawn up for age-groups, by gender, educational qualifications and any other criteria perceived as relevant. Thus, the sales manager just referred to might provide results that show that he or she is in the top 10% for numerical ability and in the top 5% for verbal reasoning. This information may be helpful if it enables comparisons to be made with existing staff with whom this person will have to work. However, it is important to ensure that the norms used are up-to-date, and relevant, to the individual or group being tested.

15. Tests typically fall into the following categories:

1. *Intelligence tests* (eg especially of logical reasoning/ critical thinking) Such tests are designed to produce a single score (an Intelligence Quotient, or IQ)

2. *Aptitude tests* (eg facility with numbers, spatial reasoning, dexterity)These tests produce a range of scores for different aptitudes

3. *Attainment tests* (eg tests of previous learning in arithmetic, spelling, keyboard skills etc) These tests also produce a range of scores

4. *Occupational preference tests* (ie which bring out a person's *preferences* for occupational choice; they do not identify whether the individual has the relevant aptitudes or abilities to fulfil their choice)

5. *Personality tests* (eg designed to provide a profile of an individual's temperament and pre-dispositions; these are often controversial and may not always be valid)

16. Answers to questions in the first three categories of tests fall into the 'correct/ incorrect' system of scoring. Answers in the last two do not, ie there are no 'correct' answers to issues of occupational choice or personality traits. Except for personality profiles, most tests in a work situation are used to provide a quick and standardised method of obtaining information about a particular aspect of an individual's abilities, in order to recruit, or place, that person in a suitable job or role. The tests are invariably used in conjunction with other information about candidates (eg from application forms, references, academic certificates and interview impressions). They are rarely taken in isolation from other forms of evidence about performance, but can be used to confirm suitability or unsuitability for a particular job or role.

Personality — definitions and theories

17. Attempting to define personality, and identify its component elements in respect of any one individual, is a controversial activity, but one that can shed light on crucial areas of an organisation's performance (eg in managerial and supervisory performance, teamworking ability, and the selection of the best candidates for jobs). Personality has been defined by Allport (1961)[4], as

    '.....the dynamic organisation within the individual of those psychophysical systems that determine his characteristic behaviour and thought.'

    The question 'What is personality, and how can its elements be identified?' has exercised the minds and hearts of psychologists ever since the days of Ancient Greece. Indeed, it was Hippocrates in the 5th century BC, who identified what he called 'the four humours' of Man. These were four basic personality types — *melancholic* (ie gloomy), *sanguine* (ie confident, breezy), *phlegmatic* (ie slow to anger/action), and *choleric* (ie bad-tempered). His view was that an individual's general behaviour fell into one or the other basic types, which coloured the way they saw themselves and the world. Much later, in the twentieth century, H.J Eysenck (1970[5], 1976[6]) pointed out the limitations of a type theory of personality by showing that individuals did not easily slot into one type or another, but tended to manifest behaviour from several types.

18. This is not a textbook for students majoring in psychology, but it is important to make some passing references to the ideas and influence of the great psychologists Freud and Jung, whose work has provided the basis of modern psychology. What students of organisational behaviour need, in particular, is knowledge of any *application* of their theories to people in work organisations. Both Freud and Jung have contributed important concepts in this respect, and their key ideas will be summarised below.

Sigmund Freud

19. Freud's major contribution to personality came in 1923[7] with the publication of his theory of a three-fold structure of personality. This was based on what he called *das Es, das Ich,* and *das uber-Ich,* now commonly referred to respectively as the *id,* the *ego,* and the *superego.* According to Freud, the *id* represents the core of our being — our instincts, drives, innate capacities and largely subconscious ways of responding to the outside world. The *ego* evolves out of the id, and is that part of personality which as well as responding to the subtle demands of the former, does so in a controlled way, using intellectual skills and perceptual powers to satisfy those demands (the 'reality principle'). Within the innermost core of the ego lies the *superego,* which represents the individual's internalised values and moral standards. The superego consists of two sub-systems — the *conscience* (ie the capacity to evaluate, criticise and reproach behaviour), and the *ego-ideal,* which is essentially our self-image. According to Freud, the *id* part of our personality seeks instinctive, impulsive solutions, the *ego* part seeks practical, realistic solutions, and the *superego* seeks moralistic, perfectionist solutions.

20. In management terms, the *id* might correspond to an instinctive and needs-based strategy, the *ego* corresponds to operational and executive management, whilst the *superego* might be represented by policy statements, employment standards and organisation culture. However, in one key respect, it is difficult to sustain such an analogy — *consciousness.* Most of the workings of the human personality, according to Freud, are unconscious, even those of the *ego* itself. By comparison, most management systems operate with a high degree of conscious decision-making and awareness of issues.

21. Freud concluded that the three elements of personality were in a dynamic, and usually conflicting, relationship with each other. Conflict produces anxiety in the *ego,* which develops defence mechanisms to enable it to cope. These mechanisms have two prime features — (1) they occur at an unconscious level, and (2) they tend to deny or distort reality in order to make it less disturbing. Defence mechanisms take various forms eg repression, denial, displacement ('kicking the cat') and sublimation (re-directing unacceptable behaviour). Such reactions undoubtedly do occur in the workplace, but four forms, in particular, have great relevance to it. These forms are as follows:

> 1   Regression — ie adopting essentially childish behaviour
>
> 2   Fixation — ie obsessively rigid behaviour linked to regression
>
> 3   Rationalisation — ie 'explaining away' motives/behaviour
>
> 4   Projection — ie attributing feelings/motives to others

Recognising such forms of behaviour can be useful to managers faced, for example, with uncooperative employees, because it enables questions to be raised and corrective action to be taken. Any kind of defensive behaviour, however, is merely an indication of some deeper malaise or dissatisfaction, and any action has to be directed at underlying causes and perceptions, as well as at the overt symptoms.

Carl Jung

22.   Jung was born some twenty years after Freud, and was considerably influenced by the latter's work. However, he broke away from Freud's models of the human personality in a number of significant ways. He rejected Freud's three-part view of personality, preferring to describe it in all-embracing terms as 'the *psyche*', which contains all the psychological processes involved in being human. Jung (1953)[8] saw the psyche as composed of a number of dynamic sub-systems, notably the following:

> 1   the *ego*, or *conscious mind*
>
> 2   the *personal unconscious*
>
> 3   the *collective unconscious* (the experiences common to all humanity eg birth, death)

23.   The psyche, according to Jung, has two basic attitudes, one of which is always dominant in any individual. These are *extraversion* (inclined towards one's *outer* world) and *introversion* (inclined towards one's *inner* world). The way in which we perceive our world, and how we react to it, are described by Jung as functions, of which there are four — *sensing, intuitive, thinking and feeling*. By combining these four functions with the two attitudes, Jung suggested that there were eight psychological types — four extravert types and four introvert. In addition to these individual types, Jung also identified a number of what he termed 'archetypes'. These are part of the collective unconscious, and are defined as universal thought forms or predispositions.

The principal archetypes, according to Jung, are:

1   the *persona* (the role we play, the mask we wear, the compromise between who we are and who we are expected to be).

2   the *shadow* (the darker self, the unsocial self)

3   the *animus* and *anima* (the masculine and feminine qualities that are present in each person)

4   the *self* (the core of the personality, the striving towards self-actualisation,   the organising force behind the psyche); the true self emerges after the others, and cannot begin to appear until people reach their forties; for most people the full realisation of the self is never attained.

24.   Like Freudian theories, Jung's ideas and concepts are complex, raising as many questions as they answer. Nevertheless, for the lay-person, the ideas of both strike many chords within themselves and their experience of the outside world. An understanding of the forces at work within the individual personality helps to explain the variety of responses that people may make, and may provide some clues as to how to counter their responses, when they are not favourable. Later, in subsequent chapters, we shall consider examples of social interventions in the workplace designed to improve such factors as team-working, leadership skills and employee counselling. For the moment, we can refer to one tool which has been employed in organisations for assessing personality types in relation to job applicants and promotion candidates— the Myers-Briggs Type Indicator (MBTI).

The Myers-Briggs type indicator

25.   The MBTI is a widely-used instrument for assessing personality types in work organisations. It was developed in the 1960's by a mother-and-daughter team as a way of sorting people into different personality types, based on Jungian concepts. The basis of the assessment is a set of four polar dimensions as follows:

Extraversion ——————Introversion	(EI scale)
Sensing ——————Intuition	(SN scale)
Thinking ——————Feeling	(TF scale)
Judgement ——————Perception	(JP scale)

The resulting framework enables sixteen types to be identified, each scored on the four basic dimensions. There is a good deal of face validity in the MBTI, as people invariably recognise, and accept, their own type. However, as Furnham (1992)[9] points out, the MBTI has yet to be validated satisfactorily on a number of issues:

> 'Although there has been a vast amount of work on the MBTI, little has examined the relationship between types and occupational behaviour such as productivity or satisfaction.'

The test has been used in work organisations to increase understanding of employee motivation, leadership styles and learning styles, as well as for the purposes of employee selection. A wider discussion of the application of the MBTI can be found in Keirsey & Bates (1978)[10].

H.J Eysenck

26. Hans Eysenck was born in Germany during the First World War, and moved to England just before the start of the Second. He has been active as both researcher and clinician in psychological matters for more than fifty years. He became interested in personality studies and psychometrics in the 1940's and has made a considerable contribution to our understanding of personality traits, or characteristics. He defined personality (1970)[11] as

> '...a more or less stable and enduring organisation of a person's character, temperament, intellect and physique which determines his unique adjustment to the environment.'

As a result of his research, he identified what he considered as the three basic dimensions of personality. These were defined in terms of collections of personality traits, combined into five inclusive traits, or *superfactors* : (I) *extraversion*, (2) *introversion*, (3) *neuroticism*, (4) *stability*, and (5) *psychoticism*. The first four of these collective traits, or dimensions, represent polar extremes, and one (psychoticism) is uni-dimensional. These make up Eysenck's basic model of personality, whose foundations are based on a number of component traits as follows (Figure 5.2):

Dimension/Inclusive Trait	Component Traits/Characteristics
1. Extraversion	Activity, Sociability, Risk-taking, Impulsiveness, Expressiveness, Practicality, Irresponsibility.
Introversion	Inactivity, Unsociability, Carefulness, Control, Inhibition, Reflectiveness, Responsibility.
2. Emotional Instability (Neuroticism)	Inferiority feelings, Depressiveness, Anxiety, Obsessiveness, Dependence, Hypochondriasis, Guilt.
Stability (Adjustment)	Self-esteem, Happiness, Calm, Casualness, Autonomy, Sense of health, Guilt-freedom.
3. Psychoticism	Solitary, Troublesome, Cruel, Insensitive, Sensation-seeking, Aggressive, Eccentric, Foolhardy, Upsetting, Anti-social, Uninvolved.

Figure 5.2   *Eysenck's personality traits*

27. The first two sets of inclusive traits can be reassembled into separate dimensions of behaviour, along which individual scores will lie in a continuum, as below:

1. *Extraversion* <————————> *Introversion*	
A tendency towards spontaneous and outgoing behaviour	A tendency to be controlled and inhibited
2. *Neuroticism* <————————> *Stability*	
Inclined to anxiety, instability and emotional reactions	Generally stable in outlook and behaviour; well-adjusted types

Thus, on these dimensions, any individual's score will provide an indication as to whether they are basically extraverted or introverted, and whether they are inclined to be neurotic or emotionally stable.

28. The third inclusive trait is one which, according to Eysenck, is present in everybody to a varying extent. It can be shown as a single scale as follows:

> *Considerably psychotic* <————> *Slightly psychotic*
>
> Disturbed, violent, antisocial   Occasional adverse reactions

The implication of this dimension is that any individual can demonstrate mildly psychotic tendencies, and a few are likely to show considerably psychotic tendencies. Where individuals lie on each continuum depends on the results of their scores in a number of questionnaires. Over a period of thirty years or so, Eysenck has built up a considerable amount of evidence to support the scores people achieve.

29. Typical questions asked in one of Eysenck's extraversion-introversion questionnaires (1976)[12,] which contains 210 separate questions, are as follows:

Do you like planning things well ahead of time?	Yes ? No
Do you become restless when working at something in which there is little action?	Yes ? No
Are you normally on time for appointments?	Yes ? No
Is your anger quick and short?	Yes ? No
Can you always be fully relied upon?	Yes ? No
Can you make decisions quickly?	Yes ? No
Do you sometimes have a tendency to be 'slapdash' in your work?	Yes ? No
Is it important to you to be liked by a wide range of people?	Yes ? No

Note that these are all closed questions, requiring a Yes, No or ? (Dont Know) response. People completing such a questionnaire are advised to respond quickly and not to dwell on their answers. In this example, analysis of the responses can be self-scored, although generally scoring is done by trained test supervisors. The results can indicate an individual's degree of possession of a key factor, such as activity, sociability, impulsiveness etc.

30. On the basis of the first two dimensions, Eysenck derived a model of personality similar to the old Greek model. The four alternative types can be deduced from the following quadrant (Fig. 5.3), which shows the dimensions on each of its axes. The component behaviour traits associated with each box can be derived from the lists shown in paragraph 26 above. The approximate Greek equivalent is indicated for each quadrant.

	Neuroticism	Stability
Extraversion	Neurotic extrovert (Choleric)	Stable extrovert (Sanguine)
Intraversion	Neurotic introvert (Melancholic)	Stable introvert (Phlegmatic)

Figure 5.3   *Eysenck's personality types*

31. Eysenck emphasised that traits in themselves are neither good nor bad. However, he suggested there are likely to be problems for individuals whose scores are particularly high or low on each continuum, since the evidence would suggest that they possess an unbalanced personality. If people decided they did not like their personality profile, Eysenck concluded (1976)[13] that there was little they could do to change it —

> 'Personality is determined to a large extent by a person's genes [ie it is primarily a matter of heredity, or genetics].....the genetic influence is overwhelmingly strong, and the role of environment in most cases is reduced to effecting slight changes...'.

Since many of his questions are aimed at elucidating physical symptoms of behaviour, it is not surprising that biological links with personality are emphasised. However, there is a good deal of research to support Eysenck's personality types, even though it has many critics. The most suitable quadrant for a typical manager in a large organisation is likely to be a stable extrovert, ie someone who combines extraversion with stability.

32. Eysenck's approach to personality is what psychologists call *nomothetic*, which is to say that it is based on the assumption that trends and regularities in an individual can be identified, and that measures can be derived which will enable the individual's 'score' to be compared with those of others (relevant norms). Nomothetic approaches assume that generalisations can be made about personality on the basis of objective questionnaires given to a wide cross-section of the population. They assume that personality is composed of a number of identifiable traits, or characteristics, which may be considered as the building blocks of the individual personality. They also assume that personality traits are given, ie they are basically unalterable.

R.B Cattell

33. Another well-known researcher of personality is R.B Cattell (1977)[14], who also adopted a nomothetic approach. Cattell defined personality (1950)[15] in strictly scientific terms as

'....that which permits a prediction of what a person will do in a given situation.'

He is particularly noted (eg Engler,1995)[16] for providing '..*an exemplary instance of a scientist who is concerned with validating evidence.*' As his definition suggests, personality is important insofar as it enables us to predict future behaviour. Cattell, like Eysenck, believes that the identification and analysis of traits is an important step in developing a theory of personality. Unlike Eysenck, however, he does allow for the influence of social factors in the development of personality. Cattell concluded that there are two main groups of personality traits — *surface traits*, which are *clusters* of overt behaviour, such as honesty and self-discipline — and *source traits*, which are characteristic tendencies that underly surface traits. He identified sixteen source traits, which have formed the basis of his efforts to measure personality using a questionnaire known as the 16PF questionnaire (Personality Factors).

34. The 16PF questionnaire is built on the following polar dimensions:

Outgoing	Reserved
More intelligent	Less intelligent
Emotionally stable	Emotionally unstable
Assertive	Humble
Happy-go-lucky	Sober
Strong conscience	Lack of internal standards
Adventuresome	Shy
Tough-minded	Tender-minded
Trusting	Suspicious
Imaginative	Practical
Shrewd	Forthright
Apprehensive	Self-assured
Experimental	Conservative
Group-dependent	Self-sufficient
Casual	Controlled
Relaxed	Tense

There is a ring of credibility about Cattell's list, which seems to square with our experience of ourselves and others. It also provides an interesting comparison with Eysenck's ideas, with which it shares several common features (eg extraversion-introversion, emotional stability/unstability). Scientifically, however, there has been much evidence to support Cattell's use of the sixteen factors as predictive of human behaviour. Over forty years or so it has been the most widely applied personality test for *occupational* groups, our prime concern here.

35. Cattell's main sources of data for the development of his theory of surface and source traits have been as follows:

a.   Life record data rated by trained observers
b.   Self-rating by means of the 16PF questionnaire
c.   Test data collected from observations of individuals undergoing specific tests

The above data has been subjected to a complex statistical technique known as factor analysis, which has enabled the researchers involved to cluster hundreds of surface traits into possible source categories, test them, refine them and re-test them, eventually as the 16 dimensions mentioned above. As well as being widely used as an aid to personnel selection, the 16PF has also been applied as a predictor of job satisfaction and employee effectiveness.

36.   The efforts of Eysenck and Cattell have attracted much attention in research circles, and, in recent years, a consensus has been emerging on the possibility of five key personality traits — known as the 'Big Five'. According to one writer (Kassin,1995)[17], the five most consistent traits identified from numerous studies over the past fifty years are as follows:

1	*Neuroticism*	eg anxious versus calm, insecure versus secure etc
2	*Extraversion*	eg sociable versus withdrawn, fun-loving versus sober etc
3	*Openness*	eg imaginative versus down-to-earth, curious versus incurious etc
4	*Agreeableness*	eg good-natured versus irritable, soft-hearted versus ruthless
5	*Conscientiousness*	eg conscientious versus negligent, well-organised versus disorganised etc

37.   Support for the Big Five concept has come from studies by Costa & Macrae (1992)[18] into personality questionnaires and ratings, such as those described above. In this case a new assessment tool — called the NEO-PI-R (Neuroticism Extraversion Openness Personality Inventory (Revised) — has been developed to test individuals in the big five traits. The overall conclusions appear to be that genetics plays the largest role in the emergence of personality, but that the role of environment, whilst lesser in effect, cannot be ignored. In the work environment, for example, an individual is usually in a subordinate position to someone else, and thus may want to try to suppress aspects of behaviour in order to please — in Jungian terms, a clear case of the *persona* overcoming the *self!*

Other research into personality

38.   A quite different approach to personality is adopted by other researchers such as Carl Rogers (1959)[19] and Erik Erikson(1980)[20]. Their approach assumes that each personality is unique (ie rather than a norm against which others may be

compared), that individual perceptions of the world and how to respond to it have to be taken into account (ie subjective rather than objective data), and that personality develops with experience (ie it is affected by environmental and social factors). The person is seen as a *whole* rather than as a combination (albeit fascinating) of individual characteristics (traits). This approach is called the *idiographic* approach to personality. This approach has had a greater impact on fields such as psychotherapy than on the world of business and enterprise, probably because it is more conducive towards a warmly-positive, client-centred attitude towards people as individuals in their own right, and is not particularly interested in the measurement of component traits, or characteristics, in the service of organisational ends.

Assumptions about behaviour

39. Our attitude towards the behaviour of others is coloured by the implicit assumptions we make about people's behaviour generally. Engler (1995)[21] points out that the theorists of human psychology also have their preferred way of seeing individual differences, or similarities, between individuals. She considers that there are five particular issues on which expert opinion is frequently divided. These are:

1	*Freedom versus determinism* —	ie people are either free to control their own behaviour *or* they are controlled by their environment (including other people)
2	*Heredity versus environment* —	ie people's reactions are determined mainly by genetics *or* by the effect of their environment
3	*Uniqueness versus universality* —	ie people are unique (and therefore cannot be compared) *versus* people are mostly similar (and can be compared!)
4	*Proactive versus reactive* —	ie people generally act on their own initiative *or* generally respond to external events
5	*Optimistic versus pessimistic* —	ie people can, and do, change their personal repertoire during their lifetime *versus* people can only work with what they have inherited.

40. By increasing awareness of our own assumptions, we can better evaluate the judgements we make about others by acknowledging our personal bias. From the Organisational behaviour viewpoint, such information is extremely helpful, since it can enable managers in a work organisation to act with greater sensitivity towards their colleagues, their advisers and their own staff. They can recognise, for example, that a Theory X management style is rooted in determinism, and that a good delegator clearly assumes that people are proactive rather than reactive. These alternative assumptions about people in organisations need to be taken into account when addressing the priorities referred to in Figure 4.4 in the previous chapter.

References

1. McEvoy, G. & Cascio, W. (1989), *'Cumulative Evidence of the Relationship betweenEmployee Age and Job Performance*, Journal of Applied Psychology,Feb 1989.

2. Institute of Personnel Management (1991) *Statement on Age in Employment*, IPM (now IPD)

3. Anastasi,A. (1988) *Psychological Testing* (5 edn), Macmillan

4. Allport, G.W. (1961), *Pattern and Growth in Personality*, Holt, Rinehart & Winston

5. Eysenck, H.J. (1970), *The Structure of Human Personality* (3rd edn), Methuen

6. Eysenck, H.J. & Wilson,G (1976), *Know Your Own Personality*, Penguin

7. Freud, S. (1953), *The Complete Psychological Works of Sigmund Freud*: Standard Edition, Hogarth Press (esp Vol. 19 - The Ego and the Id, 1923)

8. Jung, C. G (1953), *The Integration of Personality*, Farrar & Ruchart

9. Furnham, A. (1992), *Personality at Work*, Routledge

10. Keirsey,D. & Bates,M. (1978, *Please Understand Me - Character & Temperament Types*, Prometheus Nemesis Book Co.

11. Eysenck, H.J. (1970) op. cit

12. Eysenck, H.J. & Wilson,G (1976) op. cit

13. Eysenck, H.J. & Wilson,G (1976) op. cit

14. Cattell, R. B. & Kline, P. (1977), *The Scientific Analysis of Personality and Motivation*,Academic Press

15. Cattell, R.B. (1950), *Personality: a Systematic, Theoretical and Factual Study*, McGraw-Hill

16. Engler, B. (1995), *Personality Theories* (4 edn), Houghton Mifflin

17. Kassin, S. (1995), *Psychology*, Houghton Mifflin

18. Costa, P. & MacRae, R. (1992), *Revised NEO Personality Inventory*, Psychological Assessment Resources

19. Rogers, C. (1959), *A theory of therapy, personality, and interpersonal relationships as developed in the client-centred framework, in Koch (ed)*, Psychology: A Study of a Science (Vol.3), McGraw-Hill

20. Erikson, E (1980), *Identity and Life Cycle*, Norton

21. Engler, B. (1995), op. cit

Questions for reflection/discussion

1. In what ways can a person's physical qualities and appearance affect the way they are treated at work?

2. What is it that makes stereotypes so attractive when we make judgements about others? What are the dangers of stereotyping?

3. What do organisations hope to gain from employing psychometric tests?

4. How useful might Cattell's 16PF personality test be to personnel specialists engaged in recruiting people for a range of positions in production, quality control and field sales?

5. How significant for organisational behaviour are Freud's concepts of defence mechanisms (regression, fixation etc)? Give some examples of defensive behaviour from your own experience of organisations.

6. What factors in an organisation's social and business environment are the most likely to cause individuals to consider themselves as:

   a. relatively free to direct their own behaviour

   b. relatively controlled by events.

6 Individual perceptions, personal values and attitudes

Introduction

1. A key feature of every human being is his or her unique way of looking at things, based on their physical abilities, their intelligence and their personal repertoire of values and attitudes. The concept of 'perception' is extremely important in understanding human behaviour. The reason is that, for the student of organisational behaviour, it is not so much *what* people see happening around them that is important, but rather *what they think they see* is happening. In other words, it is how people *interpret* the events going on around them that is important. They may interpret things quite wrongly, according to an objective standpoint, but their reactions have to be dealt with as they are. It is useless, for example, if managers say *'They shouldn't overreact!'* when employees are angry with some apparently reasonable and logical change in procedures. What the managers have to address is the *feelings* of the employees as well as their possible misunderstanding of the new situation. Thus, the individuals we are dealing with at work operate at the feelings level as well as at rational and action levels. People feel, think and do.

2. Questions concerning perceptions, attitudes and personal values can be looked at in two broad ways — as objects of research for social scientists, or as matters of major practical interest to managers in organisations. We shall examine both perspectives, starting with the theoretical basis of perception. Look, for example at the following picture (Fig.6.1). What do you see — and old hag or a young woman? Typically most people consistently see one before the other, but having picked out both images can usually switch easily between them. A few people have difficulty in seeing both. The point is the picture is open to different interpretations, ie people can *perceive* it differently!

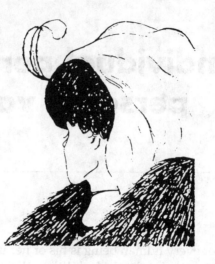

Figure 6.1   *Old hag or young woman?- a problem of perception*

Perception

3.   What do we mean when we use the term *'perception'*? A typical dictionary definition is likely to run along the following lines:

> 'the process of organising, interpreting and integrating external stimuli received through the senses; the mental process involved in identifying and subjectively interpreting objects, concepts and behaviour; the attainment of awareness, insight and understanding.'

Thus the concept of *'perception'* appears to encapsulate a mental or cognitive activity that receives, processes and interprets (rightly or wrongly) the host of external stimuli that impinge on our everyday lives. This process usually takes place instantly — we see something and jump to some immediate conclusions about it. Phrases such as *'First impressions are often misleading!'* and *'Don't jump to conclusions!'* suggest that what we 'see' (or more correctly what we understand to have seen) is often not the truth, not the reality before us. In other cases, it is not so much a question of misunderstanding reality, but merely seeing a *different* truth in it! So, for example, a man looks out over the countryside towards the sunset, and says *'Just look at that view!'*, and his companion says *'Yes, it's amazing how dark it gets in the early evening at this time of the year!'* Or, take two people listening to a brass band playing in the park, one enraptured by the sound, the other restless and wanting to move on. Same stimulus, but different perceptions and different responses.

4. If we were to draw a map of the perceiving process, it would contain at least three elements — the perceiver, the object/person/ concept perceived, and the situation or context (see Fig 6.2).

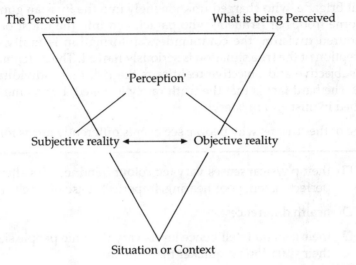

Figure 6.2   *Perception - a basic model*

Each element has its own conditions — the perceiver brings sensing qualities, motivation, attitudes and previous experience to the process; the object, or focal point, of the perception (ie what is being perceived) will reflect different qualities depending on whether it is an object, an idea or a person ; the external situation, or context, will contain conditions relating to what has gone before, as well as what is happening now. The extent to which an individual's perception (ie the *subjective reality*) of the event matches what is truly there (ie the *objective reality*) depends on:

1) factors at work in the perceiver, such as the individual's physical health, intelligence level, degree of open-mindedness, and general level of emotional well-being.

2) factors at work in the external situation, such as whether this is a new experience or a repeat of a past event, the extent of involvement of others, especially those who bring strongly positive or negative messages (eg encouragement and support, or criticism and stress), and the timescale involved.

5. The diagram in Figure 6.2 also indicates the tension between the subjective reality, which is the individual's *perception* of the truth, and the objective reality, which is the truth. Much of life is concerned with trying to judge whether our understanding of the truth is the correct one, or at least close to the truth. In military situations, for example, field commanders often have to assess the strength and deployment of the enemy on the basis of

partial or quite faulty information. Local reconnaissance, reports from prisoners and intelligence reports from the rear all help to build up a picture of what is likely to be the enemy's position. If, as in the case of the Light Brigade, who charged unknowingly into the Russian guns, or of the airborne troops at Arnhem, who parachuted into the midst of a German armoured division, the commanders' information is faulty, then their perception of the true situation is seriously flawed. The difference between the subjective and objective realities is the risk that individuals have to take. The hard fact is that the truth rarely is naked, but on the contrary is clothed in mist and mystery!

6.   Some of the reasons why people see events differently are as follows:

> ❑ their physical senses vary (eg colour blindness, less-than-perfect vision, poor hearing, imperfect sense of smell etc)
>
> ❑ health differences
>
> ❑ their general intelligence levels vary (ie some people size up their situation far quicker than others)
>
> ❑ nature, and effects, of past experiences are different for individuals (eg an experienced birdwatcher will see the camouflaged bird well before a less experienced colleague)
>
> ❑ innate abilities and learned skills are different between individuals
>
> ❑ individual values and attitudes cause people to see things differently (eg assumptions, stereotypes and 'halo effects' spring all too readily from our personal positions on people and events)
>
> ❑ personalities differ, and thus individuals tend to adopt particular stances towards outside events (eg some get very intense, ascribing all sorts of motives and feelings to the perceived event, while others are cool and detached about the same event)
>
> ❑ individual aspirations and goals also differ widely, and these affect the relative importance attached to outside events

7.   *Status* also has an effect on perception, since it colours the assumptions an individual makes about a situation. In a study reported by Zalkind & Costello (1962)[1], it was shown that status differences between perceiver and perceived led to the former ascribing different motivations for behaviour on the basis of relative status. For example, persons of high status were seen as wanting to cooperate, whereas low status persons were seen

as being persuaded to cooperate. Another point made by Zalkind & Costello, in their informative review of perception studies, was that the *visibility* of the perceived person's traits was an important factor affecting the accuracy of perception. Thus, where the other person is able to express particular traits freely, then the perceiver can judge them more accurately. Unfortunately, however, perceivers often judge traits they cannnot see (eg honesty, loyalty) but infer from what they think they have 'seen'. Judgements, therefore, usually have to be weighed against other evidence of the perceived person's behaviour. As the authors put it :

> 'Frequently the practical situation demands judgements, but we should recognise the frail reeds upon which we are leaning and be prepared to observe further and revise our judgements with time and closer acquaintance.' (p.219)

8. Differences in the situation of the perceived depend greatly on whether the object of the perception is a person (or a group of persons), an idea or concept, or a physical object. The greatest differences on this side of the triangle (Fig. 6.2) appear when the objects of the perception are other human beings, ie where *social perception* is the issue. Here all the differences just mentioned apply, in particular those relating to people's assumptions, stereotypes, attitudes and status. The effect of these is to produce certain reactions and responses on the part of the perceived group, which are themselves a product of *their* perceptions of what is happening, or being asked of them. When dealing with people, the most effective perceivers are those who display *empathy* (ie the ability (1) to see the situation from the other's point of view, (2) to do so in a non-judgmental way, and then (3), as Egan (1990)[2] insists '...*and communicating [your] understanding to the client*.') Showing empathy does not mean agreeing with what the other is saying, but accepting it at its face value. This is an important lesson for anyone in a managerial position, especially when dealing with problematic staff or customers.

9. The situation, or context, in which perception takes place can have a major bearing on the behaviour of the perceiver. Again the strength of situational variables depends on whether the object of the perception is physical, human or conceptual. Where the object is some *physical* entity, the situation is likely to affect perception in terms of problems of visual perspective, amount of light and reflection, and the clarity of the image. In the half-light it is easy to wrongly recognise a friend or relative. In the workplace accidents are sometimes caused by an individual's visual misperception of the safety of a piece of equipment, which then leads to unexpected injury. Other factors, such as the nature of people's expectations and the urgency of the situation, may also affect the perception of physical objects. This combination of circumstances is not untypical in military situations, for example, where, on a forward patrol over enemy-held territory, fighter pilots have sometimes shot down friendly aircraft in the belief that they

are the enemy. This happens partly because they are anticipating meeting the enemy, and thus liable to wrongly attribute their presence, and partly because of the danger they are exposed to if they fail to recognise the enemy.

10. When the object is *human behaviour*, the situation can be very telling. Much, for example, can depend on the timing of events. If you witness a scruffy youth running from a shop with various people in pursuit, you might perceive him to be a thief attempting a getaway. However, if you had arrived at the scene a few moments earlier, you would have spotted another individual in a balaclava sprinting from the shop with a fistful of notes — the youth is, in fact, trying to stop the real thief! In a work situation, misunderstandings (ie misperceptions) can arise for various reasons, such as:

   ❏ unclear or ambiguous message sent by management

   ❏ inadequate communication channels

   ❏ failure by management to address possible feelings aroused by their message

   ❏ the influence of powerful individuals or groups may encourage others to read an adverse meaning into an otherwise neutral message

   ❏ the form and content of the message goes against the tone of past practice (ie against the cultural norms of the organisation)

   ❏ failure of the communicating party to check out understanding before issuing the message

11. The perceptual process can also be affected by the number of parties involved. For example, it may be easier to avoid misperceptions in a one-to-one situation compared with one person to a group, or one group to another. Other factors include the importance of the issues at stake, the relative status of the parties, and the expectations arising from the dominant culture in the organisation. Clearly, the situational aspects of the perception process affect both the perceiver and the perceived, requiring each party to recognise the difference between appropriate and inappropriate cues, and then adapt their behaviour as best they can.

The practical implications of perception at work

12. If we are aware of the elements of the perception process, we can be more attentive to the cues we receive from the object of our perception, especially where this is another human being. We can learn, for example, to pay more attention to *body language* in our dealings with others, watching out for significant gestures, eye contact, head nodding, facial expressions and

body postures. Body language is less easily disguised than words, and is often a better guide to a truthful perception of events than verbal language, where people may say one thing but mean something else. In an employment interview, a candidate may answer affirmatively to a question, but indicate by body language that he is unsure of the answer, or uncomfortable with it. As Pease (1984)[3] points out

> '....whenever we call someone 'perceptive' or 'intuitive', we are referring to his or her ability to read another person's non-verbal cues and to compare these cues with verbal signals.'

13.   The extent of our acceptance of an organisation's culture (its rules, conventions and atmosphere) invariably affects how we perceive people, ideas and physical objects. For example, if the organisation's culture implies that older, senior managers know best, then one's attitude will be coloured by this acceptance in dealings with older, senior members of staff. Similarly with ideas, if the organisation is basically expansive in its view of say marketing and production, it will be difficult for a manager in one of these areas to suggest that certain activities are scaled down. Individual's status in relation to others can affect perception in significant,even tragic ways, for example when the junior flight officer in an airliner accepts his captain's bland and incorrect assessment of possible engine trouble, even though he strongly suspects something is seriously wrong, and loses his life in the subsequent crash. It is not surprising following such situations that civil airlines now incorporate assertiveness training into their pilot training, so that junior flight deck personnel are better prepared to question the judgement of senior captains in an emergency situation.

14.   The principal practical use of social perception is to assess not only how people are reacting now, but to predict how they might behave in the future. If our perceptions of others are correct, then we can assume reasonably confidently how they will perform. Thus, in work organisations, events such as employment interviews, team meetings, appraisal and disciplinary interviews can all contribute to an authentic knowledge of what is happening now, and what is likely to happen in the foreseeable future. Unfortunately, however, our perceptions often seem to be flawed, especially in the case of first impressions. Thus a manager's judgements about a new recruit, whom he has recently interviewed and appointed, can only truly be considered as an interim assessment subject to performance in the job. In such a situation, a more realistic view of the recruit's capacities and potential can only be obtained after a period of months in the post, for example when the first appraisal or job review interview takes place.

15.   Most commentators on social perception agree that the accuracy of an individual's perception is greatly enhanced if he or she has a high degree of *self-perception*. Awareness, and acceptance, of one's own strengths, weaknesses and prejudices can lead to a sharper, more truthful assessment of

another's capacities, predispositions and future behaviour patterns. It is also helpful if the perceiver is capable of exercising judgements in a relatively impartial, objective way. This is a critical skill for groups such as counsellors and the psychotherapists, but can be deployed just as usefully in the workplace as in a clinical situation.

16. A useful model for analysing self-perception is the so-called Johari Window, devised by Joe Luft and Harry Ingram (see Luft,1970)[4], which has been widely used in management and team development. As Figure 6.3 indicates, the quadrant of the self-inventory is based on the two axes of 'Known and Unknown to Self' and 'Known and Unknown to Others'.

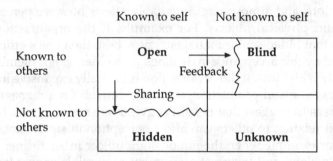

Figure 6.3   *The Johari window (after Luft & Ingram)*

The key feature of the model for development purposes is to enable individuals to extend the scope of their Open area by (1) encouraging them to share their Hidden area with colleagues, and (2) by giving feedback to them as to how they are perceived by others, thus further extending the Open area, this time at the expense of the Blind area. The information people can gain about themselves increases their self-knowledge, and, in a supportive atmosphere, can also increase their self-confidence. The benefits are improved perceptual skills, as mentioned in the previous paragraph.

17. In addition to the social skills just referred to, there are cognitive methods of improving perceptual accuracy. In using our mental powers to check out what is going on in a particular situation we can greatly enhance our prospects of assessing a situation or person correctly. What we tend to look for is *corroborative evidence* from at least one other source. Thus, in the selection process a manager will want to see the individual's application form or CV, a reference or report from previous employers, evidence of proper certification, as well as the exploiting the opportunity of interviewing the person in a face-to-face situation. Police detective work, to take another example, is principally one of finding enough information from enough different sources to bring about the successful conviction of a criminal. Thus, forensic evidence alone may not be sufficient to convince a jury, but if the forensic evidence matches witness statements, evidence from iden-

tity parades and other reasonable sources of information, then it is likely that a jury's perception of a person's guilt will be sufficient to return a verdict of guilty.

Personal values and attitudes at work

18. As was noted in the first part of this chapter, an individual's personal values and attitudes play a key role in the way people, things and events are perceived. These values and attitudes develop from early childhood onwards as a result of upbringing, education and experience of life. Some people's attitudes, it seems, become set by their late twenties/early thirties, others seem able to retain a certain flexibility throughout their life. Reasons for such differences in attitudes appear to be linked to individuals' intelligence level and personality traits.

19. What then are *values* and *attitudes?* It is important to clarify what we mean here, so that we can disentangle the concept of a value from that of an *attitude* and related concepts, such as *opinions* and *norms*. We commence with the concept of a *personal value*, which for our purposes we will define as follows:

   A personal value is an underlying acceptance of a general way of behaving that is seen as preferable to alternative ways, and usually carries notions of right and wrong within it. The development of personal values is influenced by such factors as personality characteristics (eg conscientiousness etc), the level of intelligence, childhood (and subsequent) learning, and the influence of others (eg parents, teachers, ministers, and peer-groups), as well as by life's experiences. Values tend to be more deep-rooted than attitudes and opinions. A collection of values is usually called a value-system.

20. Personal values have been categorised into a number of types. Allport et al (1951)[5], for example, distinguished between the following six types of values:

> 1 *Theoretical*, ie placing considerable emphasis on the use of reason to arrive at the truth of things
>
> 2 *Economic*, ie emphasising the useful and the practical aspects of life
>
> 3 *Aesthetic*, ie placing high value on beauty and form
>
> 4 *Social*, ie emphasising the importance of people over other aspects of life
>
> 5 *Political*, ie concerned with exercising power and influence
>
> 6 *Religious*, ie a concern for spiritual values in life

The priority given to each type of value reflects the individual's dominant concerns. Thus, ministers of religion have been found to put religious and social values high on their list of priorities, whereas managers in business have been found to give higher priority to economic, theoretical and political values. The above list identifies where people's priorities may lie, but does not tell us much about the rights and wrongs of behaviour. Yet the morality issue is a crucial dimension of personal values, which are not just about what is important in life, but what is right and wrong.

21. Rokeach (1973)[6] distinguished between two types of values — *terminal values*, and *instrumental values*. *Terminal* values refer to desired end-states, or eventual preferred outcomes such as:

    ☐ a comfortable life ☐ a world at peace
    ☐ freedom ☐ inner harmony
    ☐ pleasure ☐ self-respect
    ☐ wisdom

    Such values sum up an individual's ultimate aim in life and provide a framework within which day-to-day events are judged, and decisions reached. Such values are more likely to be held implicitly than explicitly, but will undoubtedly affect human behaviour.

22. *Instrumental* values are concerned with the achievement of terminal values and are thus a matter of modes of behaviour rather than goal-setting. Rokeach identified a number of such values, including the following:

    ☐ ambition   (ie working hard, setting personal goals)
    ☐ competence   (ie being capable, showing effectiveness)
    ☐ neatness   (ie working/ dressing tidily)
    ☐ helpfulness   (ie working for others' welfare)
    ☐ obedience   (ie being dutiful, showing respect)
    ☐ dependability   (ie seeking responsibility, showing reliability)

When Rokeach asked different groups of people to rate terminal and instrumental values, it was noticed that those in similar occupations tended to give similar ratings. However, between groups there were considerable variances, bearing out the findings of Allport's studies earlier. The list of instrumental values is one that is easier to recognise in real life than the list of terminal values. This is because individuals tend to maintain their instrumental values explicitly, and thus manifest them in their working lives. Their terminal values by comparison are usually so integrated into their behaviour that they tend to be held implicitly.

Attitudes

23. In terms of the value types just referred to, attitudes are more instrumental than terminal in nature. Attitudes are also more likely to be focused on specific issues and events than values, which act more as a general guide to preferred behaviour. A working definition of an attitude, for the purposes of this chapter, is offered as follows:

An attitude is a predisposition to make certain kinds of judgements about people, issues and events, usually in specific situations. Personal attitudes are a reflection of the broad values held by the individual. Attitudes lead to the development of personal opinions and prejudices, as well as contributing positively to an individual's exercise of judgement. Some attitudes are held firmly, and are unlikely to be changed in a person's lifetime; others are held less firmly, and are subject to change, where the individual perceives it useful to do so. Attitudes are narrower in concept than values, and tend to be focused on specific elements of the individual's external world.

24. Differing attitudes in the workplace can cause considerable disruption to the nature, pace and efficiency of work. The well-known concept *of 'Us and Them'* exemplifies the gulf that can exist between management and workers, or between one work-group and another. The implication is that the two parties are at odds with one another, and that one party, at least, is unhappy with this position. Much of the effort that goes into harmonising people's activities, creating pride in the product, and generally developing an organisation culture (see Chapter 13) is directed towards turning negative,or lukewarm, attitudes into strongly positive ones. Another well-known attitudinal problem is summed up in the expression *'Take it or leave it!'*.The implication here is that the individual or group supplying a service do not care whether the recipient is satisfied. This kind of attitude is the complete opposite of the attitudes which organisations attempt to instil in a Total Quality Management approach, or in Customer Relations training, for example.

25. Eysenck & Wilson (1976)[7] identified an important group of values-related personality factors in addition to the extrovert/introvert/ stable/ neurotic and psychotic groups referred to in the previous chapter. These values

113

were *tough-mindedness* and *tender-mindedness* — each of which comprised a range of personality characteristics, as indicated below (Fig. 6.4):

Personality Dimension	*Component Traits/ Characteristics*
Tough-mindedness	Aggressiveness Assertiveness Achievement-orientation Manipulation Sensation-seeking Dogmatism Masculinity
Tender-mindedness	Peacefulness Submissiveness Unambitiousness Empathy Unadventurousness Flexibility Feminity

Figure 6.4   *Values-Related Personality Traits (Eysenck, 1976)*

26. In order to measure individuals' responses on these two dimensions, Eysenck prepared a questionnaire of 210 separate questions, designed to draw out people's scores on the fourteen component traits. As with the earlier Eysenck questionnaires, the results place individuals somewhere along a continuum of the two dimensions:

Tough-mindedness <————>	**Tender-mindedness**
Inclined to be aggressive, manipulative and dogmatic	Inclined to avoid confrontation; preferring peace and gentleness

The questionnaire implies a number of assumptions about behaviour, and the specific references to 'masculine' and 'feminine' contain several assumptions that are likely to be challenged today. Nevertheless, there is considerable advantage in analysing the values implicit in the different traits on these dimensions, since they can provide clues to individuals' differing attitudes towards people at work.

27. It was mentioned in paragraph 23 that some attitudes are firmly held and unlikely to be changed without good cause. In work situations some entrenched attitudes can adversely affect harmony, discipline and efficiency, and it is important for managers to be able to bring about change for the better. This is no easy task. Kurt Lewin (1951)[8] many years ago argued that in order to introduce change in such a situation it was necessary to 'unfreeze' the current behaviour (see Fig 6.5) before introducing any changes. This means recognising the underlying perceptions of the target group, and the strength of their feelings, however unwarranted they might be. Then devising ways of helping them to see the benefits of the changes, and gaining their acceptance for them, albeit with some compro-

mises on the way, if necessary. Once the individuals concerned have accepted the changes in principle, then their attitudes are open to change too. So, for example, they can begin to accept that it is no longer the supervisors who have to shoulder all the responsibility for quality or safety, but that this is a responsibility that all have to share. In this case, the process of changing attitudes leads to changed behaviour, which then has to be reinforced in order to maintain the momentum of change.

| Unfreeze existing attitudes and behaviour | ——> | Introduce changes | ——> | Reinforce changed attitudes and behaviour |

Figure 6.5   *Changing attitudes and behaviour at work (after Lewin)*

Opinions and norms

28. Related to attitudes are personal *opinions*, which are expressions of our preferred way of dealing with specific problems. *Opinions* are more solution-centred than attitudes, which are more to do with inclinations than actions. Thus, we are more likely to be asked for an opinion on a specific situation (eg *'How much effort do you think we should invest in developing this product for export markets?'*), and for our *attitude* towards a category of people, issues or events (eg *'In principle, do you think we should support expansion in overseas markets?'*)

29. Related both to attitudes and values are *norms*, which are their collective form. Norms can be set out *explicitly* in the form of rules, written standards, codes of practice and laws, or *implicitly* in group attitudes and in all the unwritten standards and practices that are summed up in the 'organisation culture'.

A concluding model of values, attitudes and perceptions

30. In the light of the ideas outlined in this chapter, a model of personal attitudes, perceptions and action can be mapped out, showing the impact on attitudes of values, norms and moral principles, as follows (Figure 6.6):

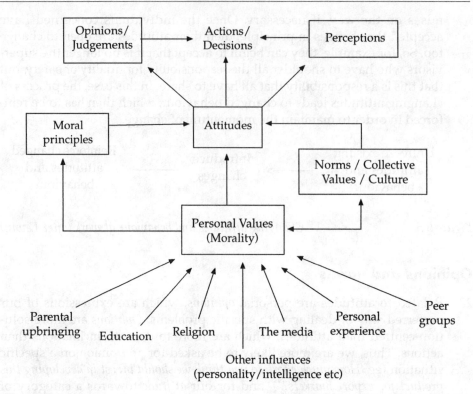

Figure 6.6   *Attitudes, perceptions and action*

31. The model simplifies the complexities of the relationships between values, attitudes, perceptions and norms, but nevertheless can help to identify the relationships between the major elements of an individual's value-system, and the actions that spring from it. The foundation of the system is the individual's primary set of values, which is formed under various influences in the *external* world, such as parents, teachers, the media etc, and by *internal* forces, such as personality and intelligence. From the basic values spring personal attitudes and one's private moral code (moral principles). Personal values also contribute to, and are influenced by, the prevailing norms of society (collective values). The individual's attitudes are influenced by the moral climate (social norms) as well as by the individual's basic values and moral code. The individual's personal attitudes are the platform from which perceptions are formed, opinions and judgements made, and actions taken. What the model does not show is the effect of the consequences of the actions that are taken, but these consequences themselves form part of life experience, which is a formative influence on the individual's basic value-system. Thus the whole process begins again from its roots.

References

1. Zalkind,S. & Costello,T. (1962) *'Perception: Implications for Administration' in Organisational Psychology* (3rd edn, 1979), eds Kolb,D.,Rubin,I. & McIntyre,J., Prentice-Hall

2. Egan,G. (1990), *The Skilled Helper* (4th edn), Brooks/Cole

3. Pease A. (1984), *Body Language*, Sheldon Press

4. Luft, J. (1970), *Group Processes : An Introduction to Group Dynamics* (2nd edn), National Press

5. Allport, G., Vernon,P. & Lindzey,G. (1951), *Study of Values*, Houghton Mifflin

6. Rokeach,M. (1973), *The Nature of Human Values*, Free Press

7. Eysenck, H. & Wilson,G. (1976), *Know Your Own Personality,* Penguin

8. Lewin,K. (1951), *Field Theory in Social Science*, Harper

Questions for reflection/discussion

1. What, in your view, are the three most important reasons for explaining why people at work may 'see' the same person, idea or event differently?

2. What is 'empathy', and how can it contribute to closing the gap between subjective and objective versions of reality in a given situation?

3. What are the problems surrounding the issue of 'unfreezing' people's current behaviour?

4. What are the most important factors influencing the development of a personal values-system? Give your reasons.

5. How far might an individual's personal moral standards affect their behaviour at work? Give some examples of behaviour and attitudes you might look for.

7 Motivation, job satisfaction and performance

Introduction

1. Previous chapters have considered some of the key aspects of personality and individual perception that underlie people's behaviour at work. These aspects of individual behaviour are important when turning to the issue of individual motivation at work, for the strength and direction of an individual's motivation are likely to be greatly influenced by personality factors as well as by individual perceptions of reality. Motivation is essentially about what drives a person to work in a particular way and with a given amount of effort and enthusiasm. We shall examine the concept more closely in a moment. Linked to motivation is the whole issue of individual satisfaction with work — so-called 'job satisfaction'— and this will be considered in the light of Herzberg's studies mentioned earlier (Chap.4). Motivation and job satisfaction are significant factors in people's performance at work, and these particular influences will be considered in terms of their contribution to organisational effectiveness and efficiency.

2. In the context of organisational psychology, the term 'motivation' tends to be looked at from two different perspectives — firstly, and principally, as a concept of human behaviour that is of major interest to students of organisational behaviour, and thus requires investigation and exploration; secondly, as a concept of management practice that needs to be understood by managers, and then applied to the work environment, even to the extent of being instilled into employees. This chapter focuses on the first perspective. Subsequent chapters will examine motivation as a means of forming employees' attitudes towards organisational goals at work (eg Chap 11, Leadership).

Motivation as human behaviour

3. What is meant by the word 'motivation' when applied in the context of human behaviour? It has been described variously as:

1   '.....a label for the determinants of (a) the choice to initiate effort on a certain task, (b) the choice to expend a certain amount of effort, and (c) the choice to persist in expending effort over a period of time......holding constant the effects of aptitude, skill, and understanding of the task, and the constraints operating in the environment.'

(Campbell J. & Pritchard, 1976)[1]

2   '...the search for motive is the search for a process of thinking and feeling that causes a person to act in specific ways.' (p.71)

(Kolb,D.Rubin,I. & McIntyre,J.,1979)[2]

3   'Processes or factors that cause people to act or behave in certain ways.'

International Dictionary of Management
(4th edn), 1990[3]

As the above definitions suggest, 'motivation' is concerned both with identifying the triggers for behaviour, and understanding how and why human beings behave in certain ways in given circumstances.

4.   In the light of the above comparisons, we can now define a working definition of motivation for the purposes of this chapter, as follows:

'Motivation' is the term used to describe those processes, both instinctive and rational, by which people seek to satisfy the basic drives, perceived needs and personal goals, which trigger human behaviour.

Motivation as defined in this way emphasises the process of motivation rather than the identification of the triggers (often called the *motivating factors)*, although these are, of course, extremely relevant. The definition includes satisfying instinctive, or semi-conscious, drives (eg hunger, sleep, sex etc), as well as rational, or conscious, needs and aspirations (eg for recognition, achievement, self-fulfilment etc).

5.   The key elements described in most of the discussions about 'motivation' are as follows:

❏ needs, drives, stimulus and triggers

❏ goals, desired outcomes

❏ approach versus avoidance (pleasure versus pain)

❏ performance (actual), response, effort

❏ valence (attractive value), incentive

..... continued

> ❏ expectations (of rewards, satisfaction)
>
> ❏ reinforcement
>
> ❏ abilities, intelligence, awareness (of options)
>
> ❏ perception of reality
>
> ❏ personality differences
>
> ❏ management attitudes/ assumptions about people

The latter point is usually only brought up in discussions concerning how to apply motivation theory in practice in the workplace.

6. These elements — with the exception of the last point — can be viewed diagrammatically as follows (Fig. 7.1):

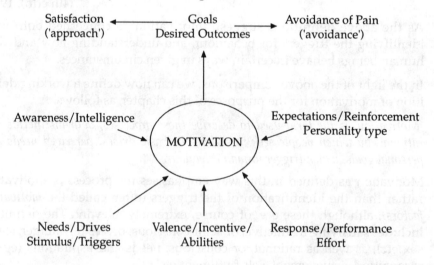

Figure 7.1   *Key elements in the concept of motivation*

7. What this basic overview of motivation shows is that, when human beings experience a need, drive or some stimulus or trigger, they set themselves (consciously or unconsciously) appropriate goals or desired outcomes, which may invite satisfaction or enable avoidance of pain. The extent to which humans set, or even recognise, appropriate goals depends considerably on their level of awareness of suitable options. Whether goals are identified consciously or not, the needs and drives produce a response in the individual, in which effort is exerted and a level of performance achieved. The level of this response is determined partly by the value, or incentive, that the person sees in performing the activity, and partly by his or her abilities. Once the response is made the success, or otherwise, of the outcome for the individual depends partly on their expectations, partly on

personality type, and partly on the extent to which earlier outcomes reinforced the expectations.

8.   The basic concept of motivation can be remodelled as follows (Fig. 7.2):

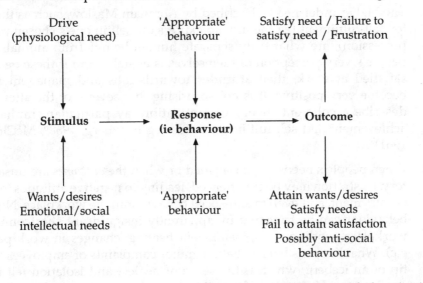

| Drive (physiological need) | 'Appropriate' behaviour | Satisfy need / Failure to satisfy need / Frustration |

Stimulus → Response (ie behaviour) → Outcome

| Wants/desires Emotional/social intellectual needs | 'Appropriate' behaviour | Attain wants/desires Satisfy needs Fail to attain satisfaction Possibly anti-social behaviour |

Figure 7.2   *A basic model of motivation*

9.   The key to the model is the stimulus, since this is what triggers the motivation process. This stimulus could be something basic like intense thirst, or something subtler such as a perceived need for success in some skill or other. In the first case, the appropriate behaviour (ie the response) is to seek water and drink enough of it to slake the thirst. In the second case, the appropriate behaviour may be to seek training in the skill, then practice opportunities, and finally opportunities to perform it. The basic physiological needs are usually described as 'drives' or 'appetites', and refer to the instinctive or semi-conscious needs that demand our attention. In the workplace this level of need is met by the provision of canteens, rest breaks, toilet facilities and welfare arrangements. Other needs, such as social contact and team membership are also met at work by giving people opportunities to share offices and workspace, and by assigning them to work-groups.

10   The satisfaction of physical needs leads to a state of equilibrium, at least until the effects have worn off. Thus a hungry person eats his fill and is no longer motivated to seek food, at least not for the next few hours. The satisfaction of *higher* needs, such as recognition and achievement, seem not to have the same temporary effect as for lower level needs. In the case of higher needs, the attainment of the goal appears to increase an individual's taste for more of the same. We often use the expression 'inspired behaviour' when trying to describe the effects of early success on individuals, which seems to inspire them to even greater efforts. These differences

in the outcomes of motivation were first identified by Maslow (1954)[4] and subsequently taken up by Herzberg et al (1959)[5], who described the former as *hygiene* factors and the latter as *motivators* (see Chap 4 above).

11. The higher order needs described by Abraham Maslow, such as the need for self-fulfilment (eg the urge to express oneself in one's chosen trade or profession), are what truly separate human beings from animals. Here people's very perception of themselves is at stake, and if these needs are satisfied at work, then attitudes towards jobs and management can become very positive. It is not surprising that several of the attempts to describe a coherent theory of motivation lay particular emphasis on achievement and self-fulfilment needs (eg Herzberg, 1968[6]; McClelland, 1961)[7].

12. When people's needs are unsatisfied or when the *outcomes* are unsatisfactory, frustration may be experienced, leading to negative attitudes towards employment, and even to anti-social behaviour in the workplace. Negative behaviour can be triggered by apparently insignificant shortcomings in workplace conditions (eg insufficient heating, changes in work patterns etc). What happens here is that the minor complaints of employees are the tip of an iceberg, which is the sense of neglect and isolation felt by the employees over a period of time. Most people, it seems, are demotivated if their contribution is neither recognised nor rewarded. On the contrary, as the Hawthorne Experiments showed (Chap 4), when employees feel that they are important, and that their work is valued by the management, they will produce high performance even if some aspects of working conditions are poor.

Factors influencing motivation at work

13. Although much of the emphasis in recent years has been on the process of motivation, most of the well-known 'theories' of motivation have focused on the triggers for behaviour. These well-known 'theories' are, in fact, only attempts at a theory, as most of their exponents would admit. The general question they have raised is *'What are the major factors that influence an individual's motivational processes at work?'* The answer to this question is not only of interest to researchers and theorists, but also to practising managers and supervisors. The former are interested in isolating the key variables that might influence both *what* a person sees as a need (*content theories*), and *how* he or she seeks to satisfy needs (*process theories*). The managers and supervisors are interested in assessing what they can, and can't, manipulate in the internal organisational environment in order to achieve a 'motivated workforce'. The most important factors are indicated in Figure 7.3, which maps out the clusters of factors that are most likely to be referred to in texts about motivation.

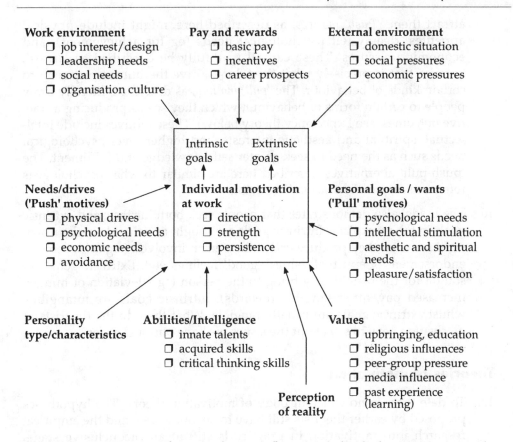

Work environment
- ❑ job interest/design
- ❑ leadership needs
- ❑ social needs
- ❑ organisation culture

Pay and rewards
- ❑ basic pay
- ❑ incentives
- ❑ career prospects

External environment
- ❑ domestic situation
- ❑ social pressures
- ❑ economic pressures

Intrinsic goals   Extrinsic goals

Needs/drives ('Push' motives)
- ❑ physical drives
- ❑ psychological needs
- ❑ economic needs
- ❑ avoidance

Individual motivation at work
- ❑ direction
- ❑ strength
- ❑ persistence

Personal goals / wants ('Pull' motives)
- ❑ psychological needs
- ❑ intellectual stimulation
- ❑ aesthetic and spiritual needs
- ❑ pleasure/satisfaction

Personality type/characteristics

Abilities/Intelligence
- ❑ innate talents
- ❑ acquired skills
- ❑ critical thinking skills

Values
- ❑ upbringing, education
- ❑ religious influences
- ❑ peer-group pressure
- ❑ media influence
- ❑ past experience (learning)

Perception of reality

Figure 7.3   *The major factors influencing individual motivation at work*

14. What the model (Fig. 7.3) demonstrates, albeit by over simplifying the complexity of the interrelationships, is that an individual's motivation is not just a matter of satisfying *needs* and *wants*, vital though these are. Motivation is also influenced (i) by internal factors such as the type of personality, perceptual and ability levels, and the individual's personal value-system, and (ii) by external factors such as the individual's work and domestic environments. Thus, managers who want to assess the motivational needs of their particular employees must take into account more than just the apparent needs and personal goals of these employees. They have to recognise the influence of other factors, such as different personality types and differing skills and talents. They also have to take into account the effect of organisational factors such as the design of jobs, the nature of the organisation culture, and the pay and rewards system. And, as if that were not enough, they also need to evaluate the employees' external environment, checking the domestic, social and economic pressures that might adversely affect job performance.

15. The model suggests that there are differences between motives that *push* people towards certain kinds of behaviour, and those that *pull* them, ie

attract them. *'Push' motives,* as described here, might include physical appetites, deeply-felt psychological needs (eg for achievement), and economic pressures. These can all truthfully be described as *'drives'*, because that is precisely what they do — drive the human organism to certain kinds of behaviour. The *'pull' motives*, as described, literally draw people to certain forms of behaviour, which they see as producing attractive outcomes (see Expectancy theory below). These motives include intellectual, spiritual and aesthetic interests, and higher level psychological needs such as the need to seek greater self-knowledge and fulfilment. The 'push-pull' alternatives described here are similar to what psychologists refer to as *'approach-avoidance'* behaviours.

16. The model also demonstrates that people seek both intrinsic and extrinsic goals in the workplace. Intrinsic goals are sought as valuable in their own right for what they produce *within* the person involved (eg achievement, endorsement of spiritual values, 'good' feelings etc). Extrinsic goals are sought for the benefit they bring to the person (eg alleviation of hunger, increased pay, other tangible rewards). Intrinsic goals are intangible, whilst extrinsic goals are usually tangible. What then do the theorists of motivation have to say about the issues we have outlined so far?

Theories of motivation

17. To date there is no coherent body of motivation theory. The hypotheses proposed by earlier theorists still have to be vindicated, and the empirical research into motivation in practice is still at an inconclusive stage. Nevertheless, a few 'theories' (ie part-theories) have found some validation from amongst the research community, and several have found some support amongst the managerial community. In the main, theories of motivation fall into two categories — *content theories*, which focus attention on the apparent needs, drives and wants of individuals, and *process theories*, which concentrate on the processes involved when individuals make decisions about things that they perceive as important to them.

Content theories of motivation

18. The leading content theories deal essentially with *what* appears to motivate people (ie what causes them to divert effort towards certain kinds of desired outcomes). Most of these theories have been mentioned in earlier chapters, but some further summaries will be useful at this point. They can be listed as follows (Figure 7.4):

Theories	Principal Features
1. F.W Taylor and Scientific Manage- (see Chap 2 paras 20-26)	Money is primary incentive. Punishment (especially in form of withdrawal of benefits or threat of dismissal) a proper part of motivation. 'Carrot and stick' approach.
2. Hawthorne Studies (see Chap 4 paras 3-12)	People need social contact at work. Management interest in employees' work can itself produce improvements in motivation.
3. Socio-technical Systems (see Chap 3 paras 37-40)	Motivation at work does not come only through efficient systems and technology, but also through attention to people's needs for social contact and a degree of decision-making autonomy in their work
4. Abraham Maslow (see Chap 4 paras 15-17)	People's needs are arranged in an hierarchy, in which basic needs generally have to be satisfied before higher needs come into play. The basic needs include physiological and safety needs, followed by social and affiliation needs. The higher needs include esteem needs and self-actualisation to which were later added 'curiosity' and the need to understand.
5. Clayton Alderfer (see Chap 4 paras 16-17)	A Modified version of Maslow's hierarchy based on existence needs, relatedness needs and growth needs seen as representing different stages along a continuum of needs. Individuals may move backwards as well as forwards along the scale. Known as ERG Theory of Motivation. Provides a more flexible approach than Maslow's.
6. D. McGregor (see Chap 4 paras 22-24)	Theory X and Theory Y, in which the former represents management's assumptions that employees only respond to inducements and threats, and the latter represents the assumption that employees can be trusted, want to achieve and can accept responsibility. Theory X encourages a carrot and stick approach; Theory Y encourages autonomy and self-actualisation at work.
7. F. Herzberg (see Chap 4 paras 28-31)	Motivation-Hygiene theory (or two-factor theory) of human motivation suggests that certain factors in the environment (eg pay, working conditions, company policies etc) do not lead to motivated employees, even when these factors are handled generously by the employer. However, such factors are often a source of lack of motivation on the part of employees. These are called hygiene factors. In contrast to these are the motivators, which include such factors as recognition, achievement and interesting work. Motivators have a positive affect on motivation. Whilst of interest as a contribution to motivation studies, this 'theory' is of greater relevance to the concept of 'job satisfaction'.
8. D. McClelland (see Chap 4 paras 32-33)	Achievement theory based on idea that the single most distinct human motive is the need for achievement (nAch). An individual's strength of this need is what most strikingly points to different levels of activity compared with colleagues. Two other key motives are the need for affiliation (nAff), and the need for power (nPow). McClelland has made considerable use of the Thematic Apperception Test as a means of eliciting this motive (see below).

Figure 7.4   *Content theories of motivation*

Achievement theory

19. Most of the above theories are described in earlier chapters, as indicated. However, McClelland's Achievement Theory can usefully be expanded at this point. McClelland's studies led him to discover people's dominant motives not by direct questioning nor by observation, but obliquely by asking them for their thoughts on the content of a number of cards on which vague pictures were shown. These cards were derived from a projective technique, known as the Thematic Apperception Test (TAT) developed by H.A.Murray at Harvard University in the late 1930's. Essentially the TAT material consists of a number of cards containing rather vague black and white pictures, and a single blank white card. Individuals taking the test are asked to look briefly (10-15 seconds) at each picture, and then write an account of what is happening in about five minutes. Over the course of twenty years or more, McClelland's research team discovered that people's reactions to the stories implied in the pictures tended to produce a number of common themes, which when analysed produced three distinct sets of motivational needs — the *need for achievement* (nAch), the *need for affiliation* or belonging (nAff), and the *need for power* (nPow). Everyone appears to have all three needs, but in different proportions. Since the Harvard studies were primarily concerned with motivation in a work context, the nAch drive was seen as especially significant. Several norms have been established for the TAT, but, according to Anastasi (1982)[8]

   '..most clinicians rely heavily on 'subjective norms' built up through their own experiences with the test.' (p.567)

20. The need for achievement expresses itself in a continual determination to do well at a task. In an article published in 1966, McClelland[9] described a simple experiment in which a group of people were given a problem and told that they could choose as a partner either a close friend or a stranger who was an expert in the issue concerned. People designated as high on nAch chose the expert in preference to their friend. Those choosing their friend were seen as high on nAff, where social relationships counted for more than achieving the task. The latter '..were not 'unmotivated'; their desire to be with someone they liked was simply a stronger motive than their desire to excel at the task.' (p.89) The need for power (nPow), it should be noted, is not the same drive as nAch. The former is more concerned with getting control and gaining attention than in improving performance. Of course, many people with a high nPow are successful achievers too, but this outcome is a by-product of their search to satisfy their dominant need for power and the exercise of control.

21. The importance of using the TAT method is that it enables the researchers to infer motives from what people say in their accounts of the different stories. As McClelland put it :

'It requires special measurement techniques to identify the presence of nAch and other such motives. Thus, what people say and believe is not very closely related to these 'hidden' motives, which seem to affect a person's 'style of life' more than his political, religious or social attitudes.' (p.90)

What has happened with the use of the TAT is that people have thought about a story in a context free from overtly personal or employment references. Their very thinking process, however, has led them to declare to the world what their priorities really are in terms of the three dominant drives of achievement, social affiliation, and power. McClelland concluded that nAch is a motivator than can be 'caught' (ie learned), and does not rely on inherited characteristics. Thus, achievement theory is being used widely to encourage development of nAch through training courses and experiential learning exercises (eg see Kolb et al, 1979[10].

Content theories — summary of motivators

22. In summarising the factors identified most strongly by the content theorists, we arrive at the following list of 'motivators' relevant to the workplace:

> ❐ security needs (eg for job security, adequate financial rewards, promotion prospects etc)
>
> ❐ social and affiliation needs (eg social contact at work, group membership etc)
>
> ❐ recognition and esteem needs (ie acknowledgement by management by word and deed)
>
> ❐ need for an acceptable level of autonomy in the job (ie power to make range of decisions about how tasks will be achieved)
>
> ❐ need to find interest and challenge in work itself
>
> ❐ need for achievement and sense of satisfaction in one's work
>
> ❐ need to achieve growth in personal repertoire of knowledge and skills
>
> ❐ need to find personal growth and development through work (ie ultimately to contribute to self-actualisation)

Process theories of motivation

23. These theories move the focus away from what motivates people in order to consider motivation from the point of view of how people become moti-

vated. The most comprehensive theory so far in this paradigm is what is termed **'Expectancy Theory',** as developed by Vroom, Lawler, Porter and others. The leading process theories are as follows:

❐ Expectancy Theory (especially the work of Vroom)

❐ Equity theory

❐ Goal theory (especially the contribution of Locke)

❐ Attribution theory (especially the work of Kelley)

❐ Reinforcement theory

We shall briefly outline each of these theories in the following paragraphs.

Expectancy theory

24. In Figure 7.2 in paragraph 8 above, we noted a basic model of motivation that suggested that *motivated behaviour* is triggered by a *stimulus*, which leads to an *outcome*, which may (or may not) be satisfactory to the person involved. Whereas content theorists focus on the stimuli to behaviour, Expectancy Theory focuses on the outcomes, and in particular on the *anticipated outcomes* of behaviour. The concept of individual perception is central to expectancy theory, since it is predicated on the basis that motivated behaviour arises from the perceived value placed by an individual on an activity, especially in terms of the benefits that are expected to flow from that activity.

The three core concepts of expectancy theory, as proposed by Vroom (1964)[11], are:

❐ **expectancy** (ie the perception of the likelihood that a particluar act will produce a particular outcome)

❐ **instrumentality** (ie the perception that performance will be rewarded appropriately)

❐ **valence** (ie the belief that attractive— valued— rewards are available)

---

25. This last concept — *valence* — is distinguished from *value* in the theory. Valence describes the *anticipated* satisfaction deriving from an outcome, whilst value is seen by Vroom as describing the actual satisfaction obtained. This emphasis on satisfaction has led at least one commentator (Locke,1975)[12] to describe expectancy theory as:

'...a form of calculative, psychological hedonism in which the ultimate motive of every human act is asserted to be the maximization of pleasure and/or the minimization of pain.'

Another commentator (Guest,1984)[13], however, sees expectancy theory as providing

'...the dominant framework for understanding motivation at work.'

26. The basic process defined by expectancy theory, as proposed by Vroom, and subsequently expanded by others (eg Lawler & Porter, 1968)[14] can be modelled as follows (Figure 7.5):

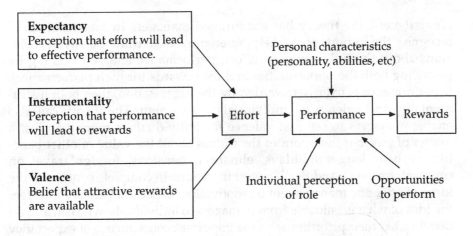

Figure 7.5   *Basic model of expectancy theory*

27. The first three concepts — expectancy, instrumentality and valence — combine together to create a driving force, designated by Vroom as *Force* (F), which motivates an individual to put in effort, achieve a level of performance, and obtain rewards at the end. Vroom indicated that Force was a multiple of Expectancy and Valence (encompassing Instrumentality) in the formula:

Force = Expectancy × Valence

This multiplicative aspect of the theory has been criticised on the grounds that it does not always follow that motivation is dependent on the connection between Expectancy and Valence. However, Vroom softens this by adding that performance is affected not just by the F factor, but also by individual characteristics (personality, skills and abilities), and by individual perceptions of role (eg how one perceives what is being asked for in a particular role).

28. The theory also takes account of environmental factors such as opportunities to perform, acknowledging that there may be constraints on an indi-

vidual's performance which are outside his control. Viewing the theory as a whole, Furnham (1992)[15] describes it as follows

> 'Expectancy theory characterizes people as rational, logical and cognitive beings who think about what they have to do to be rewarded and how much the reward means to them before they perform their jobs.' (p.148)

It is debatable how far people do act in this rational manner, especially when they are attempting to predict the *future* outcome for themselves of a particular course of action. *Needs*, as drivers, are not considered by the theory, and neither is the effect of past experience in reinforcing particular motives.

29. Nevertheless, the theory has encouraged managers in organisations to recognise the importance of helping employees to draw positive conclusions about the links between effort, performance and rewards (eg by providing both the opportunities and the rewards for high performance). If performance is overtly rewarded by the organisation, then both instrumentality and valence for individuals can be high. The theory can also enable managers to see that valence for individuals is more than just a matter of pay, but incorporates their ideas about the value of other benefits, such as longer holidays, ehnanced pensions, foreign travel on company business, and flexible working hours. In complete contrast to the ideas of scientific management on motivation, expectancy theory transfers the idea of what is valuable from managers to individuals, who can and do decide what their priorities are. One important consequence of expectancy theory is the growth of developments in work design aimed at providing opportunities for job interest, high performance and adequate feedback in the job. This point will be returned to later (see Chap. 15).

Equity theory

30. The basis of equity theory, in a work context, is that people make comparisons between themselves and others in terms of what they invest in their work (inputs) and what outcomes they receive from it. As in the case of expectancy theory, this theory is also founded on people's *perceptions*, in this case of the inputs and outcomes involved. Thus, their sense of equity (ie fairness) is applied to their *subjective* view of conditions and not necessarily to the objective situation. The theory states that when people perceive an unequal situation, they experience 'equity tension', which they attempt to reduce by appropriate behaviour. This behaviour may be to act positively to improve their performance and/or to seek improved rewards, or may be to act negatively by, for example, working more slowly (Taylor-type soldiering?!) on the grounds of being under-rated or underpaid.

31. Robbins (1993)[16] reports research that suggests that when people perceive an inequitable situation for themselves they *'can be predicted to make one of six choices:*

    1. *Change their inputs (for example, don't exert as much effort)*

    2. *Change their outcomes (for example, individuals paid on a piece-rate basis can increase their pay by producing a higher quantity of units of lower quality)*

    3. *Distort perceptions of self (for example, 'I used to think I worked at a moderate pace but now I realize that I work a lot harder than everyone else.')*

    4. *Distort perceptions of others (for example, 'Mike's job isn't as desirable as I previously thought it was.')*

    5. *Choose a different referent(for example, 'I may not make as much as my brother-in-law, but I'm doing better than my Dad did when he was my age.')*

    6. *Leave the field (for example, quit the job)'* (p.225)

32. Equity theory suggests that people are not only interested in rewards as such, but also in the comparative nature of rewards. Thus, part of the attractiveness (valence) of rewards in a work context is the extent to which they are seen to be comparable to those available to the peer-group. Such thinking, however, is best applied to *extrinsic* rewards, such as pay, promotion, pension arrangements, company car and other benefits that (a) depend on others for their provision, and (b) have an objective truth about them. Equity theory cannot apply in the same way to intrinsic rewards, such as as intrinsic job interest, personal achievement and exercise of responsibility, which by their very nature are personal to the individual, entirely subjective, and therefore less capable of comparison in any credible sense. For example, it is difficult to argue convincingly that *' I am experiencing a lesser sense of achievement at work than X.'* After all, who knows what standards of achievement X sets for himself, and how relatively satisfied he is with what he has achieved. It is all rather relative, and explains why individuals tend to distort (ie change!) their original perceptions of relative rewards.

33. Nevertheless, so far as extrinsic rewards are concerned, managers would be well advised to reflect on the ideas of equity theory, especially in recognising that subjective perceptions are extremely powerful factors in motivation. As Jaques (1961)[17] discovered more than thirty years ago, questions of equitable payment in relation to the discretion or autonomy available to an individual in the job are a key factor in achieving a sense of fairness at work. In a subsequent handbook for managers (1964)[18] he commented that:

    '....individuals privately possess common standards as to what constitutes-fair payment for given levels of work.......These norms of fair payment arerelative; ie they indicate what differentials in payment are felt to be fair in relation to differentials in levels of work.'

The 'felt fair' factor is essentially a restatement of 'individual perception of fairness'.

Goal theory

34. The thinking behind Goal Theory is that motivation is driven primarily by the goals or objectives that individuals set for themselves. Unlike in expectancy theory, where a satisfactory outcome is the prime motivator, goal theory suggest that it is the goal itself that provides the driving force. Locke (1968[19]) first proposed the idea that working towards goals was in itself a motivator. His research indicated that performance improved when individuals set specific rather than vague goals for themselves. When these specific goals were demanding ones, performance was even better. General exhortations to *do one's best* appear to be less effective than identifying *specific targets* and aiming for them.

35. Goal theorists (eg Locke & Latham, 1988[20]) also argue that an individual's motivation is enhanced when feedback on performance is available. Other important factors include goal-commitment (ie the extent to which the individual is committed to pursuing the goal even when things get rough), and self-efficacy (ie the perception that one has the ability to achieve the goal). Goal commitment is likely to be enhanced when goals are made public and when they are set by the individual rather than imposed externally. Clearly, the concept of goal 'ownership' is important here. A major aspect of management-by-objectives (eg Humble,1967)[21] is the intention that the process should attempt to harmonise individual and company goals. Self-efficacy is rather like the quality described by McClelland (1966 op cit) as at the core of those with a high nAch, ie a belief that they were capable of achieving their goals, which were set at a realistic, though challenging, level.

Attribution theory

36. Attribution theory suggests that we judge other people's behaviour by attributing meaning to their behaviour in the light of perceived internal or external forces. Internally caused behaviour is perceived to be under the control of the individual, ie they have made a *choice* in selecting the behaviour. Externally caused behaviour results from *environmental* forces that are perceived to influence people's behaviour (eg organisational rules, machinery breakdown etc), and over which the individual has little or no control. Kelley (1972)[22] suggests that when people make attributions, they do so with three major criteria in mind:

> ❑ **Distinctiveness,** ie how distinctive or different is the behaviour? How untypical?
> ❑ **Consensus,** ie how far is the behaviour typical of others in the same situation?
> ❑ **Consistency,** ie how consistent is the behaviour over time? Or is this an unusual piece of behaviour?

37. Application of the theory to an individual's lateness at work, for example, might result in the following thinking:

	Distinctiveness	Consensus	Consistency
Internal Attribution	Individual is considered to dislike work	Other people are usually on time	Individual is frequently late
External Attribution	Individual is not usually late to work	Other employees were also late	Individual is rarely late

In the case of the internally caused behaviour, we would be likely to draw the conclusion that this person was an unmotivated individual who disliked his job, and therefore 'chose' to be late. Where the behaviour was seen as essentially caused by external factors, we would be likely to conclude that this was a one-off event caused by circumstances outside his control, such as a major traffic hold-up en route to work.

38. Attribution theory is as much an issue of perception between individuals as a theory of motivation. Nevertheless, by providing another way of looking at people's behaviour, it can add to our understanding of the motivational process. The theory clearly has connections with achievement theory, since people attributed with primarily internal sources of behaviour have strong similarities with those showing high nAch needs (ie belief in their own internal strengths). People attributed with external causes of behaviour are likely to see their working lives dominated by external forces, such as the production system, actions of management etc.

Reinforcement theory

39. Whereas attribution theory has strong links with ideas about human perception, reinforcement theory, as applied to motivation, has major connections with learning theory (see next chapter), and especially the work of the behaviourist, B.F.Skinner. The reinforcement theory of motivation suggests that a given behaviour is a function of the consequences of earlier behaviour. Thus, all behaviour is determined to some extent by the rewards or punishments obtained from previous behaviour, which have

the effect of reinforcing current actions. In this sense all behaviour is caused by *external* sources, since we can have little control over the consequences of our actions. So, if an individual's efforts to contribute new ideas to a team are consistently met with an indulgent but apathetic approach by the management (ie negative reinforcement), then the individual is likely to be discouraged from making further suggestions, and may even seek to change his or her job. Where, by comparison, the individual is encouraged to share new ideas and help to develop them (ie positive reinforcement), then the person is likely to generate even more ideas.

40. Strict reinforcement theory would argue that an individual's own understandings, emotions, needs and expectations do not enter into motivation, which is purely about the *consequences* of behaviour. However, modifications of the theory (eg social learning theory) do allow for the effect of individuals' perceptions of the rewards/ punishments obtained by others as a contributor to motivation. Thus, an employee is not just affected by the consequences of his own actions at work, but is able to infer 'appropriate' behaviour from what he sees as the consequences for others of their behaviour. Reinforcement theory is not basically concerned with what motivates behaviour, or how, and is not strictly a theory of motivation. It is more concerned with control of behaviour (ie power over others).

41. Supporters of reinforcement theory (eg Jablonsky & De Vries (1972)[23] offer some important guidelines to those intending to use it as a motivating tool in the workplace. Typical suggestions include the following:

❏ Positively reinforce desired behaviour

❏ Ignore undesirable behaviour, so far as possible

❏ Avoid using punishment as principal means of achieving desired performance

❏ Provide reinforcement as soon as possible after the response

❏ Apply positive reinforcement regularly

❏ Assess positive and negative factors in the individual's environment

❏ Specify desired behaviour/ performance in quantifiable terms

The underlying assumption behind this approach is that people are there to be controlled, and that management's task is to provide the 'right' conditions to encourage high performance. This is not quite such a negative view of people as is suggested by McGregor's Theory X, but reinforcement theory is not too far removed from that concept of human motivation.

Motivation as a management goal

42. The discussion of reinforcement theory above leads us nicely onto the second meaning of 'motivation' referred to in paragraph 2 above, ie motivation as an aspect of management that requires human behaviour to be manipulated in order to harmonise individuals' goals with those of the organisation. In this context an understanding of motivation can be an important tool of management in practice. Here the stimulus is the need to gain employees' cooperation and commitment to high performance in achieving organisational goals. The 'appropriate behaviour' for management includes finding out about employees' needs and endeavouring to meet them by means of adequate pay and incentives, job enrichment programmes, briefing groups, quality circles and similar opportunities for employees to experience recognition, achievement and other higher level needs. It may also mean adopting reinforcement techniques to persuade employees to behave in desired ways, and to avoid behaving in what are deemed undesirable ways. Either way, the outcomes, if successful, are a *'motivated workforce'*, that is a group of employees willing to associate themselves and their skills with the goals of their organisation. These outcomes are the subject of other chapters (eg Chap 11 on leadership, and Chap 15 on work design).

References

1. Campbell, J. & Pritchard, D. (1976), *Motivation Theory in Industrial and Organizational Psychology*, in Dunnette, M. (1976), *Handbook of Industrial and Organizational Psychology*, Rand McNally

2. Kolb, D., Rubin,I. & McIntyre, J. (1979), *Organizational Psychology - an experiential approach* (3rd edn),), Prentice Hall

3. Johannsen H. & Page,G.T. (eds) *International Dictionary of Management* (4th edn, 1990), Kogan Page

4. Maslow, A. (1954), *Motivation and Personality, Harper & Row*. (See also 2nd edition, 1987, Harper & Row)

5. Herzberg, F., Mausner,B., & Snyderman,B. (1959), *The Motivation to Work*, JohnWiley

6. Herzberg, F. (1968), *Work and the Nature of Man*, Staples Press

7. McClelland, D. (1961), *The Achieving Society*, Van Nostrand

8. Anastasi, A. (1982), *Psychological Testing* (5 edn), Macmillan

9. McClelland, D. (1966), That Urge to Achieve, in Kolb,D., Rubin,I. & McIntyre,J. (1979), Organizational Psychology- a book of readings (3rd edn), Prentice Hall

10. Kolb, D., Rubin,I. & McIntyre, J. (1979), *Organizational Psychology - an experiential approach* (3rd edn),), Prentice Hall

11. Vroom, V. (1964), *Work and Motivation*, Wiley

12. Locke, E.A. (1975), *'Personnel Attitudes and Motivation'*, in Rosenzweig,M. & Porter,L. (eds) Annual Review of Psychology, Palo Alto

13. Guest, D. (1984), *'What's New in Motivation?'*, in Personnel Management, May 1984, IPM

14. Lawler, E. & Porter, L. (1968), *'Managerial Attitudes and Performance'*, in Vroom, V. & Deci, E. (1990), *Management and Motivation*, Penguin

15. Furnham, A.F. (1992), *Personality at Work*, Routledge

16. Robbins, S.P. (1993), *Organizational Behaviour* (6th edn), Prentice Hall

17. Jaques, E. (1961), *Equitable Payment*, Heinemann

18. Jaques, E. (1964), *Time-Span Handbook*, Heinemann

19. Lock, E.(1968), *'Towards a Theory of Task Motivation and Incentives'*, in Organizational Behavior and Human Performance, May 1968.

20. Locke, E. & Latham, G.P. (1988), *A Theory of Goal-setting and Task Performance*, Prentice Hall

21. Humble, J. (1967), *Improving Business Results*, McGraw Hill

22. Kelley. H. (1972), *'Attribution in Social Interaction'*, in Jones, E et al (eds), Attribution: Perceiving the Causes of Behavior, General Learning Press

23. Jablonsky, S. & De Vries, D. (1972), *'Operant conditioning principles extrapolated to the theory of management.'* in Organisational Behaviour and Human Performance, 14.

Questions for reflection/discussion

1. How useful is it to think of 'motivation' in terms of satisfying drives rather than as a process of developing appropriate behaviour?

2. What are the advantages of analysing 'motivation' in terms of a process that enables a person to become 'motivated'?

3. Taking into account the major factors influencing motivation (see Fig.7.3), what would you argue are the five most significant factors, and why?

4. What would you say were the pros and cons of projective tests such as the Thematic Apperception Test?

5. How far would you agree that the basic concept of Expectancy Theory is too heavily biassed towards rational, logical behaviour?

6. What part do outcomes, both intended (eg goals, objectives) and unintended (eg unexpected side-effects) play in the process of motivation?

8 Learning styles and achievement

Introduction

1. There have been several references in previous chapters to the influence of past experience and learning on such issues as individual perception and motivation. It is now time to examine some of the important aspects of individual learning in a work context. This chapter will therefore consider what we mean by 'learning', look at some well-known learning theories and their relevance to the workplace, and then consider some of the implications of different learning styles for the management of organisational behaviour.

What is 'learning'?

2. Learning is a process by which human beings become aware of themselves and their environment and the need to adapt the one to the other in order to survive, grow and prosper. For the purposes of this chapter, we can use the following working definition:

> *Learning is a process by which people acquire knowledge, understanding, skills and values, and apply them to solve problems throughout their daily life. The learning process engages an individual's emotional as well as intellectual dimensions, and enables him or her to control, or adapt to, their environment. Whilst much individual learning is put into store, most learning leads to behaviour, which can be recognised and assessed.*

Judging by the frustrations of parents and teachers, learning does not always take place — at least not in the way envisaged by these two groups. We ourselves recognise that there are some things we seem unable to learn, some skills that forever seem out of our grasp. We also recognise that others are sometimes quicker than us at seeing the crux of an issue, or demonstrating a particular skill.

3. Thus, learning is certainly not an automatic process — we both learn and fail to learn, and we do so at a different rate, and often in a different way, from our neighbour. One of the reasons for separating 'knowledge' from 'understanding' is to indicate that facts or data by themselves (knowledge) have limited value for human beings. The ability to see relationships

between facts or data, and the ability to make connections between them (ie part of the process of understanding or insight) is altogether more valuable. Many people are capable of acquiring facts; far fewer are capable of exercising understanding.

4. Nevertheless, learning — when it does take place — appears to have a number of common features between individuals. These are as follows:

> ❐ learning usually implies (observable) change
>
> ❐ learning implies relatively permanent change
>
> ❐ learning usually manifests itself through behaviour
>
> ❐ learning involves some stimulus or experience
>
> ❐ learning is influenced by personal characteristics (temperament, intelligence, motivation, health etc)
>
> ❐ learning is influenced by others (teachers, role models etc)
>
> ❐ learning is assisted by visual stimuli
>
> ❐   learning is assisted by 'doing' (sharing an experience)
>
> ❐ learning requires feedback (knowing how well you have done)
>
> ❐ learning is aided by success
>
> ❐ people can also learn from their mistakes/ failures

5. Most theorists agree that learning involves change, and change of a relatively permanent kind. Most learning is manifested in behaviour, but the two concepts are not identical. Individuals can, for example, choose to override what they have learned is a dangerous practice, and risk their health or their life in the pursuit of an experience that gratifies a strong need (smoking, unsafe sex, fast driving etc). An experience of some kind is fundamental to learning, for this is the stimulus to the learning process. The stimulus may be a formal learning event such as a textbook chapter to be studied for homework, a picture to be analysed in class, an instrumental piece to be played in a music tutorial, or a problem to be solved in a management exercise. Most stimuli are less formal than these, occurring randomly during our waking hours — finding our way to an appointment, being confronted by an angry customer, experiencing a software fault on a computer program, attending a negotiating meeting and other such events of everyday working life.

Factors affecting learning

6. Human learning is a complex process involving numerous internal and external factors (see Fig.8.1). The internal factors are those arising from the individual's person (intelligence, temperament, health etc), and from personal experience; the external factors are those arising from the individual's environment (ie the context of learning).

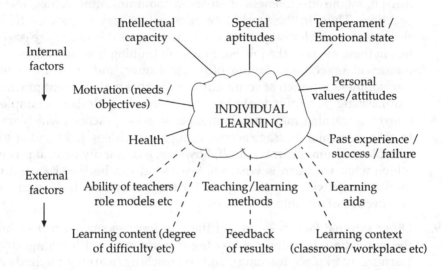

Figure 8.1   *Principal factors affecting learning*

7. As Figure 8.1 indicates, learning is influenced considerably by internal/ personal factors, such as our intellectual capacities, our state of health, our aptititudes, our dominant needs and our motivation or level of interest in the topic/ event. For example, an individual who is generally more intelligent than another will tend to perceive situations more correctly, judge behaviour more appropriately, and act more quickly than the other person. Rate of learning is affected by a variety of factors, including intelligence (especially in the sense of general problem-solving ability), general level of health, and motivation. The latter often manifests itself in enthusiasm for the task, an enquiring mind, and a willingness to persevere in the task. Also, as discussed shortly (paras 21-26 below), the way we learn differs - we have different preferences in how we tackle problems. In the words of the theorists, we have different learning styles. These are usually linked to temperament. Our emotional state, however, can also play a major role in our ability to learn, and particularly in our ability to *demonstrate* learning. The phenomenon of 'examination nerves' has frequently prevented people from doing justice to their real grasp of a subject, because their anxiety has obstructed their ability to recall facts or construct arguments. Personal values and attitudes can also affect learning, for example, is situations where a person deems a subject not worthy of his attention. Finally, there is

the role of past experience (ie previous learning). This will have comprised both successes and failures, which can contribute to understanding.

8. As well as being affected by internal (personal) factors, learning is also influenced by various external factors. These include other people, notably parents, teachers, other role models and peer-groups. Whether expressly or tacitly, we are strongly influenced both in *what* we learn, and *how* we learn it, by the effectiveness of others in communicating values, ideas and practices. Thus, in the workplace, it is just as easy to pick up (ie learn) sloppy safety or clerical practices, for example, as it is to acquire *good* practice in these areas of the job. So, much job training is aimed at eradicating inefficient practices in favour of efficient ones, and much management development is aimed at combatting ineffective management practices by emphasising (ie reinforcing) *effective* practices. In both these examples, the *content* of learning may contain models of 'good practice', which are used to get a particular message across, using films, videos, talks and any other suitable medium. Learning itself, however, is a morally neutral process, in which what we learn is what we learn — it can be 'good'/'positive' or 'bad'/'negative', depending on (a) the behaviour itself, and (b) the perspective of the onlooker.

9. Other external factors — part of the *total learning environment* — include the immediate learning context (eg classroom-based learning, distance learning, workplace learning), and the teaching/learning methods in use (eg lecturing, group discussions, problem-solving exercises etc). The use of textbooks, prepared notes and handouts, computers, and other aids to learning, such as visual imagery, also affects our ability to learn. Visual methods of learning, in particular, are widely used in formal training in educational establishments and at work, as well as less formally on advertising hoardings and television screens in our consumer society. These visual cues are considered by some theorists to represent monuments to 'passive' learning (ie the absorption of facts, abstract ideas and 'knowledge'). Yet much learning is indeed stimulated by books, pictures, computer images and other materials, which invite the engagement of the senses and the use of the individual's thinking capacity. Those theorists who talk about so-called 'passive learning' are usually reacting against the teacher-dominated, didactic methods of education that have typified most of education and training during the twentieth century. As a result they have become advocates of a problem-solving/ 'hands-on' approach to learning, which they would describe as 'active learning' (eg Rogers, Kolb et al). However, this is not to say that they deny the usefulness of passive methods as part of the total learning process.

10. The most effective learning comes about when the individual is fully committed to the task in hand, and is capable of meeting the demands raised by it. This implies not only observing and recording, and using thinking skills, but also engaging feelings and behaviour. These *passive-*

active forms of learning are often summed up by phrases such as those shown in Figure 8.2, which also indicates the dimension of commitment involved:

Descriptive Phrase	Passive/Active	Dimension
1 'Knowing about.......'	Passive	Observing,recording
2 'Knowing how to.....'	Passive	Observing
3 'Doing it/ applying it...'	Active	Behaviour (doing)
4 'Learning *what* to do...'	Passive	Observing, thinking
5 'Learning *how* to do it..'	Active	Thinking,feeling,doing
6 'Demonstrating understanding of.........'	Active	Doing

Figure 8.2   *Passive and Active Forms of Learning*

11. In present times, the word *'interactive'* is being used increasingly to describe the active learning dimension. This word has derived from computer-based learning, where the user is able to interact with the computer by responding to questions and scenarios on the screen by using the keyboard or mouse. Thus, an essentially passive learning tool can be extended to incorporate active learning. The value of engaging the whole person in learning has been known for centuries, as witness the comments of Confucius [551-479 BC]:

> *'I hear and I forget.*
>
> *I see and I remember.*
>
> *I do and I understand.'*

12. An important aspect of the learning process is *feedback*. In many practical tasks it is fairly obvious whether the end-result is correct or adequate. For example, in mathematics, physics and language tasks, there is usually one correct or best answer. Often it is clear to the individual whether he or she has achieved it. However, in tasks that involve conceptualising or making judgements, it is often difficult to state what is the correct answer, if any, and it is usually unclear to the individual whether the optimum answer has been achieved. In both situations it is important for individuals to obtain an assessment of their results, either from observing the consequences of their decisions or from the comments of parents, teachers, lecturers, trainers and others. The successful achievement of tasks at an interim level appears to motivate individuals in their learning as tasks become more complicated. Feedback is also relevant for the learning process itself, and not just its results and outcomes. This aspect of feedback

is often considered under the titles of 'learning style' (ie people's approach to problems, ability to see alternatives, ability to make generalisation etc), and 'learning environment' (ie the external conditions of learning).

The learning cycle

13. These ideas about learning can be considered against the widely-used model of the learning/problem-solving process put forward by Kolb et al (1979)[1] in their well-known work on learning styles. The basic model is as follows (Fig. 8.3):

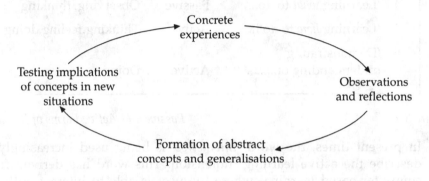

Concrete experiences

Testing implications of concepts in new situations

Observations and reflections

Formation of abstract concepts and generalisations

Figure 8.3   *The learning cycle (Kolb et al, 1979)*

The learning cycle described by Kolb and colleagues is based on a number of assumptions:

1   learning is a continuous process ('...all learning is relearning...')

2   the direction of learning is governed by the individual's felt needs and goals

3   given the importance of individual needs and goals, styles of learning *become highly individualised in terms of direction and process ('....a mathematician may.... place great emphasis on abstract concepts,whereas a poet may value concrete experience....')*

14. The unfortunately-named 'concrete' experience is the initial stimulus to the learning process. This could be an incident of some kind (eg a sudden loss of text on a computer screen), a problem-solving exercise set by a trainer (eg an exercise to explore particular aspects of some word-processing software), or a piece of reading (eg selected chapters from a user's manual). The experience is followed by the individual's efforts to clarify the problem and 'make sense' of it (ie observation and reflection). This stage leads on to the crucial cognitive (ie thinking) stage, when conceptualising and generalising takes place. This part of the cycle represents the process of *inductive learning,* ie where the individual experiences an event, attempts to puzzle it out, and then draws conclusions about it,

perhaps in terms of a guiding rule or principle (see further discussion below).

15. The second half of the cycle leads from abstract conceptualising to the testing of concepts in new situations — in other words, putting ideas and conclusions to the test. This stage is followed by further experiences — ie the results of tests — thus completing the cycle. This part of the cycle represents *deductive* learning, ie where the individual works forward from some hypothesis or other, tests it in practice and obtains results — new experiences.

The scientific method

16. The systematic search for truth, using objective observation both to arrive at principles, and to test their truthfulness, is known as the scientific method of enquiry. It originated with the thinkers of Ancient Greece, especially Plato and his pupil, Aristotle, and saw its heyday in the Renaissance period in Europe in the 16th/17th Centuries. The scientific method relies on an interplay between inductive and deductive methods of reasoning. An *inductive* process is one which commences with the study of particular experiences, which if found to be typical over a number of occurrences, provide the basis for the statement of a general rule or principle. It is in this sense that new theories are 'discovered'. This approach is sometimes known as 'Eg- rule' (ie, an example followed by the rule, or principle). Inductive reasoning always moves from the particular to the general. A modern example of the application of inductive reasoning can be found in the opinion poll. This samples the opinion of a cross-section of a population, and, on the basis of the replies received, extrapolates the results across the total population. As we know from past experience, polls are sometimes incorrect. but nevertheless there is not a politician in any democratic country who does not take them seriously. In other words they have achieved sufficient accuracy to be considered credible.

17. In the context of the *physical* sciences, inductive reasoning has led to laws (eg of gravity) which have become part of the accepted truths of our society. However, even laws which have been accepted as true for centuries can be challenged, as the impact of Einstein's General Theory of Relativity proved in 1915, when displacing Newton's theory of gravitation, which had been held to be true since 1685.

18. *Deductive* methods of reasoning, in contrast to *inductive* methods, commence with a proposed theory (a hypothesis) intended to explain one or more physical (or social) behaviours, and then test the theory by applying it to the target problem (or group) in a variety of ways and over a period of time. The results obtained form the basis for the proof, revision or rejection of the theory. Mathematics is based on deductive reasoning. This

approach is typified by a form of Aristotelian logic termed a syllogism, which is a three-part logical argument, in which a proposition, or major premise, together with a minor premise leads to a conclusion. For example:

All men are mortal (major premise).

The king is a man (minor premise).

Therefore the king is mortal (conclusion).

This form of logic is sometimes called 'Rule-eg', (ie where a general rule is found to be present in an example). Deductive reasoning always moves from the general to the particular.

Revising the Kolb model

19. The basic model described by Kolb and colleagues (see Fig. 8.3) can now be elaborated to show the inductive/ deductive dimension (Fig. 8.4):

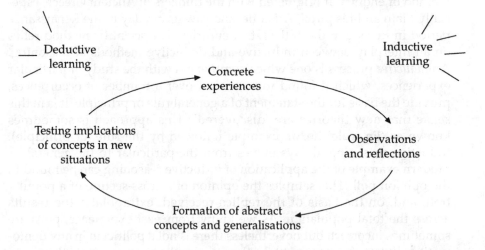

Figure 8.4   The learning cycle - inductive and deductive dimensions

20. In terms of the learning cycle, people who prefer to operate on the right hand segment are those with a preference for inductive methods of enquiry/ learning; those on the left side have a preference for deductive methods. These differences are dealt with Kolb and colleagues in terms of differing learning styles, of which there are four:

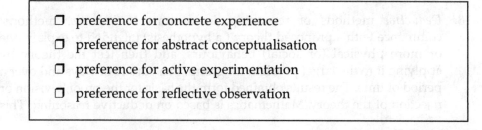

❐ preference for concrete experience

❐ preference for abstract conceptualisation

❐ preference for active experimentation

❐ preference for reflective observation

By means of a questionnaire known as the Learning Style Inventory (LSI), each individual can measure his or her *'strengths and weaknesses as a learner in the four stages of the learning process.'* As the concept of different learning styles is a useful way of considering learning theories, we shall describe two important models in the next few paragraphs, before moving on to describe leading theories, which can then be seen in the context both of learning styles and the scientific method.

Learning styles

21. First we examine the learning styles identified by Kolb and colleagues in the context of the concepts embodied in the learning cycle described above (Figs. 8.3 & 8.4). As mentioned previously, Kolb identified four stages of learning and four learning preferences. In analysing learning preferences (styles), Kolb isolated two major dimensions on which individuals could be scored, using the LSI inventory. The two dimensions were: (1) *concrete — abstract*, and (2) *reflective — active*. These dimensions were set out in grid form and labels allocated to the learning style that was appropriate to each quadrant (see Fig. 8.5):

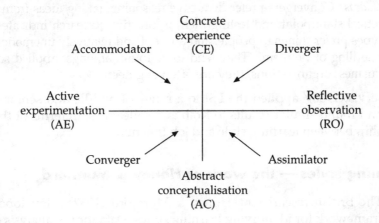

Figure 8.5   *Learning styles (Kolb et al)*

22. The four learning types were derived from both research and observation of the learning characteristics of numerous individuals, aided by use of the LSI (Kolb et al, 1979). Their justification is as follows:

Accommodator. This is an individual who has a strong preference for concrete experiences and active experimentation. Such a person prefers an action-oriented, 'hands-on' approach to learning. *'...this person tends to excel in those situations where where one must adapt oneself to specific immediate circumstances.....is at ease with people but is sometimes seen as impatient and 'pushy'.'* The accommodator likes to get fully involved and to take risks. In business organisations this style is often found amongst sales and marketing staff.

Diverger. This person also has a preference for involvement in concrete experience, but then wants to reflect upon it and puzzle things out. The diverger's greatest strengths are imagination and the ability to see issues from a number of different perspectives. '.....*a person with this style performs better in situations that call for the generation of ideas...*' Divergers tend to be people-oriented and are often found amongst people educated in the arts and humanities. In business, divergers tend to be found amongst personnel managers and organisation development specialists.

Assimilator. This style tends to be adopted by the abstract thinkers who are keen to develop theoretical models, as they swing between reflection and conceptualising. '*This person excels in inductive reasoning and in assimilating disparate observations into an integrated explanation.*' In situations where a theory does not fit the facts, an assimilator is more likely to challenge the facts rather than the theory. In organisations this style is more likely amongst research staff and planners.

Converger. This person operates between abstract conceptualising and active experimentation. '*This person's greatest strength lies in the practical application of ....ideas.*' Convergers prefer deductive reasoning, taking ideas from their theoretical standpoint and testing them in practice. Research indicates that such types prefer things to people, and are cool and relatively unemotional in their handling of problems. They tend to be found amongst applied scientists. In business organisations, they are often engineers.

23. Jervis (1983)[2] applied the LSI to a range of middle and senior managers, and found similar results to Kolb and colleagues, in terms of the relationship between learning style and job function.

Learning styles — the work of Honey & Mumford

24. The British researchers, Honey & Mumford (1982)[3], developed another framework for identifying learning styles. Data for the analysis of styles is obtained from an 80-statement questionnaire, and the results are plotted on a two-dimensional grid to produce four different styles not unlike the Kolb variety, as follows:

> 1. *Activists.* These persons learn through activity and challenge, and get bored with implementation and consolidation. (Similar to *concrete experience*).
>
> 2. *Reflectors.* These are the thoughtful, cautious types who tend to have a low profile in the organisation. (Similar to *reflective observation*).

> 3. *Theorists*. These are the logical thinkers who revel in theories, and are detached and rational in their problem-solving. (Similar to *abstract conceptualisers*).
>
> 4. *Pragmatists*. These are action-oriented persons who like putting ideas into practice. (Similar to *active experimentation*).

25. Theories about differing learning styles have particular implications for training and staff development. By recognising that different styles are available, each with their own strengths and weaknesses, trainers will not be disappointed when different people respond in quite different ways to certain training events and activities. Trainers can also prepare to build in varied training opportunities so as to appeal to a wide range of styles.

26. In the light of the chapter so far, which has considered broad issues of learning, methods of enquiry and learning styles, we can now turn to some of the leading theories of learning, which have contributed in one way or another to contemporary views about learning.

Theories about learning — the work of Gagne

27. Gagne (1970)[4] in a classic work on learning suggested that all learning can be divided into eight different types, ranging from the relatively simple (eg making simple responses) to the relatively complex (eg concept-learning, problem-solving). In the light of what follows in the outline of key learning theories, Gagne's list can provide a useful marker at this point, since it refers to several important features of leading theories. The list is as shown in Figure 8.6.

Gagne's analysis of different learning types helps to shed light on the varied nature of the learning process in all its various forms, simple and complex. Such an analysis helps to show the weaknesses in some of the theories that follow (eg Behaviourism), and the strength of modern, eclectic, theories (eg Kolb).

1. *Signal learning*

   This form of learning is closely related to basic instincts and reflexes, producing a reaction (ie behaviour) in response to some external stimulus (signal). (An example could be a drum roll at a military parade, indicating that every rank should straighten up and stand to attention; a drum roll is often used to attract our attention to some exciting event, at a circus, for example; sprint runners, for whom the starting gun is a crucial stimulus, often think they have heard the signal before it has actually fired, and get an involuntary 'false start' instead.) This sort of learning is often called a conditioned response, and was made famous by Pavlov's dogs (see below).

2. *Stimulus-Response (S-R) learning*

   This form of learning involves making a less instinctive, more voluntary response to a stimulus. A key element in this type of learning is reinforcement (eg rewards). It is also usual for the learning to take place gradually, following repetition of the act. This type of learning is sometimes referred to as operant conditioning (see below). The ability to match the sound of a word in a foreign language, when prompted by the teacher, is an example of S-R learning. Rewards can be as basic as an encouraging nod or smile, or an outpouring of praise. If an incorrect response has been given the reward is withheld rather than punishment inflicted.

3. *Chaining*

   This involves linking two or more previously acquired responses to achieve new behaviour. Learning to drive a motorcar involves chaining - first steering and basic clutch work, then use of accelerator and brake, then a combination of leg and arm movements to drive round a corner or do a three-point turn.

4. *Verbal association*

   Involves making chains with words, and is thus to be found in language development. In study and work situations, memory aids (mnemonics) are frequently employed to assist learning with such mnemonics as *SWOT* analysis (strengths, weaknesses, opportunities and threats analysis in organisations), and *GIGO* (garbage in - garbage out in reference to computer applications).

   ..... continued

Figure 8.6 (a)   *Gagne's learning types*

5. *Discrimination learning*

   This form of learning consists of building up chains (eg between different birds and their flight patterns), and then learning to distinguish between them (eg identifying different species in flight). Lecturers engage in this form of learning when learning the names of their students. The difficulty with this type of learning is that it is susceptible to interference, which leads to forgetting previous learning.

6. *Concept learning*

   This type of learning involves identifying the abstractproperties of a stimulus (an object eg a cube, a word eg 'middle') and using those properties to identify subsequent stimuli of a similar nature. This is the ability to generalise from the particular. The process involves chaining, discrimination, verbal association and rule-learning. At this point we are leaving simple forms of learning and moving into the complex forms of learning that characterise mankind alone.

7. *Rule-learning*

   Much of formal education is centred around the learning of rules (rules of grammar, mathematical theorems, laws of physics etc). A rule is basically a chain of two or more concepts, and rule learning is concerned with acquiring the idea contained in the statements of rules. Once the idea has been grasped, then the rule can be applied in a range of situations (eg use of the feminine article in plural as well as in the singular form). Rules are often expressed as 'If .... then ....' statements.

8. *Problem-solving.*

   This form of learning involves combining old rules into new rules and solving new problems with them. At the heart of this type of learning is the thinking process. It is also characterised by the phenomenon of understanding that we call 'insight'.

Figure 8.6 (b)   *Gagne's learning types*

Early theories of learning

28. The earliest theories of learning in the West originated in Greece with such influential figures as Plato and Aristotle, whose emphasis was firmly on the use of the mental processes (reason, memory and willpower). As indi-

cated earlier (para 16), these two were responsible for developing the schools of thought that led to deductive and inductive reasoning. The emphasis on reasoning, as opposed to *experiencing* and *feeling*, led to intelligence being rated the highest stimulus to learning, and thus to development as a person. The approach to learning adopted, in practice, by the adherents of intellectual athleticism led in the Western world to structured forms of learning, didactic teaching methods (ie teacher-centred/ telling/ directed learning), emphasis on rule-learning and memorising, and respect for the subject itself.

29. It was not until the eighteenth century that any real challenge was made to the intellectual discipline approach. Then Jean-Jacques Rousseau argued that mental activity alone was not the most important element in human learning and development. He emphasised the role of feelings and instinct in learning, thus paving the way for liberal approaches to education based on the needs of the learner rather than on the demands of the subject. Whilst such approaches have been limited mainly to primary education, there have been efforts in management training, in particular, to engage feelings and action as well as thinking skills. These broader approaches to personnel development tend to come under the label of 'experiential learning' (eg Kolb).

Behaviourist theories

30. During the course of the last hundred years, several studies of learning have been carried out by theorists who have focused their attention exclusively on observed behaviour. Their philosophy is essentially that learning can only be assumed to have taken place if some *action* follows from it. If no behaviour is recorded, then no learning can be assumed. More than this, the *Behaviourists*, as these theorists have become known, deliberately draw no conclusions either about the *thinking* processes involved in learning, or about the *emotional* responses of learners. They have been merely concerned with the links between a stimulus and a response in learning. Their greatest exponent was B.F.Skinner (1904-1990), whose ideas are outlined shortly.

31. Most of the learning experiments of the early behaviourists were carried out on animals (eg cats, dogs, rats and pigeons). In each case a number of key learning concepts were tested. These were:

❐	Drive	A need or motive; a readiness to respond.
❐	Stimulus	An external signal or prompt of some kind.
❐	Response	The subject's reaction (behaviour).
❐	Reinforcement	Measures applied in order to strengthen a response.

For an animal the drive was usually hunger, the stimulus was food, the response was activity aimed at eating the food, and the reinforcement could be more food, or praise, for example.

32. Two early theorists of behaviourism achieved fame for their work on 'conditioning'. First was I. Pavlov (1849-1936), who conducted experiments on dogs to see if they would respond to a neutral stimulus if it were presented at the same time as a main stimulus — in this case food. Normally, dogs will only salivate at the sight of food. However, Pavlov, introduced another stimulus - a ringing bell - which was operated at the time the food was brought to the animals. He then looked to see what the effect would be if he sounded the bell alone, but brought no food. The result was that the dogs salivated at the sound of the bell only! They had, in effect, made a *conditioned response* to the bell in a process that has become known as *classical conditioning*. The second person was E.L. Thorndike (1874-1949), who carried out experiments with cats, where a hungry cat was put into a cage, which had just one means of escape. A plate of food (the stimulus) was placed outside the cage, and the cat's behaviour observed. Initially, the cat made apparently random efforts to find a way out, eventually knocking the escape mechanism and getting at the food. When the cat was put through this exercise a number of times, it eventually went straight to the mechanism, operated it, and escaped to reach the food. This process was called *operant conditioning*. Unlike classical conditioning, where the emphasis is on the stimulus (eg food), operant conditioning is more concerned with the response (eg escape behaviour). Thorndike made a major contribution to learning theory in setting out his Law of Effect, which stated that when a response is followed by a reward, the response is likely to be repeated in similar circumstances. The relevance of rewards, as opposed to punishments, in encouraging learning cannot be underestimated.

33. Perhaps the most influential behaviourist, however, was B.F. Skinner, an American psychologist from Harvard University. Skinner's early experiments into conditioning were carried out using rats or pigeons, but then he applied his ideas to human learning (1974)[5]. His particular area of interest was operant conditioning, and especially the reinforcement aspect. His view of reinforcement was that responses could be strengthened both by the provision of *positive* rewards (eg lecturer's approval, satisfaction from obtaining correct answer etc), and by the removal of *negative* rewards (eg punishment, criticism etc). Skinner concluded that punishment was not a reinforcer, since it tended to weaken responses rather than strengthen them. By using frequent reinforcement (eg with pigeons), Skinner could mould the behaviour of his subjects so that they could perform quite remarkable feats (eg playing table tennis!). This use of reinforcers was termed *'shaping'*, and was an important feature of operant conditioning.

34. Skinner introduced the concept of *programmed learning*, which is an essentially step-by-step approach to learning based on a logically-constructed programme composed of small, discrete elements. Such an approach relies heavily on two factors - first, the establishment of clearly-defined (or prescriptive) learning aims; and second, an integrated system of feedback, so that learning outcomes can be judged quickly. Skinner's behaviourism implied, of course, that learning aims, or objectives were not only to be prescriptive, but were to be expressed in concrete (ie behavioural) terms, which could be measured readily and so provide prompt feedback. Thus, the controlled conditions of the laboratory were translated into the individual person's learning environment, and there was no scope for exploration or imagination. In Skinner's world of learning 2+2 must always equal 4.

Cognitive theories of learning

35. Many other learning theorists were appalled by the narrow and strictly behavioural approach of behaviourism. They argued that learning was more than just applying rules, or responding to small-scale problems and making connections between the basic elements of a subject. Learning, in their view, consisted of 'making sense of' issues and situations, of developing insight and understanding, and of seeing patterns in their environment. For these theorists, the whole was greater than the sum of its parts (ie 2+2 definitely equals 5!). They saw learning as a complex process involving such skills as mental mapping, use of intuition and imagination, and problem-solving. Such learning also involved individual perceptions and motivation, and could be stored until required. In other words overt, measurable behaviour was not the only evidence for learning. Their theories are known as *cognitive theories* of learning.

36. An example of a theorist opposed to the ideas of behaviourism is Carl Rogers(1979)[6]. In a seminal text entitled 'Freedom to Learn', he denounced the behaviourist view that learning is controlled by factors outside the influence of the individual and that it is only as a result of external stimuli that behaviour takes place. On the contrary, claimed Rogers, Man is free. This freedom is encapsulated in such things as '....*the quality of courage which enables a person to step into the uncertainty of the unknown as he chooses himself. It is the discovery of meaning from within oneself......It is the burden of being responsible for the self one chooses to be....It is the recognition of a person that he is an emerging process, not a static end product.*'(p.269) In promoting this essentially humanistic view of learning as centred in the individual and not in the external environment, Rogers saw the role of teachers as facilitating learning rather than directing it.

37. Rogers conclusions on learning are as follows. They were the result of an inductive process based on observations of people in many different situations:

1 Human beings have a natural potentiality for learning ie they are curious

2 Significant learning takes place when the subject-matter is perceived as relevant to the learner

3 Learning which involves change in oneself is seen as threatening and tends to be resisted

4 Learning which appears to be threatening is more easily assimilated when the external threats are at a minimum

5 Much significant learning is acquired through doing

6 Learning is facilitated when the learner participates responsbly in the learning process

7 Self-initiated learning, involving the whole person (feelings as well as intellect), is the most lasting and pervasive form of learning

8 Independence, creativity and self-reliance are all facilitated when self-criticism and self-evaluation are in place rather than external assessment

9 Learning about the process of learning, being open to experiences and being comfortable with change is the most socially-useful kind of learning

10 The role of facilitators in learning is to provide an encouraging climate for learning, to help people to clarify their purposes and build on their own motivation, to make a wide range of learning resources available (including themselves), to accept feelings as well as rationalising in the learning process, and, finally, to share in the learning process with their students.

38. Rogers' ideas are firmly embedded in the thinking of Kolb and others in their promotion of experiential learning. A considerable section of the post-experience training and development of people in work organisations has begun to adopt such principles, especially where interpersonal skills are called for. These ideas are more appropriate to higher levels of learning, but can also apply to some of Gagne's middle-range levels (eg where confidence-building on the part of the instructor can help an individual acquire key sets of responses — chaining.)

39. An important aspect of cognitive learning is that of *'insight'*, where, for example, a person suddenly sees the link between concepts, understands an issue or sees a solution to a problem. Insight is sometimes referred to popularly in such terms as 'When the penny drops' or 'When the light suddenly dawns', or simply as 'Eureka!'. The concept applies primarily to higher levels of learning, and not to lower-level activities such as routine information-gathering or memorising. Lunzer (1968)[7] describes the key characteristics of 'insight' as follows:

> ❏ a suddenness of solution
>
> ❏ an immediacy and smoothness of behaviour
>
> ❏ an ability to replicate solutions on subsequent presentations of the problem
>
> ❏ an ability to transpose the solution to similar situations but in a different context

40. Considered against Gagne's learning types, *behaviourist theories* are better suited to lower levels of learning (eg signal learning, S-R learning etc), and *cognitive theories* more appropriate for higher levels of learning (eg concept learning, problem-solving etc).

References

1. Kolb,D.,Rubin,I.,& McIntyre,J. (1979), *Organizational Psychology - an experiential approach*, Prentice-Hall

2. Jervis, P. (1983), *'Analysing Decision behaviour: Learning Models and Learning Styles as Diagnostic Aids'*, in Personnel Review,12-2

3. Honey,P. & Mumford,A. (1982), *The Manual of Learning Styles*, P.Honey

4. Gagne, R. (1970), *The Conditions of Learning*, Holt, Rhinehart Winston

5. Skinner,B.F. (1974) *About Behaviourism*, Random :House

6. Rogers, C. (1979), *Freedom to Learn*, Charles E. Merrill

7. Lunzer,E.A.(1968), *The Regulation of Behaviour: Development in Learning*, Staples Press

Questions for reflection/discussion

1. To what extent is the total learning environment (ie external factors) important in learning?

2. Argue the case for the pre-eminence of internal factors other than motivation inthe learning process. Why do you think the behaviourists avoided discussing the operation of these factors in learning?

3. Is there such a thing as 'passive' learning? Justify your answer.

4. Rank the internal factors mentioned in Figure 8.1 in order of their importance, and compare your list with a colleague. Discuss some of the reasons why your results differ. What do the differences say about how we perceive learning?

5. What are the implications of differing learning styles for trainers, lecturers and others involved in the teaching-learning process?

6. In terms of Gagne's list of learning types, how many different types apply to your present learning situation? What evidence can you bring forward to illustrate your reply?

Groups at work

Our study of Organisational Behaviour now moves away from individuals to people in groups. Many of the issues for groups are the same as those for individuals — perceptions, motivation, needs, learning etc. However, the context of having several individuals together throws up different challenges and problems for the management of organisations. Interpersonal relations are altogether more complex when the interactions are more than just one-to-one. Chapters 9 - 13, therefore, examine the following issues: the nature of groups (Chapter 9); decision-making and communication in groups (Chapter 10); leadership and power (Chapter 11); stress and conflict (Chapter 12); and the development of organisation culture (Chapter 13).

9 Groups and group behaviour

Introduction

1. The study of people in groups is a relatively modern phenomenon — part of the twentieth century fascination with the behaviour, needs and motivation of fellow human beings. So far as work organisations are concerned, it was the results of the Hawthorne Experiments in the 1920's and 30's (see Chapter 4) that triggered a major interest in the behaviour of groups — as opposed to individuals — in the workplace.

2. A group has been defined (Schein, 1988)[1] as:

   '....any number of people who (1) interact with one another, (2) are psychologically aware of one another, and (3) perceive themselves to be a group.'

   This definition helps to distinguish groups from mere collections of individuals, be they a crowd, a rabble or some random gathering, who have no real interaction between them, and who consider themselves more as individuals-*within*-a-group rather than as members-*of*-a-group.

Formal and informal groups

3. Groups are typically analysed under two main categories — *formal* and *informal* groups. *Formal* groups are the units established by the management as part of an organisation structure. They are defined in terms of their purpose and roles, they are official in the sense that they have appropriate authority, and they are provided with financial and physical resources. The principal raison d'etre of formal groups is to further the aims and objectives of the organisation as laid down in mission statements, unit objectives, policy statements and routine procedures. It is tempting to think of organisations as being mainly, or solely, composed of such formal groups. The truth is, however, that work organisations, in particular, are by no means activated just by formal groups. There are other, employee-centred groups, whose aims and intentions may even be counter to those of the official organisation — these are the informal groups.

4.   The influence of *informal* groups in the workplace was first identified clearly in the Hawthorne Experiments. These and subsequent studies have identified a number of characteristics of informal groups, which can be summarised as follows:

a.   they draw their norms (rules) of behaviour from amongst themselves

b.   their first loyalty tends to be towards their fellow group members rather than to the organisation as a whole

c.   their goals are decided more by what they feel is right for them rather than by what is laid down for them by the management

d.   their behaviour is derived more from interpersonal relationships than by any role allocated by the management

e.   their behaviour may or may not be in line with what their organisation expects

f.   group leadership is likely to be exercised on a charismatic basis rather than by legitimate authority, and power rather than authority is more influential

g.   informal groups generally meet social and security needs before other needs

h.   informal groups are likely to be less permanent than formal groups

5.   Burns and Stalker (1961)[2] in their important study of change in organisations (see Chapter 3 above) found that the formal organisation was typified by mechanistic structures, where both loyalty to the organisation and obedience to superiors was expected. However, where organic structures were in place, there were aspects of both formal and informal organisation, and it was difficult to distinguish between the two. The point about organic organisation structures is that they are deliberately less standardised in terms of allocating roles, defining tasks and agreeing authority levels. Much more of the decision-making in such organisations is left to the operating units, and this requires a level of trust by senior management in the leadership qualities of middle and junior management and in the common sense of purpose of the workforce as a whole. Nevertheless, for the purposes of this chapter, which is considering the basic building blocks of an organisation, and not the structure itself, *all* formal (ie officially-recognised) groups are described as part of the formal organisation structure, regardless of whether this is deemed to be mechanistic or organic.

6.   In recent years, with the onset of management ideas about organisational excellence (eg Peters & Waterman, 1982[3]; Goldsmith & Clutterbuck, 1984)[4] and 'empowerment' (eg Clutterbuck,1994)[5] and with the decline in trade-union dominated employee relations, many organisations have been actively seeking ways of reducing (a) the number of organisation levels and (b) the amount of supervision exercised by management. This has led

to a greater devolvement of authority to basic work-groups within a slimmed-down structure, where attainment of customer satisfaction within agreed budget targets is the key objective. The use of the term 'customer' refers both to external purchasers of the organisations goods and services, and to those internal 'customers' who are users of the services of their colleagues (eg see Cole, 1994, p156)[6]. In these conditions, it is not suprising that much attention is directed towards developing an organisation culture, which is intended to be shared throughout every level of the enterprise. The development of a corporate culture does not lead to the destruction of influential informal groups, but aims to encourage them to match their aspirations with those of the whole organisation.

Key issues in group behaviour

7. In examining the behaviour of people in groups, whether formal or informal, there are a number of key issues that have to be considered, and these are shown in Figure 9.1. Some issues (eg purpose, group tasks etc) are especially relevant to *formal* groups, others are important for informal groups (eg roles within groups), and a few are significant for both types of group (eg motivation of members, and leadership). Apart from leadership, which will be dealt with in Chapter 11, these issues will be discussed in the following paragraphs. The main focus of the points raised in the rest of the chapter will be on formal groups, since that is where management's principal responsibilities lie.

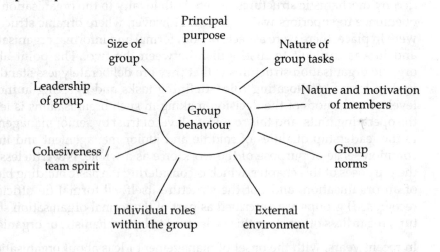

Figure 9.1   *Key issues in group behaviour*

Group size

8. The size of a group is one factor that can determine its likely behaviour. Larger groups, for example, require a higher degree of formalisation than smaller groups, and are likely to require clearer lines of communication as well. Larger groups may tend to pay less attention to the needs of individuals than smaller groups, and may well concentrate more on task requirements than personnel issues. Larger groups are more susceptible to the development of sub-groups than smaller groups, which are likely to remain more closely-knit. The Frenchman, V.A. Graicunas, in the 1930's, suggested that the number of relationships between leaders and their teams could be shown in a mathematical formula, as follows:

Number of relationships,

$$R = n\,(2n - 1 + n - 1)$$

(where n = number of subordinates)

According to this formula, where two subordinates were supervised, the total number of possible relationships was six. Where six subordinates were supervised, the number rose to two hundred and twenty two. Although Graicunas' proposal was mainly theoretical, it nevertheless pointed to the complexity of possible relationships within groups.

9. Few teams or closely-knit groups are larger than a dozen (eg a cricket eleven, a rugby fifteen, a rowing eight), and many work-groups are considerably smaller. The well-known classical theorist, L. F. Urwick (1947)[7], suggested that no manager should be responsible for the work of more than five or six subordinates whose work was interlocked. He accepted that larger groupings were possible where there was less collaboration required between the members. Size, therefore, cannot be considered in isolation from other factors, such as the nature and complexity of the task, the targets set for the group etc. A manager supervising the work of a group of research chemists is unlikely to be able to cope effectively with more than half-a-dozen fellow scientists. In contrast to this situation, a manager supervising a routine mass production operation is likely to be capable of handling as many as twenty personnel, and, to take a military example, an infantry platoon officer is expected to take command of around thirty soldiers.

10. The optimum number for a group is whatever is sufficient to provide enough resources from its own ranks to enable an effective and timely completion of the group's tasks, both to the satisfaction of the organisation and the group members. Sometimes small hand-picked groups of specialists are deployed in project teams or task-groups in order to tackle specific

problems. In this case small is beautiful. However, if a group is *too* small to meet its objectives, either because of sheer lack of numbers or for want of the necessary expertise, then an opportunity has been lost and resources wasted. For several decades, especially following the policy of full employment after World War II, many organisations in Europe and the United States were hopelessly overmanned — too many people were employed on any one task. In the last decade, however, most of the fat has been cut away, and organisations are now much leaner (Peters & Waterman, op.cit). The reasons for this are not only the rise of computer-based technology, but also the desire to use labour more efficiently than in the past. Many British firms have reduced their workforce over the past five years, and employee work-groups are now probably near their optimum membership.

Purpose of group

11. Work-groups are usually assigned a definite purpose within the organisation structure. This will be made up of a continuing aim (*eg 'to gather feedback from customers on a continuous basis throughout the year'*), and a number of supporting targets or objectives (*eg 'achieve 30% sampling of customer responses to Product X from our top 20 customers'; 'conduct one general customer survey a month to monitor retail customer satisfaction'*). These aims and objectives represent the 'bread-and-butter' responsibilities of groups at work. They are part of the day-to-day activities of the whole organisation, and will probably attract no great attention, unless they fail to deliver. As well as meeting on-going tasks, however, work-groups are often asked to focus their efforts on specific problems, usually of a short-term nature. Some groups are especially set up for this very purpose, such as task-forces, working parties and project groups. Such groups will invariably be given a definite remit or terms of reference (*eg 'Examine our failure to expand market share in X product-range, identify possible reasons and make recommendations as to the immediate and mid-term future of these products'; 'Plan and implement a programme of discussions with X and Y companies aimed at reaching a basis for substantive negotiations regarding a merger or joint-manufacturing arrangement'*).

12. Short-term tasks are usually allocated some explicit time-limit (eg three months, six months, one year). Leadership of such groups is often given to a senior person who personally spends a small amount of time on the project, contributing a policy and resourcing role, whilst the team-members carry out the detailed work. Special project groups often develop quite a high profile, unlike routine group activities, and this can benefit individual members in terms of promotion prospects. Some organisations allocate younger managers and specialists to such groups as part of their

management development. The mere fact of being selected for such a group acts as a considerable motivator for ambitious individuals.

Nature of task

13. The nature of the task will be decided in broad terms by the group's purpose and objectives. A clearly-defined purpose requiring fairly specific tasks and outcomes will demand different qualities from the group compared with, say, a generally-stated problem requiring further questions to be asked rather than solutions to be proposed. Tasks can be differentiated in several ways, including the following (Figure 9.2):

Type of Task	*Demands on Group*
1 Ongoing/ routine	Maintaining targets and quality. Avoiding boredom.
2 Attaining a target	Adequate preparation. Deploying members appropriately. Encouraging perserverance (esp if target is difficult).
3 Implementing new process/ procedures	Learning new systems. Problem-solving pressures. Declaring difficulties. Supporting each other.
4 Creating new ideas	Encouraging confidence and trust. Encouraging synergy within the group. Clustering/reorganising ideas.
5 Solving specific problems/ issues	Ensuring optimum skills/expertise available. Encouraging lateral thinking
6 Meeting a tight deadline	Maximum pressure on task requirements. Retaining sufficient attention to people-needs. Coping with stress.
7 Important negotiations with customer	Allocating roles (figure-head, information-gatherer, tactician, peace-maker etc). Keeping within policy guidelines (eg on concessions etc).
8 Important negotiations with competitor	Allocating roles appropriately. Maintaining awareness of competitive issues. Keeping to strategic guidelines.

... continued

Figure 9.2 (a)   *Task types and the demands on groups*

Type of Task	Demands on Group
9 Project requiring close collaboration between team members	Learning to trust each other. Drawing appropriately on members' skills. Handling boundary conflicts within the group. Wise leadership required.
10 Task requiring regular collaboration with other groups in the company	Developing 'customer relations' attitudes within the group. Actively seeing other groups as 'customers' or 'suppliers'. Devising effective communication and boundary management arrangements with other groups.

Figure 9.2 (b)   *Task types and the demands on groups*

14. As Figure 9.2 indicates, different tasks exert different pressures on groups. Nevertheless, certain key issues come up time after time. These are:

> ❏ allocating roles/ deploying talents effectively
>
> ❏ developing mutual support and trust
>
> ❏ devising role/ boundary conflict counter-measures
>
> ❏ keeping to targets/ policy/ strategy guidelines
>
> ❏ developing synergy (ie enabling group performance to be greater than the sum of the efforts of each individual member)
>
> ❏ encouraging learning within the group

Group leadership

15. The issue of leadership in organisations will be examined in greater detail in Chapter 11, but for the purposes of the present discussion, a few comments are necessary. In the previous paragraph, for example, a number of key issues of group behaviour in the face of the demands of a task were identified. Most of those issues have to be resolved by the leader of the group, even if he or she consults widely within the group. Even a democratic style of leadership can leave some issues unresolved by the group as a whole, and here the leader must take responsibility and make a decision for them. A group that is well-balanced in its array of talents, and with a good team-spirit, still has a need for someone to keep the group together when difficulties arise. Thus, there will always be a requirement for an effective leader, even in the closest-knit group. Figure 9.3 shows the

key variables that are at stake in group leadership. These are: the nature and composition of the group, the requirements of the task, the organisational environment (policies, procedures, other groups etc), and the attributes of the leader (personality, interpersonal skills, leadership style, technical knowledge etc).

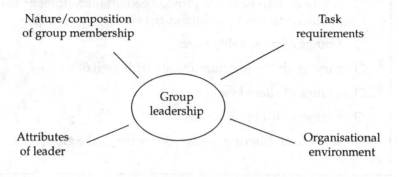

Figure 9.3   *Group leadership - key variables*

16. In formal groups the leader is officially appointed to the role, and he or she is the one who will carry responsibility for success or failure. Depending on the leader's style of leadership (see Chap.11), however, the necessary direction, encouragement and conflict resolution may also emerge from other members of the group. An autocratic leader will always take the decisions for the group, but a democratic leader will discuss possible decisions with the group before making a choice, and may even let another member take charge temporarily. Unofficial leaders, however, never carry the formal responsibility for group outcomes. The main role of the formal leader is to use the resources of the group members to the full, gain their commitment to the task, and achieve the results set by his or her superior.

Nature and motivation of group members

17. Not surprisingly, the behaviour of any group is determined to a considerable extent by the composition of its membership and by their level of commitment to the group's goals. The range of qualities contained in a group includes the following:

❑ variety of relevant technical or professional knowledge (including 'experience')

❑ a range of cognitive, interpersonal and technical skills

❑ ability of individuals to provide certain roles (thinker, leader, planner, ideas person, humourist etc)

❑ a range of personality types

❑ varying ability to communicate with each other

❑ a range of shared values

❑ a range of differing values

❑ a range of differing motives for being in the group

18. Clearly, there is a need for any group to have an appropriate mix of skills, knowledge and talents, for these represent its main resources. It is also important for certain *common* levels of knowledge and skill to be present in the group. Groups that have a specific purpose, or are under pressure, for example, will need a sufficiency of common values between them, otherwise they will fall apart and be unable to complete their objectives. Motivation is another key issue. A substantial degree of commitment to the group's tasks is needed if the latter are to be achieved successfully. Part of each individual's motivation has to be the thought that the others are relying on him or her, and that team performance is just as crucial as individual performance. It was not for nothing that the expression 'team-spirit' was chosen to describe the willingness of team members to work for each other in pursuit of their goals. This team spirit is an aspect of group cohesiveness, which is the next issue to be addressed.

Group cohesiveness

19. Group cohesiveness refers to the closeness of a group — a cohesive group has strong bonds that bind the members in loyalty to, and support for, each other. A cohesive group develops clear standards of behaviour (norms) which are accepted by the members. Sometimes this can be a positive thing, where true team-spirit and collaboration are the order of the day. It can also act negatively, in that group standards can begin to oppress individual members, especially those seeking changes in the group's behaviour. Janis (1982)[8], in a study of American foreign policy disasters in the 1970's, identified several negative aspects of cohesiveness, which he termed collectively as 'Group Think'. The characteristics of 'Group Think' can be summarised as follows:

1. A sense of the group's invulnerability (an illusion!)
2. A tendency to rationalise evidence and decisions (to fit preconceptions)
3. A belief in the inherent morality of the group
4. A strong tendency to stereotype those holding opposing views (ie they don't know what they are talking about!)
5. A tendency to put pressure on individual group members who voice doubts (a form of group censorship)
6. Self-censorship by members is the norm (maintaining the confidentiality of the group)
7. Unanimity is taken for granted — silence by members is taken to mean acceptance
8. Unanimity extends to behaviour outside the group — everyone supports the collective decision

Thus, whilst cohesiveness is something that most leaders and members desire, and whilst it undoubtedly contributes to the effectiveness of the group, it nevertheless has both healthy and unhealthy aspects to it.

20. Cohesiveness develops over time. New groups usually lack this quality precisely because they are a new assembly of people who know very little about their task and each other. An important aspect of the group leader's task is to achieve a measure of cohesiveness. Other factors which influence the degree of cohesiveness are as follows:

- ❐ similarity of tasks in achieving group goals
- ❐ the system of work (eg interdependent operations or separate tasks)
- ❐ physical proximity (eg close by or distant)
- ❐ size of group (easier to achieve in a small group)
- ❐ leadership capabilities of the appointed leader
- ❐ extent to which group goals are shared by group members
- ❐ extent to which members want to work together (motivation)
- ❐ prospect of rewards for group achievements
- ❐ prospect of threats from external sources
- ❐ competition from other groups
- ❐ key social features in common (eg age, sex, qualifications etc)

21. Groups which are very cohesive are considerably insulated against external forces, and change is unlikely to be accepted if imposed from outside. In such groups, change must come from within. The leader, or other influential person, must come to see that change is required or acceptable before the rest of the group will agree. Thus, cohesive groups, both formal and informal, can represent a threat to management's corporate aims and authority. This is particularly true for highly cohesive *informal* groups, where power to act for or against the organisation's interests as a whole can determine the success or otherwise of a change in operational goals or processes. In such circumstances it is easy to understand why weak managements often prevent bonding in groups, adopting a policy of 'Divide and Rule' in order to retain control. Confident managements, on the contrary, actively stimulate team-spirit in work-groups, but do so in the context of a carefully-tended organisation culture. Peters and Waterman (op cit) refer to this approach as 'simultaneous loose-tight properties'.

Group norms

22. Norms are the standards adopted by a group. Most of these standards will be *formal* (ie officially adopted by the organisation). Such standards will be contained in written policies, operating procedures, operating manuals, blueprints, safety notices and similar material. They will also be encapsulated by the oral instructions and personal behaviour of managers and supervisors. Part of the role of the latter is to insist on adherence to official norms. Part of the function of organisation culture is to encourage adherence to organisation-wide norms (eg attention to quality, listening to the customer, safety-consciousness etc). In a new group, or in an experienced group where new standards have been introduced, there is a period when the norms come to be challenged or questioned before they are 'owned' by individuals and the group. Sometimes new norms may be rejected, and effectively referred back to the management. In a recent case in the sporting world, the captain of the England Rugby team was sacked by the Rugby Football Union senior management for making some ill-advised public criticism of their behaviour. Another team-captain was sought from amongst the players, but the team was so united behind their former captain that noone was prepared either to accept the captaincy, or any other captain. The entire team urged the RFU Board to reconsider its verdict, which it did. The captain was reinstated, after making a suitable form of apology in public. It is important to recognise that, even when arising from official sources, all norms are *interim* measures for securing the human resources of the organisation in the attainment of organisational goals. There is very little that is written in stone in the world of organisational behaviour!

23. *Unofficial* norms are those which arise from amongst the members of a group. These may be to do with relatively trivial matters such as the decoration of an office with plants, or the gathering of group members at lunchtimes. They can also be aimed at more serious matters such as the group's attitude towards work targets or work rostering, the treatment of members by management, and the treatment by members of customers. Where the official norms lay down the *letter* of the law, unofficial norms represent its *spirit*. Thus, a particular issue such as customer relations can be dealt with in grudging fashion by a group, or by wholehearted acceptance of customers' priorities. Managements cannot stop unofficial norms from developing, but what they can do is to (1) recognise them when they arise, (2) encourage them if they are in line with organisational interests, and (3) aim to transform them if they appear to be working against the organisation's interests (which involves recognising what perceived threat or advantage lies at the heart of the norm). Ultimately, management has the power to disband and reform groups, if they appear to be getting too far out of line.

Roles within groups

24. Roles are the particular parts played by individual members of a group. The parts (their scripts) are determined partly the expectations of the management (eg through job descriptions), partly by the employee's personal perceptions of how the job is to be performed, and partly by the expectations of others in the group (eg leader, other group members). In *formal* groups the parts are mostly allocated in conjunction with job functions, but are also derived from the individual's personal qualities (eg enthusiast, peace-maker, humourist etc) and how these are seen and exploited by other members of the group. In informal groups, roles are likely to spring from (a) the relevant knowledge or skills possessed by individuals (ie what Handy,1985[,9] calls 'expert power'), and (b) their personal qualities (ie 'personal power'). Personal qualities have a stronger influence on *informal* groups, where, for example, a 'natural' leader may emerge (ie the person with the greatest influence, or personal power, over the others). In formal groups, it is the allocated job position (ie 'position power') that usually predominates since this includes the authority allocated to the leader,.

25. A widely-respected analysis of roles in teams was developed by Belbin (1981)[10] and colleagues following research into management teams undergoing experiential learning in groups. The analysis is based on eight key team-roles, ie parts that need to be played out in successful teams, summarised as follows:

❏	Company Worker	Conservative, dutiful, predictable types
❏	Chairman	Calm, self-confident, controlled types
❏	Shaper	Highly-strung, ougoing, dynamic types
❏	Plant	Individualistic, serious-minded, unorthodox types
❏	Resource Investigator	Extroverted, enthusiastic, curious, communicative types
❏	Monitor-Evaluator	Sober, unemotional, prudent types
❏	Team Worker	Socially-orientated, rather mild, sensitive types
❏	Completer-Finisher	Painstaking, orderly, conscientious, anxious types

Each role has its positive and weaker qualities, but a combination of all the roles is likely to lead to the development of a successful team, ie one that not only produces results but also provides satisfaction for the members. Belbin (op cit) mentions that predicting which teams would be 'winners' in their experiments was not easy. It was much easier to pick out those teams that looked likely to 'fail'. Winning teams appeared to have the following characteristics:

> '...the most positive indicators were the attributes of the person in the Chair, the existence of a good Plant, a spread in mental abilities, a spread also in personal attributes laying the foundation for different team-role capabilities, a distribution in the responsibilities of members to match their different capabilities, and...an adjustment to the realisation of imbalance.'
>
> (p.94)

26. In any group an individual does not act out his or her role in isolation, but in the context of a role-set. Figure 9.4 illustrates the kind of role-set that might be applicable to a Market Research Manager in a large consumer goods company. As indicated, the Market Research Manager's role requires the ability to handle a complex of relationships, ranging from line matters (work targets, quality issues, budgets etc) and staff management (recruiting, allocating tasks, appraising performance etc) to consultation and advisory responsibilities with senior colleagues from sales, production and R&D, collaboration with brand managers and other marketing colleagues, and maintaining relationships with relevant external agencies. This kind of role requires an individual who is not only good technically, but also has the interpersonal skills to establish and maintain effective working relationships with people at the same level, or senior to, the role itself and in circumstances where there may be considerable differences of

opinion.between the managers concerned (eg between sales and production, R&D and Market Research etc).

Figure 9.4   *Role-Set for a market research manager*

External environment

27. The context in which a group operates can be described from the perspective of (1) the physical environment, and (2) the social context. Most of the issues described earlier refer to the group's *internal* environment — its organisation, personnel, role requirements etc. However, the group life that springs from that internal environment influences, and is influenced by, what goes on in the external environment. First, we consider the physical environment. Clearly, if a team are working in close proximity, there will be ample opportunity to develop an understanding of each other and experience collaboration. If problems arise they can be dealt with quickly, and everyone can be consulted.

28. Conversely, where a team is scattered, then it is more difficult to build up team spirit, assess each others strengths and weaknesses, and confront problems speedily. Hence the pressure on team managers to call regular meetings of the team, and to maintain close contact by telephone, fax etc. Regular information bulletins are sometimes used by sales managers to help keep everyone in the team aware of what is happening elsewhere in the company. Occasionally, a managing director or function head will gather all their key staff at a country house or some other suitable off-site location in order to spend a day or two reviewing strategy or dealing with particularly difficult problems in an atmosphere designed to reduce stress to the minimum, and to encourage creativity.

29. The social context is extremely important in the life of groups. The organisational environment in itself is a reflection of people and their needs and intentions. Much depends on (a) the dominant leadership style of the management, (b) the influence of key individuals, and (c) the influence of external stakeholders such as customers, suppliers etc. Typical pointers to the nature of the social environment are:

- ❑ sense of common purpose (mission) evident amongst employees
- ❑ extent of reminders, exhortations to staff (eg re safety, quality, customer relations etc)
- ❑ degree of formality/ informality in relationships between management and staff
- ❑ extent to which management is task or people-oriented
- ❑ extent to which staff appear to be committed to achieving organisation goals
- ❑ the nature of the organisation structure (hierarchical, flat, organic etc)
- ❑ extent to which employees are encouraged to participate in problem-solving, decision-making etc
- ❑ extent of reliance on published rules and procedures
- ❑ extent to which technology and technical systems predominate over people-systems
- ❑ the dominant idea of what constitutes 'success' in the organisation

30. Whilst most of what appears in the above list is down to the management to decide, and here the quality of the managers and their preferred styles is critical, it is often the case that particular individuals can create their own mark on the way the organisation behaves. Thus, individual managers can buck the normal trend in terms of management style and implement what they find works with their own team. Other individuals with no formal authority can exert the power of their own personality in order to achieve particular forms of behaviour both within their own work-group and sometimes *across* groups. An example could be the power exerted over a whole section of a factory by a charismatic shop steward or trade union representative.

31. Outsiders, such as customers, can make an impact on the social environment by insisting on certain standards of employee behaviour, or partic-

ular arrangements for structuring relationships between themselves and the employees they have to deal with. Firms such as Marks and Spencer, for example, when assessing possible suppliers, lay down quite clear guidelines as to what is wanted, and how it is to be presented. Supplier firms, anxious to win a large order, seem quite happy to reorganise their production arrangements in order to meet Marks and Spencer quality guidelines. Some British firms are exerting pressure on suppliers of certain consumer goods in parts of Asia, to change a situation where children are being employed under very poor conditions to produce goods for export to the West. Ultimately, any outsider has the right to withdraw their custom if the supplying organisation does not come up to requirements, whether in terms of technical quality, delivery times or even civil rights.

The formation of groups

32. One of the fascinating aspects of the study of groups is how they came to be formed and develop as a group of people with certain common interests and purposes. Tuckman (1965)[11] devised a useful model for considering how groups changed over time. He identified four key stages in group development, which were later joined by a fifth stage — Adjourning (Tuckman & Jensen, 1977)[12], as follows:

Stage 1 — Forming
↓
Stage 2 — Storming
↓
Stage 3 — Norming
↓
Stage 4 — Performing
↓
Stage 5 — Adjourning

33. The first stage — forming — refers to the initial formation of the group, where tasks have to be understood, resources and information acquired, individuals have to get to know one another, and there is considerable reliance on the leader. The storming stage represents that period when problems begin to be faced more openly than in the earlier stage, individuals begin to question or challenge the task and have to confront emotional issues between themselves. This period of relative upheaval then moves into a more considered stage where conflicts are settled, new standards are developed and owned by the members, and cooperation really takes off. This stage opens the way for the most productive stage — Stage 4 — when the group is working effectively both in terms of its goals and its internal

173

relationships. Teamwork develops and solutions are found. The last stage — Stage 5 — underlines the fact that a group's life will eventually come to an end, as people move on elsewhere in the organisation or as the original purpose is attained and the job is completed.

34. Tuckman's analysis can be compared with that of Woodcock (1979)[13], who also adopted a four-stage sequence of development, as follows:

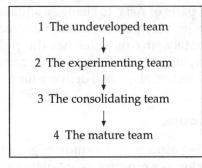

1 The undeveloped team

2 The experimenting team

3 The consolidating team

4 The mature team

The *undeveloped* team is one where there is uncertainty about objectives, where feelings are avoided, and where the leader takes most of the decisions. The *experimenting* team is one where issues are faced more openly, where individuals listen to each other, and where the emphasis is on the internal needs of the group. The *consolidating* team is one where personal interaction and collaboration are present, where the tasks and other objectives are clearer, and where tentative procedures are set in motion. The *mature* team is one where aims are clear, working methods are agreed, individuals work easily together, there is openness and flexibility, the leadership function tends to be shared, and the group recognises its responsibilities to the rest of the organisation.

35. What such analyses demonstrate is that group/team development can only take place over time. Initially, the group is more like a collection of individuals with little or no idea what they are there for, and who depend heavily on the leader for guidance and support. At this stage they have no sense of team-spirit, no knowledge of each other's strengths and weaknesses, and no mutual norms of behaviour, apart from those laid down at the outset by the leader. Over time, however, the group will gradually develop a sense of itself, its purpose and prime tasks, the capabilities of its members, the roles they might be able to play, and will develop norms of behaviour capable of carrying it through the foreseeable future. The key role in the development of a group from a state of immaturity to one of mature readiness is that of the leader, who has the task of shaping the individuals into a cohesive team able to perform with competence.

Effectiveness of teams

36. Team effectiveness can be looked at from a number of different perspectives, such as :

> ❏ How well is the team fulfilling its overall purpose?
>
> ❏ How far is it achieving its objectives?
>
> ❏ How efficiently does the team use its resources?
>
> ❏ How well does the team cope with internal difficulties (role conflict etc)?
>
> ❏ How closely does the team collaborate with other groups when it is necessary to do so?
>
> ❏ How effectively is the leadership function handled within the team?
>
> ❏ To what extent are members motivated to attain group targets etc?
>
> ❏ How cohesive is the group (ie what level of team-spirit is evident)?
>
> ❏ How enjoyable and/or beneficial is team membership to its members?

37. As can be seen from the above list, some of the questions focus on team outcomes, whilst others focus on team processes. McGregor (1960)[14] distinguished between effective and ineffective groups in terms of how well they handled their internal processes. His key points were as follows Figure 9.5).

Effective Groups	Ineffective Groups
The atmosphere is informal and relaxed	The atmosphere may be bored or tense
There is much relevant discussion, in which most members share	Discussion is often irrelevant, and tends to be dominated by one or two individuals
The group task is clearly understood, and members are committed to it	No common objective is evident, and the members are rather aimless
Members listen to each other	Members tend not to listen to each other
Conflict is brought constructively into the open	Conflict tends either to be avoided or develops into open warfare
Decisions are generally reached by consensus	Decisions are made on the basis of majority votes rather than consensus
Ideas are expressed freely and openly	Ideas and personal feelings are frequently suppressed for fear of criticism
Leadership is not just reserved to the appointed leader, but is shared when appropriate	The leader retains tight control
The group frequently examines its own progress and behaviour	The group avoids discussing its progress and behaviour

Figure 9.5   *Characteristics of effective and ineffective groups*
(after McGregor, 1960)

Conclusion

38. This chapter has focused primarily on formal groups, and has outlined the impact on groups of such matters as group size, group purpose, group tasks, leadership, group membership (motivation, cohesiveness, norms etc), roles within groups, and the external environment (especially the external social environment). The chapter has also considered the stages groups pass through in progressing from immaturity and relative ineffectiveness to maturity and effectiveness. So far we have not considered how groups communicate within themselves, how they behave when in competition with other groups, how they handle decision-making, how they resolve conflicts, and how they experience leadership. These further matters will be examined in the next three chapters. The section will end with a review of the concept of 'Organisation Culture'.

References

1. Schein, E. (1988), *Organizational Psychology* (3rd edn), Prentice Hall
2. Burns,T. & Stalker, G.M. (1961), *The Management of Innovation*, Tavistock
3. Peters, T. & Waterman, G. (1982), *In Search of Excellence*, Harper & Row
4. Goldsmith, & Clutterbuck, D. (1984), *The Winning Streak*, Penguin Business
5. Clutterbuck, D. (1994), *The Power of Empowerment*, BCA/ Kogan Page
6. Cole, G.A. (1994), *Strategic Management*, D P Publications
7. Urwick, L.F. (1947), *The Elements of Administration*, Pitman
8. Janis,I. (1982), *Victims of Group Think: A Psychological Study of Foreign Policy Decisions and Fiascos* (2nd edn.), Houghton Mifflin
9. Handy, C. (1985), *Understanding Organizations* (4th edn), Penguin
10. Belbin, R.M. (1981), *Management Teams - Why They Succeed of Fail*, Butterworth Heinemann
11. Tuckman, B. (1965), *'Developmental sequence in small groups*, in Psychological Bulletin, 63.
12. Tuckman, B. & Jensen, N. (1977), *'Stages of Small Group Development Revisited'*, in Group and Organizational Studies, vol 2 pp 419 et seq.
13. Woodcock, M. (1979), *Team Development Manual*, Gower
14. McGregor, D. (1960), *The Human Side of Enterprise*, McGraw-Hill

Questions for reflection/discussion

1. What are the primary characteristics of formal groups?

2. How far do current preferences for 'excellence' and 'empowerment' weaken the position of *informal* groups in the workplace?

3. Which of the key issues in Figure 9.1 are consistently likely to influence the behaviour of a group? Give reasons for your choice.

4. To what extent does the type of task to be achieved affect the pressures on the members of a group?

5. In what respects might the members of a work-group be expected to share common characteristics (eg professional knowledge, skills etc)?

6. What factors in a group are likely to encourage a healthy team-spirit? Whatare the dangers of an *unhealthy* team-spirit?

7. On the basis of any model of group development, discuss which stage you think is the most likely to present problems for the group leader. Suggest reasons.

10 Decision-making and communication in groups

Introduction

1.   One of the purposes of groups is to make decisions about matters within their sphere of competence. Indeed some groups (eg Boards of Directors, executive groups) are established especially to make decisions. The kinds of decisions that are made in groups and how are they dealt with depend considerably on the existence of effective methods of communication. These matters are the subject of this short chapter, which will also include an outline of the processes involved when groups are in competiton with one another.

Decision-making in groups

2.   Whilst many day-to-day decisions are made by individual managers and employees, there are certain kinds of decision which are generally handled by groups. These tend to be the kinds of decisions that require a number of minds to wrestle with them either (a) because of their complexity, or (b) because they need to be acceptable to a majority of those responsible for implementing them. Complex decisions clearly benefit from the old idea that 'two heads (or more) are better than one.' The more analysis that is conducted about the decision-situation, the more varied the options proposed, and the more thorough the assessment of the consequences, then the better will be the final decision. Handy (1993)[1] highlights ten major uses of groups or teams, of which three have a direct bearing on problem-solving and decision-making:

       'Organisation use groups, or teams and committees........

       3 For problem-solving and decision-taking....................

       6 For testing and ratifying decisions............................

       9 For negotiation or conflict resolution........................' (p.151-2)

3.   Groups such as committees are brought into existence precisely for the purpose of making decisions, or at least making recommendations for subsequent decisions. A committee usually comprises *political* forces in the first instance, ie the first people who are chosen to sit on a particular committee are selected because of the interest groups they represent (eg powerful or influential departments or functions). This ensures that people with power in the organisation will be party both to the discussions about key issues, and the subsequent decisions taken to meet them. Such powerful people will share the responsibility for decisions and for getting the commitment of their staff to fulfilling them. It will be assumed by other committee members that any individual's reservations or contribution will have been catered for during the decision-making process, either by being accepted, or by being argued down. Thus members 'own' the decisions made by their committee, or resign.

4.   Once the political interests have been catered for, committees usually look for *expertise*. Thus, the membership is expanded to ensure a sufficiency of expert knowledge and skills in the relevant areas of the business. Thus, a strategic review committee, composed mainly of senior functional heads (the 'politicians'), will nevertheless want to include an economist, a financial adviser and any other specialist thought to be needed to provide relevant information about conditions in the external environment of the business. Firms operating in high-technology markets will usually include specialist electronics and engineering staff; firms operating in fast-moving consumer goods markets may include market research specialists, and even social psychologists; firms engaged in complex operations, involving mutli-disciplinary work-teams composed of several nationalities may include personnel specialists, 'cultural advisers' and even language specialists.

5.   Some committees and similar groups also look for *representatives* of relevant interests. These may be the same people as those selected because of their political power, but usually they consist of others with no particular political power, but whose presence is important, even in a low-key observer/ information role, to ensure the democratic nature of the group's decisions. Representatives may, or may not, have voting rights on a committee. If they do have such rights, then clearly they have an element of power which can be exerted on the processes of the group, but overall they do not carry anything like the political 'clout' of those who come to the table with the backing of powerful interests. Committees which are set up to examine a particular issue, such as making a senior appointment or considering the impact of a new highway on a local community, usually ensure that they draw their members from representative sources as well as from the political and expert sources.

A basic model of decision-making

6. The decision-making undertaken by formal groups such as committees tends to follow a fairly rational path. As indicated by Figure 10.1, this suggests that problems are addressed, solutions sought and consequences assessed in a reasonably systematic way.

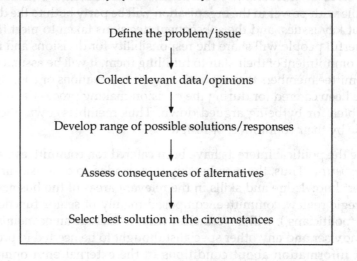

Define the problem/issue

↓

Collect relevant data/opinions

↓

Develop range of possible solutions/responses

↓

Assess consequences of alternatives

↓

Select best solution in the circumstances

Figure 10.1   *A rational approach to decision-making in groups*

7. Committees and similar formal groups have first to confront the problem or issue they are attempting to respond to. They need to ask such questions as *'What is the real problem/issue here?'*, *'What further information do we need to clarify the problem-situation?'*, *'Who is affected by this problem/issue?'*. It is also sometimes helpful to ask *'What is **not** the problem?'* The answers to such questions are likely to be generated from two main sources — (1) the members themselves, and (2) their expert advisers. This step leads neatly to the second stage which is the collection of relevant information and opinions from interested or affected parties. Sometimes it is necessary to set up a sub-group of the committee (eg working party) to collate and examine relevant documentation, seek the views of people who may be affected by the problem/issue, and make a full summary of findings available for the principal group. Sub-groups usually have no political power, and therefore may not take decisions in their own right. What they are expected to do is to summarise a situation, draw interim conclusions about it and either make recommendations, or submit a proposal for ratification. The ultimate action to be taken will always be reserved to the full committee. The main contribution of sub-groups is to move the decison-making process from the fact-finding stage into the development of possible solutions — the third stage.

8. It is important for groups to weigh up the consequences of possible solutions before opting for what in the circumstances appears to be the best way forward. At this stage the various interest groups that are represented around the table can put their point of view, and the experts can illustrate how they see the impact of particular solutions. It is then possible for the group to select the optimum solution, where the viewpoints of the political members of the group will be critical. The best solution will generally be one that is not only technically the best, but which will command the greatest degree of support from amongst those affected by it.

9. The degree of formality in a group's decision-making processes can vary. Many ad hoc groups only need a chairman, clear terms of reference and a time-scale to be able to work effectively. Formality is kept to a minimum, with members contributing on an 'expert'/'informed colleague' approach, and where reports of meetings are kept short and crisp with perhaps only action points referred to. These informal groups (often called 'task-forces') can be operated in an organisation's domestic context, where external accountability is not called for, and where the topic under scrutiny is relatively narrow in scope. Another example of a less-formal group is the creative ideas, or 'brainstorming', group. This kind of group, which is not strictly a decision-making group, actively encourages ideas and suggestions, which are not subject to scrutiny or rejection at this stage. Any ideas are welcomed, and to achieve a fruitful session, it is necessary for the leader to have created an atmosphere of trust, in which no ideas, however far-fetched, will be subject to ridicule.

10. Where, however, accountability to external groups (eg the public, government departments, professional bodies, trade unions etc) is concerned, then a much more formal arrangement must be made to ensure that decision-making is an open, consultative and accountable process. This arrangement usually takes the form of a formal committee, since this type of group contains the full spectrum of political, expert and representative interests. Formal committees probably spend as much time ratifying other (sub-) groups decisions as they do in generating their own decisions.

Committees as formal groups

11. A formal committee can take account of the interests of external stakeholders as well as of its own members and their constituents because it incorporates the following measures designed to ensure a full and fair debate about the issues that it addresses:

1 A *chair-holder* (chairman/ chairperson etc), who may be independent,whose role is to guide discussion and debate, ensure that members get a fair share of the talking, and who ensures that the necessary paper-work is available both prior to, during and after each meeting.

2 A *secretary,* who takes notes during the meeting, drafts the minutes,and generally provides administarive support to the committee.

3 An *agenda,* which sets out the subects for debate/ discussion/ decision,thus enabling members to prepare in advance to address certain issues.

4 *Minutes* of meetings are kept to ensure a summary record of the debate and decisions taken, which is presented to the members at each meeting to receive their approval or to be qualified in some way.

5 Committee *papers/ reports* are ways in which written information can be made available to assist in the decision-making process; these are sometimes provided by administrative staff, sometimes by sub-committees, and sometimes by external advisers/ consultants.

6 *Rules of procedure,* which ensure that the group acts within its powers, acts fairly towards its members, and prevents debate turning into a shouting match.

12. The existence of the above elements of formality does mean that decisions reached by committees tend to take longer than those resulting from less formal groups. Nevertheless, so long as only major or far-reaching decisions are reserved for committees, there are numerous advantages in submitting decisions to such a formal process. These advantages are summarised in Figure 10.2.

Communication processes within groups

13. Communication processes within mature groups tend to dominated by what Leavitt (1951)[2] called 'all-channel' networks, ie where all the members of the group communicate freely with each other (see Figure 10.3). Another form used in groups, especially those which are newly-formed, and where communication channels are somewhat tentative, is the 'circle', where individuals tend to communicate with one or two other

☐ Their organised nature means they can handle greater complexity than less formal groups

☐ Committees can call upon the services of sub-groups, administrative staff and consultants more readily than informal groups

☐ Decisions are reached only after extensive discussion and debate, during which different interests and arguments are considered and then accepted, modified or rejected

☐ Decisions represent the views of a group rather than just one or two powerful individuals, as is more likely in an informal group

☐ Because they invite the participation of key interest groups within an organisation, committees perform a powerful coordinating role between departments and functions

☐ The decisions reached by a committee tend to have considerable political 'clout' in an organisation, because of the select nature of the members and the relative thoroughness of the decison-making process

☐ Committee decisions, being open to scrutiny by the members, their constituents and sometimes the public at large, have a high degree of accountability in them, which contrasts with decisions taken in less formal groups with little direct accountability outside their immediate interests

Figure 10.2   *Advantages of formal committees*

members only. These channels of communication contrast strongly with the more centralised channels found in organisation-wide systems of communication, where the hierarchical 'chain' is the most common form. In decentralised channels, the role of the leader is primarily that of 'chairman' or 'catalyst' rather than 'manager' or 'gate-keeper'. In centralised channels, the leader's role is clearly that of 'controller' — managing the members, the task and the decision-making process, and acting as a clearing-house for resources and agreement to progress proposals put forward by members. This approach is typified by the 'wheel'.

14. Leavitt's illustrations of the various options open to organisations form the basis of the summary shown in Figure 10.3:

'Chain'

Here the communication flows are vertical, with the downwards channel dominating. This form is adopted in every hierarchy, and the role of leaders is to control.

'Circle'

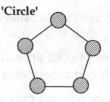

Members tend to communicate with those nearest them. Leader's role is likely to be seen as unclear, ie member of the circuit, yet 'in charge'.

Likely at the 'forming' stage of team development.

'All-channel'

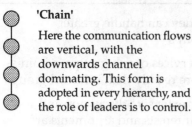

Members communicate freely, using all the resources of others to expedite tasks. Leader adopts democratic style by acting as one of the points on the circuit. Most likely to be adopted in mature groups.

'Wheel'

The leader is the central figure in the group. This style is more likely in the 'forming' and 'norming' stages, when reliance on the leader is at a premium.

Figure 10.3   *Communication channels (after Leavitt,1951)*

15. In addition to the channels of communication used by members of a group, there is also a variety of individual behaviours that can be manifested in the communication processes within the group. Rackham & Morgan (1977)[3], building on earlier work by Bales (1950)[4], distinguished more than a dozen separate categories of behaviour in groups, which can be summarised as shown in the table on the following page (Figure 10.4).

16. It is particularly important for group leaders to be aware of these alternative forms of behaviour, so that they can (a) recognise the behavioural styles of their group members, and (b) adopt a wide range of behaviours in their own right. The dominant style of an individual is likely to be reflected in the person's role within the group. Thus, an 'ideas person' is more likely than not to show open behaviour, a tendency to make proposals and a facility for contributing information. By comparison, the group 'sceptic' is likely to adopt blocking/ difficulty-stating behaviour and to test understanding frequently. The leader of a group is likely to adopt building and supporting behaviours in the early life of the group, encouraging members to contribute freely and to be positive in their attitude towards issues. As the group grows in maturity, however, the leader may prefer disagreeing and difficulty-stating, confident that individuals will not take things personally, but see constructive disagreement as a positive step towards optimum solutions. The total range of behaviours in a group should enable individuals to express feelings and opinions as well as thoughts and facts.

❏ Proposing, eg actions, ideas, recommendations

❏ Building, ie taking up and developing another person's ideas/ suggestions

❏ Supporting, eg another person's viewpoint

❏ Disagreeing

❏ Defending

❏ Attacking, ie more than just disagreeing

❏ Blocking/ Difficulty Stating, ie with no positive alternative

❏ Testing Understanding, eg asking questions

❏ Summarising, ie re-stating earlier arguments/ latest position etc

❏ Seeking Information

❏ Contributing Information

❏ Open behaviour (risking ridicule etc)

❏ Shutting-out behaviour (eg interrupting, turning away from etc)

❏ Bringing-in behaviour (ie engaging/ involving other members)

Figure 10.4   *Behaviour categories in groups*

Body language in groups

17. In the whirl of communication that can take place in a group using all its available channels, some of the communication will be expressed by body language rather than in words. An alert group leader will be on the lookout for non-verbal signs within the group, since they can give a fair indication of supporting/building/bringing-in behaviours on the one hand, or disagreeing/shutting-out behaviours on the other. Examples of body language that might indicate a person's attitude towards a discussion in a group are shown in Figure 10.5. Useful examples of body language, especially in one-to-one relationships, are given in Pease (1984)[5].

Behaviour category	Non-verbal forms of communication
Supporting	Head nodding, making direct eye-contact
Disagreeing	Shaking head, pulling faces, raising eyebrows
Attacking	Leaning forward, wagging or pointing finger
Shutting out	Deliberately turning aside from the person concerned, placing hands in flat open position as if to push away, refusing to make eye-contact
Bringing in	Making direct eye contact, turning towards the other, opening one hand in gesture towards the other

Figure 10.5   *Examples of non-verbal communication*
                                                                 (body language) in groups

Conflict in groups

18.   Some conflict is inevitable, even desirable, in groups. Whilst conflict may be at its height at the Storming stage of development, it is likely to be present from time to time at any stage. Conflict is not necessarily a bad thing, for it can force members of a group to recognise the deep feelings of one individual, or of a minority, and make efforts to resolve the issue which appears to be divisive. Sometimes, the lone individual has in fact got the 'right' answer to a problem, and everyone else is 'wrong' but at that stage cannot see it. If the lone individual is not articulate enough or lacks political clout, then the weight of his or her disagreement takes time to break down the resistance of the others, and, of course, may fail to do so, to the detriment of the group. The leader's role in handling conflict is crucial. If disagreements get out of hand, if individuals start making personal attacks on each other, then the group can easily descend into chaos. On the other hand, if all conflict is avoided, or smothered at birth, then major issues are likely to be submerged, and an unsatisfactory compromise solution reached — the lowest common factor. As noted in the previous chapter (paragraph 19), the dangers of Group Think are that crucial issues are likely to be ignored in the effort to maintain solidarity. Leaders have a difficult task at the best of times, and here they have to tread a middle path, not avoiding conflict and dis-agreement but aiming to use them constructively.

19.   Thomas (1976)[6] identified five characteristic styles of handling conflict on the basis of the degrees of assertiveness and cooperativeness shown by individuals in response to questionnaires. The five styles are essentially

conflict-handling alternatives, and are indicated in Figure10.6. They range from collaboration, which is seen as the optimum way of handling conflict, to complete avoidance of conflict, which is seen as the weakest response to conflict. In between these two extremes are a competitive response and two forms of compromise behaviours ('compromising' and 'accommodating').

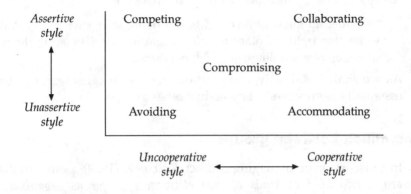

Figure 10.6   *Conflict-handling types in groups*

20.   The use of the two scales of *assertiveness-unassertiveness* and *cooperativeness — uncooperativeness* enables five separate ways of handling conflict to emerge. An assertive style is one where the individual takes positive steps to pursue his own interests. Where this is accompanied by a cooperative approach, which recognises the interests of others too, then the person is adopting a collaborative style of handling conflict, which is the optimum style. Where an assertive style is accompanied by an *un*-cooperative attitude (a less-than-ideal form of assertiveness), then the individual's preferred way of handling conflict is to compete with the other(s). Where an individual is basically *un*-assertive, ie weak in pursuit of personal interests, and this is accompanied by an uncooperative attitude, an avoiding tactic is likely to be adopted (ie a refusal to admit to conflict/ disagreement by *'burying one's head in the sand.'*). Where the unassertive approach is accompanied by a cooperative stance, then the way forward is seen to be by accommodating the other(s) (*'bending over backwards to please'*). Where an individual is reasonably assertive and reasonably cooperative, then a compromising style is produced — *'If you will do X, then I will agree to this point.'* Naturally, these five styles simplify a complex range of alternative behaviours, but they do help to identfify some of the major options open to people in groups.

21.   The use of the expression 'assertive' in Thomas's model of conflict-handling does not quite equate to the meaning ascribed to the term by those engaged in assertivenes training (eg Back & Back, 1994)[7]. They would only call the collaborative approach true assertiveness, for

competing would be regarded more as an aggressive response. The Backs'
definition of assertion includes:

> '......Standing up for your own rights in such a way that you do not violate
> another person's rights.......The aim of assertive behaviour is to satisfy the
> needs and wants of both parties.......'

An aggressive reponse, according to the Backs, is :

> 'Standing up for your own rights, but doing so in such a way that you
> violate the rights of other people.......Ignoring or dismissing the needs,
> wants, opinions, feelings, or beliefs of others........'

As we shall see shortly, competition frequently causes groups to adopt
essentially aggressive tactics against other groups.

Competition between groups

22. In a discussion on managing conflict, Kolb et al (1979)[8] point out that there
     are '...*two distinct kinds of competitiveness as far as organizations are
     concerned....'*and go on to comment that *'Competitiveness internal to an orga-
     nization usually results in energy being expended at the expense of the overall
     mission......Competition between organizations is the essence of the marketplace.'*
     Thus, they clearly distinguish between healthy and unhealthy competi-
     tion. The former has its place in providing incentives, and excitement, as
     between organisations — be they international companies or national foot-
     ball teams; the latter should have no place in the internal workings of
     groups, where it is seen to have destructive and demoralising effects.
     Within groups a competing style is not good enough, and what is needed
     is a collaborative style.

23. However, even competition between groups can prove counter-produc-
     tive. Schein (1989)[9] addresses the problem of inter-group competition in
     terms of the challenge of

     > '...how to establish conditions *between groups* which will enhance the
     > productivity of each without destroying intergroup relations and coordina-
     > tion....This problem exists because as groups become more committed to
     > their own goals and norms, they are likely to.......seek to undermine their
     > rivals' activities, thereby becoming a liability to the organization as a
     > whole.'

     Schein concludes, on the basis of several experiments into inter-group
     competition conducted by fellow researchers (eg Sherif et al, 1961[10]; Blake
     & Mouton, 1961[11]), that certain common patterns of behaviour emerge
     within groups and between groups.

24. Behaviour *within* competing groups tends to develop as follows:

❐ the group becomes more closely knit (cohesive), elicits greater loyalty from its members, and closes ranks; some differences are buried. [NB It is easy to see the seeds of Group Think in this situation.]

❐ the group climate changes from informal and easy-going behaviour to a focus on the task and a lower regard for members' needs.

❐ leadership becomes increasingly autocratic, and the members accept this.

❐ the group becomes more highly structured and organised.

❐ the group demands conformity as well as loyalty in order to present a united front. [NB Another feature of Group Think].

The key to the behaviour patterns within groups depends on the extent to which the leader can achieve a balance between the negative and positive aspects of cohesiveness and attention to task. As Adair (1973)[12] illustrates, in his action-centred model of leadership (see Chapter 11), it is vital to ensure attention to individual's needs and the needs of the group as well as focusing on the requirements of the task.

25. The behaviour *between* groups in a competing situation tends to develop the following characteristics:

❐ each group begins to see the other as a threat

❐ each group begins to develop (negative) stereotypes about the other

❐ each group's perceptions both of themselves and their competitors become increasingly distorted

❐ communication and interaction between the groups weakens substantially

26. In any competition there are winners and losers, and the effects of the result are sometimes striking. It does not take a genius to see which crew has won the Oxford and Cambridge Boat Race — the winners have their arms in the air, are smiling and look fresher than the losers, who are usually slumped over their oars, their heads down and looking thoroughly dejected. In work organisations such obvious emotions are not often to the fore, but the effects of winning or losing can be just as significant — a huge increase in turnover and profits for the winners, and possible liquidation

for the losers. However, at the level of the work-team genuine behavioural symptoms become apparent. For example, winning groups tend to grow ever more cohesive and more informal in their working methods, they pay even more attention to members' needs than those of the task, and complacency is never far away. Losers, by comparison, become introverted in a negative sense — internal conflicts resurface, scapegoats are sought and there are negative attitudes towards members' needs. However, losers tend to use the opportunity to regroup, reexamine their stereotypes and their working methods, and then apply themselves to the task with a renewed sense of urgency. Thus, the losers may learn more from their lack of success than the winners, if the latter fail to halt the drift towards complacency.

27. Schein suggests that the way to avoid the negative consequences of inter-group competition are as follows:

> ❑ ensure that greater emphasis is given to *overall organisational effectiveness*, and the role that units play in that, rather than to individual team effectiveness [NB this is one of the aims of organisation culture]
>
> ❑ stimulate a high level of interaction and communication between groups, and distribute rewards partly on the basis of help given to others
>
> ❑ arrange for the frequent rotation of members between groups, so as to develop better mutual understanding
>
> ❑ avoid situations where groups are put into a 'win-lose' position in relation to other groups

One other tactic that is sometimes adopted to avoid inter-group stress is to identify some common enemy (eg 'waste', foreign competitors etc), and to use that enemy as a rallying point for group collaboration. Governments are know to use this tactic, especially when undergoing a sustained attack by opposition groups, and thus urge everyone's attention on combatting inflation, or organised crime, or international terrorism, or whatever.

Guidelines for successful groups

28. This and the previous chapter highlight the complexities of working in, and leading, groups in the workplace. Groups clearly possess qualities that are at once helpful and constructive on the one hand, and unhelpful and destructive on the other. In their advice to teams that do outstandingly well — 'superteams' — Hastings et al (1986)[13] include ten 'golden rules' of effective team-working, broadly summarised as follows:

❑ The leader should prepare adequately for team meetings

❑ The leader and the members agree on the purpose of the meeting

❑ The timing of the proceedings should allow for adequate discussion of issues as well as covering all the required ground

❑ Team members should be encouraged to communicate regularly with one another, listening skills and the confidence to ask for clarification should be developed

❑ Team discussions should remain focussed, and any change of topic should be consciously agreed

❑ The talents and skills of group members should be recognised and exploited

❑ The team should develop its creative problem solving capacity, frequently questioning old solutions and testing new ones

❑ Agreement of members should checked by the leader, and silence should not imply agreement

❑ Conflict is recognised and accepted as useful, so long as it is constructive — 'Properly managed conflict also provides energy for a team and prevents complacency'

❑ The working of the team should be reviewed regularly with the participation of all the members

❑ Decisions taken and actions agreed should be implemented without delay

Whilst the above list applies particularly to the conduct of group meetings, much of the advice applies equally to the working of groups generally and can thus help to optimise group performance and minimise the effects of negative behaviour.

References

1. Handy, C. (1993), *Understanding Organizations* (4th edn), Penguin Business

2. Leavitt, H.J. (1951), *'Some effects of certain communicative patterns on group performance'* Journal of Abnormal Psychology

3. Rackham, N. & Morgan, T. (1977), *Behaviour Analysis in Training,* McGraw Hill

4. Bales, R. F. (1950), *Interaction Process Analysis,* Addison-Wesley

5. Pease, A. (1984), *Body Language,* Sheldon Press

6. Thomas, K.W. (1976), *'Conflict and Conflict Management',* in Dunnette,M. (ed) Handbook of Industrial and Organizational Psychology, Rand McNally

7. Back, K. & Back, K. (1994), *Assertiveness at Work* (2nd edn), BCA/McGraw Hill

8. Kolb,D. et al (1979), *Organizational Psychology - an experiential approach* (3rd edn), Prentice Hall

9. Schein, E.H. (1989), *Organizational Psychology* (3rd. edn), Prentice Hall

10. Sherif, M. et al (1961), *Intergroup Conflict and Cooperation - The Robbers Cave Experiment*, University Book Exchange

11. Blake, R. & Mouton, J. (1961), '*Reactions to Intergroup Competition under Win-Lose Conditions*, Management Science 7 (pp 420-435)

12. Adair, J. (1973), *Action-centred Leadership*, McGraw Hill

13. Hastings, C. et al (1986), *Superteams - A Blueprint for Organisational Success*, Gower/Fontana

Questions for reflection/discussion

1. To what extent might there be conflicts between the political, expert and representative forces on a committee?

2. Why are committees so often the target of cynicism despite their widespread use as a crucial means of decision-making?

3. What advantages does an 'all-channel' approach to communication have over other types of channel?

4. How far is the significance of body language under-rated in group discussions?

5. Why is competition within groups likely to have a greater negative impact than competition between groups?

11 Leadership and power in organisations

Introduction

1. In any organised group the issue of leadership is crucial. One of the most striking differences between two otherwise seemingly equal groups often lies in the effectiveness of their leadership. This chapter looks at the meaning and nature of 'leadership', considers what leaders do that is different from other members of a group, and discusses the nature of power in organisations.

The meaning of leadership

2. Leadership is essentially a process in which one individual, or sometimes a small group of individuals, influences the efforts of others towards the achievement of goals in a given set of circumstances. Thus, the key variables in any leadership situation are as follows (Figure 11.1):

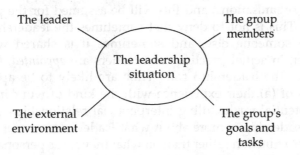

Figure 11.1   *The key variables of leadership*

3. The components of the leadership situation illustrated in Figure 11.1 comprise:

   ❑ the leader (or leading group)

   ❑ the members of the group (both as individuals and as a whole)

❏ the goals and tasks set for the group (primarily from external sources)

❏ the external environment in which the group operates (eg structure, culture)

Effective leadership amounts to finding the optimum balance between these four sets of variables, which are described in more detail throughout this chapter, which focuses primarily on leadership activities within small groups and work-teams.

4. At this point it will be helpful to propose a working definition of leadership in relation to small groups and work-teams, as follows:

> *Leadership is a social process in which one person in a group harnesses the knowledge, skills and motivation of the other members in the attainment of group goals. This process implies the consent — willing or grudging — of the group. Leadership involves managing the external boundaries of the group, as well as dealing constructively with the members' internal responsibilities, roles and relationships. Leaders are especially required to identify the need for change, and to use their influence to re-direct the energies of group members accordingly. In work-teams this usually refers to changes in group processes rather than in group goals, which is the responsibility of senior management to change.*

The key leadership variables

5. Taking the first variable — the *leader* — we are discussing a role that is fundamental to the success of a group, since the leader has the responsibility to develop the group, harness their skills and motivate them to achieve their tasks and goals. The leader is usually appointed to the role in modern organisations, and this will be assumed for the purposes of this chapter. This is not to deny that sometimes the leadership role is taken over by someone else, and sometimes it is shared within a group. However, in actual practice most leaders are *appointed*, for better or for worse, to the leadership role. They are likely to be appointed on the grounds of (a) their experience with the kind of work involved and (b) their potential for handling interpersonal relationships. As will be seen below, leadership is more about what leaders *do* in order to maintain the leadership function rather than on what they *are* as personalities. There has been some discussion (eg Zaleznik,1986)[1] about the possible differences between 'leaders' and 'managers', but for our purposes, whilst accepting that the term 'leader' has slightly wider implications than 'manager', we will assume that such distinctions are academic, and, as emphasised above, confirm that 'managers' are indeed 'appointed leaders'.

6. The nature of the membership of the group is a factor in the total leadership equation, since the leader's behaviour will be influenced strongly by the nature of the group members, their skills, their strengths and weak-

nesses, the roles they play, their personalities and their motivation. Since the interaction between the leader and the group members is a dynamic one, each party will set off reactions in the other. As Drummond (1992)[2] points out

> 'no power relation is absolute, or one way', noting that 'although an employee may be highly dependent on his manager for his job and promotion, the manager is dependent on the employee's skill, energy and integrity, all of which reflect upon him.' (p.31-32)

The extent of the interplay between the leader and the group will also depend partly on the shared values of the group, and partly on the maturity of the group, as mentioned in Chapter 9 (paras. 17-18 and 32-37).

7. The effect of the group's *goals* and *tasks* on the leadership situation is especially significant for work-teams. In a formal organisation, goals and key tasks are set by outsiders, usually senior management. Thus, there is relatively little scope for the group leader to introduce changes, except in the *way* tasks are completed, and no scope for individual members to challenge either the goals or the tasks — they are part of the *'givens'* in the situation. However, where a group is able to set at least some of its goals and key tasks, then there is flexibility and scope for the group to adapt its behaviour around its goals. The only group that is usually empowered to revise its own goals is the senior management team, for whom the need to assess opportunities and threats in the environment and then revise organisational goals to meet a new challenge is paramount. For lower-level groups down the line no such flexibility is likely, but then neither is there the same degree of risk involved for the leaders. A modern trend aimed at increasing the discretion of lower-level groups is called 'empowerment', and is mentioned below.

8. Unofficial (informal) groups do determine their own goals, and these can work against goals set officially by the management, as was shown during the Bank Wiring stage of the Hawthorne Experiments (see Chap 4 paras.8-10). However, in a well-managed group, there is less chance of this occurring because the official leader will (a) insist on adherence to the formal goals of the organisation, and (b) seek to meet group members' fears and doubts. Much of the power wielded unofficially by trade union representatives in many British manufacturing organisations in past decades was due to management's inability to (a) demonstrate firm leadership, and (b) win the confidence of their employees, admittedly at a time of full employment and when there were few legal restraints on trade union activity within firms.

9. The general situation in which a group finds itself, ie its *external environment*, also has an impact on the leadership exercised in the group. No work-team exists in isolation, as Likert (1961)[3] illustrated over thirty years ago when describing his 'linking pin' model of organisation structure (see

Figure 4.3, p.76). This idea was developed from Likert's views on supportive relationships, which he saw as facilitating relationships *between* groups as well as enabling effective relationships *within* groups. In the model each head of a unit (function, department, section etc) interacts with other heads at the next level up in the hierarchy, as well as providing the leadership of the base unit. The shape of the organisation is still that of the hierarchical pyramid adopted by the classical theorists, but nevertheless operates on the basis of interlocking teams, which provides a degree of lateral collaboration and cooperation. Where such support is available to group leaders, this is advantageous; where it is lacking, then the leadership situation becomes more problematic — resources may be hard to obtain, unhelpful competition from neighbouring groups develops, and individual's needs may be difficult to meet.

10. Other factors that have a bearing on the *environment* of a group include:

> ❐ The extent to which decision-making authority is delegated down the line (ie where authority is delegated, the group has to address decisions that would otherwise be made for it by a higher authority)
>
> ❐ The nature of the organisation's business (eg routine administration, fast-moving consumer goods, specialist one-off capital goods etc) affects the organisation and pace of work, the opportunities for applying technology, and the extent of the requirement for training etc
>
> ❐ The demands exerted on the group by external customers/ clients etc (ie where customers are in a powerful position to state their terms, this puts great pressure on the team members to meet deadlines, quality standards and other customer demands)
>
> ❐ The demands exerted on the group by other groups within the structure (ie where 'internal' customers or neighbouring teams in the production process are placed to make time and quality demands)
>
> ❐ The nature of the organisation culture (eg in terms of personnel policies, quality management, health and safety consciousness, customer relations, 'excellence' etc) affects the manner in which a group is expected to conduct itself by other members of the organisational community
>
> ❐ The time-scale within which objectives/ targets have to be achieved (eg the pressures in a daily newspaper office are immediate and energetic compared with those in a university research unit, which are long-term and where energy is expended over months rather than minutes)

The general effect of these particular factors is to increase the task and competitive pressures on a group, which, as was noted in the previous chapter contain as many dangers as positive advantages both for groups and for the organisation as a whole.

11. The scenario presented to a leader confronted by all these issues of goals, tasks, group membership and environment is complex. At best the scenario can be seen as exciting and challenging, at worst as stressful and daunting. How a particular leader responds to the situation will depend considerably on the support received from the rest of the organisation (supportive management and culture, adequate resourcing etc), and on the leader's own resourcefulness. The latter usually manifests itself in an individual's leadership style, or preferred way of managing. This question of style has been of great interest to researchers and practitioners alike.

Leadership styles

12. An individual's leadership style refers to their preferred manner of tackling task and personnel issues in delivering the goals set for their group or team. Chapter 4 has already referred to some of the primary choices available to managers in their leadership role. These choices are in two main groups — (1) between task-orientation and people orientation (or a combination of these), and (2) between the personal use of power (eg autocracy) and varying degrees of delegated power (eg democracy). Two of the early models of leadership style were those of McGregor (1960)[4] and Likert (1961, op.cit), which were referred to in Chapter 4, and are summarised in Figure 11.2.

Model	Exponent(s)	Basic Premise
Theory X & Theory Y	D. McGregor	Theory X implies a need to *drive* people to achieve group goals; Theory Y implies an opport unity to *encourage* people to contribute to group goals.
Systems 1-4	R. Likert	System 1 — leader as *powerful driver,* using threats and punishment; System 2 — leader as *benevolent driver,* using rewards as well as threats; System 3 — leader as *consultative driver;* System 4 — leader as *participative driver.*

Figure 11.2   *Summary of early models of leadership*

13. Other early studies of leadership were carried out in Michigan and Ohio in the 1950's. The Michigan studies, with which Likert was involved, looked at the differences between high-producing and low-producing groups to see if they could identify any differences in leadership behaviour. What they found was that supervisors in *high*-producing groups were *employee-centred* in their approach to their work targets, whereas supervisors in *low*-producing groups were *production*-centred. This was an ironical result, yet it was clear to the researchers that where supervisors paid attention to interpersonal relationships, exercised less direct supervision and encouraged participation, the outcomes were more productive than in cases where the supervisors were directive and focused more attention on the task than on employee needs. Some supervisors adopted characteristics of both extremes, and the resulting model of leadership styles was presented as a continuum of alternatives (see Figure 11.3):

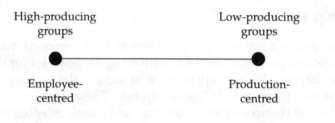

High-producing groups	Low-producing groups
Employee-centred	Production-centred

Figure 11.3   *The Michigan Continuum*

14. The Ohio studies[5] were conducted shortly after the Michigan research. They also concentrated on leadership behaviour, using a 150-item Leadership Behaviour Description Questionnaire. Results obtained from the completed questionnaires suggested that two distinctive types of behaviour appeared to be dominant. These were (1) behaviour that was essentially relationships-orientated (ie where employees needs were taken into consideration), and (2) behaviour that was principally concerned with organising the task, and thus where task-requirements were given priority. The two types of behaviour were called 'Consideration' and 'Initiating Structure' respectively. However, unlike the Michigan studies, the Ohio results showed that there were two separate dimensions at work in the leadership situation, and that supervisors could score highly on *both* dimensions. Thus supervisors could be placed in one of four quadrants on a grid developed on the basis of the two dimensions (see Figure 11.4).

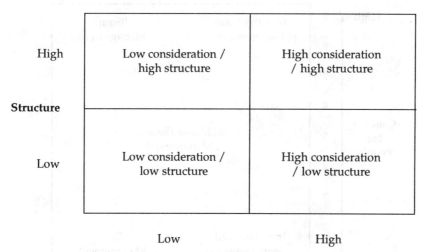

High	Low consideration / high structure	High consideration / high structure
Structure		
Low	Low consideration / low structure	High consideration / low structure
	Low	High
		Consideration

Figure 11.4   *The Ohio Quadrant*

15. The quadrant shown in Figure 11.4 suggests that the optimum style is one where the tension between high consideration and high structure has been successfully resolved — the leader pays thorough attention to people's needs and organises the work very efficiently. In complete contrast to this style is the low consideration/ low structure style, which must be considered a minimal style — inefficient yet autocratic. The approach taken in the Ohio studies was taken up subsequently by Blake & Mouton (1985)[6] in their so-called 'Managerial Grid', which was used for management development purposes as a means of clarifying individual's leadership styles. On the strength of questionnaires, group discussions and practical exercises, individual managers were able to identify a style that seemed to be consonant with their own perceptions and those of colleagues. The basic Grid is depicted at Figure 11.5

16. The Grid uses two dimensions — Concern for People (equivalent to 'Consideration') and Concern for Production (similar to 'Structure'), and individuals are scored on two scales each of 1-9. Like the Ohio quadrant, the Grid also displays an optimum and a minimal style. The Team Management style is the optimum style, where there is full attention to both people's needs and production concerns. The minimal style is unsurprisingly called Impoverished Management. A concern for people at the expense of production is termed Country Club Management style (ie where the object is to keep the customers happy above all else). An over-concern for production and little concern for people leads to a Task Management (ie taskmaster) style. Unlike the Ohio version, the Managerial Grid allows another dominant style to emerge — the Middle-of-the-Road Management style — where the emphasis is on compromise to keep every one reasonably happy. As a development device the Grid has proved quite useful.

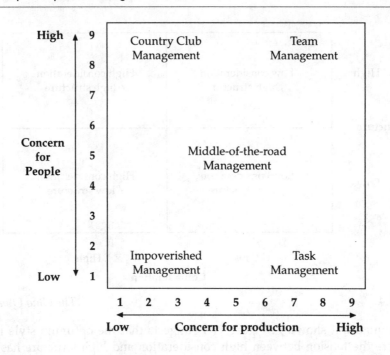

Figure 11.5   *The Managerial Grid (after Blake & Mouton, 1964,1985)*

17. A development of the Managerial Grid entitled the 'three-dimensional model of managerial behaviour' was made by Reddin (1970)[7]. The 3-D model also includes concern for people (Relationship Orientation — RO), and concern for production (Task Orientation — TO), but adds an Effectiveness/ Appropriateness dimension, which has the effect of producing *eight* management styles, depending on whether the style is applied appropriately and effectively. Underpinning these eight are four basic styles, or 'stances' might be a better expression, which arise from the strength of an individual's attitudes towards task and people. The basic styles are unexcitingly termed *'Related'* (High on people, low on task), *'Separated'* (Low on both people and task), *'Dedicated'* (Low on people, high on task), and *'Integrated'* (High on both people and task). The eight key management styles that arise from these four basic stances are more interestingly named Missionary, Deserter, Compromiser, Autocrat, Developer, Bureaucrat, Benevolent Autocrat and Executive. All the alternative styles are as set out in Figure 11.6, which shows the principal features of each.

18. Compared with the Blake Grid, Reddin's model has four effective styles to Blake's one, which allows for a greater flexibility of style. Nevertheless, although both the Blake Grid and the Reddin model are of interest in helping individuals and their organisations to think about leadership styles, and apply the models to management development, they have not been validated by research. Therefore their contribution to our understanding of the leadership process is rather limited.

Basic Styles/ Stances (4)	Features
Related	High concern for People, low concern for Task
Separated	Low concern for both People and Task
Dedicated	High concern for Task, low concern for People
Integrated	High concern for both People and Task

Key Management Styles (8)

Missionary	Basically Related, but inappropriate and less effective
Developer	Basically Related, appropriate and *more effective*
Deserter	Basically Separated, inappropriate and *less effective*
Bureaucrat	Basically Separated, but appropriate and *more effective*
Autocrat	Basically Dedicated, but inappropriate and less effective
Benevolent Autocrat	Basically Dedicated, appropriate and *more effective*
Compromiser	Basically Integrated, but inappropriate and less effective
Executive	Basically Integrated, appropriate and *more effective*

Figure 11.6   *Management styles — from Reddin's 3-D model*

19. Another set of university studies of leadership carried out in the United States was the work at Harvard under R.F.Bales. Their research into group behaviour suggested that, like the Michigan studies, leader's preferences are uni-dimensional rather than two-dimensional, or more. The Harvard team identified two separate styles of leadership — (1) task leaders, who emphasised the task needs and structuring, and (2) the socio-emotional leaders, who showed concern for supportive relationships. The team concluded that a person could *not* be both a task leader and a socio-emotional leader at the same time, a conclusion which goes against the thinking implied in the Blake and Reddin models.

20. The question of how useful it is to study leadership from the point of view of styles is one that appears to divide academics from practitioners. The former find little use in the approach for the purposes of understanding the nature of leadership, whereas the latter seem to find it very useful as a means of management development. The truth is that style is only one aspect of the leader's position in a group, which is strongly influenced by

the amount of authority granted to the leader by the organisation, as well as by the other variables depicted in Figure 11.1 above. It will be well, therefore, to widen our discussion of leadership.

Contingency approaches to leadership

21. Reddin's allusion to appropriate and inappropriate situations in determining the effectiveness of management style reminds us of the need to consider the *context* of the leadership role. Some theorists have broadened out the study of leadership from a relatively narrow base of personality traits and/ or personal style of leadership to a more contextual view of leadership. Their approach has been termed (Fiedler,1967)[8] a *'contingency'* approach to leadership, since it recognises that leadership, and the way it is exercised, depend on a range of variables rather than on just one or two. The contingency approach takes account of at least six major variables in the leadership situation, as shown in Figure 11.7.

22. Fiedler (op. cit) was the first theorist to employ the expression 'contingency' in the context of leadership. His *'leadership contingency model'* suggested that leadership performance depends on the leader adopting a style that is appropriate according to the favourableness of the situation, which is determined principally by three key variables:

❏ leader-member relations

❏ degree of structure in the task

❏ power and authority of the position

According to Fiedler, the most favourable situation for the leader is when (1) he has good leader-member relations, (2) the task is highly structured, and (3) he has a powerful position. The least favourable position is one where the leader is disliked by the team, where the task is relatively unstructured, and where the leader has little power.

23. A more recent development of contingency leadership is the Functional Leadership model devised by Adair (1968[9], 1983[10]). This proposes that leadership is a question what the leader does in order to meet the requirements of the task and the needs of the team, both as a group and as individuals. Adair points out that it is important to separate individuals' needs from group needs, otherwise there is a tendency for the group's needs to dominate individuals. He argues (1983 op. cit.) that

'....leaders should always be aware of both the group and each individual, and seek to harmonise them in the service of the third factor — the common task.' (p.34)

❑ *the nature of the task or goal -*
- ○ complexity/ simplicity
- ○ short/ long timescale
- ○ demands made on team members
- ○ cost of failure/ rewards for success

❑ *the social interaction of team as a whole*
- ○ high/ low morale
- ○ good/ poor team-spirit
- ○ high/ low degree of mutual support
- ○ high/ low recognition of each individual's talents/ contribution

❑ *the characteristics of individual members*
- ○ wide/ narrow range of skills and experience
- ○ preferred role within the group
- ○ relative ability to work with others

❑ *the attributes of the leader*
- ○ general intelligence
- ○ temperament
- ○ expertise
- ○ relative ability to perform the leadership role

❑ *the power or authority given to the leader*
- ○ wide/ limited authority granted to the role (position power)
- ○ power arising from personality (charismatic power)
- ○ power arising from knowledge/ skill (expert power)
- ○ power arising from acceptance by the group/ team (personal power)
- ○ power arising from external sources other than management (position power)

❑ *the external environment of the team*
- ○ the culture of the local organisation
- ○ the overall organisation culture
- ○ the physical environment (eg close/ scattered, dangerous/ comfortable etc)
- ○ the impact on team of external groups (customers/ suppliers etc)

Figure 11.7   *Contingent variables in leadership*

24. Adair's model is based on three overlapping circles, which make up the primary contingencies required to be balanced by the leader, as follows (Figure 11.8):

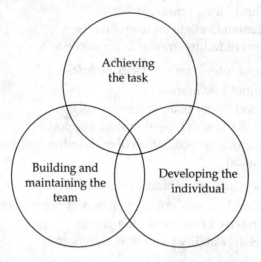

Figure 11.8   *Adair's functional leadership model*

The value of perceiving leadership as achieving the best balance between the three overlapping areas of task, group and individual needs is that it becomes clear that failure to meet any one area will adversely affect the chances of success. So, for example, if a leader concentrates on Team and Individual needs to the neglect of the Task, then both the former will be less than completely satisfied. If the task is not completed satisfactorily then both team and individual morale are likely to suffer. The reason for this is partly that people come together in groups precisely to achieve tasks that they are unable to fulfil on their own. Thus, if the task is not met, there will inevitably be disappointment. Of course, many leaders, especially those who are appointed to their role, prefer to focus on the needs of the task, since those are easier to handle — they don't answer back! Such leaders neglect, or overrule, individuals' needs, and the needs of the group as a whole, in order to achieve the task laid on them by their superiors. Inevitably, this leads to a self-defeating position, where the task is not achieved adequately because individual and group needs have not been met.

Leadership and decision-making

25. An influential paper published by Tannenbaum & Schmidt in 1958[11] suggested that a leader's decision-making style could be plotted on a continuum from relatively authoritarian to relatively democratic (see Figure 11.9). The paper took decision-making rather than 'leadership style'

as its focal point, and suggested that the extent to which the leader involves the group in decisions depends on a number of situational factors, especially the relative maturity of the group (see Chapters 9 & 10 above on topics of Group Formation and Channels of Communication). The continuum was revised slightly later by the authors (see Harvard Business Review May/Jun 1973)[12].

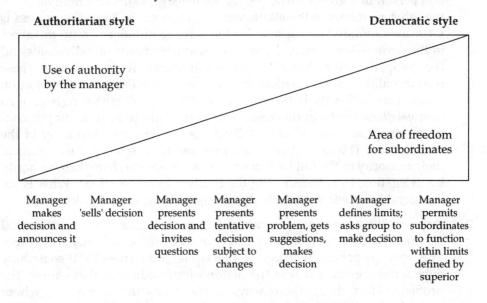

Authoritarian style   **Democratic style**

Use of authority
by the manager

Area of freedom
for subordinates

| Manager makes decision and announces it | Manager 'sells' decision | Manager presents decision and invites questions | Manager presents tentative decision subject to changes | Manager presents problem, gets suggestions, makes decision | Manager defines limits; asks group to make decision | Manager permits subordinates to function within limits defined by superior |

Figure 11.9   *Leadership patterns in decision-making*
                                        (adapted from Tannenbaum & Schmidt,1958)

26. As indicated in Figure 11.9, when the manager uses the full extent of his authority, the area of freedom (ie of decision-making) for subordinates is effectively nil. As the manager gradually shares his authority, so he moves from complete autocracy through two forms of what might be termed 'benevolent autocracy' into two stages of consultation and, finally, into two stages of joint decision-making. There is a flexibility of managerial action implied in the continuum, and a manager can move between styles depending on the situation. For our purposes the model proposed by Tannenbaum & Schmidt offers an opportunity to consider the difference between leadership, authority and power, since the continuum illustrates a range of uses of authority (power conferred by the organisation) in leadership.

Power, authority and leadership

27. Much of this chapter has been concerned with questions of authoritarian versus participative approaches in leadership. The assumption has been that leadership is exercised within the limits of the authority granted to the

leader by his or her superiors as representatives of the corporate organisation. However, it will be fairly obvious by now that *leadership* is not necessarily synonymous with *authority*, let alone *power*. What are the differences between these three concepts?

28. *Leadership*, as was noted in paragraph 4 above, is a social process in which one person in a group harnesses the knowledge, skills and motivation of the other members in the attainment of group goals. Since the process is ultimately founded on consent, leaders have to influence group members in the desired direction, and meet the reasonable needs of individuals and the group, as well as handling task requirements. To assist them in these responsibilities, formal leaders have a degree of *authority* conferred upon them. This authority is essentially *the power to act within certain, often closely-defined, limits*. In this case *power* is the right to implement personal decisions, granted to selected individuals by the upper hierarchy of the organisation. The individuals concerned can choose to exert the limits of their authority to the full (autocracy) or can choose to share their authority by delegation, thus transferring their power to act to others. What is *not* transferable is their accountability, or *responsibility*, for the task in hand.

29. *Responsibility* is personal and cannot be removed except by an authorised superior. Neither can it be delegated to others, unlike authority and power. This why the person in charge of a group is 'held responsible' if something goes wrong, even if it was the action of subordinates that caused the problem. Thus, delegation always carries a risk that those with whom authority has been shared may fail in their efforts and bring criticism or retribution on their leader from above. They themselves cannot be held responsible, since the burden of responsibility was laid on the leader. This is why the classical theorist, Lyndall Urwick (see Chapter 2 para. 18), insisted on the Principle of Correspondence in his list of management principles. Authority, argued Urwick, should be commensurate with responsibility. In other words, if you give someone a job to do, and are holding them accountable for its achievement, you must give them enough power to act to enable them to carry out the job.

30. Power has to be seen as a separate concept from leadership, authority and responsibility. *Power* is essentially a matter of getting other people to do things they might not otherwise have done. Power is usually discussed in terms of (1) the ability to act, and (2) the ability to control resources, including people. It implies also the ability to exercise control whether others like it or not. Leadership, by comparison, generally implies consent. The decision-making continuum referred to above shows that, apart from the extreme authoritarian style, all the remaining approaches to decision-making suggest that some deference is being made to the rest of the group (ie to the subordinates referred to by Tannenbaum and Schmidt). The link between power and leadership is that power is a resource that leaders can call upon in order to influence or control others.

31. Most of the current theories about power use as their starting point the analysis conducted by French & Raven[13] nearly forty years ago. This analysis suggested that there were five principal sources, or bases, of power — coercive power, reward power, legitimate power, expert power and referent (charismatic) power. Briefly these can be summarised as follows:

    ❑ *coercive power* — this is the crudest form of power, which uses threats and punishment to achieve its ends; examples include (1) the threat of sanctions against suppliers, if they do not conform to a particular policy, (2) the threat of dismissals for non-cooperating staff, and (3) physical demonstrations such as mass walk-outs by employees.

    ❑ *reward power* — this is the use of rewards to influence people's compliance; to be effective the rewards must be desired by the target group; an example would be where a firm offered financial inducements to a group under pressure in order to maintain their commitment to the task, but failed in this because the group valued time off more highly than extra monetary reward.

    ❑ *legitimate power* — this is what is generally known as 'authority', ie power conferred on an individual by the organisation; it implies the power to act as well as power over resources, and is invariably limited in some way; this is the form of power referred to by Weber in his use of the concept of 'rational-legal authority' (see Chapter 2, paras 32-35)

    ❑ *expert power* — this is the power that comes from possessing specialised knowledge and skills; Handy (1993)[14] describes this as

    '...for many, the least obnoxious of the sources of power. In a meritocratic tradition people do not resent being influenced by those whom they regard as the experts.'

    Expert power is dependent on the expertise being recognised by those concerned, thus 'credibility' is vital otherwise noone will take any notice!

    ❑ *referent power* — this is what is generally known as personal power, or charisma; the individual's power comes from the high regard he or she is held in by others; should that regard falter, or wane, then this form of power vanishes; thus, referent power is often employed in conjunction with other power sources.

32. Other sources of power include knowledge (as information) and personal contacts and alliances. Legitimate power as 'authority' usually ensures that an individual has access to information and internal contacts (other 'linking pins', advisers etc) as well as permitting some use of reward power. Thus legitimate power carries with it elements of other sources. This situation enables individuals to continue in their post even when

some of their power to influence is weakened by the countervailing power of others. By comparison, a charismatic leader relying principally on referent power may one day find that his power base has become eroded and he disappears from the scene due to the lack of supporting sources of power. This frequently happens to informal leaders, whose names may have gone down in history, for example, for some strike they led against the employers, yet who slipped into early anonymity once the strike was over.

33. Power, therefore is not the same as leadership, nor is it the same as authority. In one sense it is larger than both, and in another it is the servant of both. In the first sense it has a free-ranging role, which is not subject either to authority or to responsibility, and it can be used to counter the power of others. In the second sense, it acts as the motive force for leadership and authority, and has other useful characteristics, as Morgan (1986)[15] points out *'Power is the medium through which conflicts of interest are ultimately resolved. Power influences who gets what, when and how.'* Judging by the work of McClleland(1961)[16], as mentioned in Chapter 7 para 20, the need for power is an important motivator for managers. Here the power refers especially to the power to control events and resources. Finally, it has to be said that neither is power the same as responsibility, which is the accountability (and usually the formal accountability) that each individual has for his or her job in the organisation. Responsibility is always owed to another, whereas power can be exerted in its own right, unless curtailed by situational forces, such as limits of authority, others' dependence on rewards etc.

34. There is currently much interest in the concept of 'empowerment' in the workplace. Clutterbuck (1994)[17] offers several definitions, such as: (1)

> '...finding new ways to concentrate power in the hands of the people who need it most to get the job done — putting authority, responsibility, resources and rights at the most appropriate level for the task...'

and (2)

> '...the controlled transfer of power from management to employee in the long-term interest of the business as a whole.'

Peters[18] (1988), in typically bold fashion describes it as follows:

> 'Empowering really boils down to 'taking seriously'. No one denies where the answers are: on the firing line. How do we get people to come forth and give the answers, to take risks by trying new things....?'

His answers to the question are (1) by listening to staff, (2) by deferring to the front line, (3) by delegating — *'the sine qua non of empowerment'*, and (4) by installing a 'horizontal' style of management.

35. A more academic view of empowerment is provided by Thomas & Velthouse (1990)[19], who see it as a process that increases an employee's intrinsic motivation (ie those things that are valued in their own right by that individual). They suggest that management's contribution to this kind of empowerment is to:

   1. enhance the *impact* of employees' jobs
   2. develop employees' *competence* at a range of tasks
   3. enhance the perceived *meaningfulness* of the job for each employee
   4. extend the employee's *choice* in determining how to perform the job

   These suggestions seem to reside more in the field of 'job enrichment' (see Chapter 15 below) than empowerment, which is primarily about increasing an individual's discretion to act. Nevertheless, by focussing on impact and choice, in particular, there is scope for a genuine transfer of power from management to individual employees.

36. Power in organisations mostly comes from the top down in the forms of legitimate power (authority), reward power and expert power. As mentioned several times earlier, power such as this is invariably limited in some way. This enables those handing down the power to retain an element of control over the way it is employed, otherwise, it could be argued, anarchy and confusion would prevail. One of the problems associated with the issue of 'empowering' people at work is precisely the problem of control. Even the enthusiastic Peters (op. cit) realises that in order to empower people down the line, managers have got to have a clear sense of vision and a strong nerve to 'really let go'.

37. Therefore, if organisations want to empower their staff, they have first to ensure that their management are people with a clear sense of direction and commitment, who possess and expect high standards of performance, and who are prepared to accept the risks that failure of their staff might bring. Over time a culture of empowerment might develop, in which power might become a *'bottom-up'* phenomenon instead of *'top-down'* as at present. The Japanese experience with the use of Quality Circles has shown that it is possible over time to generate a culture of shop-floor decision-making that is effective, reliable and 'empowering'. (Note: Quality Circles are shop-floor teams charged with discussing, *and implementing*, improvements in quality, productivity and safety — see Cole,1993, p.285)[20]. When all is said and done, 'empowerment' is all about making the best use of the organisation's investment in people.

References

1. Zaleznik,A. (1986), *'Excerpts from 'Managers and Leaders: Are They Different?''* in Harvard Business Review, May/ June 1986

2. Drummond, H. (1992), *Power - Creating it,* Using it, BCA/ Kogan Page

3. Likert,R. (1961), *New Patterns of Management,* McGraw-Hill

4. McGregor, D. (1960), *The Human Side of Enterprise,* McGraw-Hill

5. Stogdill,R & Coons, A. (1957), *Leader Behaviour: Its Description and Measurement, Research Monograph No. 88,* Ohio State University

6. *Blake, R. & Mouton, J. (1985), The Managerial Grid III, Gulf Publishing* (Previously published in 1964 as The Managerial Grid, Gulf Publishing)

7. Reddin, W. (1970), *Managerial Effectivenesss,* McGraw-Hill

8. Fiedler, F.E. (1967), *A Theory of Leadership Effectiveness,* McGraw-Hill

9. Adair, J. (1968), *Training for Leadership,* Gower Publishing

10. Adair, J. (1983), *Effective Leadership,* Gower Publishing

11. Tannenbaum, R. & Schmidt, W. (1958), *'How to choose a leadership pattern',* in Harvard Business Review,Mar/Apr.

12. Tannenbaum, R. & Schmidt, W. (1973), *'How to choose a leadership pattern - Retrospective Commentary',* in Harvard Business Review, May/Jun

13. French,J. & Raven,B. (1958), *'The bases of social power'* in Cartwright,D. (ed) *'Studies in Social Power',* Institute for Social Research

14. Handy, C. (1993), *Understanding Organizations,* Penguin Business

15. Morgan, G. (1986), *Images of Organization,* Sage Publications

16. McClleland, D. (1961), *The Achieving Society,* Van Nostrand

17. Clutterbuck, D. (1994), *The Power of Empowerment,* BCA/ Kogan Page

18. Peters, T. (1988), *Thriving on Chaos,* MacMillan

19. Thomas, K.W. & Velthouse, B.A. (1990), *'Cognitive Elements of Empowerment: An 'Interpretive' Model of Intrinsic Task Motivation',* in Academy of Management Review,October 1990

20. Cole, *G. A. (1993), Management: Theory and Practice (4th edn),* D P Publications

Questions for reflection/discussion

1. In what ways can the *external* environment of a group affect the successful fulfilment of the leader's role?

2. To what extent is a leader dependent on the members of his/her group, and what factors increase or decrease this dependency?

3. What might group members legitimately expect from their leader in order to play a full part in the group's activities?

4. Why do you think *academics* are less enthusiastic than *practitioners* about studying leadership from the point of view of leadership style?

5. Explain the differences between the following concepts:

   a) power b) authority c) responsibility

6. What forms of power are likely to be available to an appointed leader in a large organisation?

7. How far might the process of 'empowering' employees lead to role conflict for managers?

12 Stress and conflict in organisations

Introduction

1. Given the complex nature of organisations, it is not surprising that the people who work in them are subject to a range of conflicting pressures, some of which will lead to individual stress. This chapter looks at the nature of stress and its causes, and identifies some of the actions that can be taken to reduce or avoid stress both by individuals and by their organisation. The chapter also includes some discussion of the nature of conflict in organisations.

The nature of stress

2. The nature of stress is graphically described by de Board (1978)[1] as follows:

    'Stress is a condition in which the body reacts to danger in the sameway as our hunting ancestors, but spread over a long period.....Whenman the hunter had fled from a bear or fought for his life, he slept in order to recover from the effects of his body's internal action. In a stress situation today, people are likely to feel continually tired, because they are never able to fully recover from the effects of their bodies' internal activity.'

    He comments that the increased heartbeat, tensed muscles and extra adrenalin in the bloodstream that were all part of early Man's reaction to danger were biologically directed towards two immediate options of 'fight or flight'. In our modern situation, people face dangers that are not only of a subtler kind, but where neither of the two primitive options are available in any realistic sense. Worse still for modern man is the fact that stressful situations are likely to continue over weeks and months and not just for a few intense moments. If individuals' reactions continue at the primitive hunter level over these extended periods of time, then they are going to develop chronic side-effects from them. Typical illnesses known to have links with stress include coronary heart disease, high blood pressure, gastric ulcers, back pain and clinical depression.

3. Marshall & Cooper (1981)[2] point out that one reason why executives often do not want to do anything about stress in their organisations is because

they see it albeit mistakenly, as something beneficial. The authors argue that this is partly due to terminology, and emphasise that 'stress' is a different phenomenon from 'pressure', whereas many managers draw no such distinction. They comment as follows:

'If....we distinguish between everyday pressures and stress, where individuals experiencing the latter are unable to cope and anxious, suffer symptoms of physical and mental ill-health, then the concept of stress becomes much less appealing!' (p.xii)

Stress, therefore, is something more than mere pressure. It carries strong overtones of the breakdown of normal human performance. In an earlier work, Cooper & Marshall (1978)[3], the same two authors concluded that

'stress is essentially individually defined and must be understood with reference to characteristics of both the ...individual and his environment, as it is the outcome of the two.' (p.4)

4. The argument goes as follows: (a) the external pressures on individuals vary substantially, (b) individuals' also differ substantially (eg phlegmatic personality types are much more likely to react calmly in a range of situations than neurotic types); therefore, (c) individuals' reactions to pressure (the 'stress reaction') will also differ, leading in some circumstances to the ability to cope, and in other circumstances to long-term ill-effects. As Figure 12.1 indicates, stress in a limited form, ie as 'pressure' can provide a positive spur to performance. However, when stress increases (ie 'real stress') beyond a certain point the individual is likely to find it difficult to cope with, and thus performance is adversely affected.

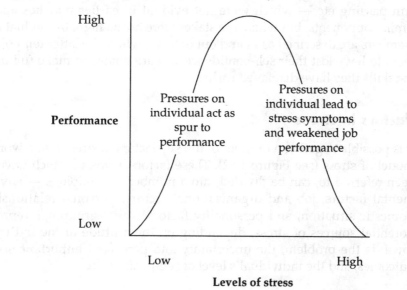

The logic of the diagram is that at lower levels of stress an individual functions perfectly capably, even better than under normal conditions, but at higher levels the individual begins to develop stress symptoms and performance declines over time.

5. Most of the modern discussion about stress focuses on the latter situation, ie where a person is unable to cope and develops dysfunctional behaviour leading to substantially-reduced performance at work. Most researchers now acknowledge that stress is a personal, subjective reaction to pressure. It depends on an individual's *perception* both of the scale of the problem and their own ability to cope with it. So, where an individual perceives that (1) the problem is manageable, and (2) is confident in his or her ability to handle the problem, then the symptoms of stress are unlikely to appear, however much pressure is exerted by the problem. However, if the same individual perceives the problem as difficult to manage, and is lacking self-confidence in their ability to handle it, then stress will result.

6. A further factor in stress, in addition to personal perceptions of the problem and of self, is that the possible outcomes (eg of relative success or failure) are seen as both uncertain and important. Stress is unlikely where the outcome is not considered to be important to the individual. However, where the outcome is seen as important (eg clinching a major sale, producing a vital report, or just being able to 'please the boss'), then stress is more likely, and if the outcome itself is seen as uncertain, then stress is definitely more likely. The sporting world often provides us with examples of stress, as when a team meets well-matched opponents in a World Cup match, and displays evidence of tension and anxiety — mistakes, uncertain passing etc — which were not evident in earlier matches against similar opponents, but where the stakes were not so high. Individual team members are described as in and out of form, where the latter temporarily seem to have lost their self-confidence and are unable to make full use of the skills they have displayed earlier.

Key factors in stress

7. It is possible to gather a number of the key factors in stress into a working model of stress (see Figure 12.2). These factors, some of which have just been referred to, can be divided into a number of groupings — environmental factors, job and organisational factors, personal relationships, domestic situation, and personality factors. These groupings represent potential sources of stress, depending on the attitude of the individual towards the problem, the uncertainty and perceived importance of the outcomes, and the individual's level of self-confidence.

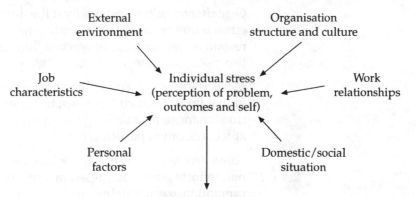

8. Important examples of specific factors that have been found to contribute to stress are set out below under each of the main groupings illustrated in Fig. 12.2 above.

Sources	**Examples of Factors**
1 *External environment*	*Economic situation* for the industry (especially where the industry is in decline and redundancies are common-place)
	Competitive situation for the organisation (eg uncertain market position may lead to withdrawal/ vulnerability to take-over/ possible retrenchment of the business)
	Arrival of new technology (may lead to reduction in jobs and/ or skill requirements; or pressure to acquire new knowledge and skills)
	Political changes may affect organisations vulnerable to political influence (eg state-owned businesses, key industries in energy, military equipment etc)
2 *Organisational factors*	*Organisation structure* (especially where the pattern of jobs, and the attendant rules and regulations, constrain the individual's range of choices in how to do the job)
	Communication system (where this does not facilitate communication with colleagues)

Organisation culture (especially if the dominant ethos is one of internal competition for resources, rewards etc, or where a 'hire and fire' policy operates)

Management style (especially where the individual finds it difficult to adapt to his superiors' management style eg because it is too autocratic or too participative)

Career development (especially where individuals' efforts are unrecognised in terms of promotion, extra training etc)

3 *Job characteristics*   *Physical conditions* (where these are adverse)

Intrinsic job demands (ie where the nature of the tasksrequire repetition, or offer insufficient challenge, or are simply too excessive for one person)

Degree of autonomy (where this is insufficient to meet either the demands of the job and/ or the expectations of the job-holder)

Role conflict (ie where the organisation's expectations of the role either (1) lead to confusion with related roles, or (2) do not meet the job-holder's expectations)

Contractual terms (especially where these provide for rewards on a high-performance basis eg meeting targets, production quotas etc, or where the rewards are seen as poor in relation to the demands of the job)

4 *Work relationships*   *Superiors* — especially where individuals fail to achieve a reasonable working relationship with their immediate superior

Colleagues — an inability to get on reasonable terms with fellow team-members or colleagues from other sections can be source of considerable unhappiness; women, in particular, may suffer from male patronage or sexual harassment (Davidson & Cooper,1983)[4]

Own staff — many people appointed to their leadership role in the organisation find it stressful to deal with the demands of their own staff

Customers/ suppliers/ other outside people — these stakeholders can be a source of stress eg especially for those dealing with customer complaints all day long

5 *Domestic situation*

Home life — upheavals at home due to family illness, care of elderly parents, unhappy marriage, debt problems etc are problems that can overflow into the workplace and adversely affect an individual's performance and attitude

Outside social life — individuals with a rich social life (eg active in Rotary etc) may find that work and leisure clash, especially if their organisation expects them to work unsocial hours or to be available at short notice.

6 *Personal factors*

Individual perception of role/ job etc — as noted above, the individual's perceptions of tasks etc and their difficulty is a key factor in the stress formula

Personality type — research suggests that certain types (eg Type A personalities) are much more vulnerable to stress symptoms than others (eg Type B)

Ability to adapt to change — adaptable individuals are less prone to stress than those who are inflexible

Motivation — ie where a person is deeply committed to his or her work, they are more likely to find ways of coping with potentially stressful situations than someone with a low commitment

Tolerance for ambiguity — where an individual can tolerate uncertainty (eg role/ task ambiguity), stress is less likely

9. Given that stress is essentially related to personality and personal perceptions, the references above to Type A and Type B personalities is important. Friedman & Rosenman (1974)[5] identified the Type A personality in their researches into coronary patients. Type A's are the people who were identified as at great risk of heart disease. They are characterised by excessive competitiveness, a chronic sense of urgency of time, a constant search for achievement, and behaviour that tends to be aggressive, impatient and restless. Such personalities are constantly engaged in activity and express

guilt feelings if they try to relax. Type B personalities have none of these characteristics, are altogether calmer and more relaxed. Furnham (1992)[6], reviewing a range of studies into workplace studies of stress, comments that American studies point to a situation where

> '...the workplace for men rewards Type A behaviour which leads to considerable stress. The Type A person is a workaholic with an exaggerated success ethic.' (p.271)

The symptoms of stress

10. Symptoms of stress are typically analysed under three headings — physiological, psychological and behavioural. Common symptoms are as follows:

Physiological — in addition to the short-term reactions of increased heart beat, tensed muscles and extra adrenalin secretion mentioned earlier as a human being's instinctive reaction to danger, the chronic (ie longer term) effects of stress are associated with such unhealthy conditions as coronary heart disease, high blood pressure, indigestion, gastric ulcers, back pain and even cancer. Stress is also likely to be manifested in less serious infections, allergies and physical disorders.

Psychological — in chronic situations the psychological symptoms of stress tend to become manifest in anxiety states (phobias, obsessions etc) and depression. In less serious cases, stress emerges in the form of tension, irritability, boredom and job dissatisfaction.

Behavioural — ultimately the physiological and psychological symptoms lead to generalised changes in behaviour such as loss of appetite, increased cigarette smoking and alcohol consumption, and sleeplessness. In the workplace behaviour may take the form of increased absences (flight), aggression towards colleagues (fight), committing more errors than normal and taking longer over tasks. In utterly intolerable conditions individuals may leave the organisation and seek work elsewhere or sink into despair at home. The loss to the community resulting from stress-related conditions is estimated to be substantial.

Coping with stress

11. Strategies for coping with stress can best be analysed under two headings — personal strategies and organisational strategies. The former include actions that individuals can take at work and outside of work to increase their ability to cope with sustained pressure and thus avoid the symptoms of stress. The latter include a number of organisational steps that can be taken to reduce the likelihood of stress due to structural and style problems.

Personal coping strategies

12. In their study of women managers, Davidson and Cooper (op. cit) asked their respondents to give their answers to a number of questions relating to 'positive coping strategies' . These included such questions as 'How often do you use the following to relax?' on a 1 (Never) — 5 (Always) scale:

    ❑ relaxation techniques?

    ❑ exercise?

    ❑ talking to someone you know?

    ❑ using humour?

    ❑ leaving the work area?

    These questions provide some clues as to the sort of actions at a physiological and psychological level that individuals themselves can take to reduce the effects of stress in their lives. However, the responses implied by these particular questions are more concerned with external aspects of stress. What is especially important in becoming more stress-free is to examine one's own attitudes towards personal strengths and weaknesses, and this is more a matter of assertiveness and personal planning.

13. Back & Back (1994)[7], on the topic of assertiveness at work (see earlier remarks in Chapter 10 para 21 above), draw attention to what they describe as people's 'faulty thinking' in contributing to stressful situations. Such thinking, they argue, is *'irrational, not always honest, and [an] often inaccurate reflection of the situation.'* (p.79) Their answer is for individuals to challenge their faulty thinking processes, as the following example illustrates:

Faulty thinking process	Flaw	Challenge
I'll get sucked into lots of arguments that I will lose.	Exaggeration and assumption	'Lots' or only some arguments? Will you necessarily lose them?
That would undermine my position.........	Illogical	Is this probable or merely possible?
I'll really show them up if they try to catch me out	Relinquishing control of yourself	Or could you respond assertively if you chose to?' (p.80)

14. A good deal of stress could be avoided if people paid more attention to their own rights. Assertiveness, as noted earlier (Chapter 10) is a question of standing up for your own rights, but in a way that does not violate another person's rights. Assertiveness is also concerned with expressing (ie making known) personal wants, feelings and opinions in honest and appropriate ways. This latter point is important because, if other people do not know how we are feeling about a particular action, or decision, made on our behalf, how can they appreciate our problem and how can they begin to address it? Stress, according to Back & Back (op. cit), will result

'....if there is a continuing conflict between what you want or would like and what is actually happening to you.' (p.141)

The addition of the word conflict to the stress equation is significant. Stress is not just about excessive pressures and individual self-image, but also about personal conflicts of interest. Thus, a young and ambitious manager with a young family and a wife at home is likely to find a conflict of interests occurring if he is frequently asked to be away on business overnight and at weekends. To take another example, if an individual is in a highly-paid job, in a comfortable office and with a congenial boss, but is offered little opportunity to use his or her professional skills and knowledge, there will undoubtedly be a conflict of feelings about the job sooner or later.

15. What sort of rights should a person be able to assert at work? Clearly, there are statutory rights to do with conditions of employment. There are rights arising from the organisation's policies (eg flexible working hours, appropriate training etc). These are written rights, which are easy to identify and defend, if necessary. Much stress, however, is caused by the individual's failure to obtain unwritten 'rights', or 'assertive rights' as they are often called. At work, such rights could include the following (see Figure 12.3):

General rights	❑ to be treated with respect as a person
	❑ to be permitted to express personal opinions and ideas
	❑ to be given a fair hearing in a discussion or argument
	❑ to be permitted to make mistakes (eg Peters,1988[8], 'supporting fast failures')
Job-related rights	❑ to be clear about what is expected of me
	❑ to be given sufficient resources (including authority) to undertake the job satisfactorily
	❑ to be able to do the job in my own way, subject to necessary constraints and meeting targets
	❑ to be consulted about matters affecting my job and of my team, where appropriate
	❑ to make mistakes occasionally

Figure 12.3   *Assertive rights at work*

16. Once a person has made satisfactory headway in negotiating their assertive rights, then they can employ other ways of coping with stress at a personal level, such as time management and personal planning. In these

respects, Atkinson (1988)[9] suggests several ways of avoiding stress at work, which can be summarised as follows:

> ❑ decide on your priorities and get agreement for them
> ❑ be assertive (eg by expressing your state of overwork and seeking assistance)
> ❑ be aware of yourself (especially in terms of your Type A or B characteristics) and act accordingly to reduce stress
> ❑ do not procrastinate, but act now
> ❑ examine your deadlines and inform others if you think you are going to be late
> ❑ take a step by step approach to big tasks — do not try to do everything at once
> ❑ talk to others about your problems
> ❑ do not take yourself too seriously
> ❑ use time management techniques to deal with problems of meetings, paperwork, interruptions etc
> ❑ take up a sport or hobby

17. The conclusions that can be drawn from the above coping strategies are that individuals can help themselves significantly to avoid, or at least reduce, stress at work by asserting their personal and job-related rights, by planning their priorities and use of time, and by taking appropriate steps to relax and take exercise.

Organisational strategies for handling stress

18. When an organisation's employees suffer from stress, the results are likely to take the following forms:

> ❑ high levels of absenteeism
> ❑ lower productivity and missed targets
> ❑ increased accident and error rates
> ❑ increased number of internal conflicts
> ❑ excessive staff turnover

Assuming that these overt manifestations of stress are merely the tip of an iceberg, then it is likely that the organisation is going to be faced with a range of subsidiary symptoms indicating dissatisfaction with work.

Overall, the costs to the organisation are likely to be substantial. It is, therefore, in the interests of the senior management to set about reducing the overall levels of stress for individuals so that the organisation as a whole can function properly. What steps can organisations take?

19. The steps they can take to reduce the experience of stress among their work-force can be considered under two main headings — (1) stress *avoidance* measures, and (2) stress *reduction* measures. The former are aimed at removing the potential for stressful situations, while the latter are aimed at containing stress within reasonable bounds when it does occur. Both sets of measures are implemented at an organisational rather than individual level.

Stress avoidance by organisations

20. It was suggested earlier (Figure 12.2) that among the sources of stress for individuals are their job characteristics, work relationships, organisation structure and the organisation's culture. Given that a certain amount of pressure (Fig. 12.1) can have a positive effect on employee performance, what can organisations do to ensure that pressure does not lead to stress? It is a difficult balance for a healthy, active organisation to achieve. However, there are certain steps that can be taken to provide the necessary incentives for employees without building up chronic stress. These can be summarised as follows:

Source of Stress	Avoidance Counter-measures
1 *Job characteristics*	*Design jobs* to permit use of skill and discretion by job-holder; incorporate sufficient task variety and challenge to maintain employee interest; ensure that tasks are sufficiently related to form a coherent job; provide mechanism for giving early feedback on performance.
	Design work so as to allow the exercise of responsibility by the job-holders, provide sufficient authority to enable job-holders to carry out their responsibilities adequately, allow job-holders to share in decisions that affect their work, allow for learning opportunities through work; and ensure clear work goals and targets that do not conflict with those set for others.
2 *Work relationships*	*Superiors* can develop participative management styles that allow for discussion of issues, where appropriate, and real delegation of authority; leaders pay attention to individual's

needs as well as those of the task and the group; leaders required to deal immediately with cases of bullying, sexual harassment, racist behaviour etc.

Colleagues/workmates accept fellow team-members in a cooperative spirit; team-members support each other; individuals valued for their role.

Own staff (ie for managers and supervisors) — adequate training in handling staff is provided; immediate superiors able to provide diplomatic support where necessary; implementation of proper disciplinary procedures to cater for uncooperative or disruptive employees.

3 *Organisation structure*

Hierarchy of jobs is reduced to the minimum (ie flatter structure) to permit wide use of skill, discretion and authority.

Communication systems are designed to encourage communication *between* departments/ sections as well as vertically through the management chain; grievance procedures are rapid and discreet; positive feedback is encouraged (eg by job results, staff appraisal etc).

Decision-making processes in the organisation are delegated as far as is reasonable down the organisation; people at every level are able to share in decisions affecting (a) their work and (b) their future prospects; results of decisions affecting employees are notified as soon as possible.

4 *Organisation culture*

Attitudes towards employees are positive, even when customers are regarded as the 'number one priority'; where attention to product/ service quality is paramount, this should reflect itself in respect for employees' knowledge, skills and contribution; reasonable risk-taking is encouraged, and mistakes seen as learning opportunities rather than grounds for criticism; employees are regarded as the organisation's best asset in meeting the wants and demands of customers and other external

stakeholders; training, development and counselling opportunities are available for every
employee; conditions of employment (eg
salaries, wages, holiday arrangements, shift-
working) are fair.

Stress reduction in organisations

21. Despite all the actions that might be taken to prevent stress in the first
place, it is inevitable that some individuals will experience stress from time
to time. This is because individuals' stress levels are determined by such a
wide variety of factors in their personal make-up, their work environment
and their social and domestic lives. Moss Kanter (1989)[10], in reviewing the
pace of life in the modern American workplace, concludes that there are
three common explanations why some people work such long hours.
These can be summarised as follows:

   ❐ they are addicted to work — they are 'workaholics' unable to let go of
   work

   ❐ organisations make greedy demands on individuals, forcing them to
   subordinate their lives to its demands

   ❐ some people like to put up a good show at work by 'working' long
   hours, even though in many cases the extra time is totally unproductive

   Moss Kanter does not entirely agree with these conclusions, commenting
   that working longer is due to changes taking place in what she calls 'post-
   entrepreneurial workplaces'. Such changes include restructuring leading
   to job losses and thus a sense of insecurity among employees, who work
   hard to keep their jobs. Leaner organisations tend also to be meaner, thus
   fewer people are required to do the same level of work as before. The new
   workplace also increases the challenge *'When work is more exciting, people
   want to do it longer'*. Thus the products of the Peters age, thriving on chaos,
   are under great pressure to work harder and longer.

22. Such a work environment inevitably means that some individuals will
crack up under the pressures, moving from the left hand segment into the
right hand segment of Figure 12.1 above. Stress reduction facilities can
help move them back into the healthier left-hand element. Moss Kanter
suggests three ways in which workloads can become less burdensome:

   ❐ when authority is delegated along with responsibility

   ❐ when the number of simultaneous changes are minimised

   ❐ when simplicity is observed over complexity

The first item has already been referred to above in the stress avoidance measures. The other two could form part of a response to stress in individual cases by reducing (1) the number of changes expected of any one individual or team, and (2) the procedural and other complexities associated with the tasks to be achieved.

23. As noted above, in the discussion on assertiveness, a key reduction factor in stress is the ability to express one's feelings and anxieties to someone else. If the organisation has (a) provided adequate communication channels, and (b) appropriate leadership training, then the first person a stressed individual should be able to talk to is his or her boss. Where supportive relationships *within* work groups is encouraged it need not go as far as the boss, since colleagues will be able to supply the necessary listening skills and task/ role flexibility to ease the strain from any one individual. Talking to one's spouse or partner may also help to offset the burden of stress, and for those who believe in the power of prayer, there is another outlet which may help to retain the individual's sense of proportion about their perceived problems.

24. However, it is becoming increasingly common nowadays for organisations to provide professional counselling facilities for employees. According to the Institute of Personnel & Development, in a Statement on Counselling in the Workplace (1992)[11], counselling at work is

> 'where one individual uses a set of techniques or skills to help another individual take responsibility for and to manage their own decision-making whether it is work-related or personal.'

The individual here is either a professional counsellor or a manager trained in counselling techniques. The IPD statement notes that colleagues whilst being sympathetic may unwittingly make quite unhelpful suggestions to the person under stress. Therefore trained helpers are required, and since most managers do not possess either the talent or the training for counselling, the most they can be expected to contribute is an awareness of when counselling may be appropriate for an employee.

25. Egan (1990)[12] describes counsellors as 'skilled helpers' who are effective

> '...to the degree that their clients [eg a person under stress], through client-helper interactions, are in a better position to manage their problem situations and/or develop the unused resources and opportunities of their lives more effectively.'

The implication that individuals have within themselves the potential to overcome their problems is significant, for counselling can enable people to find their personal reserves, identify external opportunities and then deploy both to work successfully through stressful situations.

26. The counselling process is one in which the counsellor assists the client to:

1. identify what is their problem (which may not necessarily be just what appears on the surface of a situation)

2. agree what they want ideally to achieve, or what they would prefer

3. consider alternative ways by which the desired outcomes might be achieved

Of course, the very opportunity of talking about a problem with someone who is prepared to listen without making judgements or telling them what they ought to do, is a powerful aid in its own right. Some organisations employ counsellors within their organisation. Some employ external specialists who operate what are known as Employee Assistance Programmes, which can offer free telephone counselling to employees at any time of the day or night (eg rather like the Samaritans), or provide opportunities for face-to-face interviews off-site. In each case complete confidentiality is maintained, although the number of cases of help sought and the time spent is recorded for the purposes of charging the employing organisation.

27. A few organisations also provide assertiveness training, relaxation classes and other helpful activities such as team-building, all of which can contribute to a lessening of stress, especially in organisations that operate in a hectic environment. It is often in an employer's interests to provide services that can off-set the symptoms of stress, whilst maintaining a high-pressure environment and culture. Sports and social facilities are less common nowadays, since they tend to be associated with paternalistic attitudes of earlier years, but a few organisations still provide them. If fitness and exercise can play a part in reducing stress in individuals then such facilities may represent a useful additional means of enabling some employees to cope better with pressure in the workplace.

28. The main strategies for avoiding or reducing stress can now be summarised. As Figure 12.4 illustrates, these can be prioritised as follows:

❐ design work around individuals, so far as is reasonably practicable (see Chapter 15 below)

❐ ensure adequate job resources, especially authority and/ or discretion

❐ minimise the amount of bureaucracy (rules, procedures etc)

❐ provide adequate communication mechanisms, especially within the individual's role-set (see Chapter 9 para 26 above)

❐ ensure adequate rest periods during the working day, and insist on employees taking their holidays

❐ provide counselling facilities as back-up where needed

❐ provide appropriate training opportunities, especially in skill updating, assertiveness, and team-building etc

There is nothing outstanding about such measures, which are likely to be found in any well-managed organisation that sees its employees as its biggest single investment as well as one of its principal stakeholders.

29. Figure 12.4 shows the immediate, inner arc, of conditions as consisting of the design of the job together with resourcing and appropriate basic conditions of employment (especially rest periods and holidays). The middle arc provides for the administrative and organisational structure, whilst the outer arc provides for counselling and training, which only make sense if the other two sets of conditions are in place. The effect of implementing all these conditions is to substantially reduce the prospect of stress among the workforce.

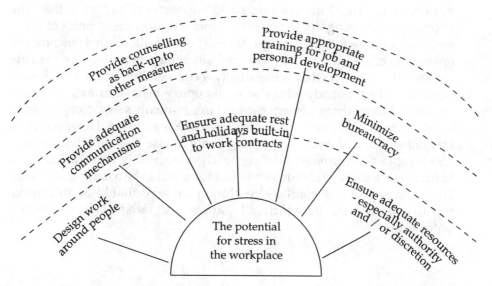

Figure 12.4   *Relieving individual stress at work*

Conflict in organisations

30. Conflict is more than just mere disagreement based on differing views and opinions. It is more than just healthy competition. There is something negative about the term 'conflict', which suggests that it is unproductive at least and possibly even destructive. And yet, as Handy (1993)[13] points out

> 'Paradoxically, differences are essential to change. If there were no urge to compete and no need for disagreement the organisation would be either in a state of apathy or complacency....' (p. 313).

Where then does one draw the lines between disagreement, competition and conflict? As Figure 12.5 suggests, the basis of conflict lies in disagreement, but that the degree of disagreement can vary from milder to stronger forms, each provoking different behaviour and having different outcomes. For our purposes in this chapter, the following working definition of conflict is proposed:

> *Conflict is a condition that arises whenever the perceived interests of an individual or a group clash with those of another individual or group in such a way that strong emotions are aroused and compromise is not considered to be an option. Conflict, when managed effectively, can contribute to organisational effectiveness, but when mishandled can give rise to counter-productive behaviour, in which both sides lose.*

31. The model illustrated in Figure 12.5 simplifies the subtle processes of disagreement and conflict in order to show the major options that are available if one goes down one route rather than the other. Outright conflict can produce extremely destructive behaviour, equivalent to organisational warfare, but 'considered disagreement' suggests that the opposing sides recognise the positive aspects of the others' point of view, and a willingness to seek a compromise. The main alternative outcomes of open conflict are either (1) a 'win-lose' situation where the stronger side comes out on top in what is essentially a competition, or (2) a 'lose-lose' situation, where nobody wins due to disruptive behaviour or a stalemate situation. Milder disagreement can lead to a mutually satisfactory solution — a 'win-win' situation — in which everyone is satisfied. However, even this milder form of conflict can bring about a 'lose-lose' situation, where, for example, a compromise has been reached too readily, and what appears at first to be a successful outcome in fact turns out to be a failure. In overall terms the aim of any conflict—resolution strategy should be to achieve positive outcomes, in which all parties are satisfied (ie 'win-win' outcomes).

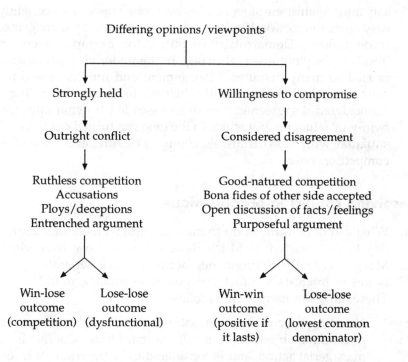

Differing opinions/viewpoints

Strongly held   Willingness to compromise

Outright conflict   Considered disagreement

Ruthless competition   Good-natured competition
Accusations   Bona fides of other side accepted
Ploys/deceptions   Open discussion of facts/feelings
Entrenched argument   Purposeful argument

Win-lose   Lose-lose   Win-win   Lose-lose
outcome   outcome   outcome   outcome
(competition) (dysfunctional)   (positive if (lowest common
                                 it lasts)   denominator)

Figure 12.5   *A simplified conflict model for organisations*

32. As Figure 12.5 indicates, outright conflict can be totally uncompromising with behaviour ranging from ruthless competition to entrenched argument with accusations and deception thrown into the behavioural mix. The inevitable outcome is that either one side will win, or there will be a stalemate situation in which both sides will lose. The UK's industrial relations history in the post-war years provides an example of considerable inter-necine strife, in which powerful trade unions and uncertain managements were locked in battle for the control of the workplace. Demarcation disputes, strikes, overtime bans and other trade union-led actions eventually brought a number of proud British industries to their knees - shipbuilding, coal-mining and motor vehicle manufacture were among the victims of lose-lose outcomes, in which neither side would budge from their entrenched positions. Some industries never recovered their former trading position, although others (eg motor vehicles) have re-emerged as powerful business sectors in a re-shaped economy. However, it is important to ask why collective trade union power was able to inflict so much damage on major British companies, instead of acting as a spur to enhanced working conditions and labour productivity.

33. There are several reasons for what happened, including the high demand for labour in the economy, managerial ineffectiveness at the highest level, lack of attention to quality and reliability, inadequate control of costs, excessive attention to status levels, and few laws to restrict trade union

sanctions against employers. However, one reason was certainly the too-easy compromises on key issues that were made by managements to the trade unions. Demarcation disputes, for example, were frequently 'resolved' without any real change in the underlying job inflexibility that caused so many disputes. Management and unions agreed to cosmetic changes, which subsequently helped to bring down the industry. 'Considered disagreement' in these cases led to what appeared to be a 'win-win' situation, but which in the long run turned out to be a 'lose-lose' situation, with mass dismissals, company closures and a loss of business to competitors overseas.

Resolving conflict in organisations

34. What can organisations do to manage disagreement and conflict in their day-to-day existence? Much depends upon how they view conflict. Morgan (1986)[14] distinguishes between three separate approaches to issues of interests, conflict and power — unitary, pluralist and radical. These three alternatives are as follows:

   1. *Unitary perspective* — organisation seen as collaborating in the pursuit of common objectives as *'a well-integrated team.'* Conflict is avoided by managerial action, and is considered to be the result of troublemakers when it does occur. Power in its raw sense in disregarded in favour of authority and leadership in achieving common goals.

   2. *Pluralist perspective* — organisation seen as a loose coalition of a range of different interest groups. Conflict is seen as *'...an inherent and in-eradicable characteristic of organizational affairs...'*, and which has positive aspects for the organisation. Power is regarded as the crucial medium by which conflicts of interest are both alleviated and solved.

   3. *Radical perspective* — the organisation is seen as composed of opposing forces of a 'class' nature. Conflict is regarded as inevitable as part of social changes in the class structure, and power is seen as important but reflective of divisions in society (eg as illustrated in the previous paragraph).

35. The first two perspectives are the most important for our present discussion, since most organisations display characteristics either of the unitary or of the pluralist approach in the way they are managed. Paternalistic, family-oriented businesses, for example, tend to be unitary organisations, whereas competitive firms seeking excellence in all aspects of their business strategy are more likely to take a pluralist perspective. The use of power is an important factor in handling conflict, according to Morgan, who considers that power *'is the medium through which conflicts of interest are ultimately resolved.'* In unitary organisations power is exercised primarily through the authority granted to individuals through the chain of

command. In exercising their authority managers will stick to the organisation's rules and procedures — in cricketing terms, they play a straight bat. By comparison, pluralist managers tend to be good at 'playing politics', ie they use power for their own ends, both proactive and defensive. Thus they may seek to include combatting staleness, stimulating innovation and releasing emotional pressure among their power uses, as well as ensuring that they 'win' appropriate resources when in competition with others.

36. A key problem for such pluralist managers, suggests Morgan, is

> '..to find ways of maintaining just the right level of conflict......too much conflict can immobilize an organization by channelling ...efforts.....into unproductive activities, too little conflict may encourage complacency and lethargy.' (p.191)

Pluralist managers are more likely than unitary managers to make full use of the conflict management styles mentioned earlier in Chapter 10 (see Fig. 10.6). The latter are likely to prefer collaborative styles, which implies that as well as deploying the optimum style, they will tend to prefer accommodation and compromise. Pluralist managers will tend to choose whatever style seems to suit their purpose and their power position at the time, although generally preferring more assertive options.

37. Other suggestions for handling conflict have been put forward by Peters (1988), whose advice is not to stifle disagreement, but to encourage it. This implies a culture in which:

❐ openness is encouraged (concerning feelings as well as factual issues)

❐ leaders are trained to accept and use disagreements within their teams in order to arrive at optimum solutions to problems

❐ mistakes are used as learning opportunities rather than as causes of criticism

❐ serious mistakes are dealt with quickly, again with no recriminations

❐ assertiveness is encouraged as a way of expressing individual and team views

❐ a framework of clear objectives, good communications and adequate fail-safe systems (ie controls) are set in place

---

38. The last point applies especially to conflict-management, since once strong disagreement occurs, it is important to be able to contain it and/or redirect it. An effective framework of objectives, communications and

control systems will help to provide that constraint. Much of the comments so far have assumed that conflict is essentially between one group and another within the organisation — between employees and the management, between one function or department and another. However conflict can arise between two individuals at any level — two senior managers in conflict over the implementation of some policy, or between two skilled tradesmen about how to tackle a particular operational problem. In such one-to-one situations it is essential that the individuals' senior managers or supervisors are able to recognise when to step into the argument. Conflict can also occur *within* individuals, for example when a person experiences role-conflict (ie when his or her expectations of the role clash with the expectation of others such as the boss, colleagues or functional specialists). In this situation, the individuals' managers can take the kind of stress avoidance measures referred to in paragraph 20 above.

39. The range of conflict resolution methods typically available to organisations can also include the following:

> ❑ use of the formal grievance procedure to handle individual grievances (ie by formally giving time to hearing an employee's problem, identifying the key issue and the role of any other persons concerned, allowing the employee to be accompanied by a colleague or trade union representative, agreeing to specified action within a specified time-limit, and allowing for the grievance to proceed further up the management chain, if necessary.
>
> ❑ *inter-departmental meetings* can be called to permit disagreements to be aired, usually under the chairmanship of a senior person.
>
> ❑ *regular team meetings* are, of course, an important means of avoiding conflict in the first place by enabling team members to clarify objectives, identify points of disagreement and thrash out problems together before they develop into unproductive conflict.

40. Where disagreements develop into entrenched conflict, then the following options are open to organisations, additional to those referred to above:

□ *negotiation and conciliation* (ie the parties get together, perhaps under an independent chairman, to negotiate about their differences with a view to achieving their own resolution of the issue).

□ *mediation* (ie where a third party — internal or external — acts as a broker or peacemaker between the warring factions, seeing each side independently, trying to assess the nub of their disagreement, and then trying to provide a basis upon which the two sides are prepared to return to the negotiating table; mediators sometimes put forward specific proposals for the parties to agree on; ultimately, however, the final agreement has to be made by the parties themselves).

□ *arbitration* (ie where a third party hears the arguments of both sides, examines the evidence, and then makes the decision for the parties; this frequently entails a decision that is favourable to one party and not to the other; by going to arbitration the parties in conflict realise that they cannot reach agreement themselves and give the responsibility to an outsider, whose judgement they agree to accept; arbitration, therefore, is very much a matter of last resort).

References

1. de Board, R. (1978), *The Psychoanalysis of Organizations*, Tavistock Publications
2. Marshall, J. & Cooper, C. (1981), *Coping with Stress at Work*, Gower
3. Cooper, C. & Marshall, J. (1978), *Understanding Executive Stress*, Macmillan
4. Davidson,M. & Cooper, C. (1983), Stress and the Woman Manager, Martin Robertson
5. Friedman,M. & Rosenman, R.H. (1974), Type A Behaviour and Your Heart, Alfred Knopf
6. Furnham, A. (1992), *Personality at Work*, Routledge
7. Back, K. & Back, K. (1994), *Assertiveness at Work*, BCA/ McGraw Hill
8. Peters, T. (1988), *Thriving on Chaos*, Macmillan
9. Atkinson, P. (1988), *Achieving Results through Time Management*, Pitman
10. Moss Kanter, R. (1989), *When Giants Learn to Dance*, Simon & Schuster
11. Institute of Personnel & Development (formerly Institute of Personnel Management), Statement on Counselling in the Workplace,1992, IPD
12. Egan, G. (1990), *The Skilled Helper* (4th edn), Brooks/ Cole
13. Handy, C. (1993), *Understanding Organizations* (4th edn), Penguin
14. Morgan, G. (1986), *Images of Organization*, Sage Publication

Questions for reflection/discussion

1. How realistic is the distinction between 'pressures' and 'stress' in the workplace?

2. What potential sources of stress are likely to be the most important for:

   a. a police officer in an inner-city area?

   b. a teacher in a rural primary school?

3. a. In what ways can an individual's job become a source of stress?

   b. What can the individual's manager do to reduce the stress factors you have identified?

4. How can assertiveness training help people to overcome potentially stressful situations at work?

5. What are the main differences between unitary and pluralist approaches to conflict in organisations?

6. How is it possible for senior managers to reconcile a desire to permit disagreement and competition within the organisation, with wanting to prevent unproductive stalemate and violent conflict?

13 Organisational culture

Introduction

1. There have been numerous references to 'culture' in other chapters of this book, and the general meaning ascribed to the word has been that of 'the organisation's values-system', ie 'culture' sums up the dominant values, visions, perspectives, standards and modes of behaviour that typify any one organisation. This chapter takes us a little further into the concept of culture and considers some of its implications for work organisations. A key concept in any discussion about 'culture' is that of 'stakeholders', ie the people who have an interest — at stake — in the activities and outcomes of the organisation. Typically, these consist of shareholders, employees, customers, suppliers, competitors, banks and other creditors, and those representing the 'public interest' (see Figure 13.1). All are likely to be affected, in one way or another, by the dominant culture of the organisations they deal with.

The community interest

2. The cascading effects of culture serve an ever-widening group of interests as illustrated in Figure 13.1. Initially culture serves the visionary interests and priorities of the founders. Then it widens to encompass the interests of the inner group of like-minded persons around the original founders. As the new organisation begins to bud, then the interests of customers and employees come into the picture. With growth of activities suppliers become more important and sources of financial support are required, thus producing further demands on the organisation culture. At this stage, too, there is a need to develop the organisation structure, which will both reflect and form the implementation of the founders' vision. Once the early days of the organisation are behind it, then further funding is required, and, for commercial undertakings this usually means going to the stock market and issuing shares, thus creating yet another powerful interest group. As the organisation picks up speed, as it were, there are considerations of the wider public interest to be accounted for — the payment of taxes, obedience to legal requirements, respect for environmental issues etc. At this stage too there are likely to be relationships with competitors

that make demands on the culture, ie whether to adopt a deliberate price-cutting strategy to drive out competitors, whether to build alliances to split the competition, whether to engage in industrial espionage etc. Ethical considerations, it can be noted, form an important part of business practice and business culture, which is not just about marketing and production practices.

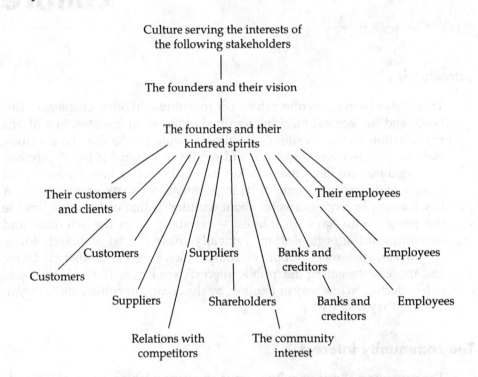

| Figure 13.1 | Culture and the organisation's stakeholders |

3. A mature and effective culture will be capable of serving the interests of a full spectrum of stakeholders. Not that organisations necessarily set out to meet cultural demands on a 360° basis, for they usually have one or two key priority groups, such as customers and employees. In fact, excellent companies, according to Peters & Waterman (1982)[1], in their study of 'excellence' in American companies, have got where they are

    '...because of a unique set of cultural attributes that distinguish them from the rest.'

    In a similar study in the UK, Goldsmith & Clutterbuck (1985)[2], also discovered that

    '......it became clear that there were...common characteristics of management style between the companies. What differed was the emphasis they placed on each.......it also became clear that organisational culture was a crucial element in the ability to maintain these characteristics consistently.' (p.6)

What then is 'culture'?

The meaning of 'organisation culture'

4. According to Mintzberg & Quinn (1991)[3],

> 'Culture arrived on the management scene in the 1980's like a typhoon blowing in from the Far East. It suddenly became fashionable in consulting circles to sell culture like some article of organizational clothing......'. (p.351)

They themselves see culture as *'not an article of fashion, but an intrinsic part of a deeper organizational 'character'......'* in which the collective interest and unity of an organisation is built up through shared beliefs, habits and traditions. The point they are making is that 'culture' should not be the subject of a temporary fad, but the focal point of long-term research into the workings of organisations.

5. Morgan (1986)[4], in typically illuminative manner, sees corporate (ie organisational) culture as :

> 'Shared meaning, shared understanding, and shared sense making.......In talking about culture we are really talking about a process of reality construction that allows people to see and understand particular events, actions, objects, utterances or situations in distinctive ways. These patterns of understanding also provide a basis for making one's own behaviour sensible and meaningful.' (p.128)

He sees the development of organisations in itself as a cultural phenomenon, and suggests that as between several national cultures (eg Britain, USA, Japan etc) there is a common culture of industrial society that distinguishes them from other societies which are predominantly rural. Within each of these industrial societies, however, there are significant differences in organisation cultures arising from past history (class conflict, rise of competitive individualism, Protestant work ethic etc). Thus, industrial competitors worldwide have both common and unique features, which enable them to adapt to the competitive challenge in relatively successful, or less successful, ways.

6. Handy (1993)[5] also has an imaginative way of looking at organisation culture when he comments

> ' ....anyone who has spent time with any variety of organizations, or worked in more than two or three, will have been struck by the differing atmospheres, the differing ways of doing things, the differing levels of energy, of individual freedom, of kinds of personality. For organizations are as different and varied as the nations and societies of the world....They have

differing cultures — sets of values and norms and beliefs — reflected in different structures and systems.' (p.180)

He subsequently goes on to identify four main types of culture to be found in organisations, which are summarised as follows (Figure 13.2):

Type	Metaphor	Characteristics
Power Culture	A web	Control/ power emanate from the centre; very political and entrepreneurial; resource powerand personal power predominate. This culture serves the figure head and the leader.
Role Culture	A Greek temple	Classical structure; bureaucratic nature; roles more important than the people who fill them; position power predominates, and expert power tolerated. This culture serves the structure.
Task Culture	A net	The focus is on completing the job; individuals' expertise and contribution are highly valued; expert power predominates, but both personal and position power are important; the unifying force of the group is manifested in high levels of collaboration.
Person Culture	A cluster or galaxy	A loose collection of individuals —usually professionals — sharing common facilities but pursuing own goals separately; power is not really an issue, since members are experts in their own right. This type of culture serves the individual.

Figure 13.2   *Four types of culture in organisations (based on Handy, 1993)*

7.   Handy's model considerably oversimplifies the realities of organisation culture, which more likely than not is composed of elements of all *four* types. He himself admits that his typology is impressionistic and imprecise, commenting that

'A culture cannot be precisely defined, for it is something that is perceived, something felt.' (op.cit. p.191)

This point is taken up even more strongly by Schein (1992)[6] in his leading text on culture and leadership, when he comments that:

'The word *culture* has many meanings and connotations. When we apply it to groups and organizations, we are almost certain to have conceptual and semantic confusion because groups and organizations are also difficult to define unambiguously....In talking about organizational culture....I often find we agree 'it' exists and 'it' is important....but that we have completely different ideas of what 'it' is.' (p.8)

Schein argues that superficial models of culture should be avoided in favour of *'deeper, more complex anthropological models'*, since culture is the result of a complex group learning process, in which leaders in particular play a key role.

8.   Compared with terms such as *norms, values, traditions, rituals and behaviour patterns,* all of which are used in discussions about *culture,* the latter, according to Schein, adds two other critical elements to the concept of sharing — (1) some level of *structural stability* (ie culture is not only what is shared openly but what is deep-rooted and subconscious), and (2) *patterning or integration* (ie joining the separate elements of culture into a whole — the essence, according to Schein, of what we mean by 'culture'). He then offers his own definition of culture as follows:

'A pattern of shared basic assumptions that the group learned as it solved its problems of external adaptation and internal integration, that has worked well enough to be considered valid and, therefore, to be taught to new members as the correct way to perceive, think, and feel in relation to those problems.'

9.   Schein concludes that there are three different levels of culture, and employs an archaeological analogy to describe them. On the surface, as it were, are the *artefacts* of culture — the signs that are visible, but often hard to decipher. These are the explicit, often written, aspects of culture. Digging deeper into the cultural soil, to continue the analogy, one comes across the *espoused values* that underlie these artefacts. These values represent the rallying points of the group, which are being tested in experience (learning) and may or may not be implemented in practice. Thus, at the first two levels, it is not easy to sort out organisational rhetoric from organisational reality. Does the organisation really mean what it proclaims to believe? Only by going deeper still, according to Schein, can one find the implicit, taken-for-granted assumptions — the *basic assumptions* — about what works and what is acceptable to the group, and thus what subconsciously guides its behaviour and outlook.

10. The effect of these basic assumptions is to provide the anchorage and stability necessary for a coherent culture to emerge and flourish. The implication is that once these assumptions have become rooted, they are extremely difficult to change. Thus, culture whilst acting as a unifying and integrating influence, also carries strongly conservative messages to the group members. This has important implications for leaders. They are the individuals whose ideas and vision are the original sources of those beliefs and values that have become part of the fabric of the culture, but they are also the people whose role requires them to challenge, and be prepared to change, the existing culture or aspects of it. Thus, an important aspect of managing culture is to ensure that the current leadership is always open to change and aware of the need to re-adapt as external conditions change. On this point, Goldsmith & Clutterbuck (op. cit.) noted that

> 'In the long-established companies, the culture is constantly evolving, with each generation making its mark. Although it carries many of the basic tenets of its founder......the culture of a Sainsbury or a Marks and Spencer today has moved with the times to reflect modern values......' (p.162)

The components of organisation culture

11. Most business enterprises and most voluntary organisations (eg major charities) begin life as an idea in the minds of one or two individuals. One only has to think of Michael Marks and Tom Spencer in the retail world, and of Octavia Hill and her fellow co-founders of the National Trust, to recall two examples of small groups of individuals who started organisations that have become both respected and successful. More recently, such individuals as Bill Gates of Microsoft and Richard Branson of the Virgin Group have left an indelible mark on the business world. In another field, lawyer, Peter Benenson, concerned about the injustice of individuals held without trial, founded Amnesty International in 1961 to work for the release of prisoners of conscience. This is now the world's largest voluntary human rights organisation. With over one million members in more than 150 countries, the organisation is both respected and feared by governments in every continent. What is it that these charismatic people brought to their infant organisations many years ago? What is it that they bring now that enables their adult organisations to survive in changing circumstances, but yet still to bear the cultural marks of the founders?

12. The answers to the first question can be found mainly in the beliefs implicit in the initial vision of those charismatic individuals who developed famous enterprises on the basis of nothing more than what seemed to them to be a good idea or a desperate need. Michael Marks, for example, had a vision of selling cheaply-priced everyday goods in vast quantities. Joining up with Tom Spencer in the 1890's, a network of retail shops was born on which this vision could be carried. Soon the idea of promoting

product reliability was added to the cheapnesss of price. Goods were still restricted in range, but they were of consistent quality and within the reach of ordinary folk, both in financial terms and in their availablity. These few simple ideas formed the bedrock of a company that is consistently one of the best-performing retail businesses in the UK/ world?

13. It was the belief of giving unparalleled support to customers in terms of reliability and service that enabled IBM to achieve its success against competitors who often had lower prices and sometimes had better technology. It was a belief in product quality that put Procter & Gamble on the road to success. It was a deep concern for wounded soldiers that enabled Jean Henri Dunant and his five Swiss fellow-citizens in the 1860's to draw the world's attention to the need for rules for the treatment of the wounded and prisoners. The resulting International Committee of the Red Cross has since spread the symbol and the spirit of the Red Cross — and its Muslim equivalent, the Red Crescent — to more than 160 national societies.

14. Once the initial beliefs have been established, then habits and traditions follow them. In other words, once the founders have floated their idea in the marketplace, or in the public conscience, they can then decide *how* the product, service or cause is to be provided, or promoted. At the outset, the originators usually gather a small nucleus of like-minded people around them before the organisation proper begins to take off. This step is then followed by a number of crucial culture-building activities that move the organisation from its conception to the budding stage, as illustrated in Figure 13.3:

Figure 13.3   *Culture-building Activities in a Budding Organisation*

15. The culture-building activities shown in Figure 13.3 highlight the different ways by which a distinctive culture can be developed in a new organisation, and go some way to answering the second question raised in paragraph 11 above. Some of the activities are likely to overlap in practice (eg the development of group norms with statements of espoused values, and policy/ mission statements), but for our purposes it is useful to see as many as possible of the separate elements of culture between the first visionary ideas of the founders to the eventual reflection on, and learning about, the events of the budding organisation, as it develops. The reference to organisational learning is extremely important, since this is how a culture not only comes to be owned and accepted by all, but also is able to be adapted in reponse to change in the external and internal environments. The issue of organisational change is dealt with in the next section of the book (especially Chapter 14).

16. Figure 13.3 shows the initial steps that are likely to be taken in the earliest stages after the visionary idea has been sown. These will include:

❐ *the recruitment of like-minded individuals* (ie fellow-travellers, kindred spirits) — such persons will be attracted instinctively to the founders' vision and aims; they are usually willing to accept the founders' views on how things should be done as well as what should be done; thus, an important consensus is achieved at the crucial early stage.

❐ *the development of group norms* (ie standards of behaviour such as 'working for each other') — these are likely to be strongly influenced by the founders in the formative stages.

❐ *statement of espoused values* (ie the publicly-stated values claimed by the organisation such as 'Never knowingly undersold' (John Lewis Partnership) or 'Patients first!' (National Health Service) — the founders or initiators will have the greatest influence on these values in the early stages; subsequently, the organisation's leadership must demonstrate to other stakeholders that what it is saying it truly believes, and act accordingly.

❐ *production of mission statements* ('why we are in business, and what are our intentions towards our stakeholders — customers, suppliers, employees etc') — such statements provide visible evidence of espoused values and norms, and are the platform for the organisation's relationships with the various stakeholders.

17. These initial steps are likely to be followed by habit and tradition-building activities, aimed at embedding the culture in the day-to-day activities of the organisation by means of procedural and ritualistic measures, such as:

> ❏ *the introduction of appropriate communication systems and decision-making arrangements* (ie the organisational structure) — these measures are designed to assist the internal integration referred to by Schein earlier (para.8 above).
>
> ❏ *the installation of organisational procedures and rules* (ie 'the way things are to be done here') — these also promote integration by setting standards for members to follow.
>
> ❏ *promotion of organisational symbols* (eg company logo, staff uniforms, vehicle livery etc) — like battle flags and national emblems, such symbols demonstrate the unity of the organisation; they come to embody a certain reputation (eg Red Cross/Red Crescent, IBM, the National Trust acorn etc)
>
> ❏ *development of key rituals* (eg recruitment rituals, reward ceremonies for sales/ production employees, the annual staff lunch etc) — these help to establish the organisation's ethos (ie that part of culture to do with the organisational climate — 'business-like', 'thorough', 'paternal', 'friendly', 'encouraging' etc etc.)
>
> ❏ *the production of policy statements* on key issues (eg staff relations, business integrity, customer relations etc) — these like mission statements lay the basis for relations with stakeholders.

18. Finally, there will be activities aimed at:

> ❏ *assisting learning throughout the organisation* — such activities include the induction of new employees/ members, group meetings, training sessions, mentoring etc.

Newcomers will be initiated into the organisation's practices, whilst the original staff members will endeavour to interpret the founders' vision in practice through staff meetings, training sessions, appraisals and other activities aimed at the maintenance of norms and espoused values. Eventually, the culture will become established until events force some change of emphasis. Where learning opportunities have been encouraged, change is likely to be easier to facilitate; where such opportunities have been denied or neglected, then change may not occur, or if it does, will proceed more painfully.

19. It is possible for the purposes of illustration to suggest possible culture-building responses that an organisation might make towards its various stakeholders. Given that culture acts as a unifying and stabilising force within organisations, and that this has a conservative effect on values and the actions that support them, it is reasonable to assume that in most situations cultural change will tend to be evolutionary. Changes to cultural responses are likely to follow the organisation's life-cycle (ie birth and early life, prime of life, old age and decline etc) as it adapts to the changing demands of internal growth and the pressure of external forces in its environment. The list in paragraph 21 below suggests some typical responses that might be expected of a manufacturing organisation in its early life. The assumption in the example is that this company intends to create a culture that is favourable to its major stakeholders, and will do all that is necessary to ensure that its cultural aims are fulfilled.

20. The responses in each case are set out under two headings as follows:

    a) *slogans/ oral messages* (ie those public exhortations and spoken messages that are passed around the organisation, and reflect some of its artefacts and espoused values)

    b) *systems/ procedures* (ie the mechanisms designed to translate cultural messages into actions).

    Competitors are not referred to, since they have rather a different stakeholder relationship to the organisation compared with customers, employees, suppliers, shareholders and banks, all of whom have a direct interdependency with the organisation. The community interest is, however, mentioned even though there is not usualy the same level of interdependence. For further information on stakeholder issues in the external environment see Cole (1994)[7], Chapter 3.

21. The list of possible cultural responses to stakeholders in the early life of a manufacturing organisation is as follows:

Stakeholder Category	Typical Cultural Response
Customers	*Slogans/ Oral messages* — 'Customers are our life's blood. Without them the business cannot survive. Therefore we will listen to our customers, we will aim to give them the products and the quality they want at a price they are willing to pay, and will provide an after-sales service that will build our reputation. We will aim to provide customers with the value they seek.'

Systems/ Procedures — sales staff training, customer relations training, reliable ordering and invoicing procedures, competitive pricing analysis, quality procedures etc.

Employees

Slogans/ Oral messages — 'Every employee plays an important role in this organisation. We have no room for passengers. Newcomers will be given every chance to perform to an acceptable standard, and will be rewarded accordingly. Those unable to attain the required standard will be dismissed after their probationary period. Employees will be encouraged to see other people in the organisation as their customers, and a cooperative attitude towards colleagues will be expected. Rewards will be on the basis of group results. Employees will be encouraged to develop their skills and experience in the service of the customer.'

Systems/ Procedures — Role descriptions and performance standards published. Systematic recruitment and selection procedures established. Induction of new employees. Briefing and training of line managers and supervisors. Reward system operated. Basic appraisal system to assess performance and identify promotion prospects.

Suppliers

Slogans/ Oral messages — 'Suppliers are vital to our production process. Quality of components is even more vital. We will therefore build up a range of suppliers and ensure that they meet our requirements. We will expect fair but competitive prices from suppliers. Suppliers are entitled to be paid on time. They are also entitled to expect an efficient ordering system from us.'

Systems/ Procedures — Internal monitoring of suppliers. Quality standards and specifications to be clearly stated in contract negotiations and ordering procedures. Installation of an efficient ordering and payments system. Purchasing department will be on constant look-out for potential alternative sources of supply for major components/ supplies.

Shareholders

Slogans/ Oral messages — 'Shareholders are entitled to a fair reward for their investment in the company. This includes seeing a growth in the value of their shareholding, as well as adequate dividends payable during the year.'

Systems/ Procedures — Directors' reports, financial statements (statutory and other) made available. Efficient

245

despatch of dividend payments and other share-holder information. Formal company meetings organised.

Banks/creditors   *Slogans/ Oral messages* — 'Banks and other creditors are entitled to sufficient information to enable them to make appropriate decisions in the company's interests for the funding of its commercial activities. It is recognised that banks and creditors are themselves in a competitive marketplace, and thus the company will aim get optimum benefit from financial arrangement with third parties.'

Systems/ Procedures — Effective procedures in place for capital investment and other major financial proposals. Adequate controls on borrowings and repayments.

The Community   *Slogans/ Oral messages* — 'We recognise that we have a role to play in the local community. We also recognise the value of good relations with the local community to our reputation as a company. We accept our responsibility as an employee of local people. We acknowledge our responsibility towards the local environment. We will sponsor a limited number of local events each year as a direct contribution to the community.'

Systems/ Procedures — Appoint one senior person as the company's link with the local community. Recruitment procedures to ensure advertisement of all vacancies in local channels (Press etc). Maintain budget for community relations.

Frameworks for examining organisation culture

22. Schein (op. cit. p.147) suggests that there are

> 'basically two reasons for wanting to study and decipher an organization's culture: (1) scientific reasons that pertain to the building of theory and (2) action research reasons that relate to helping leaders manage cultural issues in their organizations.'

For our purposes here we are principally interested in the second reason, for which Schein provides the following broad schema for *'deciphering cultural assumptions and evaluating their relevance to some group purpose...'*. This is essentially a managerial intervention (using an external consultant to assist the process of analysis) which can be summarised as follows:

❐ Obtain leadership commitment to the study, and establish that there is a real issue or problem at stake from their viewpoint

❐ Conduct a large group meeting with the people who will be affected. This will be addressed by a senior manager who will state the issue/ problem to be discussed, introduce the consultant (process consultant) who will assist the group in their analysis of the issue and the extent to which the group's culture helps or hinders a solution to the issue.

❐ Process consultant gives short talk on how to think about culture (using his three-tier approach as mentioned in paragraph 9 above)

❐ Group describes the visible artefacts of its culture.

❐ Group identifies its espoused values (ie why they do certain things), and the consultant notes down the degree of agreement between individuals.

❐ The consultant gets the group to begin to identify the underlying assumptions behind their espoused values and visible artefacts. This is not an easy process, but once a few items are brought to the surface, they tend (a) to shed further light on their values and artefacts, and (b) to trigger the discovery of other implicit assumptions.

❐ At this point the group is broken down into subgroups, possibly reflecting the presence of sub-cultures based on function, geography etc. These groups futher refine the assumptions identified earlier, add any that may have been missed, and then assess to what extent these assumptions help or hinder the issue/ problem being addressed.

❐ Subgroups report back on their findings which are shared and analysed jointly.

❐ If the conclusion is reached that important shifts in culture are required, then the consultant explains a number of change mechanisms that are available, and a new set of subgroups may be formed to develop an appropriate change strategy (NB This topic will be dealt with in Chapter 14).

23. There are several focal points that groups can home in on when making an assessment of their organisation culture. These focal points will initially be the visible artefacts of the culture (eg office/ factory layout, people's dress, published lists of values, observable rituals etc), and then the espoused

values of the organisation (eg the values promulgated by the founders and/ or senior management, and the values expressed by individual managers and other employees). The latter may not always be consistent, and there is always a sense in which espoused values are under discussion, and not yet part of the underlying fabric of the culture as embedded in the basic assumptions of the organisation.

24. A number of starting points for the assessment of culture that have been employed in organisations include the following, which, it should be noted, tend to focus mainly on artefacts and, to a lesser extent, on espoused values:

> ❏ investigate dominant management styles (ie internal focus)
>
> ❏ assess organisation's behaviour towards its stakeholders (internal and external focus)
>
> ❏ examine strategic instruments, such as mission statements, corporate goals, strategy statements (eg on product-markets, financial, and personnel/ organisational matters) and policy statements (comprehensive focus)
>
> ❏ use of McKinsey 7-S framework (see below)
>
> ❏ use of Goldsmith & Clutterbuck key characteristics (see below)
>
> ❏ use the model proposed by Schein (see above)

25. It is not easy to interpret and write about culture, for there are difficulties for outsiders in joining a group that has already been established. Quite apart from the difficulties of understanding what is going on, let alone what it all means, there is the issue of how the outsider's role is perceived by the group members, and how far he or she influences what is said and done during the study. As mentioned in paragraph 19 above, Schein points out that a different approach to cultural assessment is required depending on whether the aim is to interpret the culture for the benefit of the insiders (ie action research), or for outsiders (ie the research community). Some studies, such as those by Peters & Waterman in the United States, and Goldsmith & Clutterbuck in the United Kingdom are written for a wider external audience — directors and senior managers as well as fellow academics. These studies tend to adopt analytical frameworks that appeal more to managerial audiences than academic, but although they may not be considered as scientifically rigorous as researchers would like, they nevertheless can make a major contribution to our understanding of how organisations work, and, in this case, how culture both forms, and is formed by, organisational behaviour.

26. Peters & Waterman, in their study of 'excellence' (op. cit) chose to follow what has become known as the McKinsey 7-S framework of organisation analysis. This framework is based on the following parameters:

> ❐ Shared values (ie the essential culture of the organisation)
>
> ❐ Style (ie management style)
>
> ❐ Strategy (ie goals and corporate strategic plans)
>
> ❐ Structure (ie organisation structure)
>
> ❐ Systems and procedures
>
> ❐ Staff (all employees)
>
> ❐ Skills (ie people's talents, levels of competence etc)

The seven variables are seen as interdependent, with shared values placed at the core of the group.

27. In their use by Pascale & Athos (1981)[8], certain variables were described as 'hard' (ie strategy, structure and systems), meaning that these were the more easily measurable and predictable dimensions, and to some people more convincing as sources of evidence about organisational performance. The others were seen as 'soft' (ie shared values, management style, staff and skills), in that they were less tangible, less predictable, and implicit rather than explicit. The irony is that the so-called 'soft' variables have shown themselves to be more significant to success than the 'harder', quantifiable elements. Peters & Waterman, in *their* study, found that the so-called 'soft' aspects of organisational behaviour were the most striking in their effect:

> 'We have observed few, if any, bold new company directions that have come from goal precision or rational analysis. While it is true that the good companies have superb analytic skills, we believe that their major decisions are shaped more by their values than by their dexterity with numbers. The top performers create a broad, uplifting, shared culture, a coherent framework within which charged-up people search for appropriate adaptations.....Such high purpose is inherently at odds with 30 quarterly MBO objectives, 25 measures of cost containment.......[etc]..' (p.51)

28. Peters (1988)[9], in a follow-up text, concludes that the successful firm in the 1990's will have the following characteristics, most of which, it will be noticed, can be considered as 'soft' features:

> ☐ a flatter structure (ie having fewer layers of organisation)
>
> ☐ more autonomous units with greater authority to introduce and price products
>
> ☐ strongly differentiated in their markets, and producing high added-value
>
> ☐ a quality-conscious and service-conscious approach
>
> ☐ a more responsive stance
>
> ☐ faster at innovation
>
> ☐ using highly-trained, flexible people as the principal means of adding value

29. Goldsmith & Clutterbuck, in their study of successful companies, isolated a number of key characteristics of good management, which were elicited from a framework that comprised the following features of organisation:

> ☐ *leadership* — especially (1) in the presentation of, and commitment to, a clear vision of where the organisation is going by top management, and (2) where managers at lower levels *'have and espouse understandable objectives and the resources and support to pursue them.'*
>
> ☐ *autonomy* — especially what might be considered 'selective autonomy', where different companies *'...have different areas where they need to encourage entrepreneurial spirit.'* This is similar to Peters (1988) 'simultaneous loose-tight properties'.
>
> ☐ *control* — ie seeking a balance between strict controls on certain issues (eg capital spending) and flexibility elsewhere (eg operating budgets). The successful companies tended to *'enforce the control perception by practice and by consensus that particular procedures are 'the right way of doing things'* rather than by hefty rule books.'
>
> ☐ *employee involvement* — ie generating a high level of employee commitment by means of a variety of extrinsic and intrinsic rewards. Such companies are *'...not afraid of being labelled paternalistic....they see their behaviour as both enlightened self-interest and a necessary part of an efficient organization.'*
>
> ..... continued

> ❏ *market orientation* — this is basically an acceptance of the primary importance of the customer to every function of the company
>
> ❏ *zero basing* — this refers to the practice of going back to first principles on every major aspect of the organisation's activities — *'These companies habitually take an introspective look at what they are doing and why, and relate this to their core objectives.'* (p.10)
>
> ❏ *commitment to innovation* — ie innovation as a means to an end: customer satisfaction and related goals.
>
> ❏ *integrity* — ie adopting an honest and consistent approach to all the company's major stakeholders (employees, customers, suppliers and the community).

30. The above summaries of analytical frameworks designed to aid an organisation's assessment of its culture give some idea of the complexities of the undertaking. It is by no means easy to 'capture' the length and breadth and depth of a culture, let alone to experience its implicit features. The danger is that people will identify and evaluate the visible aspects of their culture, and mistake them for the full picture. However, as Schein points out, it is necessary to dig deeper in order to reach the implicit, embedded assumptions that make up the heart and soul of culture. In the final analysis, culture is much more than the sum of its parts.

References

1. Peters, T. & Waterman, R. (1982), *'In Search of Excellence: Lessons from America's Best-Run Companies*, Harper & Row

2. Goldsmith, W. & Clutterbuck, D. (1985), *The Winning Streak*, Penguin Business

3. Mintzberg, H. & Quinn, J. (1991), *The Strategy Process - Concepts*, Contexts and Cases, Prentice Hall International

4. Morgan, G. (1986), *Images of Organization*, Sage Publications

5. Handy, C. (1993), *Understanding Organizations* (4th edn), Penguin Business

6. Schein, E. H. (1992), *Organizational Culture and Leadership*, Jossey Bass

7. Cole, G.A. (1994), *Strategic Management*, D P Publications

8. Pascale, R. & Athos, P. (1981), *The Art of Japanese Management*, Penguin

9. Peters, T. (1988), *Thriving on Chaos: Handbook for a Management Revolution*, Macmillan

Questions for reflection/discussion

1. What visible 'artefacts' of culture might you expect to find in the following two organisations:

   1 a top football club?

   2 a company engaged in the manufacture of prestige motor cars?

2. Why is it that so-called 'espoused' values held by senior individuals in an organisation need to be treated with some caution by those assessing the organisation's culture?

3. Which culture-building activities (see Fig. 13.3) are likely to be the most influential in the early stages of development in the following types of organisation:

   1 an elite team of Customs officers set up to combat illegal drug trafficking?

   2 a new chain of electrical retail superstores?

4. In what ways are newcomers to an organisation encouraged to share in its culture?

5. Taking the 7-S Framework as your model for assessing an organisation's culture, say what aspects you consider are most likely to produce relevant information, giving your reasons. Discuss with a colleague how you would decide whether your information under each aspect was 'hard' or 'soft'.

6. Why do cultures vary between organisations?

14 Organisational
change and
development

Organisational Change

Human organisations are never static entities. They are, on the contrary, constantly changing and adapting. In Chapter 2 it was noted that an organisation structure is 'an intangible web of relationships between people, their shared purposes and the tasks they set themselves.' This web of relationships as between individuals and between groups at work has been described from several different perspectives so far. Now, in the penultimate section of the book, we can examine the process of change and how it can be managed. Chapter 14 outlines the process of organisational change and development, Chapter 15 looks at issues involved in designing work and jobs, and Chapter 16 considers the Personnel role in Organisational Behaviour.

14 Organisational change and development

Introduction

1. As stated in Chapter 2 (para.12), organisations rarely stand still, but are in a more or less constant state of flux, where change and adaptation in one part of the organisation has a knock-on effect elsewhere. Like any other environment in which human beings predominate, there are always subtle changes taking place in the relationships between people. In work organisations these changes take place on a large scale, sometimes in response to external pressures and sometimes in response to planned change. This chapter looks at some leading theories of change in work organisations, examines some practical ways of introducing change, and considers some of the issues involved when there is resistance to change. Finally the chapter ends with a review of actions that senior management can take to encourage the acceptance of planned change throughout the organisation.

2. Before proceeding it might be useful to take another look at the model of organisation structure developed in Chapter 2, since the structural variables it contains represent key points of attention in any discussion of organisational change. The revised model (Figure 14.1) for the purposes of this chapter comprises the following aspects of an organisation model in which structure both reflects change in the other variables and serves to change one or more of them as well: organisational purpose and goals (strategy), tasks and work, people, technology, organisation structure (ie how the preceding variables are deployed), organisation culture (the spiritual glue that holds the organisation together) and the external environment.

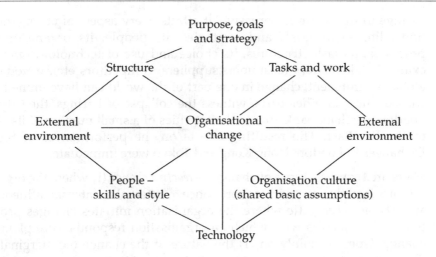

Figure 14.1   *Major variables in organisational change*

The theory of change

3.   The concept of 'change' implies that a situation, person or thing has altered in some way. Change implies difference, adaptation, innovation and renewal. Organisations as relatively permanent and structured groups of people engaged in the pursuit of common goals (see Chapter 1 para 10) are as liable to change as any other natural phenomena in our world. In their early study of innovation in British companies, Burns & Stalker (1961)[1] described dynamic organisations with network structures and flexible attitudes towards jobs as 'organic', and noted that they were suited to conditions of change. These organisations contrasted with 'mechanistic' organisations which had an hierarchy of jobs and roles where tasks were specialised. Such organisations were considered to be suited to conditions of stability. The rigidity of mechanistic types of organisation can be a strength (eg there are clear definitions of jobs and duties, clear lines of command and communication, and clear procedures for processing the work of the organisation). However, these qualities can also constitute a weakness (eg an inability to adapt to rapid change, slow adaptation to less immediate change, and suppression of individual initiative). Organic types of organisation, because of their in-built flexibility, are much better able to adapt to change, whether sudden or planned, and are better able to utilise the talents of their employees.

4.   Moss Kanter (1984)[2] discusses change in terms of 'innovation', which she describes as

> '....the process of bringing any new, problem-solving idea into use.......
> Innovation is the generation, acceptance, and implementation of new ideas,
> processes, products, or services.' (p.20)

255

Change in this sense is pervasive, it affects every aspect of an organisation's life — its goals and strategies, its people, its organisational processes, its task structures, its choice and use of technology, and its external stakeholders (customers, suppliers, competitors etc). In today's global environment, change in one part of the world can have immediate consequences in other parts, witness the collapse of Barings, the City of London merchant bank, due to the activities of a small number of its staff in the Far East. The resulting effects on the performances of Stock Exchanges in London, Hong Kong and Tokyo were immediate.

5. There are two basic types of change — *reactive change* (ie where the organisation is forced to respond at short notice to external or internal influences) and *planned change* (ie where the organisation initiates changes proactively). The success with which an organisation responds to unplanned change depends mainly on (1) the nature of the change (eg marginal or devastating), (2) the flexibility of its decision-making mechanisms, and (3) the time available to produce alternative products or services. Much can also depend on the organisation's ability to predict major changes, which is an important aspect of strategic management. Issues which have caused major grief at short notice include: a sudden and unexpected rise in interest rates, a sudden devaluation of the national currency, the collapse of a market due to political upheaval (eg coup d'etat), and the discovery of major adverse side-effects in a leading drug.

6. Most of the triggers of change are not as drastic as those just mentioned, and are more likely to appear as trends in a market, or as a development in technology. In the public sector major changes are signalled by legislation or government action. Thus the privatisation of an energy industry or the reorganisation of a health service are always preceded by public debate and discussion. Subsequent changes, even if revolutionary in content, can be introduced in a planned, evolutionary way. Many of the external sources of change are working away under the surface, so to speak, and astute organisations are not only aware of their existence but are preparing to make arrangements to deal with them when they do surface. Change which develops slowly gives organisations time to assess its implications and decide how to respond in a considered way.

7. The first priority for business organisations, in particular, is to study their *external* environment, where the triggers for change are usually out of their control. Thus, businesses have to conduct regular reviews of the following:

❏ their business environment (eg their industry and its life-cycle, their competitive situation, the nature of their customer/client base etc)

❏ the general economic situation (eg terms of trade, interest rates, tax levels, demand for consumer/ capital goods etc)

❏ the political situation (eg change of government, pending legislation on relevant issues, such as employment, equal opportunities, pollution etc)

❏ social trends (eg population changes, expenditure patterns, new fashions etc)

❏ technological developments (especially those affecting production methods, delivery of a service and the efficiency of internal administration)

Some of the above environmental factors are assessed regularly as part of routine marketing feedback, but others may only be examined annually as part of a thorough-going strategic review.

8. Although many of the triggers of change originate in the external environment, it is important that the *internal* environment of the organisation is not neglected. Leavitt (1964)[3] suggested that organisations could be changed by altering one or more of three major variables — *people, structure* or *technology*. People changes could include changing roles, relationships and attitudes. Structural changes could include changing the managerial hierarchy and the work flow. Technological changes could include changing machines, engineering processes and research. Peters and Waterman (1982)[4] widened the range of variables in their adoption of a seven-item framework in their analysis of 'excellence' in major American companies. This so-called McKinsey 7-S Framework (see Chapter 13 paras. 26-27) comprised the following elements of organisation: *strategy, structure, systems, staff, style, skills and shared values (culture)*. Other factors that could be included in a review are *technology* and *work/ task design*. The major factors likely to be examined in a review of an organisation's external and internal environments are shown shortly in Figures 14.2, 14.4, which form a useful basis for considering potential forces for change in the organisation.

Reviewing the external environment

9. Changes in the external environment are particularly liable to affect business organisations, since this is where their customers and their competitors are. However, all organisations — business, charitable and public

sector — are influenced to some degree by conditions in their external environments. What sort of factors are likely to be significant? As Figure 14.2 suggests, these can be analysed according to which external stakeholder is providing the changes.

Stakeholder Group	Examples of changes in behaviour
Competitors	Launching new products or updated versions of current products Introducing price changes, special discounts etc Seeking takeovers, mergers, collaborative arrangements
Shareholders	Agreeing to takeover terms offered by competitor Raising sensitive issues (eg directors' bonuses, conservation matters etc) at Annual General Meetings
Customers	Switching allegiance to others' products or services Demanding higher standards of quality, after-sales service etc Changing their expenditure priorities (eg less on cars and housing and more on fast foods, holidays etc)
Suppliers	Unable or unwilling to meet changes in specifications demanded by the primary producers Unable to meet delivery deadlines due to internal problems (staff changes, machine breakdowns etc) Switching to competitors due to better price, credit terms etc
Government	Increasing or decreasing tax on purchases Granting or withdrawing licences (eg to drill for oil, extract minerals etc) Promoting or withdrawing subsidies (eg for 'greenfield' manufacturing developments, promotion of UK educational books to Third World nations etc) Devaluing or revaluing the national currency
Pressure Groups	Making an issue of an environmental problem affecting the organisation's business (eg Shell and dumping of disused oil drilling platforms) Taking direct, perhaps illegal, action against the organisation's premises or employees

Figure 14.2   *Sources and examples of change in the external environment*

10. Other factors than the behaviour of stakeholders in the external environment include social and technological changes. Examples of changes in these two factors are shown in Figure 14.3.

Social Changes	Changes in the population profile (eg growing proportion of elderly, areas of ethnic minority groups, short-term burst in teenage population — 'baby-boomers')
	Changing attitudes towards work (eg dislike of shift work, unsocial hours etc)
	Changes in spending patterns among key social groups
	Changes in take-up rates of undergraduate courses in key skill/knowledge areas (eg lack of engineers and scientists)
Technological Changes	Availability of effective new process machines to aid manufacturing or provision of a service
	Effect of developments in information technology designed to control and/or measure industrial processes
	Effect of information technology on administrative procedures
	Introduction of improved raw materials (eg new metals, plastics etc)
	Application of newer forms of energy (eg nuclear power, liquefied petroleum gases, solar batteries etc)

Figure 14.3   *Examples of social and technological changes*

11. The external forces for change in an organisation's environment are substantial, as indicated in the items listed in the previous two paragraphs. This is why Figure 14.1 shows the external environment twice in the model, just in case it might be thought that the most important changes come mainly from within. Unlike matters affecting the organisation's employees, over whom there is considerable control, and the organisation's strategic and tactical decision-making processes, for which the organisation's own management are responsible, external events are largely impossible to control. External stakeholders can, of course, be influenced by what the organisation's management do, but there is not the same level of control over, and responsibility for, any actions taken by such groups. Similarly, unless the organisation itself is spear-heading technological or other innovations, it has little control over such developments ouside its borders. Social changes generally tend to be evolutionary, and so may

259

creep up on an organisation, but here again there is little opportunity to influence wider changes in society. Control, therefore, is rarely a feasible option! However, what is possible is for the organisation to make a reasonably accurate prediction of (1) future actions by major stakeholders, and (2) trends in the wider business, political, economic and social environment. Much of the effort involved in strategic management is focused precisely on this point - examining the external environment (eg as in Figures 14.2 and 14.3), predicting what is likely to happen and then taking steps to address the consequences.

Reviewing the internal affairs of the organisation

12. Most of the variables shown in Figure 14.1 above relate to the *internal* affairs of the organisation. This does not imply that the most important forces for change arise from such sources, but only that they are important and should be given attention by anyone studying organisational change. Figure 14.4, therefore, illustrates some examples of decisions/ issues that can arise from internal sources and are likely to bring about change in the organisation.

Internal Source	Examples of decisions/ issues
Strategy development	*Product strategies* (eg maintain existing products or introduce new range; improve inventory controls; build for permanence or short shelf-life? etc) *Market strategies* (eg consolidate current markets or seek new markets; maintain existing brands or seek new brands; aim for price advantage based on lower costs or go for higher price for better quality; aim for market leadership or market share? etc) *Financial strategies* (eg maintain tight controls over all expenditure or allow delegated budgets with local flexibility; choose between tight credit arrangements with suppliers/ customers or generous terms; increase amount of reinvested profit or distribute to shareholders) *Personnel strategies* (eg develop and train own staff or buy in skills from the market place; retain market leader-ship in pay and conditions or aim for middle of road policy; encourage or discourage trade union membership and activities; establish procedures for reviewing organisational structure and processes on a regular basis or meet changes as they come) ... continued

Structure and Systems	Implement structural revisions aimed at reducing the number of levels in the hierarchy; reorganise along divisional instead of functional lines; establish new cost-centres among headquarters functions; reorganise production facilities (staff, machine tools, robots etc) so as to benefit from technical developments; streamline budgetary planning process; redesign documentation for purchases, invoicing etc
Tasks and Work	Change jobs of key individuals by giving greater responsibility for achievement of tasks; reallocate tasks in the light of technical innovations; reallocate tasks to achieve better sequencing of work etc; introduce quality circles to improve total quality standards in the basic production units
People	Appoint new people to fill key senior management positions; introduce revised staff appraisal scheme based on 360° approach (ie where individual's perform-ance is appraised by everyone in the role-set, including subordinate staff); change incentive bonus scheme from an individual to a group incentive; provide new skills training programme for customer service staff.
Technology	Introduce new micro-processor controlled machines into key production areas; set revised skill standards for operators; introduce new software application for order processing and train staff; introduce teleconferencing facilities for field sales staff.
Organisation Culture	Introduce policy aimed at switching emphasis from cost-consciousness to price-consciousness; introduce incentives to encourage pride in product/ service quality; set targets for customer satisfaction with after-sales service; increase empowerment of lower-level management roles; encourage management staff to adopt more participative styles.

Figure 14.3   Sources and examples of changes in the internal environment

Strategies for change

13. Once the need for change has been identified steps can be taken to adapt the appropriate organisational variable (as shown in Fig.14.1). In many cases the changes required are relatively small and can be dealt with on a day-to-day basis as part of the normal activities of management. Some forces for changes, however, are considerable and require a matching response from the organisation. In such cases a planned approach, usually at a corporate strategic level, is required so that the necessary adaptations can be made to products, processes, people etc. Planned change requires targets to be set, implementation policies to be agreed, and appropriate steps taken to prepare employees, in particular, for the impact of change on

their own working lives. A systematic approach to change using behavioural science methods is 'Organisation Development', which will be elaborated shortly. Before considering the practical aspects of introducing change, some further comment on the theory behind change is appropriate.

Models of change

14. Schein (1980)[5] is one of several theorists who have developed an earlier idea of the change process formulated by Kurt Lewin (see Figure 14.5). This proposes a three-stage approach to change involving 'unfreezing' existing behaviour, then introducing the new behaviour, and finally 'refreezing' or reinforcing the new behaviour.

Unfreeze existing behaviour	$\longrightarrow$	Change to new behaviour	$\longrightarrow$	Refreeze new behaviour

Figure 14.5   *Summary of Lewin's Model of Change (1947)*

The 'unfreezing' stage is primarily a question of giving people a motive to change so that they see it as desirable as well as perhaps necessary. Once the motivation is there people will accept the change. The second stage involves explaining what new behaviour is required (eg actions, attitudes, values etc) and gaining the participation of the individuals concerned in working through the practicalities of change. The final stage involves taking appropriate measures to embed the changes in peoples' thinking and feelings (eg by financial rewards, promotion, praise etc). The most difficult stage is usually the first one, where one has to overcome the inertia of comfortable practices and complacency to convince others that change is not only necessary but desirable too. It is important to point out that change, unless revolutionary, takes place in stages. Thus, one does not have to undo *all* previous behaviour in order to bring about required changes! It is important for senior management to recognise what is still useful in present practices and retain that element, whilst at the same time introducing the new behaviour.

15. Chin & Benne (1976)[6] see three principal alternative strategies for introducing change, as follows:

1. Empirical-rational — where it is assumed that people will accept changes if they see that it is in their self-interest to do so

2. Normative-reeducative — where change is introduced gradually by means of a process of re-education in which old norms (ie standards of behaviour) are replaced by new norms over a planned period of time

3. Power-coercive — where change is forced through by virtue of the power held by the management, and where sanctions can be threatened against non-compliance

Of the three alternative strategies the most likely to be incorporate in planned change are the first and the second, where the lead strategy is the second alternative backed up by an effort to encourage people to see the reasonableness of the proposed changes.

16. Tynan (1980)[7] suggests that there are certain conditions that appear to favour the change process in work organisations. These are as follows:

☐ The enterprise is financially viable and seen as secure by the employees (ie jobs are not under immediate threat, as in the case of a declining business which is the subject of a take-over by a competitor)

☐ Scope exists for change to jobs and the organisation of work (ie changes are going to be more than cosmetic)

☐ Management is aware of the value of participative approaches to problem-solving

☐ There is a good degree of trust between management and other employees

☐ There are effective mechanisms for consultation and negotiation

☐ The senior management is publicly committed to the changes

☐ Conditions of employment are reasonable (eg no serious deficiencies in pay levels compared with going rates)

☐ Provision will be made for appropriate action on manning levels, job security and pay.

Over the course of the last fifteen years economic conditions have changed significantly in many European countries — the customer rather than the employee has become the major focus of managerial attention in both the private and public sectors of the economy. The deference paid by Tynan to employee interests (pay, job security etc) is unlikely to be followed today. Nevertheless, even where managements have the coercive power to force through change, the process of achieving major change will always be eased where there is a climate of trust between management and other employees, and where there are effective means of consultation and discussion of changes that may bear adversely on particular groups of employees.

Resistance to change

17. Even if the general acceptance of change is relatively high, there is still a possibility of resistance in particular quarters or on particular issues. It is therefore important to understand some of the issues involved in resistance to change. Lewin (1951)[8] contributed the interesting idea of a 'force-field theory' to explain the two sets of forces that maintain equilibrium in a situation. His argument was that any situation settles down at a particular point when a state of equilibrium occurs between opposing forces. The latter consist on one hand of forces for change, and on the other forces seeking to maintain the status quo. Change can be achieved either by exerting stronger pressure on the forces for change in order to overcome resistance and thus push through change, or by weakening the forces for the status quo, thus permitting change to flood gently in. Power-coercive approaches act as push forces, while empirical-rational and normative-reeducation approaches act more on the restraining forces than on the push forces. Lewin's theory can be presented diagrammatically as follows (Figure 14.6):

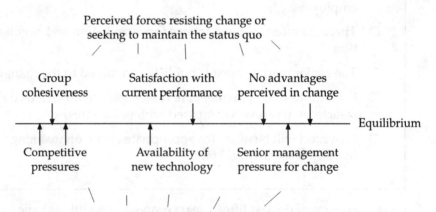

Figure 14.6   *Force-field theory of change (based on Lewin, 1951)*

18. The model indicates the pressures exerted on both sides of the point of equilibrium, or balance, and suggests that as one side pushes harder at any particular point, so the other side resists correspondingly. It all works rather like a well-balanced scrum in a rugby match. Of course, the model greatly simplifies what actually happens in practice, for in human affairs it is peoples' perceptions and (mis)understandings that count more than real events. However, by qualifying the forces so as to include perceptions, it is possible to bring the model a little closer to reality. The upshot of the opposing forces is that the state of equilibrium cannot last forever, and eventually one side begins to push more strongly, while the other weakens its

resistance. Senior management could, for example, employ sanctions in order to force through the desired change.

19. Alternatively, since we are talking mainly about ideas in the context of human activity, the side that is pushing may prefer to find a way of convincing the resistors to abandon some of their opposition and thus open the way towards change. Thus, in the above example, the senior management would need to find some evidence to convince the opposing group that change is indeed in their interests. However, as political leaders and third parties often discover (eg in Northern Ireland and the former Yugoslavia), it is not an easy task to persuade people to make concessions (ie to drop their resistance to core changes) even when the benefit could be lasting peace. When resistance is deeply entrenched it is vital for the negotiators or conciliators involved to get to the heart of the concerns of each side — mere attention to surface issues is never enough, for it is the underlying fears of each that are the real obstacle to forward progress. It is also worth noting that some of the positive factors in developing group performance (eg cohesiveness) can become obstacles to change at some future date.

Implementing organisational change

20. In practical management terms there are two basic approaches to change - tactical/ operational and strategic. The first approach is aimed at responding both to planned and sudden change at the operating levels of the organisation. *Planned* changes will have been discussed previously, timetables and targets agreed with middle management, resources allocated and progress-review mechanisms installed. Some major changes are introduced 'piggy-back' fashion, where the existing system (eg production control system or computerised warehouse inventory system) is continued at the same time as the new system is introduced, until the latter takes over fully. On other occasions changes are introduced fully on an agreed date. In both situations the staff involved will have to be prepared for the changes. For some this may mean extra training and possibly promotion or enhanced pay; for others it may mean loss of a job and possible redandancy, if no alternative work is available. Thus, there are winners and losers in change, and fear of losing is one of the biggest obstacles to the acceptance of change.

21. *Sudden* changes pose different problems for middle management. In some cases the type of change is an eventuality that has been prepared for (eg when a price increase in a price-sensitive market does lead to an early decline in sales of the product or service concerned). In this example, the business can quickly introduce an incentive to soften the blow (eg offering customers a larger discount or longer credit terms), or can promote sales of an alternative product/ service in order to off-set the lost sales of the 'over-priced' item. There are other cases where sudden change of a certain kind has not been foreseen and the management concerned are faced with an immediate problem. Ice-cream manufac-

turers, for example, in Britain's generally mild climate, are sometimes caught out by a sudden and prolonged heatwave which produces a heavy and sustained demand for their products, which they are not able to meet at very short notice. It takes days rather than hours to increase productive capacity, even with modern machinery, because the management and staff have to be organised to cope with the extra work. In situations like this, it is important for the middle management to be given sufficient authority to commit additional resources in order to make the required provision.

22. In some cases it just has to be accepted that the organisations' operating core (see Figure 2.1 Chapter 2) cannot respond effectively and has to accept lost opportunities at the very least and short-term disaster at the worst. The Bhopal crisis in India in December 1984, when Union Carbide's factory caused a massive leak of deadly gases to fall on the local population was a sudden disaster, for which no proper contingency plans had been laid. Although the management were aware of the risks of leaks due to accidents, the Company's Bhopal factory showed evidence of under-trained staff, poor maintenance and lack of investment in computerised warning systems. The company had proceeded on the basis that any such risk was small and as a consequence no effective emergency plan had been worked out. The resulting tragedy cost some 2000 lives and over 100,000 injuries among the local population, while the Company lost $800m in market value in one week and suffered a major blow to its reputation.

23. Change at the *tactical/ operational* level, whilst sometimes immediate in its effects, is rarely as significant to the long-term interests of the organisation as change at the *strategic* (corporate) level. It is at this level that the organisation's senior management bring about planned change on major issues as well as responding to key changes in their external and internal environments. Strategic level changes focus on the core elements of the business and on the key recipients of the organisation's investment resources. If things go wrong at this level, they tend to go badly wrong, since the decisions made at strategic level are predicated on a planned deployment of people, materials and finance to the appropriate sectors, and thus have repercussions right down the organisation. Examples of major strategic misjudgements of change in the external environment have included the following:

❐ A major airline acquired a smaller foreign competitor primarily to obtain access to the latter's internal routes in the USA, but misjudged the ability of the company to maintain a commercially and technically viable airline in its own right and had to bear major losses and unfortunate publicity (due to flight crashes).

❐ A large building society decided to extend its operations downstream by entering the estate agency market at a time of buoyant house sales in the UK, but failed to see that the national economy was about to suffer a severe depression leading to a collapse in the housing market, and after only two years the society had to sell off the new business at a substantial loss.

Organisational change — a managerial model

24. Implementing change, whether tactical or strategic, is not just concerned with deciding what to do and resourcing the decisions that are made. As Figure 14.7 illustrates, it is also about gaining commitment to change, reviewing the progress of change and making appropriate adjustments. The elements shown in the cycle assume a planned approach to changes where the whole process is tackled rationally. The first four stages of the cycle commencing with the environmental review have been referred to earlier in this chapter. The fifth stage — obtaining employee commitment — is of crucial importance, for no change can be implemented satisfactorily unless the employees are motivated to see it through to fulfilment. Not surprisngly, therefore, a good deal of effort is put into this aspect of change by both the senior manqgement responsible for initiating the changes and the change agents who smooth the process of change. The depiction of the model as a cycle of change is intended to emphasise the dynamic nature of organisational change — things never stand still.

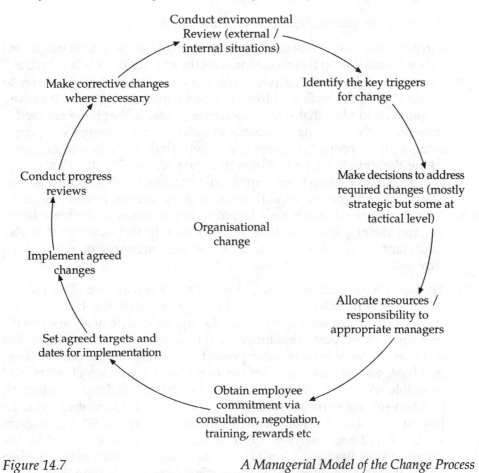

Figure 14.7   *A Managerial Model of the Change Process*

25. This key stage can involve the management in several change-building activities, including the following:

❑ *systematic consultation* with all those affected (eg by special briefing groups, use of the normal line unit team meetings, introduction of quality circles, use of joint management-trade union committees etc)

❑ *negotiation* with key individuals or groups (eg line department heads, functional heads, joint management-union negotiating panel etc)

❑ *cost-benefit analysis* (ie in which the estimated costs of rewards, training, redundancies, new technology etc are agreed and weighed against the estimated benefits of the changes)

❑ *action research* (ie a collaborative programme of change directed usually at specific issues in specific areas of the organisation — see below)

❑ *Organisation Development programme* aimed at corporate-wide changes (see below)

❑ *training programmes* aimed at providing new skills

26. Early consultation is essential when planning change. The management style adopted during this process will set the tone for the whole exercise. If the style is fully participative, employee commitment will be easier to obtain than if the style is autocratic (see Chapter 11 Figure 11.9 above). Negotiation implies that senior management realise that there are certain concessions they will have to make in order to carry enough key people along with the proposed changes. They will aim for a 'win-win' outcome, taking the right-hand path shown in Figure 12.5 in Chapter 12 above. A key element in management's approach to planned change is information — not only information about the external environment, but also about the costs of personnel, machinery, technical improvements, accommodation etc, and the anticipated pay-off to be gained. In this situation it is also important to assess what might be the consequences of not making changes!

27. The reference to 'action research' needs further explanation. This usually refers to an approach to change in which an external person, often an academic, works with a team from within the organisation to analyse a specific problem, suggest possible solutions, test them out and evaluate them. The result at the very least is some powerful learning on the part of those involved, and at best provides the organisation with an effective and workable solution to the problem. Action research follows a systematic problem-solving sequence in which (1) the problem is identified, with the help of the external person acting as guide and catalyst, (2) data is gathered, collated and analysed, (3) feedback on progress is shared by the group on a regular basis, so as to facilitate 'ownership' both of the problem and of possible solutions, (4) action is taken to test, revise and then imple-

ment approved solutions, again with the aid of the external person, and (5) both achievements and the process itself are evaluated by the group members. Although not as widely used as other methods of handling change, action research can be a valuable way of assisting learning among key specialist and line management staff as well as contributing to improvements on specific issues.

Organisation development

28. Organisation Development (OD) is an altogether more comprehensive approach to organisational change. French & Bell (1984)[9] define organisation development as follows:

> '.....a long-range effort to improve an organisation's problem-solvingand renewal processes......through a more effective and collaborative diagnosis and management of organisation culture.....with the assistance of a consultant-facilitator and the use of the theory and technology of applied behavioural science, including action research.'

Important points to note about this definition are that OD is long-range (ie strategic), is primarily concerned with enhancing organisational processes rather than producing outcomes (although these are certainly not neglected), requires the intervention of a change agent in the form of a consultant-facilitator (a skilled, neutral outsider), and utilises behavioural science knowledge. Not surprisingly, as a corporate-wide activity, OD is concerned with adapting the organisation's underlying assumptions — its culture — as the prime vehicle for achieving change elsewhere in the system.

29. There is a typical pattern to an OD programme, which reflects its importance as an organisation-wide effort to introduce planned change, as follows in Figure 14.8.

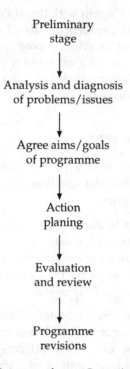

Figure 14.8   _Typical Sequence for an Organisation Development programme_

The first stage is primarily for the top management of the organisation to decide what kind and what level of changes are required. The discussions at this preliminary stage may have been prompted by threatening conditions in the external environment, or, more positively, by new opportunities for expansion of markets or product-range. Issues may also have arisen as a result of obvious weaknesses in the organisation's internal situation — perhaps in employee knowledge and skills, perhaps in the structuring of jobs or perhaps in the way the organisation structure itself is deployed. Whatever the reasoning, grounds for change will have been identified, some provisional goals will have been set, and, crucially, a change agent (see below) will have been appointed.

30.   The change agent role is crucial in any OD programme. The role is principally to guide and facilitate the change process once the initial approval to proceed has been given by the top management. However, there is a range of options depending on the extent to which the change agent is perceived as directing or facilitating change (see Figure 14.9). Directive approaches in which change agents are seen as experts, leaders and consultant-advisers are more likely to be employed in a rational-empirical strategy, for example. Normative-reeducative strategies will prefer the roles of facilitator-counsellor and problem-solver. Power-coercive approaches will tend to favour the leadership aspect of the role.

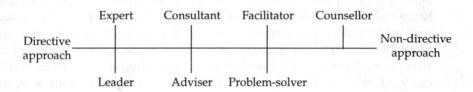

Figure 14.9   *Alternative Change Agent Roles*

31. The change agent is usually someone from outside the organisation, especially where internal politics are likely to play an important role in the change process. As Thakur and others (1978)[10] have pointed out, in this situation an outsider is less constrained by organisational politics and conditioning. Such a person has to be skilled in analysing situations, communicating effectively with a wide range of people, and offering a range of possible solutions to problems and issues. A skilled change agent will also bring a greater sense of objectivity to discussions — challenging existing norms and cultural forms, acting impartially between individuals and groups, and introducing experience and insights gained from similar exercises in other organisations. Schein (1969)[11] in an earlier classic on organisational change refers to the change agent as a 'process consultant' who *'seeks to give the client 'insight' into what is going on around him, within him and between him and other people.'*

32. The second principal stage of an OD programme is the analysis and diagnosis of problems and issues. This is essentially the 'finding out' stage in which facts, opinions and feelings are brought into the open. This will be progressed by means of document analysis (previous budgets, reports, published memos etc), questionnaires (aimed at all or sections of the staff affected by potential changes), one-to-one interviews and small group meetings. The change agent usually drafts and implements the questionnaires, interview outlines and meeting procedures so as to reach the widest possible number of people and to achieve consistency of treatment between individuals and groups. In a large-scale set of interviews and meetings the principal change agent will have several assistants, usually a few from outside and some from inside the organisation (eg as in the original Hawthorne Experiments -see Chapter 4 paras 3-11). Once the basic information has been obtained, the top management team use the services of the change agent to help with the diagnosis of the problems and issues. Management need to 'own' the diagnosis, so that they are motivated to give the change process their full backing. This step quickly leads on to stage three — the agreement of principal aims and goals for the programme. These may include intentions in respect of any of the variables mentioned earlier (structure, systems, personnel, management style, culture etc).

33. Since OD is a systematic approach to organisation-wide change, it is essential for action plans to be approved right down through the management chain. Top management in consultation with the change agent usually

agree what the priorities are to be, what OD activities are to be utilised (eg team-building, Transactional Analysis, empowerment of line units, skills training etc), who is to responsible for what steps in the process and what timetable is to be set. A programme may take anything from six months to two years, depending on the scale of the operation and the relative difficulty of the problems to be confronted. During the course of the programme the change agent and top management team monitor progress, make adaptations as necessary and then review the whole programme at key points in the timetable.

OD Interventions

34. Jusifiably, OD activities are usually described as 'interventions', since they are deliberate and planned efforts to bring about change. Such interventions are aimed at one or more of the following:

> ☐ changing the behaviour of teams and groups (eg improving problem-solving abilities, improving collaboration between teams etc)
>
> ☐ changing relationships between individuals (eg key colleagues, leader and team-member etc)
>
> ☐ changing organisation structures (eg removing layers, changing to divisional form. setting up new profit-centres etc)
>
> ☐ changing individual behaviour (eg management style, developing new attitudes to customers etc)
>
> ☐ changing the dominant culture of the organisation (eg introducing a major switch of emphasis)

35. Typical interventions aimed at changing the behaviour of teams or groups include:

☐ *process consultation*, where an external consultant helps a group to examine its behaviour, understand it and replace it with alternative behaviour if appropriate; the consultant acts as diagnostician, adviser, counsellor and catalyst.

☐ *team-building exercises*, which are similar is some respects to process consultation, but where the emphasis is on nurturing the team by improving relationships, developing team roles and generating team-spirit; a team in this context is more than just a group of employees engaged in related work, for it is composed of *'players who have a reciprocal part to play and are dynamically engaged with each other.'* (Belbin, 1993)[12]

❏ *sensitivity training (or T-groups)*, in which a trained consultant helps the members of a group to cope with the emotional aspects of group membership by examining inter-relationships and individual feelings about group processes; this approach is less popular than it used to be, mainly because individuals have found it too stressful, and organisations now find that they have to select people before exposing them to this type of intervention; however, in professions such as counselling and psycho-therapy such exposure is essential as part of the necessary preparation for professional qualification.

36. Activities aimed at changing relationships between individuals include the following:

❏ *coaching* (ie as between senior/ more experienced person and a junior/ less-experienced colleague); most coaches require to be trained for this role, and in an OD programme this will generally be provided by the change agent or some other external training source.

❏ *leadership training* (eg using Managerial Grid exercises or Adair functional leadership model as mentioned in Chapter 11 above).

❏ *Transactional Analysis*, where a consultant helps individuals in one-to-one or one-to-small group situations to understand the nature of the interactions between them based on a Parent-Adult-Child model of responses; an understanding of the interactions can lead to better ways of responding and thus enhance work relationships.

❏ *conflict-management techniques*, using role-play and other exercises, to improve an individual's handling of conflict with others.

37. Activities aimed at changing the organisation structure range from de-layering the organisation to restructuring individual jobs. The main alternative structural forms have already been described in Chapter 3 (especially paras. 21 - 33), and the issue of work and job design will be the subject of Chapter 15.

38. Activities aimed at changing individual behaviour include the following:

❏ *coaching* (as above)

❏ *counselling* (ie where a trained person enables the employee to understand his or her situation more clearly, become better informed of personal strengths and weaknesses, and be able to make wiser decisions about work responsibilities)

❏ *appraisal programmes* (ie where staff performance is assessed regularly by their managers and where individuals receive appropriate feedback on their personal results)

❐ *training programmes*, especially those aimed either at improving employee performance in present roles, or at providing knowledge and skills for future roles

❐ *provision of suitable rewards* (eg greater responsibility, enhanced pay, bonuses, promotion and career development prospects etc)

❐ *imposition of sanctions* (ie in cases where individuals refuse to cooperate in changes —after due consultation and negotiation— they may have to suffer the loss of their job or be moved to another position not of their choosing)

39. Culture change was referred to briefly in the previous chapter. Changing a culture means focusing on strategic priorities in respect of stakeholders, especially customers, employees, shareholders, suppliers, and the community at large. Where a commercial undertaking decides to shift its emphasis from being a paternalistic business with a product-orientation to one that serves customers first and rewards employees for effective performance, a large shift in basic assumptions is called for. How can this be achieved? The following activities are likely to be considered:

❐ revising *mission statements*, promulgating them and getting them discussed in team meetings

❐ publishing *brochures and other documents* aimed at spelling out what are the new priorities for the business, stating the likely benefits and pointing out the costs of failure

❐ *active 'selling'* of the new culture by top management to show that it will be more than mere lip service

❐ *develop key slogans/* cultural messages (see Figure 13.4 in previous chapter)

❐ *recruiting like-minded people* to key positions in the organisation, some by promotion from within, others by external recruitment

❐ preparation and publication of *revised procedures, communication and decision-making arrangements* in any re-structuring

❐ *utilise services of Personnel and Training specialists* to provide appropriate rewards system for new culture and back-up training opportunities for relevant groups of employees

❐ *develop key rituals* to support cultural change (eg departmental quality awards, customer service awards, annual directors' presentation to the staff etc)

Completing the cycle of change

40. Whether a major change is introduced using an OD programme, action research or some other vehicle for change, the cycle referred to in Figure 14.7 above has to be completed. Thus, once the change factors have been triggered and decisions made concerning new priorities, and once the employee commitment programme is under way, then the relevant targets and timetables must be prepared, subsequent progress reviewed, formally as well as on a day-to-day basis, and corrective changes made as required. Introducing major change in any organisation is never an easy task — vision is needed at the outset, staff need to be consulted and involved in much of the decision-making, the fears and feelings of people need to be expressed and dealt with, and the administrative machine has to match the demands of the change programme. The change has to be properly resourced in human, material and technological terms, all of which must be paid for in order to gain the benefits that are sought. In the final analysis all major change programmes carry a risk of failure, conflict and confusion. To minimise the risk managements have to consider every aspect of the change cycle, with the addition, perhaps, of a little cunning and a large measure of patience.

References

1   Burns, T. & Stalker, G.M. (1961) *The Management of Innovation*, Tavistock

2. Moss Kanter, R. (1984) *The Change Masters*, Unwin

3. Leavitt, H. (1964) *'Applied Organizational Change in Industry: Structural, Technical and Human Approaches'* in Cooper W. et al (eds), New Perspectives in Organization Research, John Wiley

4. Peters, T & Waterman, R. (1982) *In Search of Excellence*, Harper Collins

5   Schein, E.H. (1980) *Organizational Psychology (3rd edn)*, Prentice Hall

6. Chin, R. & Benne, K. (1976) *'General Strategies for Effecting Changes in Human Systems'*, in Bennis, W. G. et al (eds), The Planning of Change (3rd edn), Holt, Rinehart & Winston

7. Tynan, O. (1980), *'Improving the Quality of Working Life*, WRU Occasional Paper No 16, Work Research Unit

8. Lewin, K. (1951) *Field Theory in Social Science*, Harper

9. French, W. L. & Bell, C.H. (1984) *Organization Development: Behavioral Science Interventions for Organization Improvement* (3rd edn), Prentice Hall

10. Thakur, M. et al (1978) *Personnel in Change*, Institute of Personnel Management (now IPD)

11. Schein, E.H. (1969) Process Consultation: Its Role in Organization Development, Addison-Wesley

12. Belbin, M. (1993) *Team Roles at Work*, Butterworth Heinemann

Questions for reflection/discussion

1. What factors in the *external* environment are likely to make the biggest contribution to change in the following organisations:

   a. a large travel agency specialising in up-market tours and cruises

   b. a community health trust serving the population of a residential seaside town

2. Why is it important for business organisations, in particular, to be aware of trends in their external environment?

3. Discuss the statement that 'Strategic changes, whilst triggered by change in the external environment, nevertheless have their greatest impact on an organisation's *internal* affairs'.

4. Why do individuals and groups tend to resist change, and what can senior managers do to overcome their resistance?

5. Why is it helpful to think of change as a cyclical process?

6. How far are Organisation Development programmes really necessary in order to effect major change in an organisation?

7. What skills would you look for in a first-class change agent?

15 Designing work and jobs

Introduction

1. Having considered many of the key issues involved in the design of organisation structures, the motivation and perceptions of people at work, and the behaviour of groups, we can now turn to the problems of designing work itself to meet the needs of enterprises in the closing years of this century.

2. Earlier chapters have examined differing attitudes and differing solutions to the problem of effective organisation design. Wrestling with this problem has spanned the twentieth century from its earliest decades. The basic problem of designing an appropriate (ie workable) organisational form is still with us. What has been learnt from the past, and how can 'better' structures be devised for the information age that is coming rapidly upon us as we approach the turn of the century? We have also examined the challenging issues posed by human behaviour in work organisations. Individuals' needs, skills and contribution have been considered, so too have the needs and behaviour of people when organised in groups. We have also made a brief survey of the effects of technology and the organisation's external environment on human behaviour at work. In this particular section of the book, we have examined some of the leading issues of organisational change. The question now is, 'What does all this mean for the design of work, ie the jobs and their constituent tasks that make up the delivery system of an organisation's output?'

3. Unlike Handy (1984)[1] in his thoughtful text on the future of work, which in his view encompasses more than just 'employment' (ie paid work), the assumption in this chapter is that 'work' means paid employment. It might be useful at this point, therefore, to refer back to the definition of a work organisation given in Chapter 1. This went as follows:

A work organisation consists of a group (large or small) or groups of people who collaborate in a structured and relatively permanent way in order to achieve one or more goals which they share in common, and which they could not achieve by acting on their own. Such an organisation is structured in a manner which formally recognises, and places, the tasks and roles that individuals are expected to fulfil. The operation of work organisations implies a considerable degree of control over individual members, especially those most junior in the task structure. The predominant values and standards of the members of an organisation develop over time to form an organisation culture, which is a preferred way of doing things. The particular form and culture adopted by an organisation is considerably affected by technological and environmental factors.

4. The core of the above definition is the formal structure that recognises, and places, the tasks and roles that individuals are expected to fulfil, and which places restraints on people's behaviour. The definition also recognises the significance of technological and environmental factors in the kind of structure that is devised, and the way in which it is implemented.

The pressures for change in jobs

5. The way in which work, and specifically the network of jobs, is organised is affected fundamentally by two of the key factors referred to later in Figure 15.2 — (1) the potential for change in external environment, and (2) the impact of technology. The external environment, whether it is relatively calm or quite turbulent, represents a major source of change at the level of the individual job. This is partly because of changes introduced by governments in the form of legislation and administrative rules, partly because of changing trends in society at large (personal preferences, fashions etc), partly because of economic factors (global as well as national), partly because of changes in the organisation's competitive position, but mainly because of the behaviour of those who are currently purchasing (or intending to purchase) the organisation's products or services. Customers, clients, patients, users of goods and services of all kinds have the biggest single impact on the way most commercial and many public and voluntary bodies behave. Since jobs are the means by which organisations actually deliver their goods and services, they are in the front-line for any significant changes that occur in their respective user-communities. Given the fact that Britain and other advanced economies are moving rapidly from a manufacturing base to a services base, there is increasingly a direct face-to-face relationship between customer and provider at the most basic element of the organisation — the job-holder.

6. If change in the external environment is the biggest single influence on the network of jobs in an organisation, then change in technology is a close second. The introduction of machines in bygone times usually led to the loss of jobs. Nowadays, that threat is less likely, but there is another in its place — a change in the knowledge and skill requirements of jobs. When new technology is introduced tasks that were done previously by people are now taken over by machines. Of course, this has brought benefits in that many dirty and/or repetitive tasks have been mechanised, leaving human beings to carry out the control and monitoring functions. The challenge for individuals is to acquire the new knowledge and skill that modern technology demands.

7. New technology has become widely available due to the incredible effciency and compactness of the micro-processor. Computers and computer-controlled machines are transforming factory and office work all over the world. Some

idea of what this can mean in changes to jobs can be gleaned from the wheel diagram shown in Figure 15.1, which illustrates the radical change from manual to electronic systems in the office (see Birchall & Hammond, 1981)[2]. As the wheel implies, technology has not *reduced* the availablity of jobs in offices but has changed them, calling for revised task needs, new skills and revised job descriptions. What is clear from the diagram is that the different office systems (writing, copying, computing etc) are gradually converging into one electronic office. The likely result for many office workers is that all their work transactions will be processed through a keyboard and computer screen. They will tend to become chained to their 'workstation' unless attention is paid to social and physical health needs.

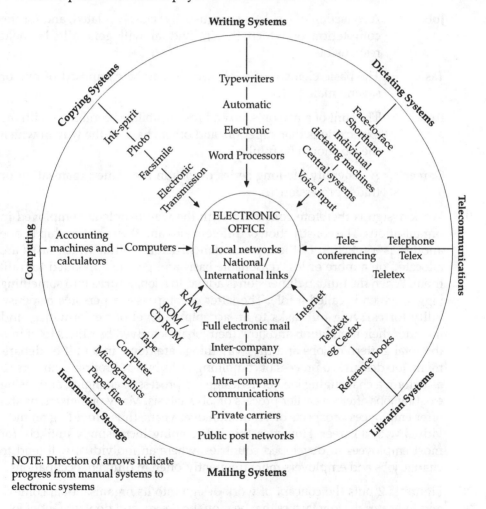

NOTE: Direction of arrows indicate progress from manual systems to electronic systems

Figure 15.1   *Impact of technology on office systems (adapted from Birchall & Hammond, 1981)*

Key issues in work design

8. Having considered some aspects of two of the principal influences on work and job design, we can now concentrate on the formal recognition of tasks and roles as contained in the definition of a work organisation referred to above, and examine key issues affecting the design of work. Figure 15.2 maps out these key issues.Firstly, however, it may be useful to set out some simple definitions of the key concepts of work, job, task, role and career, as follows:

    Work   Activities in which people are gainfully employed in jobs, usually for money, in the service of another individual or an organisation

    Job   A collection of tasks that are (usually) closely related, and for the completion of which the individual will generally be held responsible

    Task   The basic element of a job, which may be composed of one or several main tasks

    Role   The sum of a person's job and responsibilities combined with the expectations that superiors and others have of the way in which the job should be fulfilled

    Career   A generally life-long series of jobs in the same organisation or trade/profession

9. Work design is therefore concerned with the way people are employed in organisations. The construction of different jobs and their relationship to one another is a function of the organisation structure within which tasks are allocated on a more or less reasonable basis and people appointed to fulfil them. When the human dimension is added to a job, it turns into something bigger, which is called a role. The latter encompasses a person's responsibility for carrying out tasks to an acceptable level of performance, and includes their motivation and how their job is perceived by others to fit into the total pattern of jobs and the 'way things are done' in a unit or department. Job design is a process of combining tasks into appropriate clusters so as to form a challenging job. Job redesign is a process of changing or revising existing jobs after an earlier process of job analysis. Many organisations still offer employees prospects of promotion over years, thus providing an individual with a career. However, this is becoming increasingly unlikely for most employees in developed countries, where an individual will tend to change jobs and employers more frequently, often in different occupations.

10. Figure 15.2 puts the concept of work design into its organisational context, and indicates the key factors that bear on the design and deployment of jobs in an organisation. As can be seen these key factors include wider organisational factors such as the demands of customers and clients, and the requirements of the law, as well as the organisation's strategic plan, which gives rise

to operational objectives and targets. Included in these wider factors is the organisation culture, which pervades the network of jobs and roles like a breath of wind on a summer's day. The model, or 'work design map', also includes factors that have a direct and often immediate impact on jobs and roles — the operational objectives and targets, the knowledge and skills of the employees concerned, the skills and style of their managers, the technology employed, the quality standards applied and the organisation structure itself.

Figure 15.2   *Key factors in the design of work*

11. The wider organisational factors in work design can be summarised as follows:

    ❒ *customer/client demands* make the biggest single impact on the nature and type of jobs likely to be required to enable the organisation to meet its strategic or business plan; their effect is greatest when they *change* their demands (eg on range, quality, price etc)

    ❒ *legal obligations* (eg on health & safety, employment conditions etc) can also affect the nature and type of jobs required as well as the *context* in which those jobs are carried out

    ❒ *social pressures* (eg on conservation issues) may also affect the nature and conduct of jobs, if not their type

- ❐ *strategic plan/ goals* reflect in part the first three items above, and thus play a dominant role in the structure of work in the organisation, and the way in which it is carried out

- ❐ *new technology* (ie technology that is available but not currently in use by the organisation) is also likely to have a major impact on the nature, type and number of jobs, as more and more activities are undertaken by machines and computers even in what were once labour-intensive industries (eg banking, insurance etc)

- ❐ *labour market conditions* (ie the availability of sufficient numbers of suitably skilled and qualified people ready for employment in the organisation); an assumption has to be made here that the organisation can offer potential recruits an interesting job at an attractive wage

12. The immediate factors that affect the design of work are:

- ❐ *operational objectives/ targets*, since this is the point at which strategic and business plans are spelt out in much greater detail (output figures, product range, personnel numbers, capital and budget allocations, price bands etc) and where the skills required and technology to be employed are determined

- ❐ *organisation structure* (ie the network or hierarchy of jobs and the formal links between them), including the mechanisms and procedures for communication and decision-making

- ❐ *technology currently employed* (eg *hardware* such as machinery and computers, *software* for process controls and office systems, production *workflows*, service *delivery systems* etc)

- ❐ *quality standards employed* will affect the nature, type and conduct of jobs in terms of what is required and to what standard

- ❐ *employee skills and motivation* are not only a *product* of the work requirements of an organisation, but also affect the possibilities for changing the structure and content of jobs and tasks

- ❐ *managerial skills and style* have a significant impact on the *way* in which jobs and tasks are carried out currently and how they could be improved in the future; these factors also have a major effect on employee attitudes and overall level of motivation

The design of jobs

13. Once decisions have been made concerning the overall structure of jobs and tasks, then attention can be paid to the detailed construction of individual jobs in the light of the personnel available, the technology in use and the objectives to be achieved. Initial questions that need to be asked include:

❐ What are our task requirements?

❐ How should these tasks be divided between people and machines?

❐ How should tasks be allocated between individuals? On grounds of efficiency, personal satisfaction or some other reason?

❐ How best can tasks be grouped into manageable and effective jobs?

❐ Who should decide how jobs are constructed — supervisors? managers? prospective/ existing job-holders?

❐ Should jobs be fitted to technology or technology fitted to jobs?

❐ How best can individuals' social and psychological needs be met through the range of tasks they are given?

❐ How best can the range of tasks and jobs be assembled into a collaborative framework in any one unit or department?

14. In answering the above questions there are a number of possible alternative approaches (see Figure 15.3), each of which will be discussed below. They range from 'engineering' type approaches such as 'scientific management' and 'efficiency management' to 'employee-friendly' approaches such as 'job enrichment' and the 'quality of working life'.

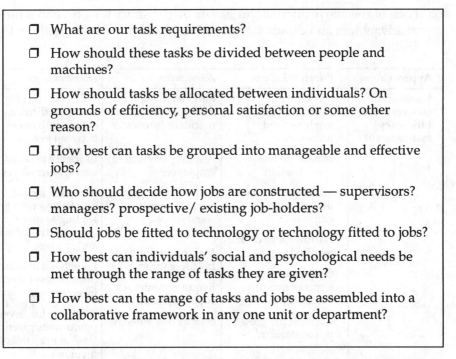

Figure 15.3   *Alternative approaches to job design*

15. Each of the above alternatives has its own distinct features and a number of advantages and disadvantages, which are summarised briefly in Figure 15.4:

Approach	Principal features	Advantages	Disadvantages
Scientific management/ Efficiency management	People are subordinate to machines and processes	Rational method of matching people to machines/processes	Inflexible use of; labour; difficult to switch employees between jobs
	Maximum task specialisation	Requires less skilled employees	Incidence of boredom amongst employees
	Minimum degree of discretion for employee	Requires less training to reach acceptable standard of performance	Increased lack of satisfaction with job leading to more absenteeism, lateness and sickness
	Narrow range of skills required	Makes work outputs precisely measurable	Likelihood of more disputes over pay, incentives etc
	Output measured in terms of quantity versus time	Requires minimum supervisor control	
	Cost-effectiveness is prime standard	Seen as cost -effective	Relatively low level of productivity given the level of investment involved
Job rotation	Switching people between jobs involving similar tasks and levels of responsibility	Creates opportunities to increase employee interest	Benefits of increased interest and reduced boredom likely to be marginal at best
		Reduces monotony and boredom	
Job enlargement	Allocating extra tasks to an existing job (ie extending it sideways)	Employee appears to be given more work and more responsibility	This is another version of 'more of the same thing' and is unlikely to bring increased motivation except in a few cases
	Usually not involving any extension of responsibility	Keeps employee busy	
		Supervisor feels he is being fair to employee	
		Depending on the extra tasks, then a bonus system employee could achieve higher earnings	
		Some evidence to suggest that certain groups of employees appreciate it	

Figure 15.4 (a)   *Job design - The pros and cons*

Approach	Principal features	Advantages	Disadvantages
Job enrichment	Sometimes known as 'vertical job loading' Involves building motivators into jobs eg achievement, recognition, job interest etc Usually does involve an addition to personal responsibility Changes to any one job are likely to affect others around it, especially the job next up the line (usually the supervisor)	Increases individual motivation at work Reduces absenteeism, sickness and other behaviour due to boredom and lack of interest Improves employee performance (Paul & Robertson, 1970)[3]	Requires considered approach to existing jobs in job-sets One man's job enrichment can be another's job impoverishment Supervisors have a lot to lose if their job responsibilities are allocated to their own staff It may not be easy to match pay etc to new responsibilities Job enrichment can be costly to introduce
Autonomous work groups	Unlike job enrichment which focuses on individual jobs, the design of autonomous work groups is aimed at work teams Complete flexibility of jobs and tasks within groups Considerable discretion within groups to plan schedules, allocate tasks, appoint leader etc	Achieves committed workforce Consistently high quality and output Builds a spirit of flexible attitudes towards work (Emery, 1979)[4] Encourages the idea of a 'learning organisation'	Needs considerable planning Team members need to be selected with care at the outset Task and role flexibility needs to be acquired through briefing and training Costly to set up Involves taking risks on part of senior management
Socio-technical systems	Work environments are composes of two interdependent elements - a social system, and a technical system The socio-technical system is affected by the organisation's culture and by the external environment (Davis & Trist, 1974)[5]	Enables technology to be utilised more effectively Meets the social needs of employees in a technical environment Encourages the informal relationships to collaborate with the formal versions	Usually requires the assistance of a trained consultant Requires considerable planning Requires major consultation and negotiation effort

Figure 15.4 (b)   *Job design - The pros and cons*

Approach	Principal features	Advantages	Disadvantages
Socio-technical systems	The social system includes informal relationships as well as formal ones	Indicates to people that they are more important than machines, but that technology is important too Leads to improved productivity when designed effectively	
Quality of working life (QWL)	High priority given to meeting employee needs in relation to technology (machines and processes) Tasks should contain variety of pace, method, skill etc Jobs should provide scope for learning People should be able to contribute to decision making about their work Personnel policies, including pay	Allows for a comprehensive approach to work design - task design, job construction, participative consultation and adequate personnel policies Enhances employee motivation Increases job interest Provides realistic work-based learning opportunities Improves attitudes towards labour flexibility Is likely to become embedded in the organisation culture Pay and conditions can be seen to move in concert with job changes	Requires substantial commitment from top management given the strategic nature of QWL Require ongoing consultancy support, even if supplied from internal source Implies ongoing support from the personnel and training functions

Figure 15.4 (c)   *Job design - the pros and cons*

16. Several of the above design alternatives have links with earlier references (Chapter 7) to Herzberg's 'motivation-hygiene theory' and 'expectancy theory'. Herzberg (1959)[7], for example suggested several practical points for introducing job enrichment, which can be summarised as follows:

☐ remove some controls over the job, but retain accountability

☐ increase the accountability of individuals for their own work

☐ give an individual a complete unit of work

☐ give additional authority where appropriate

☐ give feedback to employee direct rather than always through supervisor

☐ gradually introduce new and more difficult tasks

☐ assign tasks which will enable individuals to become experts in their field of operations

17. Lawler (1969)[8], from the expectancy perspective, suggested that intrinsic rewards were the most likely to produce the desired outcomes sought by employees, and proposed that jobs should allow for meaningful feedback, test the individual's valued abilities, and permit a considerable degree of self-control over the way the job is performed. Hackman (1977)[9] from a similar perspective devised a model (Figure 15.5) based on his observations of the psychological states and outcomes experienced by people in response to given job characteristics. These can be summarised as follows in Figure 15.5, which presents an optimistic conclusion to the provision of the selected job characteristics, several of which appear in the quality of working life section above.

Job characteristics	Critical psychological states	Personal/work outcomes
Skill variety Task identity Task significance }	Experienced meaningfulness of the work	High motivation
Autonomy	Experienced responsibility for results	High quality work performance
Feedback	Knowledge of results	High job satisfaction Low absenteeism Low labour turnover

Figure 15.5   *Job characteristics — personal and work outcomes*
(adapted from Hackman, J.R., 1977)

18. A paper by Sell (1983)[10] for the Work Research Unit of the UK Department of Employment usefully summarises the job characteristics that are essential if a job is to satisfy human needs. Briefly these characteristics are as follows:

- ☐ the job should contribute to some definite goals

- ☐ the job-holder's role should be clear both to the job-holder and to the members of his or her role-set

- ☐ individuals should be responsible for their own work and for the resources they use

- ☐ there should be some degree of autonomy over the way in which tasks are to be achieved

- ☐ the job should contain an element of variety, so as to permit variations in task, pace and method

- ☐ work cycles should be longer rather than shorter, and repetition should be kept to a minimum

- ☐ the job should enable the job-holder, wherever possible, to complete a piece of work

- ☐ the job-holder should be given feedback on performance

- ☐ the job should provide learning opportunities for the job-holder together with an element of challenge designed to extend the individual's repertoire of knowledge and skills

- ☐ the job should allow for some social interaction with others

---

Competency approaches to job design

19. Allied to national initiatives in the UK to address the state of vocational education and training, there has been considerable interest over the past decade in designing work and jobs around the concept of 'competency'. Whilst there has been some argument, even confusion, about the meaning that should be ascribed to the word 'competence', it is generally agreed that it is concerned with a person's *performance* at a task. Thus, as a concept, it is closely related to the idea of 'skill', or, more precisely, 'skill at' performing some task. The definition adopted by the UK Employment Department is as follows:

'...the ability to perform activities within an occupation or function to the standards expected in employment'.

Underlying this definition is an employment-led model of job competence expressed in terms of four interrelated components:

1. *Task skills*, ie the performance of relevant tasks

2   *Task management*, ie the skills required to manage a group of tasks within a job

3. *Contingency management skills*, ie the skills required to respond to breakdowns in routines and procedures

4. *Job/Role environment*, ie skills in responding appropriately to the wider aspects of the job or role (eg dealing with people)

20. When examining ways of describing *management* jobs in competency terms, it was found necessary to use a further model in order to describe other competencies that were also important. This further model, known as the Personal Competence model, focuses on the personal behaviour of the job-holder in carrying out his or her work. The model (eg see Fowler, 1994)[11] is based on four sets of personal competences as follows:

1. *Planning* to optimise the achievement of results

2. *Managing others* to optimise results

3. *Managing oneself* to optimise results

4. *Using intellect* to optimise results

Each set is broken down into a number of personal dimensions, for example:

Planning   ❏ *'Setting and prioritising objectives'*

           ❏ *'Monitoring and responding to actual against planned activities'*

Managing oneself

           ❏ *'Managing personal emotions and stress'*

Each dimension is then further analysed under a number of specific associated behaviours, which means the job requirements are described in detailed terms.

21. A body called the Management Charter Initiative (MCI) was established in the late 1980's to examine and develop occupational standards for managers, primarily with a view to rationalising the range of educational and training qualifications for managers, although this was subsequently broadened to encompass other issues such as job design, appraisal etc. Standards, in this context, are expressed in terms of units and *elements of*

competence supported by appropriate *performance criteria* and statements of context (*'range statements'*). Some examples are given below to illustrate the detailed breakdown of managerial jobs at first-line management level (MCI, 1991)[12], from which it is possible to see the generic competencies required to carry out the job satisfactorily (Figure 15.6).

Key role	Unit of competence	Elements of competence	Performance criteria
Manage operations	Maintain and improve service and product operations	Maintain operations to meet quality standards	*' ... consistently meet design and delivery specifications.'* *' Systems to monitor quantity, quality, cost and time specifications for service/product delivery are fully and correctly implemented and maintained.'* *'Corrective actions are implemented without delay and ... staff and customers informed of any changes which affect them'* *etc ...*
Manage people	Develop teams, individuals and self to enhance performance	Develop and improve teams through planning and activities	*'All individuals within the team are encouraged and assisted to evaluate the team's overall development needs and to contribute to the discussion and planning of how these will be met.'* *'Team building and development plans contain clear, relevant and realistic development objectives for the team as a whole.'* *'Any unproductive friction between team members is minimised.'*

Figure 15.6   *Examples of occupational standards for first-line managers (MCI, 1991)*

22.   The *benefits* claimed for the competency approach to job design are that:

> ❒   it is employment-led, ie arises directly out of work-related needs
>
> ❒   it analyses jobs in terms of the basic competency or skills required
>
> ❒   it is outcomes-orientated, ie competencies are expressed in terms of doing things
>
> ❒   it encourages the identification of appropriate and realistic criteria of satisfactory performance of key elements in the job
>
> ❒   it provides the basis for national qualifications on the strength of performance against nationally-recognised occupational standards

23. The *problems* associated with the competency approach include the following:

> ❏ it is often difficult to define realistic outcomes and/or performance criteria for jobs requiring action on the strength of knowledge and experience
>
> ❏ it is quite likely that inflexible, and even inappropriate, standards may be developed for higher-level jobs (ie where the application of knowledge is vital, and where judgement is required)
>
> ❏ it is possible for jobs to be seen as composed entirely of sub-components, whereas some jobs, when taken as a whole, acquire synergy (ie where the whole job is greater than the sum of its parts)
>
> ❏ the system can become very complex and therefore time-consuming, which may discourage organisations from reviewing and updating jobs from time to time
>
> ❏ it raises questions about how far organisations should check individuals' competencies to ensure that they are sustaining their performance (eg as in the case of airline pilots or air traffic controllers, where competency has to be demonstrated every six months or so in order to continue practising in the profession)

Implications of job design approaches

24. The approaches to job design just described indicate a range of assumptions about the relationship between people, work-requirements, technology and organisation structure, points which were included firstly in Chapter 2 in our discussion of basic issues in organisation structuring (see especially Figures 2.3 and 2.4), where tasks were seen as a key variable. The job design issue also has implications for the human aspects of organisations, which were discussed in Chapter 4 (see especially the references to Immaturity-Maturity theory, Theory X & Theory Y, Motivation-Hygiene Theory, and Achievement Motivation). The chapter on motivation, job satisfaction and performance (Chapter 7) also raised a number of issues relevant to work and job design (especially the references to Achievement Motivation and Expectancy Theory).

25. What will be clear to readers of this book is that work design in general, and job design in particular, are geared to improving the contribution of

human beings to their employing organisations. People are seen as one element, albeit a vital one, in the operation of work organisations. The art of the organisational manager is to mix all the elements of the organisation together (people, technology, culture, environment etc) in order to produce the optimum result in terms of the organisation's strategic mission and goals. These strategic features are aimed at balancing, and satisfying, the competing needs of all the organisation's stakeholders — customers, shareholders and others as well as employees. Sociologists such as Burrell & Morgan (1979)[13] do not necessarily accept the premises on which current work design approaches are based. In what they define as the 'functionalist paradigm', practically all the theoretical studies of organisations can be found — classical, Weberian, human relations and social psychological (eg as in Chapters 2-4 in this book). Their views provide a counter-balance to the essentially managerial perspective to be found in every chapter in this book

26. Burrell & Morgan describe the functionalist paradigm as

> '...a perspective which is firmly rooted in the sociology of regulation and approaches its subject-matter from an objectivist point of view.'(p.25)

In other words they see organisational theory, as described throughout this book, as being concerned mostly with regulating behaviour in organisations, and approaching organisational behaviour as if organisations were machines or biological organisms, and as if organisations structures were physical rather than social entities. Their comment on the quality of working life movement, for example, to bring their arguments into the subject-matter of this chapter, is somewhat dismissive:

> 'In essence this movement seeks to apply the insights of open systems theory, particularly through.....socio-technical systems theory and the theory of job design, to the problems which its followers see as characterising post-industrial societies. It is based on a philosophy of piecemeal social engineering which seeks to solve the problems posed by the transition fromthe industrial to the post-industrial society......'(p.182)

They conclude that:

> 'The quality of working life movement is often seen and presented as a radical action-orientated response to the current problems facing Western industrial societies. However, their stance is essentially a regulative one...... invariably geared to the contribution which this [humanitarian concern] will make to the stability and survival of the system as a whole.'(p.183)

27. Burrell & Morgan look to a future in which radical and humanistic approaches to the study of 'organisations' based not on mechanical or biological concepts but on interpretive approaches grounded in people's meanings, perceptions and attributions. They agree that such an approach represents 'virgin territory' at present. In the meantime, ordinary individ-

uals at work will be seeking adequate intrinsic and extrinsic rewards for themselves, whilst their senior managers will continue to seek to satisfy the often conflicting interests of their major stakeholders. Given the nature of people's economic imperatives, however, it is unlikely that change will occur in the foreseeable future. At best work will continue to be a source of income for most, a source of interest and challenge for some, and a deep source of pleasure and self-fulfilment for a few.

References

1.   Handy, C. (1984) *The Future of Work*, Blackwell

2.   Birchall, D. & Hammond, V. (1981) *Tomorrow's Office Today*, Business Books

3.   Paul, W.J. & Robertson, K. (1970) *Job Enrichment and Employee Motivation*, Gower

4.   Emery, F. (1979) *'The Assembly Line - Its Logic and our Future'*, in Design of Jobs, Goodyear

5.   Davis, L. & Trist, E. (1974) *'Improving the Quality of Working Life:* Some Technical Case-studies', in O'Toole, J. (ed), Work and the Quality of Life, MIT Press

6.   White, G.C. (1982), *Technological Change and Employment*, WRU Occasional Paper No. 22, Department of Employment

7.   Herzberg, F., Mausner,B. & Snyderman, B.(1959), *The Motivation to Work*, John Wiley

8.   Lawler, E.E. (1969), *'Job Design and Employee Motivation'*, in Gruneberg, M (ed), Job Satisfaction, Gower Press

9.   Hackman, J.R. (1977), *'Work Design'*, in Hackman & Suttle (eds), *Improving Life at Work*

10.   Sell, R. (1983), *The Quality of Working Life*, WRU Paper, Department of Employment

11.   Fowler, B. (ed) (1994), *MCI Personal Competence Model: Uses and Implementation*, Research Report No. 24, Employment Department

12.   Management Charter Inititiative (1991), *Occupational Standards for Managers - Management I*, NFMED & Employment Department

13.   Burrell, M. & Morgan, G. (1979), *Sociological Paradigms and Organisational Analysis*, Heinemann

Questions for reflection/discussion

1. In what ways might external pressures lead to changes in the requirements for jobs in (1) a manufacturing firm, and (2) a High Street bank?

2. What steps would you take to ensure that your office workers were not left with totally repetitive and boring jobs as a result of changes brought about by the use of electronic technology on a large scale?

3. To what extent might the following influence the type, nature and content of jobs in either a manufacturing concern, or a provider of a service :

   ☐ quality standards?
   ☐ management style?
   ☐ organisation culture?

4. How far is it possible for *people* to be fitted to the demands of *technology* rather than the other way round?

5. If scientific management approaches to work design are so rational, why is it many organisations prefer to adopt other approaches, such as job enrichment and autonomous work groups?

6. How far do you agree that the outputs of Work and Job Design activities merely soften management's control over their staff, and do little to increase individuals' self-respect and personal growth?

7. What would you say were the strengths of the 'competency' approach to the design of jobs?

16 Human resource management, personnel policies and organisational behaviour

Introduction

1. Work organisations at their simplest level are essentially networks of relationships between people. In the pursuit of their common goals, the members of an organisation need to make provision for (1) sustaining and/ or renewing their membership, (2) deploying and adapting their knowledge, skills and competencies, and (3) meeting their intrinsic and extrinsic needs. These three sets of needs make up the bedrock of human resource, or personnel management, policies, which are decided by the senior management of the organisation, aided in many cases by Personnel specialists, and implemented by all managers throughout the structure. In one sense every manager is responsible for the acquisition, maintenance and development of human resources (HR). In practice, however, line managers tend to see their HR management role more in terms of providing effective leadership for their own work-teams than in contributing personnel services, training and personnel planning to the organisation as a whole, which is seen as the role of Personnel specialists. As in so many other instances of organisational life, it all depends on the dominant culture of the organisation and the way this is reflected in the structures and styles adopted, and the extent to which people's contribution is valued.

2. Human resource policies arise out of the corporate strategic plan by which the organisation seeks to achieve its key product-market and other objectives. These objectives are aimed at satisfying all the organisation's principal stakeholders — customers, employees, shareholders, suppliers, creditors and the community at large. Seen in purely economic terms, people are the human resources that contribute along with financial, material and technological resources to meet the demands of customers and other users of the organisation's goods and services. Since line managers, in particular, have the responsibility for the efficient delivery of the organ-

isation's goods and services, they are fully concerned with managing all the economic resources available to them. They may, therefore, accept that the personnel aspects of their resonsibilities indeed merit the term 'human resource management' (HRM). Porter (1985)[1], in an influential text on competitive advantage, included human resource management as one of the four key support activities in his model of a 'value chain' in which the primary activities of taking in resources, converting them into goods and services, marketing them to customers, delivering them to the marketplace and engaging in after-sales service (ie the line function) are supported at every stage by the HRM function. In his view HRM

> '...affects competitive advantage in any firm, through its role in deter-mining the skills and motivation of employees and the cost of hiring and training. In some industries it holds the key to competitive advantage.'

3. If the management of people is looked at from a humanistic perspective, however, the expression 'personnel management' may be preferred on the grounds that employed people (ie 'personnel') form the focus of the activities rather than the somewhat instrumental concept of people as resources. Thus, personnel management is concerned with such matters as the motivation and development of the members of the organisation, and with their fair and equitable treatment, as well as with their general efficiency and effectiveness in providing goods and services. Porter's (op. cit.) comments on the supporting role of HRM encompass its motivational and develop-mental aspects, but significantly make no reference to fair and equitable treatment of employees. Given that human beings are unlike any other resource used in an enterprise in that they have an ethical dimension attached to their behaviour, and given the central importance of people in every work organisation, it provides a less than comprehensive view of 'human resources' if this dimension is overlooked. The use of the concept of 'personnel management' enables such ethical concepts as 'dignity', 'respect', 'integrity' and 'fairness' to be included in the language and behaviour of management, as well as instrumental concepts such as 'efficiency', 'productivity' and 'cost-effectiveness'.

4. In this chapter the term ' personnel management' will be used to describe the ethical-practical framework for managing the human resources of the organisation. Since leadership has been examined elsewhere (see Chapter 11), the main emphasis in this chapter will be on the contribution and activities of senior management and their personnel specialists. Before moving on to describe these activities, however, it might be useful to note the line manager's role in managing human resources, since in many respects it is this line role which is supported by personnel specialists in implementing personnel policies throughout the organisation (and fits into Porter's value chain).

The line manager's role in personnel management

5. The main elements of the line role in HRM, or personnel management, is depicted in Figure 16.1:

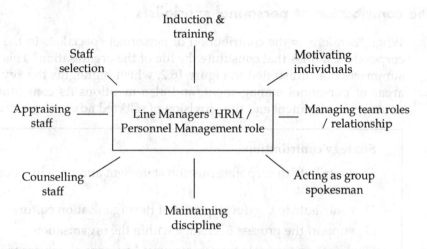

Figure 16.1   *Line Managers' HRM/ Personnel Management Role*

6. The role indicated in Figure 16.1 shows that as well as managing team roles and relationships, maintaining discipline and motivating individuals — all aspects of leadership — the line manager also engages to a greater or lesser extent, depending on the organisation, in a personnel role — selecting staff, providing induction and other training, and counselling staff . The responsibilities implied in the various activities shown in the figure reflect several of the roles of a manager referred to by Mintzberg (1973)[2], especially those of Figurehead/ Leader, Spokesman/ Negotiator, and Disturbance-handler. The support given to the line by personnel specialists focuses primarily on line management's personnel role rather than on their leadership role, although this too is supported by means of management training, for example. The support usually takes the following forms:

❏   provision of direct services (eg recruitment facilities, staff selection, induction programmes, training opportunities at several levels, wage and salary administration, personnel records and employee welfare)

❏   advice on staff selection, staff training, grievance-handling, operation of the disciplinary procedure and staff appraisal

❏   strategic leadership in key areas of HR management, such as HR planning, trade union negotiations, management development and organisation development

At the basic operating level of the organisation, it is the first two forms that are most likely to be encountered, for it is usually only at higher management levels that the strategic leadership aspect of Personnel Management comes into play.

The contribution of personnel specialists

7. What, therefore, is the contribution of personnel specialists to the wider, corporate activities that constitute the life of the organisation? This can be summarised as illustrated in Figure 16.2, which highlights the key policy areas of personnel management, and also mentions its contribution to strategy development and the provision of selected advisory services.

Strategy contribution

❏ contribute to corporate mission statement and principal goal statements

❏ contribute to the development of the organisation culture

❏ support the process of change within the organisation

❏ devise appropriate human resource/ personnel policies to sustain the implementation of corporate strategy

Policy development

❏ ensure full range of relevant HR/ personnel policies (ie statements of the manner in which the organisation intends to pursue its mission/ goals)

❏ such policies to encompass most if not all of the following:

    ❏ recruitment and employee selection

    ❏ induction of new employees

    ❏ practice regarding internal promotions and transfers

    ❏ wage and salary administration

    ❏ employee benefits (eg pensions, health care, car purchase etc)

    ❏ staff consultation/ grievance procedures

    ❏ employee relations (eg trade union recognition, negotiating procedures etc)

    ❏ training provision (skills, competencies etc)

    ❏ management succession and development

    ❏ employee welfare practices

Continued...

Figure 16.2 (a)   *Personnel specialists' contribution to corporate life*

Advisory Role

☐ advise Board on an optimum organisation structure, including arrangements for the design of jobs

☐ advise Board and line management on human aspects of all policy implementation

☐ advise Board and line management on legislation affecting employment (eg health and safety, equal opportunities, employment contracts, dismissals etc)

Executive Role

☐ ensure adequate personnel plan to ensure sufficient numbers of suitable employees available to meet line management needs

☐ ensure adequate programmes of employee development to maintain or extend employee competencies

☐ establish a management development and succession plan

☐ represent the organisation in major consultations or negotiations with trade unions

☐ ensure the provision of a full range of personnel services throughout the organisation (recruitment, , grievance and disciplinary procedures, pay/ salary procedures, PAYE procedures, staff records, welfare arrangements etc)

☐ represent the organisation in dealings with external bodies (eg government departments, pressure groups etc) on employment-related matters

---

Figure 16.2 (b)   *Personnel specialists' contribution to corporate life*

8. It is important to point out that whilst the above list (Fig. 16.2) has been set in terms of the roles of personnel *specialists*, the personnel activities referred to would have to be implemented even if there were no personnel department. Most organisations still maintain a formal personnel function, sometimes headed by a Personnel Director, but an increasing number are developing a dispersed personnel function operating through line units in flatter organisation structures. In this situation a line unit has to identify one or more persons as responsible for the recruitment of staff, administration of wages and salaries, and maintenance of employee records, for example. In many respects these are the less attractive aspects of the personnel function, compared with elements such as training, staff appraisal and job design, which line managers are often keen to control.

9. The extent to which corporate personnel departments can continue to exist, and even flourish, depends on a number of key factors (see Figure 16.3), some of which act to strengthen the role of personnel specialists, and others which weaken it.

Strengthening factors	Weakening factors
1 Board-level support	1 No real top-management support
2 Director on Board	2 No direct representation on the Board
3 Political/visionary skills of Director and other senior personnel staff	3 Inadequate and ineffective leadership of the Personnel department
4 High reputation for skills and competence of personnel staff	4 Personnel staff perceived as ineffective or incompetent
5 Centralised structure	5 Devolved structure
6 High demand for labour in several job categories	6 Little requirement for new staff
7 Lively process of change taking place in the organisation	7 Stable and/or complacent environment
8 Introduction of new technology requiring intensive training / re-training programmes	8 No demand for new technology, and existing technology well understood and routinised
9 Presence of active trade union representing employees	9 No trade union activity
10 Increase in employment	10 Current legislation well understood and catered for legislation/ codes of conduct

Figure 16.3   Key factors in the power position of personnel specialists

Personnel, strategy and change

10. Assuming that the personnel specialists are supported at the top and are reasonably competent, then the Personnel department is likely to be able to play an influential role in the life of the organisation. In the best

scenario, personnel specialists will play a key role in developing and implementing the corporate strategy of the organisation. Strategic management (Cole,1994)[3] can be defined as follows:

'......an organisational process designed to sustain, invigorate and direct the organisation's human and other resources in the profitable fulfilment of the needs of customers and other principal stakeholders......the process once started is an organisation-wide collaborative effort to satisfy the expectations of all its stakeholders.' (p.210)

Thus, involvement in the strategy process not only empowers personnel specialists in respect of the personnel aspects of the organisation's efforts, but also allows them to influence the way the other resources are procured and used (eg technology, materials, time etc). Thus an impact can be made on corporate culture. For example, the Body Shop, a company which produces hair and skin products, will only use preparations that have not been tested on animals, and insists that their suppliers confirm in writing that they have not so tested.

11. Purcell (1985)[4] suggested that the corporate personnel department could make a notable contribution to corporate culture and communications, becoming a kind of custodian of the organisation's value-system. Such a role could certainly be a possibility in respect of how *people* are employed in the organisation, including the effect on people of machines and materials, as well as the terms of their employment. It is less certain that personnel could fulfil the role in respect of the effect of the organisation's activities on the community (eg in terms of damage to the natural environment), although they could point out the adverse consequences to a community if the company were to close a factory in an area of high unemployment.

12. Given that culture whilst pervasive is difficult to pinpoint, it is somewhat easier to identify the contribution of personnel specialists to the *process of change* in the organisation. In organisations where the personnel function is both represented on the Board and has a valued reputation, it is likely that personnel specialists will be asked to play a change agent role, either singly or alongside an external consultant. Either way, it puts personnel people in a highly influential position in respect of organisational change, both in terms of what changes are to be proposed, and how they are to be implemented, if and when agreed. If the process of change is driven by line management, or by another function (eg marketing), then personnel's role may be less influential, but much will depend on the persuasive skills of the latter. Where an external consultant is given the leading change agent role, it is usually possible for the organisation's own personnel specialists to maintain a useful dialogue at a professional level with the external person. Where Personnel staff are well-qualified, well-experienced and well-respected they can usually count on being involved in the change

process at an early stage. Thus, when diagnostic activities such as organisation analysis, employee attitude surveys or job analysis are put into operation, personnel specialists can contribute their analytical skills and their inside knowledge of the organisation's mechanisms and its people.

13.   At the early stages personnel staff can often point out key issues and/ or likely stumbling blocks, if certain changes are made. These, of course, are most likely to refer to the impact of changes on the *employees*, but could also allude to effects on the other departments or functions, and on the community. Once certain changes have been proposed and agreed in principle by the Board, then personnel specialists can begin to spell out the consequences in terms of such issues as the recruitment of newcomers, perhaps in different job categories compared with the past, and the pros and cons of employing a core-and-cluster approach to staffing (ie where a core of employees are employed on permanent full-time contracts, whilst others are part-time and/or temporary). Any significant changes to the structure of jobs means that not only will different categories of employee be required, but that additional wage/ salary scales will have to be fitted into the present payments structure, and this may require the use of job evaluation studies to ensure fairness and consistency of treatment, and avoid unfair discrimination. In all these areas affecting employment conditions, personnel specialists are in their element, and can clearly take a lead role in the implementation of change.

14.   The implementation of a change programme invariably means attending to the process itself as well as to the required end-results. Personnel specialists can assist the process of change by contributing to the training involved in developing new skills and in aiding the understanding of new processes, especially where these involve inter-personal relations. They can also contribute to the consultation processes required for managers to brief and/ or motivate their teams. Where personnel staff are experienced in process consultation skills, appraisal interviewing or interpersonal relationships techniques (eg Transactional Analysis), their skills and sensitivity can be deployed in bringing key groups to a willing acceptance of change. As the organisation moves from the status quo into the new situation, matters such as the recruitment of new staff, transfer/ redeployment of existing staff, revised pay and conditions have to be dealt with effectively. Here again personnel is in the strongest possible situation for implementing the results of change as reflected in both the current members of the organisation and the potential newcomers about to be employed in the organisation.

Personnel Policy development

15.   The development of personnel policy a major factor in the implementation of organisation change is where personnel specialists play the leading role.

A policy can be defined as 'a statement of the *manner* in which a goal will be achieved'. Unlike a strategy which is essentially a corporate plan, a policy acts as a guide to behaviour. Policies are intended to apply to all levels in the organisation, and to conform to any legal requirements where they apply. Some examples of the kind of personnel policies that might be found in a typical business organisation are shown in Figure 16.4.

16. Policies are set for every functional area of an organisation — Production/Operations, Marketing, Finance, Procurement etc as well as Personnel. The intention is that the organisation shall conduct its affairs in accordance with a range of published rules and not on the basis of arbitrary behaviour by managers or directors. Policies help on the one hand to prevent the organisation from engaging (knowingly) in illegal or unethical behaviour, whilst positively promoting certain basic values to all its stakeholders on the other. A Customers' Charter, for example, is an example of a marketing policy directed towards an external stakeholder group. Others may ensure that taxes are collected and paid over to the Inland Revenue, that funds are invested safely on the money markets, and that suppliers are paid within agreed time-limits. In every way, therefore, policies make a considerable contribution to the development of the organisation's value-system, or culture.

The advisory role of personnel specialists

17. In terms of their *advisory* role personnel specialists are likely to be called upon to:

(1) comment on the implications of strategic change,

(2) suggest how the personnel aspects of the change can best be implemented,

(3) provide an advisory service on personnel matters to operational managers on a day-to-day basis.

The role in respect of strategic change is basically one of identifying the personnel implications of the changes and suggesting how they can best be addressed. For example, where major changes in the organisation structure are to be introduced in order to achieve greater empowerment and accountability for those producing the goods or delivering the services, there are considerable implications for pay structures, staff promotions and transfers, changes in individual terms and conditions of employment etc., all of which depend on the efficiency and effectiveness of the personnel function.

- ❏ 'Every vacancy in the company will be filled on the grounds of merit only, and the company will take all possible steps to avoid any unfair discrimination against applicants, whether they are internal candidates or applicants from outside the organisation'

- ❏ 'Every vacancy below Board level will be advertised internally in addition to any recruitment measures that may be taken externally'

- ❏ 'The standards to be achieved in order to qualify for any bonus payment, whether for group or individual effort, shall be clearly established and made known to the groups and individuals concerned before any payments are made'

- ❏ 'All employees shall be entitled to at least one formal appraisal from their immediate superior each year, during which meeting the individual employee shall have the opportunity to discuss past performance, present progress and future prospects'

- ❏ 'Published time-limits for action by superiors shall be expressly included in the company's grievance procedures, so as to prevent any unwarranted delays in responding to an employee's grievance'

- ❏ 'All employees at every level of the organisation will be encouraged to develop their knowledge and skills in areas of relevance to the company's activities, and opportunities shall be granted on the grounds of individual merit or department need and not related to age, sex, seniority or any other qualifying consideration'

- ❏ 'No major organisational changes will be made without thorough consultation with the staff affected either through the management chain or through joint consultation procedures'

- ❏ 'Any employee whose behaviour is deemed to constitute misconduct will be given full details of the charges made against him or her, will be permitted to be represented at a hearing with the appropriate level of management, will be given full opportunity to explain the misconduct, and will only have sanctions taken against them on the grounds of the evidence brought before the hearing by both sides; following a decision of the disciplinary meeting, the individual concerned may appeal against the sanctions to the next senior level of management; no individual shall be dismissed on disciplinary grounds except in the case of proven gross misconduct'

Figure 16.4   *Typical policy statements on personnel matters*

18. The policies that are developed in the other functional and operational parts of the organisation as part of strategic change may have personnel implications. For example, where a new policy on service quality is promulgated, there are likely to be transfers between supervisory jobs to enable key individuals to take charge of the new arrangements, as well as staff training implications to enable individuals to reach the new standards. A new policy on software applications in the headquarters' administration, to take another example, is likely to lead to demands for updating training, discussions about employee health as a result of long-term exposure to visual display units, and possible demands from key staff for improved salaries. These are all issues on which personnel specialists can offer advice and guidance.

19. An important area of any organisation's business is that of employment legislation. It is usually expected that advice and guidance on such matters will be available from the personnel specialists. The topics on which line and other managers may well seek advice include the following:

   ❐ operation of employment contracts (especially since in most cases there is no written contract but instead a series of documents and oral promises)

   ❐ procedures for dealing with cases of misconduct by employees

   ❐ procedures for staff dismissals and their outcomes

   ❐ problems of a more general nature arising from individual grievances

   ❐ relationships with recognised trade unions

   ❐ relationships with trade unions seeking recognition (ie for the purposes of collective bargaining on behalf of particular groups of employees)

   ❐ equal opportunities legislation, especially in regard to recruitment and promotions

   ❐ aspects of health and safety at work

20. Other matters on which personnel staff may give advice to line and functional managers are likely to include:

   ❐ staff recruitment and selection

   ❐ wage and salary matters (eg confirming relevant scales for new posts, confirming limits of movement within scales etc)

   ❐ job grading and job evaluation (especially important where the job structure has been changed and former pay relativities are unclear)

   ❐ personnel/ manpower planning issues (eg for a large department or major profit-centre)

❏ staff training and development

❏ issues arising from collective agreements with recognised trade unions (eg interpretations of particular clauses/ practices)

❏ dealing with problems of staff lateness, sickness and absenteeism

❏ employee welfare matters

Managers are less likely to seek advice and assistance on matters which are dealt with directly by personnel specialists as part of their servicing of the organisation's personnel requirements. The situation is determined largely by the role allocated to the specialist personnel function by the top management — where personnel is centralised, then most personnel issues will be handled directly by the specialists; where the personnel function is dispersed between the centre and the line units, then it is much more likely that managers will need to seek advice of their specialist personnel advisers.

Personnel in an executive role

21. Where the personnel function is given an organisation-wide brief supported from a central base it can carry out a significant executive role in personnel matters. Although line managers may not always be willing to accept the specialist functional role, which they may consider as interference in their line operations, it is clear from a corporate perspective that a central function can take a broader view of personnel matters. Whereas line and other managers are chiefly concerned with their own department or section, the corporate personnel function is concerned with the operation, and consequences, of personnel decisions across every department and section.

22. Where personnel can take a leading role in key executive areas such as the design of work and jobs, and the personnel/ manpower planning necessary to meet the demands of the job-structure, then it can deal proactively with related issues such as:

❏ recruitment planning (eg advertising, short-listing, interviewing etc)

❏ establishing or confirming the relative worth of jobs (through job evlu-ation)

❏ setting a framework for establishing pay relativities between jobs and individuals

❏ agreeing the rules for bonus arrangements for groups or individuals

❏ preparing effective training programmes in collaboration with the user-departments (eg induction training, job competency training etc)

❏ arrangements for shift-working, part-time workers etc

Conclusion

23. Taken as a whole, the selection, deployment, motivation, utilisation and leadership of people is the most critical function to be undertaken in any work organisation, and it is often by far the most costly. Success in managing the human resources of the organisation is an essential prerequisite for success, however measured. The function can be carried out in a dispersed manner throughout the organisation, so long as there is an adequate strategic framework based on organisation-wide policies to ensure consistency of treatment across departments and functions. In most cases the best results are likely to be gained from having a strong, reputable and credible Personnel function, providing leadership and guidance in all the key areas of human resources.

References

1. Porter, M.E. (1985), *Competitive Advantage*, The Free Press
2. Mintzberg, H. (1973), *The Nature of Managerial Work*, Harper & Row
3. Cole, G.A. (1994), *Strategic Management*, D P Publications
4. Purcell, J. (1985), *'Is anybody listening to the corporate personnel department?'* in Personnel Management, September 1985

Questions for reflection/discussion

1. In what ways does the concept of 'Human Resource Management' offer a different perspective on the management of people in an organisations compared with 'Personnel Management'?

2. To what extent does a typical line manager in a decentralised structure carry out a 'personnel function'?

3. Why might business enterprises benefit from the involvement of personnel specialists in the development of corporate policies?

4. How can a corporate personnel function contribute to the culture of an organisation?

5. How far is it realistic to expect personnel specialists to protect the interests of the employees in their organisation? What conflicts of interest might arise?

6. On what employment aspects of business might line and other managers seek the advice of personnel specialists?

7. If you were the newly-appointed Managing Director of a medium-sized company with an ineffectual personnel department, what steps might you take to develop a powerful and effective personnel function?

17 Organisational behaviour and strategic management

Introduction

1. There is a considerable overlap between the subject-matter of Organisational Behaviour and the issues addressed in the strategic management process. Indeed in many respects the study of Organisational Behaviour is a study of strategic management. This short penultimate chapter, therefore, provides an opportunity to pull together some of the organisational models used earlier in this book and compare them with the strategic management process. This may serve to emphasise the comprehensive organisation-wide nature of Organisational Behaviour as a study of the behaviour of people as individuals, and in groups, within a cultural framework of goals, policies and plans established by the strategic management process.

The strategic management process

2. In an earlier text (Cole, 1994)[1], the author concluded with a model definition of strategic management (ie in its ideal form). The definition of strategic management which follows is fairly lengthy, but by quoting it in full, one can see the scale of the topics that overlap between strategic management and the subject of this particular book - Organisational Behaviour. The definition is as follows:

    'Strategic management is an organisational process designed to sustain, invigorate and direct the organisation's human and other resources in the profitable fulfilment of the needs of customers and other principal stakeholders. The process is guided by the organisation's value system, or culture, which is manifested not only in the organisation's mission statement, policies, and strategic goals, but also in the behaviour of top management and other key managers in the organisation. The process of strategic management involves setting goals and objectives, and assessing the organisation's prospects for attaining these in the context of its internal resources and external environment. It involves deciding which customers to serve, with which products or services, and meeting those customers'

legitimate needs and wants by allocating resources in the most advantageous way. Strategic management also involves decisions about stakeholders other than customers. It is particularly concerned to meet the needs of the organisation's shareholders for an adequate return on their investment. It is concerned to treat all its employees fairly and to make reasonable efforts to ensure that they are provided with satisfying jobs. It is concerned to deal fairly, as well as cost-effectively, with all its suppliers. It is concerned to act responsibly towards its major creditors. Finally, it is concerned to act as a responsible corporate citizen in the communities within which it operates. Directing and implementing the process of strategic management is the responsibility of the organisation's board of directors, or equivalent top management. However, the process once started is an organisation-wide collaborative effort to satisfy the expectations of all its stakeholders.' (p.210)

3. As can be seen from the above definition, there are references to such topics as: *human/ other resources, principal stakeholders, culture or value-system, policies, management behaviour,* and the *external environment.* All these are topics of central interest in the study of behaviour in organisations. Whilst a major element in strategy formulation is the study of the *external* environment of the organisation (social, economic conditions etc), it is also true that any strategic review must take account of the state of the *internal* environment, which implies attention to such aspects of organisation as:

❐   the appropriateness of the current *organisation structure* given a new strategy or changed external circumstances

❐   the capability of the current *systems* in use (esp. communication systems)

❐   the appropriateness of the present *management style* given a new strategy

❐   the attitudes, motivation and performance of *current staff*

❐   the current profile of *skills* amongst staff

❐   the appropriateness of the current *culture* in the light of a new strategy or change in external conditions

❐   the continuing relevance of the organisation's present policies towards its various *stakeholders*

❐   the impact of current and new *technology* on the organisation's internal systems

❐   the contribution of *support functions* (esp personnel, procurement and finance)

❐   an assessment of present *efficiency* in the use of assets and the generation of sufficient cash flow

---

These internal issues are all of great concern to the study of Organisational Behaviour.

Organisational behaviour

4.   It is clear from the above definition of strategic management, and the list of its component activities, that most of the priorities of strategic management are contained in Organisational Behaviour, which was defined in Chapter 1 as follows:

.................a term applied to the systematic study of the behaviour of individuals and groups in the workplace, including an analysis of the nature of groups, the development of structures between and within groups, and the process of implementing change. The rationale of Organisational Behaviour is to predict and/ or control the behaviour of individuals and groups in the pursuit of management goals, which may, or may not, be shared throughout the organisation. (p. 3)

This definition indicates that the principal issues addressed by the study of Organisational Behaviour are those of (1) individual behaviour and performance at work, (2) the nature and working of people in groups, (3) the nature of social structures and organisation design at work, and (4) the processes involved in adapting behaviour to meet changing conditions. These issues are dealt with in the context of work organisations and the goals that have been set for the members by their leaders, and which, it should be noted, the former may not always share.

5.   The nature and design of the 'organisation' is of major concern both to strategists and students of Organisational Behaviour. The following definition of a work organisation, also taken from Chapter 1, indicates that (1) the process of becoming 'organised' and (2) the outcomes in terms of organisation design, are of central interest to strategic management and organisational theorists alike:

A work organisation consists of a group (large or small), or groups, of people who collaborate in a structured and relatively permanent way in order to achieve one or more goals which they share in common, and which they could not achieve by acting on their own. Such an   organisation is structured in a manner which formally recognises, and places, the tasks and roles that individuals are expected to fulfil. The operation of work organisations implies a considerable degree of control over individual members, especially those most junior in the task structure. The predominant values and standards of the members of an organisation develop over time to form an organisation culture, which is a preferred way of doing things. The particular form and culture adopted by an organisation is considerably affected by technological and environmental factors. (p. 5)

6.   The nature and form of the organisation structure are at once a product of, and an influence on, the strategic management process and organisational behaviour. However, whereas the strategic process is primarily concerned

with designing the best structure, the study of Organisational Behaviour is concerned with both the design and the operation of the structure, at individual and group interaction levels. Both perspectives share an interest in the development and maintenance of the organisation culture, and in the technological and other environmental forces that help to shape it.

The organisation as a system

7. Strategic management focuses on providing a framework for activities designed to direct, sustain and invigorate the organisation's resources. It is more concerned with *effectiveness,* or 'Doing the right things', than with *efficiency,* which is concerned with 'Doing things right'. This does not mean that strategic decision-making is unconcerned with processes and consequences, but only that its main priorities are directed towards vision, direction and achievement in the context of the external environment. It is the role of *operational* management, or what Mintzberg (1983)[2] calls the Middle Line, to implement the strategic plan and focus attention on resourcing, deployment and efficiency issues. Whilst the operational role is secondary for strategic management, it is of great importance to studies of Organisational Behaviour, since it is concerned with the process by which the strategic framework is brought to life.

8. The notion of the organisation as a system was referred to in Chapter 3 paragraph 35. This concept implies that the organisation operates in an environment from which it draws various inputs, which it then processes to produce outputs in the form of goods or services. In order to maintain the stability (or balance) of the system, the organisation utilises various forms of feedback on its performance in order to determine (1) the effect of its activities on the environment, and (2) the nature and size of the next round of inputs. Figure 17.1 illustrates this relationship as described earlier in Chapter 3.

9. Strategic concerns are firstly to decide on a strategy (a fundamental input), which means deciding what to produce in which market with what desired returns. Strategy is also concerned with the form and integrity of organisation structure, the discipline of financial controls, the guidelines of policies and the challenge of competitiveness. These are all *vital* inputs to the organisation's life as an open system. Strategic thinking draws on the external environment to assess product-market strategies and the competitive situation. It also looks to external sources for the resourcing of its plans (the labour market, suppliers etc). Finally, strategic management is concerned both with results (ie outputs) and feedback on those results, which is not just restricted to financial information, but with data such as customer satisfaction surveys, staff turnover figures and the organisation's 'reputation' in the wider community. From the Organisational Behaviour perspective, the grand scale of strategic activities is of considerable interest

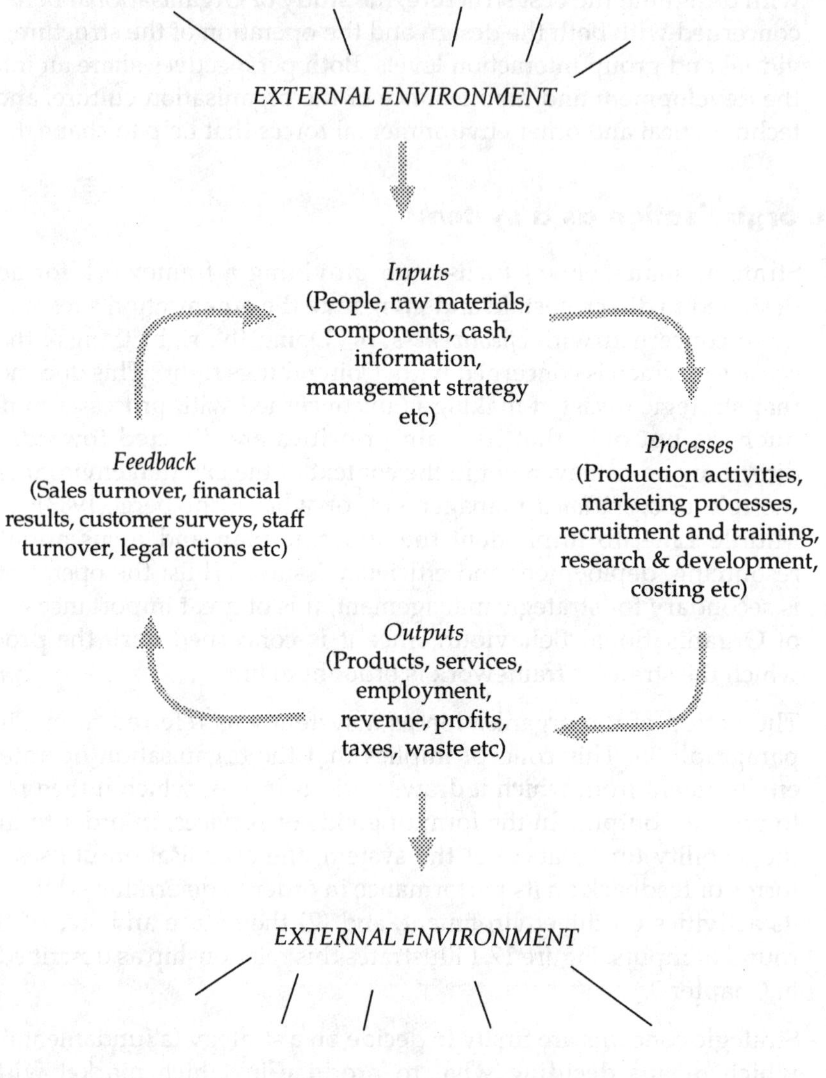

EXTERNAL ENVIRONMENT

Inputs
(People, raw materials, components, cash, information, management strategy etc)

Processes
(Production activities, marketing processes, recruitment and training, research & development, costing etc)

Feedback
(Sales turnover, financial results, customer surveys, staff turnover, legal actions etc)

Outputs
(Products, services, employment, revenue, profits, taxes, waste etc)

EXTERNAL ENVIRONMENT

Figure 17.1   The Organisation as an Open System

and value in evaluating behaviour in organisations, since it provides the raw material for assessments of the organisation structure, the values-system or culture, the dominant management style and the management of change.

10.   The *process* phase of the organisational system is predominantly the domain of operational management, which also shares an involvement with strategic management in the outputs and feedback phases. The principal concerns of operational management are those of routinisation, realisation and efficiency. Strategic concepts have to be turned into practicalities by means of resourcing, standard-setting, routines and procedures. The precise details of

such activities are of lesser interest to students of organisational behaviour than their effect on (1) the managers responsible for initiating them, (2) the employees who are required to adhere to them, and (3) external stakeholders who are affected by them (eg customers, suppliers etc). The behaviour of management is of great concern to studies of Organisational Behaviour, involving concepts such as leadership, management style, conflict management and employee motivation. The effect of management style and organisation culture on employees is of equal concern, since here we are able to assess, and attempt to predict, the behaviour of individuals as well as of people in groups. The impact of the organisation's operational activities on *external* stakeholders generally receives less attention in Organisational Behaviour, except for people with a strong interest in Marketing. However, all three groups contribute to, or resist, the processes of change in the organisation, which, of course, is an enduring concern of studies in Organisational Behaviour.

11. The *output* phase, which is shared with strategic management, is critical to operational management, since although the ground-rules are laid down by the top management, this is where operational managers are judged for their performance. Within the limitations of the resources and policies handed down from the top, they have to achieve a cost-effective delivery of goods or services on time to their consumers at a price that provides an agreed contribution to the enterprise. Students of Organisational Behaviour are less concerned with the minutiae of timeliness and cost-effectiveness, but are interested in the behavioural implications for individuals, managers and groups of the productive effort of the organisation. Similar considerations apply to the *feedback* phase, which is vital both at strategic and operational levels — for the evaluation of long-term plans and short-term operations respectively — but represents a different priority for Organisational Behaviour studies, which are principally interested in the impact of outputs on the motives and behaviour of all the employees of the organisation.

Strategic management and change

12. An area of major common interest and attention between strategic management and studies of Organisational Behaviour is that of change and how it is managed. Strategists tend to see change in general as a challenge, and particular changes as a desired objective. In fact any strategy is, in effect, a plan for change, whether modest or revolutionary in scope. Depending on the senior management concerned, a strategy will be mainly reactive (ie responding to changes in the external environment) or a mixture of reactive and proactive (ie responding to emergencies but planning change on issues previously identified). A reactive strategy puts enormous pressures on operational managers, who have to react to sudden change in their environment by 'crisis management' or 'firefighting'. A far better option from their point of view is a planned

approach to change, which gives them time to prepare alternative measures, whilst ready to deal with unexpected change should it occur.

13. The key variables in the process of organisational change were mentioned in Chapter 14, and these are reproduced again here in a slightly different format (Figure 17.2) in order to illustrate the respective roles of strategic and operational management within the whole framework of change that is one of the prime interests of organisational behaviour. Each variable is identified as being predominantly strategic or operational in its implications for change, and some are seen as shared. So, for example, structure is shared in the sense that the overall framework of the structure is defined by strategic management, but that the operation of the structure is primarily an operational matter. Technology is also shared in that strategy decides which forms of technology will be used and in what quantity, but that the application and adaptation of the technology is the responsibility of operational management.

Figure 17.2   *Organisational change, strategy and operations*

14. Whilst the most important triggers for change may be located in the *external* environment (eg due to customer behaviour, competitor activity, government legislation etc), there are independent triggers to be found in *internal* sources (eg due to inappropriate selection of individuals for key positions, illness of key person, development of bad feelings between key groups, unexpected success of sales etc). Usually, it is the role of strategic management to attend to the external causes of change and produce ideas for dealing with them, whilst operational management have to deal with the internal sources of change. The student of Organisational Behaviour is primarily concerned with the impact of change on the members of the organisation regardless of the source. In this introductory text the general emphasis has been on strategic perspectives with just some attention to operational matters. This enables the subject-matter to reflect a broad view of Organisational Behaviour, whilst omitting some of the detailed aspects

of peoples' behaviour at the operational end of the enterprise, be it commercial, voluntary or public sector.

15. In their American study of how small companies became medium-sized, Clifford & Cavanagh (1985)[3], identified six 'winning' characteristics in the way the companies dealt with the change process. These characteristics were as follows:

> ❏ they instilled a strong sense of 'mission' and 'shared values' in their workforce
>
> ❏ they paid 'relentless attention to business fundamentals' (eg careful watch on the external marketplace and competition, identified key priorities and supported them strongly etc)
>
> ❏ they avoided bureaucratic structures
>
> ❏ they encouraged reasonable experimentation and were prepared to accept the risks of failure on the basis that 'the greater sin was not to try at all'
>
> ❏ they studied their customers to determine what they wanted
>
> ❏ they selected staff carefully, spent time motivating them (ie getting their commitment) and rewarded them well if they succeeded

It is clear that the same variables crop up time and time again when examining how organisations behave in practice — mission, values/culture, structure, staff skills and motivation, external stakeholder interests etc.

16. In his view of the dynamic organisation of the future (ie now!), Peters (1988)[4] suggests that business organisations will have to adopt the following characteristics if they are to thrive rather than merely survive:

> ❏ a decentralised structure where decision-making is diffused throughout the organisation
>
> ❏ an organic rather than mechanistic form of organisation structure
>
> ❏ stability will be maintained not by uniformity or standardisation but by adherence to a set of common values, or culture
>
> ❏ innovation will be encouraged but in manageable amounts
>
> ..... continued

> ☐ reasonable risk-taking will be encouraged, and failures or mistakes will be used as learning opportunities
>
> ☐ strategies will be primarily determined on the basis of customers needs and wants
>
> ☐ within the firm each group will be seen as the potential customers of the other groups, and vice versa
>
> ☐ whilst allowing for failures and mistakes, the overall aim will be towards total quality management and 'getting things right first time'

Peters, as ever, promotes his ideas with enthusiasm and conviction. His idealistic approach, however, is based on the notion of common vision and common commitment in all those involved in the enterprise, and nowhere in his book does he refer to conflict. In terms of the conflict perspectives mentioned in Chapter 12 paragraph 34, Peters stands firmly in the unitary camp. In practice, a pluralist perspective is probably more realistic, and this requires conflict-resolution measures to be added to the above list.

Strategic management and senior management competence

17. In respect of the ideas about successful management contained in the previous two paragraphs, the competence standards being developed for senior management by MCI (see earlier reference in Chapter 15 paragraph 21) are of considerable interest. They exemplify an analytical approach to strategic management, and express many of the behaviours mentioned by Peters, Clifford and Cavanagh. The draft standards (MCI, 1994)[5] are based on nine *units of competence*, each with their supporting *elements, performance criteria* and *range statements*. In addition each element notes the requirements in terms of *'underpinning knowledge and understanding'* and *'personal competences'*. The inclusion of these additional items is intended to reduce the kind of problems referred to in Chapter 15 paragraph 23 (eg inflexibility of standards).

18. The range of underpinning knowledge and understanding requirements is set out — in very broad terms — in clusters under the following headings (Figure 17.3):

Reading/ analysing situations — local, internal/ external

eg — *situation of organisation in relation to outside environment*

Concepts/ theory/ cerebral

eg — *managing change, strategic planning, creative thinking*

Political

eg — *managing relationships, facilitating, making alliances*

People

eg — *communication, individual/ group psychology, team management*

'Technical' Managerial

eg — *legal, finance, marketing/ commercial awareness, negotiating, managing meetings, problem-solving, human resource management, risk assessment*

Figure 17.3   *Senior Management Standards — Examples of Underpinning Knowledge and Understanding Requirements (MCI, 1994)*

The five components of underpinning knowledge are intended to allow for subtle cognitive and social skills to be recognised as well as the so-called 'technical' skills, which are acquired through management training and experience, and are more widely accepted as constituting part of a manager's job. The *'reading/ analysing'* reference is to the manager's interpretive skills, whilst *'concepts etc'* refers to other cognitive (ie thinking) skills. The references to *'political'* and *'people'* requirements are clearly concerned with the possession of appropriate social skills.

19. The personal competences are fewer in number than the requirements for knowledge and understanding, but are equally broadly-stated. They are founded on the knowledge and understanding requirements mentioned above, but are to be judged in terms of observed behaviour, albeit behaviour that is more likely to be implied than explicit. The repertoire of personal competences is as follows:

judgement	*self-confidence*	*strategic perspective*
achievement focus	*communication*	*information search*
building teams	*influencing others*	

It is recognised that these competences are affected by the context in which they may be used, and that effective managers 'tend not to be equally strong in every competence, but display a variety of different profiles of strengths, styles and preferences.'.

20. Compared with our subject-matter here, there is a clear congruence of ideas and themes between the knowledge, understanding and personal competence requirements in the draft standards and the range of topics covered in this book. This amount of common ground only serves to high-light the senior management/ strategic perspective that influences so much of the scope of Organisational Behaviour.

21. The nine units of competence identified by the draft MCI standards, together with a few examples of their elements can be summarised as follows:

---

1. **Read/ influence external trends** (eg develop systems to review markets)

2. **Read/ influence internal assets** (eg review and improve the organisation's structures, systems and conditions)

3. **Read/ influence stakeholders** (eg identify the current and likely future interests of stakeholders)

4. **Set strategy and gain commitment** (eg develop a mission to guide the organisation)

5. **Plan and implement programmes, projects and plans** (eg submit porposals for programmes, projects and plans to meet strategic objectives.....)

6. **Plan and implement delegation** (eg agree targets for people and units...)

7. **Plan and implement an organisation culture** (eg consult and provide guidance on the ways in which values are to be expressed in work and working relationships)

8. **Plan and implement controls** (eg select key financial and other indicators to control programmes, projects and plans)

9. **Evaluate and improve performance** (eg develop measures and criteria to evaluate achievement of mission, objectives and policies)

The nine units provide a core framework for capturing the essence of senior management roles. They may also provide a useful framework for senior management development and assessment, the latter being facilitated by the use of explicit *performance criteria* and *statements of alternative contexts (the range).*

22. To take one example from the nine units — 'Setting the Strategy and Gaining Commitment' — this contains four elements (which is typical) as follows:

   1. *'Develop a mission to guide the organisation'*

   2. *'Formulate objectives and goals to carry out mission'*

   3. *'Draw together values and policies to guide the organisation'*

   4. *'Gain support for the organisation's mission, objectives, goals, values and policies'*

Of particular interest to students of Organisational Behaviour is the item concerning gaining support for the mission etc. Here typical performance criteria include:

   a) *'Consultation and negotiation are conducted at a time and in a manner which allows mission, objectives .....to be influenced by and made more consistent with the interests of stakeholders*

   b) *'Where the interests of stakeholders are in conflict, realistic and rational compromises are found ....*

   c) *'Mission, objectives.....are presented to stakeholders in such a way to attract their support..............'. etc etc*

23. Interestingly, whilst few people would argue with the basic items of strategic management described in the elements of competence, the performance criteria stated for this level of management could be contentious. For example, the first criterion concerning consultation assumes a particular approach to strategic management, which whilst it concurs very much with the ideas of Peters and the other gurus of 'excellence', may not necessarily apply in organisations adopting a less open and comprehensive approach to the development of strategy. Like so much of the subject-matter of Organisational Behaviour, it is impossible to avoid imparting particular sets of values about the treatment of individuals and groups at work. If one is to take a pluralistic perspective, which recognises legitimate differences in values and approaches, then a variety of actions and performance criteria can be accepted. What is avoided in this perspective is the likelihood of prescriptive approaches telling people what they ought to do. We saw in Chapter 13, that there are numerous choices of culture that can be made in organisations, and as the next and final chapter shows, these different concepts of organisation culture can be greatly affected by the national culture of the host country.

References

1. Cole, G.A. (1994), *Strategic Management*, D P Publications
2. Mintzberg, H. (1983), *Structure in Fives*, Prentice Hall
3. Clifford,D. & Cavanagh, R. (1985), *The Winning Performance*, Sidgwick & Jackson
4. Peters, T. (1988), *Thriving on Chaos — Handbook for a Management Revolution*, MacMillan
5. MCI (1994), *Draft Senior Management Standards*, Management Charter Initiative

Questions for reflection/discussion

1. How far is it true to suggest that the study of Organisational Behaviour is focused on the management of people rather than on the working of organisations?

2. Given that strategic decisions set the tone of an organisation's lifestyle, in what ways do strategic concerns sometimes differ from those of interest to students of Organisational Behaviour?

3. What, in your opinion, are the benefits to be gained by senior managers from the study of Organisational Behaviour?

4. In what ways might the study of Organisational Behaviour lead to the design of organic rather than mechanistic forms of organisation structure?

5. To what extent should the subject-matter of Organisational Behaviour be present in competence standards for (1) senior managers, and (2) first-line managers?

18 International aspects of organisational behaviour

Introduction

1.   This final chapter in Part One looks briefly at the international dimension of organisations. Although public sector organisations are domestic in their operation, many business enterprises and some voluntary organisations conduct their operations in more than one nation, and have a diversified, multinational workforce in many of their establishments. Not surprisingly, perhaps, there are some major differences of management style, organisation culture and attitudes towards authority — to name but a few varieties of behaviour — between different national cultures. These differences affect the internal operation of different sections of the same company in different parts of the world, as well as affecting intra-organisational dealings.

2.   In respect of Organisational Behaviour, in particular, it is significant to note the comment by Robbins (1993)[1] that *'Most of the concepts that currently make up the body of knowledge we call organisational behaviour have been developed by Americans using American subjects within domestic contexts.'* He quotes a 1983 study by Nadler which revealed that of more than 11,000 articles published in 24 management and organisational behaviour journals over a 10-year period, about 80% derived entirely from American studies. This situation is unlikely to continue as firms everywhere become increasingly international in their outlook and in their structures. The last twenty years have been marked by the increasingly *global* nature of business enterprises, in particular, with developments such as:

❏   international politico-economic structures such as the European Community and the looser alliances being formed in the Pacific Basin

❏   international commodity groupings such as OPEC (Oil Producing & Exporting Countries)

❏   growth of large multinational enterprises with major manufacturing/distribution operations in several nations (eg IBM, Toyota, BP, Cable & Wireless etc)

❏ increasing number of joint ventures between companies across national borders (eg Airbus Industries — France, Britain & Germany)

❏ increasing number of strategic alliances, where one business buys a major stake in a similar business in another country (eg British Telecom purchasing a 20% share of the American MCI company)

❏ availability of microprocessor-based technology, which is becoming ever cheaper to purchase and operate, and which favours developing countries with low labour costs

❏ the speed and sophistication of world-wide telcommunications, matched only by their increasing accessibility to firms of all sizes and their falling prices in the global market-place

3. Given that Organisational Behaviour is concerned with the study of individual and group behaviour in the workplace, the development of structures between and within groups, and the process of change, it is highly likely that national cultural differences will emerge in these manifestations of human behaviour at work. Perlmutter (1986)[2] has distinguished three contrasting attitudes of managers towards the internationalisation of business enterprises, as follows:

❏ *ethnocentric* — where the primary attitude is that the home country's practices and styles are best, and should be applied abroad

❏ *polycentric* — where the home managers acknowledge the diversity of practice, and agree that local managements should retain local practices with little or no interference from the home country

❏ *geocentric* — where similarities of practice are recognised as well as differences, and where through compromise the most effective practices are adopted whatever their origin

4. Clearly, whatever the differences in organisation structures, strategy and environments, to take just three important organisational variables, if the development of joint ventures or multinational enterprises are to succeed, then some sort of understanding about styles, values and culture must be reached. It is not so much *what* people work with — technology, operating systems, skills, tasks etc — that matters but rather *how* they work — expectations, motivation, leadership etc. Interestingly, Japanese companies operating manufacturing units in Britain have sought to recognise the positive values present in the workforce (eg pride in one's work, team-spirit etc), whilst at the same time introducing practices such as single status, company uniforms and other cultural symbols from Japan. Compromises have been made on both sides to achieve considerable success in motor vehicle manufacture, electronic components assembly and the production of silicon chips, for example.

Key culture differences in organisational behaviour

5. An early study of cultural differences between nations by Kluckhohn & Strodtbeck (1961)[3] developed an analytical framework based on six dimensions, each having three possible variants, as follows:

   1. *Relationship to the environment* — domination, harmony or subjugation

   2. *Time orientation* — past, present or future

   3. *Nature of people* — good, mixed or evil

   4. *Activity orientation* — being, controlling or doing

   5. *Focus of responsibility* — individualistic, group or hierarchical

   6. *Conception of space* — private, mixed or public

   The thinking behind the framework can best be explained by applying it to examples of different cultural groups, for example Americans and Japanese.

6. Americans tend to see themselves as dominating their environment, whereas Japanese tend to cooperate with their environment. Americans look for early results in terms of time, and are thus more interested in what can be done now (the present), whereas Japanese are prepared to wait for results, and thus are more concerned with future prospects than immediate pay-offs. Perceptions of people as 'good' (eg honest, trustworthy etc) are more likely to be held in Japan than in the United States, where a mixed view of people is likely to be taken. In terms of activity orientation, both Americans and Japanese display a 'doing' attitude (ie they work hard and get involved). There are differences between Americans and Japanese in how they see responsibility. The former tend to see it as primarily residing in the individual, whereas the latter see it primarily in terms of the group. The way space is used in Japan is for everything to be open and shared (eg open-plan offices, shared restaurant facilities etc), whereas in America greater privacy is sought, and the facilities tend to reflect an individual's status.

7. In a further study, which has become a classic in the study of cultural differences, Hofstede (1980)[4] investigated value differences between over 11,000 employees of a single multinational company (IBM) in some forty countries. Culture, according to Hofstede,

   'determines the identity of a human group in the same way as personality determines the identity of an individual' (p.26).

   He sees values as the building blocks of 'culture', which he applies exclusively to the characteristics of a society, using the expression 'sub-culture' when referring to organisations, professions and families, for example. In effect, therefore, Hofstede's study was focused on the influence of national culture on the sub-culture of organisations and their behaviour, as elicited from questioning and observing the employees of a large multi-national corporation.

8. From the analysis of his data, Hofstede selected four key dimensions against which to differentiate differing values and attitudes in each of the forty national cultures towards work-related issues. These were quite different from the dimensions selected by Kluckhohn and Strodtbeck, and on the whole more subtle. Hofstede's key dimensions can be summarised briefly as follows:

    1. *Individualism versus collectivism* (ie where individualism is a national culture attribute that favours people looking to themselves and their families as their first priority, and collectivism is an attribute that expects people to give loyalty to, and find protection in, the wider group)

    2. *Power distance* (ie the extent to which different cultures accept different distributions of power within the society; a high power distance society accepts wide differences of power between those at the top of society and those at the bottom; a low power distance society sees power as being shared much more equitably, leaving less of a power gap between the top and the bottom ranks)

    3. *Uncertainty avoidance* (ie the extent to which a society is tolerant of uncertainty and therefore feels either less need to avoid it (low avoidance) or feels threatened by it (high avoidance)

    4. *Masculinity versus femininity* (ie where a nation either prefers assertiveness and materialism (masculinity) or a concern for relationships and the welfare of others — femininity)

9. Hofstede found that, when comparing the results obtained from the forty different countries against the criteria of the framework, it was possible, using the technique of statistical cluster analysis, to allocate them to eight 'culture clusters', each of which had a particular profile of characteristics under the four dimensions. These clusters were labelled according to geographical area (Asian, Near Eastern, Germanic & Nordic) or language (Latin & Anglo) and are summarised as follows (Figure 18.1):

Figure 18.1   *Cultural Clusters Arising from Hofstede's Research*
                       (adapted from Hofstede (1980),p.336)

I — More developed Latin

High power distance
High uncertainty avoidance
High individualism
Medium masculinity

   Belgium
   France
   Argentina
   Brazil
   Spain
   (Italy)

II — Less developed Latin

High power distance
High uncertainty avoidance
Low individualism
Whole range of masculinity

   Columbia
   Mexico
   Venezuela
   Chile
   Peru
   Portugal

III— More developed Asian

Medium power distance
High uncertainty avoidance
Medium individualism
High masculinity

   Japan

IV — Less developed Asian

High power distance
Low uncertainty avoidance
Low individualism
Medium masculinity

   Pakistan
   Taiwan
   Thailand
   Hong Kong
   India
   Philippines
   Singapore

V — Near Eastern

High power distance
High uncertainty avoidance
Low individualism
Medium masculinity

   Greece
   Iran
   Turkey
   (Yugoslavia)

VI — Germanic

Low power distance
High uncertainty avoidance
Medium individualism
High masculinity

   Austria
   Israel
   Germany
   Switzerland

VII — Anglo

Low power distance
Low-medium uncertainty avoidance
High individualism
High masculinity

Australia
Canada
Great Britain
Ireland
New Zealand
USA
(South Africa)

VIII— Nordic

Low power distance
Low-medium uncertainty
avoidance
Medium individualism
Low masculinity

Denmark
Finland
Netherlands
Norway
Sweden

10. As a result of his researches Hofstede concluded that it was impractical to produce a unified managerial approach that could be adopted worldwide to meet the needs of individuals and groups, their structures and the requirements of change. A contingency approach is clearly called for in these circumstances, which means that organisation structures, management styles, organisation cultures and programmes of change have to be adapted to the dominant cultural attributes of the host nation. This is of major significance to multi-national organisations and others that employ or collaborate with nationals of a foreign country. Japanese companies investing in Great Britain, for example, have learned to work with British management and workers by accepting the latter's high sense of individualism whilst at the same time seeking compromise on uncertainty avoidance. Such international collaboration may well hold important clues to future developments, as each nation's managers learn to adapt their cultural values in the light of their experience of working together.

11. Another individual who has made an important contribution to the international dimension is Ouchi (1981)[5] who studied the characteristics of Japanese and American organisation, principally to see if selected practices from Japanese industry could be translated to the United States. Among the findings from his research Ouchi discovered the following differences in the behaviour of Japanese and American organisations:

Japanese Organisations

❏ Offer lifetime employment
(Core workers only)

❏ Promote from within

❏ Career paths are non-specialised

American Organisations

❏ Offer (generally) short-term employment

❏ Recruit from outside

❏ Generally specialised career paths

❐ High degree of mutual trust /loyalty between managers and employees	❐ Varying degrees of trust/loyalty between the two sides
❐ Importance of collective responsibility	❐ Individual responsibility for results
❐ Long-term performance appraisal	❐ Short-term performance more important
❐ Success seen in terms of cooperative efforts	❐ Success seen in terms of individual achievements

12. Ouchi proposed what he called 'Theory Z' (eg as opposed to McGregor's Theories X and Y)[6] as a means by which American companies could imitate certain features of the Japanese approach to managing people. He argued that American firms could make changes in the following areas of human resource management:

   1. They could offer more secure employment prospects and better prospects of a career

   2. They could extend employee participation in decision-making

   3. They could place greater reliance on team-spirit and on recognising the contribution of individuals to team effort

   4. They could encourage greater mutual respect between managers and their staffs

   Such an approach would have to be supported from the top, and would require appropriate consultation measures and a substantial training commitment, especially for managers and supervisors.

13. It is worth pointing out that the Japanese can only afford to offer lifetime employment to their core workers by also employing vast numbers of part-time and temporary staff, whose conditions of employment are greatly inferior to full-time employees. Also, given the difficulties of developing careers in today's dynamic business enterprises (see Chapter 15 above), it seems less likely that firms will want to offer guarantees of long-term prospects. The other three items just referred to can be, and are being, extended in many companies, and indeed would be regarded as merely following 'good practice' by many successful British and American firms. What, perhaps, is different is that whilst Japanese companies clearly prefer collective responsibility and collaborative effort, British and American instinctively prefer to acknowledge individual responsibility and achievement, even where tempered by a generally collaborative approach in teams.

14. In a report published in 1984[7], a representative of the management of a British manufacturer of television sets (Thorn-EMI) reported that in terms of production technology his firm was ahead of the Japanese, but that

production volumes were well behind the latter. Japanese companies had a much more flexible labour force than the British company, and only produced a limited range of models compared with the large range produced by the latter. There were striking differences in company culture between the two, with the Japanese putting great effort into gaining commitment of their staff to the company culture, compared with the much weaker sense of company culture at Thorn's. The British firm concluded that in terms of *design and production technology* it had nothing to learn from the Japanese, but that in terms of *employee commitment and personnel management* it had much to learn, especially by eliminating unnecessary status barriers between managers and staff, improving communications right down through the chain, encouraging greater individual responsibility for work quality and the work environment, and improving training for management succession.

15. In case it might be thought that all cultural changes have become one way, it is worth noting that the Japanese themselves in the immediate post-war period listened to the ideas of people such as W. Edwards Deming, the American quality management expert, who enabled the Japanese to take up some of the efficiency features of F.W. Taylor and the scientific managers, adapt them and blend them into a participative team effort within a total quality management approach to manufacturing. Deming eventually produced a list of what he called 'Fourteen Points for Total Quality Control' (1986)[8], which contains his ideas on how a total quality approach can be brought to bear on every aspect of manufacturing. His ideas include such key points as:

❑ commitment to the company's mission

❑ develop team-work and lateral cooperation across the organisation

❑ introduce participative leadership styles

❑ provide adequate training both of employees and suppliers

❑ continuously improve the production system, use statistical control techniques, inspection processes and other quantitative methods for *improving the system* rather than for *controlling people*

❑ adopt the new approach from top to bottom in the organisation

16. Although Deming's approach includes some specific references to quantitative techniques and 'hard' systems, such as production planning, his main emphasis is on human resource management, and such 'soft' issues as teamwork, communication, leadership and culture development — all principal features of the study of Organisational Behaviour.

17. More recent work on cultural issues has been provided by Graen & Wakabayashi (1994)[9] and Erez (1994)[10]. The former have studied cross-cultural issues in leadership behaviour between American and Japanese

managers, concentrating on Japanese 'transplant' operations in the US (ie where Japanese companies have invested in manufacturing plants in North America using mainly American employees). They point out that Hofstede's findings concerning the cultural differences between Japanese and American organisations indicate that the two cultures are polar opposites on several dimensions. They also highlight the fact that Japanese companies use the Toyota, or lean organisation, system, whilst Americans have experience only of scientific management or mass production systems. The two systems are distinguished by the following characteristics, according to the authors (Figure 18.2):

American	Japanese
(The scientific management approach)	(The Toyota system)
Job-holders seen as variable costs	Employees seen as assets to be enhanced
Minimal amount of on-the-job training	Significant training and retraining to enhance career prospects
Individual competition encouraged	Team cooperation and team interests seen as more important than individual self-interest
Tall hierarchies and clear job definitions	Shallow hierarchies and ambiguous team definitions
Basic contract seen as giving services for pay	Basic contract seen as mutual obligations for pay
Focus on quarterly profits	Long-term focus on market position

Figure 18.2　　　　　　　　*Contrasting management styles: Japanese vs American*

18. The main conclusion reached by the authors is that there is a wide gap between Americans and Japanese in terms of their approach to management in organisations, but that there is much less of a gap between American *leadership* styles and Japanese behaviour. In this respect it is interesting to note that Peters and others (see Chapter 17) have suggested that successful US companies do treat employees as assets, do train them, do encourage team-working, do encourage participative leadership styles and do take a longer rather than short-term perspective. Graen and Wakabayashi conclude that 'culture' could be seen

> '...not as a system of predispositions but as a set of conceptual tools to be used to solve different kinds of problems.'

They suggest that these conceptual tools can be learned by someone from a different culture. In the long-term they see that people from different cultures will set about:

☐ understanding each other's cultural techniques
☐ learning to become comfortable with them
☐ ntegrating them into a new set of cross-cultural tools

19. Erez, in her analysis of cross-cultural issues in industrial and organisational psychology, comments that

> 'The lack of a cross-cultural perspective on organizational behaviour has limited our understanding of the reasons why motivational approaches and managerial practices are not smoothly transferred across cultures....'.

She draws attention to a number of questions concerning such cross-cultural perspectives, such as whether it is possible to develop models that integrate cultural factors into employee behaviour, and how to assess the effectiveness of similar managerial and motivational techniques across cultures. The need for cross-cultural understanding, according to Erez, is becoming all the greater because of the following developments:

1. the increasing cultural diversity of workforces
2. the widening scope of the work environment from local to global and international
3. mergers and acquisitions
4. organisational restructuring (eg where headquarters is in one country, manufacturing in another, and sales in yet another!)
5. greater customer orientation leading to greater team-work in order to satisfy customer requirements
6. the emergence of high technology and telecommunication systems, speeding up communications and enabling simultaneous computer-translation of foreign language texts
7. the growing globalisation of shareholding unbounded by national borders
8. political changes affecting the unification of some parts of the world (eg in Europe, East-West Germany, North-South Korea etc) and the de-unification of others (eg Soviet Union, Yugoslavia).

Managing cultural diversity

20. In his book on global paradox, Naisbitt (1994)[11] refers to the growth of the global economy in the wake of such developments as electronics, telecommunications, worldwide tourism, the growing acceptance of English as the language and the lowering of trade barriers between nations and regions. However, he argues, as we become more universal, so there are important

counter-balancing trends which are developing alongside this universality. He calls this phenomenon 'tribalism', which he defines as *'belief in fidelity to one's own kind, defined by ethnicity, language, culture, religion...or profession.'* It is not to be confused with nationalism, which he sees as *'a belief that one's nation-state is more important than international principles or individual considerations'*. Thus, he sees increasing tribalism developing alongside increasing universalism. At business enterprise level this manifests itself in such actions as deconstructing large, and often bureaucratic, structures into smaller semi-autonomous units, able to reflect local/ regional values/ know-how whilst operating within a limited range of financial and cultural controls from the centre. Naisbitt quotes the Chief Executive of Asea Brown Boveri (ABB), the world's largest power-engineering group based in Switzerland, as saying *'We are not a global business. We are a collection of local businesses with intense global coordination.'*

21. The most likely scenario in the next century is of (1) a multiplicity of small/ medium-sized companies supplying goods and services on a global basis, and (2) a small number of large, decentralised multinational companies, emphasising their basic mission and values and exerting minimum control over financial resourcing, whilst encouraging local/ regional autonomy (empowerment) within that framework. In this way companies can compete internationally on the basis of their cultural strengths as well as on the nature and quality of their goods and services and the speed with which they can deliver them to the marketplace. In these endeavours the combined processes of digital electronics, telecommunications and computer software will supply the communication needs of the global suppliers and their customers in an almost instantaneous manner. One of the least differentiated aspects of a national culture, therefore, will be the use and application of micro-electronic technology!

Conclusion

22. It is not too much of an exaggeration to suggest that the next decade will see an enormous increase in trading and economic collaboration between all parts of the globe. Far Eastern countries will increasingly be investing in European countries, collaboration between Japan, her Eastern neighbours and the Antipodes will develop strongly, and the nations of Africa and South America will become the target of suppliers of consumer goods as well as of heavy engineering. Whatever scenario develops it will certainly be true that customers, in the light of technology, will be ever more accessible to their suppliers. Few business enterprises will be able to survive merely on a domestic market, and a strategy for the international dimension will be essential. Firms that invest overseas will have to study the cultural inclinations of their employees and their suppliers, as well as developing an awareness of customer needs and wants and the attitudes of governments. A readiness to respond to the cultural implications of all these stakeholders will be vital to success.

References

1. Robbins, S. (1993), *Organisational Behaviour(6th edn)*, Prentice Hall
2. Perlmutter,V. & Heenan, D. *'Cooperate to Compete Globally'*, in Harvard Business Review,64 (Mar/Apr 1986)
3. Kluckhohn,S & Strodtbeck, (1961), *Variations in Value Orientations*, Row Petersen
4. Hofstede, G. (1980), *Culture's Consequences: International Differences in Work-related Values* , Sage Publications
5. Ouchi, W. (1981), *Theory Z: How American Business Can Meet the Japanese Challenge*, Addison-Wesley
6. McGregor, D. (1960), *The Human Side of Enterprise*, McGraw-Hill
7. WRU Paper *'Learning from Japan'*, 1984, Work Research Unit
8. W. Edwards Deming (1986), *Out of the Crisis*, MIT Press
9. Graen, G. & Wakabayashi, M., 'Cross-Cultural Leadership Making: Bridging American and Japanese Diversity for Team Advantage', in Triandis, H., Dunnette, M. & Hough, M. (Eds), (1994), *Handbook of Industrial & Organizational Psychology*, Vol 4 (2nd. edn),
10. Erez, M. 'Towards a Model of Cross-Cultural Industrial & Organizational Psychology', in Triandis, H., Dunnette, M. & Hough, M. (Eds), (1994), *Handbook of Industrial & Organizational Psychology*, Vol 4 (2nd. edn),
11. Naisbitt, J. (1994), *Global Paradox*, BCA/ Nicholas Brealey Publishing

Questions for reflection/discussion

1. Why is it necessary to study Organisational Behaviour in an international as well as in a local context?

2. In what ways might different national cultures lead to contrasting forms of behaviour in respect of:

    a. attitudes towards *authority* in work organisations?

    b. ideas about *responsibility* in the workplace?

    c. attitudes towards *results/outcomes*?

3. In your opinion, how viable is Theory Z as a cross-cultural form of employee motivation? Give your reasons in each case.

4. What aspects of organisation culture are more likely to be able to contribute to a *universal* culture as opposed to a *local*, purely organisation-wide culture?

Part two

The workbook

This part of the book contains more than forty different questions aimed at encouraging students to give further consideration to facts and issues raised in each chapter and in previous chapters. Compared with the questions for reflection and discussion located at each chapter-end, these further questions generally require readers to apply the knowledge and understanding they have gained from their earlier reading, reflection and class discussion. In selected cases a number of scenarios have been developed to provide a practical context within which to answer questions on specific issues.

Some of the questions will be supplied with outline answer-guides for bona fide lecturers/tutors on application to the publishers.

Chapter 1   The scope of organisational behaviour

Question 1

Scenario   Issues in organisational behaviour

Your university department has been awarded a major research study into key issues in organisational behaviour in the 1990's. The field work for the project is to be carried out in a representative sample of commercial and manufacturing organisations together with a small number of public sector organisations. The private sector organisations range from a multinational company in petro-chemicals and a large High Street bank to medium-sized companies in engineering and the travel agency business.

You are a member of the research team and have been asked to help prepare a list of key questions that will be used, suitably adapted, in questionnaires and interviews with *management* staff in the organisations concerned.

Task

1. Draw up your list of questions (not more than twenty), assembling them in clusters if this makes sense.

2. Compare your list with another member of your tutorial group, and discuss any differences.

3. Then decide between you which six or eight questions you think are the most crucial.

Chapter 2   Organisation structures I

Question 2

To what extent does Mintzberg's model of organisations (see Fig. 2.1) make sense for any organisation with which you are familiar (eg where you have worked or studied)? Explain your answer and, if necessary, re-draw the model to show the profile you see in the organisation you are describing.

Question 3

What is the relationship between the external environment of an organisation and each of the following features of its internal life:

- ❐ its mission or purpose?
- ❐ its strategic goals?
- ❐ its use of technology?
- ❐ its tasks/ jobs?
- ❐ its employees?
- ❐ its culture?

Question 4

Max Weber described 'bureaucracy' as 'rational-legal authority', but how far could it be said that bureaucracy is more an issue of *organisation structuring* than one concerned with the *nature of authority*?

Chapter 3   Organisation structures II

Question 5

Scenario   The structure of an organisation

Your organisation manufactures and distributes consumer electronics goods, including stereo systems, video-recorders and personal computers. It has a healthy market share in the UK and is well established in Western Europe. Distribution is mainly via retail chains, but a mail-order service has recently been started as a result of an acquisition. Competition in all markets is intense with resulting pressure on prices and costs. Sales peaked last year and net profit is in slow decline.

Structurally the organisation has operated along functional lines with a key director in charge of all production at the principal factories, and several powerful functional directors, notably for Marketing & Sales, Purchasing and Finance. There are also key adviser roles for Personnel and Corporate Planning.

Following consultation with his fellow directors, an external consultancy company and the company advisers, the company chairman, who is also the managing director, has decided that the company should be restructured so as to obtain better synergy from the production departments.

Task

You are the external consultant who has been advising the firm. Write a report to the Board setting out the advantages and drawbacks of moving from a functional structure to a divisional structure, in which the production areas will be re-established as three separate divisions each with its own range of functional services. Existing functions may be slimmed down, but will retain a strategic and policy role.

Question 6

What basic structure would you recommend, with reasons, for one of the following types of enterprise:

a.   High Street books/stationery retail chain?

b.   District General Hospital?

c.   Large accountancy practice?

In your answer make specific reference to the following structural forms:

- ❏ high or low degree of specialisation
- ❏ tall or flat structure
- ❏ narrow or wide structure
- ❏ centralised or decentralised structure
- ❏ tight or loose control procedures

Question 7

Devise a matrix, based on the ideas of Trist, Emery and Mintzberg, which could be applied to the analysis of the external environments of organisations, and then use it to describe the nature of the environment for two contrasting types of organisation (commercial/public sector, manufacturing, service industry, charitable organisation etc).

Chapter 4   Organisation structuring — The human aspects

Question 8

Many of the investigative methods employed by the Hawthorne researchers would not be considered satisfactory today. In particular, the following methods have been criticised:

a. the use of specific groups of employees as 'guinea pigs' (eg Relay Assembly Test Room),

b. the frequent changes in the working conditions of the experimental groups,

c. the use of workplace observers (eg Bank Wiring Room).

Why do you think that the above methods could be problematic when investigating peoples' behaviour at work?

Question 9

Taking into account the ideas expressed by theorists such as Maslow, Alderfer, Argyris and Herzberg, what would you say were the ten most important needs of people at work?

Question 10

What is the essential difference between *formal* and *informal* behaviour at work? In what specific ways does *informal* behaviour manifest itself in groups, and how can managers and supervisors best deal with such behaviour? Draw up your answer in two columns, with the indications of behaviour in the left-hand column and the managerial/ supervisory response in the right-hand column. Compare and discuss your results in a small group.

Chapter 5   The individual at work: physical characteristics, skills and personality

Question 11

In what ways may an individual's *physical* characteristics (age, sex, race, size, shape etc) cause his or her supervisor/ manager and colleagues to have particular expectations about that individual's behaviour at work? What does your answer suggest about our attitudes to others at work, and what can organisations do to dissuade employees from jumping to false conclusions about fellow workers?

Question 12

Scenario   *Personal attributes in staff selection*

You are the personnel manager in the two situations described below. In each case you have discussed with the line managers concerned what *personal* attributes they see as essential for the potential job-holders (ie in addition to relevant professional knowledge and abilities). A consultancy firm, which specialises in psychometric testing, is standing by to assist in the selection of candidates suitable for short-listing for the posts, brief details of which are supplied.

Post to be filled	Psychological attributes required
1. Training Captain able to prepare foreign airline pilots to gain their certificates to fly twin-engine passenger jets, having previously flown small prop-jet aircraft. All training undertaken in the Company's £20m simulator.	*Patient attitude to trainee's difficulties / failures.*

Post to be filled	Psychological attributes required
2. **Senior Geo-physicist** to lead small team as part of the British Antarctic Survey, which requires people to live in very restricted conditions for six months at a time in sub-zero temperatures often with 20 hours of darkness.	*Emotionally capable of handling inter-personal tensions among team-members.*

Tasks

1. Prepare an initial outline of the essential attributes looked for in the candidates, so as to give the consultants some idea of the most appropriate tests to employ.

   (NB In each case one example is already provided in the following layout)

2. Consider why personality testing of potential applicants is of critical importance in these cases.

Chapter 6   Individual perceptions, personal values and attitudes

Question 13

Discuss how differences of perception between managers can prove to be an *advantage* (eg in reaching a better understanding of a problem, finding a better solution etc). Use the cases outlined in the following situations to give examples of how differing perceptions may be put to good use:

1. where a competitor suddenly and unexpectedly launches a rival product at a lower price

2. where a candidate for a senior management development role is seen as 'very suitable' by one interviewer and only 'fairly suitable' by another

3. where a sales manager, having achieved the targets set for him by his superior, cannot see why he should be criticised for slightly higher-than-budgeted sales expenses, but where the superior is under orders to keep costs tightly within budget.

Question 14

Taking Allport's six value-types as a yardstick (see p112 in Part One), what *three* groups of values — in order of priority — would you expect to assume the greatest importance for the following employees:

1. a social work manager?

2. a senior partner in an architect's office?

3. a branch manager of a High Street bank?

4. a skilled technician working in the production of aero-engines?

Chapter 7 Motivation, job satisfaction and performance

Question 15

Take *one* of the following situations and summarise what you would see as the dominant motivational requirements of each set of the employees concerned:

1. A group of insurance staff — and their supervisors — employed to deal with customer queries and complaints regarding motor vehicle insurance. (NB Two groups in all)

2. A small team of skilled maintenance engineers, working on both emergency and routine repairs, and the semi-skilled production workers whose areas they service. (Two groups in all)

3. The full-time reception staff at a busy community health centre, and the visiting community nurses attending two afternoon sessions a week to assist with minor treatments. (Two groups)

Question 16

Explain how Expectancy Theory might apply to the motivation of one of the following:

1. A Grand Prix racing driver in one of the top teams

2. A newly-appointed features writer on a national newspaper

3. A management trainee employed by a large supermarket chain

In your answer try to put yourself in the shoes of your chosen example. Compare your version of expectancy-theory-in-practice with those of others in your group, and discuss any differences.

Chapter 8   Learning styles and achievement

Question 17

Taking the principal factors of learning as a guide (see Fig. 8.1), suggest appropriate steps that might be taken by a training manager responsible for graduate entrant training in a large consumer products organisation that prides itself on its year-long graduate induction programme. Assume that the graduate recruits are given experience of working in production, marketing and sales areas as well as an introduction to the work of finance and personnel. Assume also that the recruits include graduates of various disciplines — engineers, business studies graduates and social scientists.

Question 18

Draw up a *Code of Good Practice in Training & Development* for the training staff in a large manufacturing organisation employing mostly technical graduates and skilled technicians in closely-knit teams that are required to work cooperatively with adjacent teams, and where considerable effort is put into developing supervisory and management skills. Accompany your Code with a supplementary document explaining the rationale behind each item in your code, and include references, as necessary, to learning styles, teaching aids, staff attitudes and learning theory.

Chapter 9   Groups and group behaviour

Question 19

Scenario   Issues in building a team

Your company — a recently-privatised public utility — is undergoing a massive restructuring of all its operations in order to position itself more favourably in the newly-competitive marketplace. The organisation structure has been reduced in shape, and the flatter structure has resulted in greater responsibility being pushed down the line in both line operations and support functions. The senior management have also decided that the former autocratic style of management which dominated the management chain is to be replaced by a much more participative style. Behind all these changes is a major cultural shift away from bureaucracy, and its obsession with efficient administration, towards a customer-orientated approach in which the satisfaction of customer needs is seen as the raison d'etre of every job in the company.

As a direct result of these changes you have been appointed to the role of district customer services manager with responsibility for some 50 staff, including 6 supervisors, who represent your management team.

Task

Taking Figure 9.1 as your starting-point, draw up a list of the issues you think you will have to face during the coming weeks as you brief your team and build them into an effective group. Against each key issue identify some action that you propose to take, and then discuss your lists with a colleague who will assume the role of your own manager.

Question 20

If you were the newly-appointed manager of a group of technical specialists who had developed an elitist and inwardly-looking attitude in relation to other parts of the organisation, what steps might you take to rid the group of its 'groupthink' behaviour, and yet still retain their motivation as individuals and as a group?

Compare your ideas with those of colleagues and share the results between you.

Question 21

Imagine that you are an external consultant called in by *one* of the following organisations to comment on the effectiveness of key groups, what general issues would you look out for and what examples would you supply to your clients as evidence of effective behaviour?

1. a production team consisting of a supervisor and ten semi-skilled operators on a bottling line in a cosmetics factory;

2. a small team of clerical recruitment specialists in the central personnel department of a large financial services company with branches in every major town;

3. a group of telephone-based mail order clerks working evening shifts as part of a 24-hour customer ordering service.

Chapter 10   Decision-making and communication in groups

Question 22

Scenario   Selecting people for select committees

You are the Personnel Director on the main Board of a large charitable organisation devoted to relieving the suffering of children in nations affected by famine and war. The charity has a strong central headquarters in the UK, which provides the overall strategy for the organisation, together with its main policies. Its operations in the field are supervised by regional directors (eg Middle East, Central & Southern Africa etc), who have small staffs responsible for identifying and delivering agreed aid in conjunction with the national authorities and local aid agencies concerned. The organisation's policies include *'always working with local people and organisations to assess problems and propose solutions'*, and a statement that the organisation *'will never expose its staff knowingly to danger caused by military actions'*. The Board has recently considered an appeal from its regional director in central Africa for urgent advice and assistance concerning its work in a nation currently suffering a civil war, mainly based on tribal loyalties.

You have been charged by the Board to set up a special international committee to consider urgently whether to take steps to support the regional director's appeal or to order him to withdraw until the military situation on the ground is resolved. As well as the regional director and his local staff in the country concerned, the headquarters organisation includes a logistics officer, an appeals officer, a director responsible for overseas strategy, a liaison officer responsible for maintaining links with other aid organisations (eg Red Cross/ Green Crescent), and a financial adviser. The HQ also retains a legal adviser and has contacts with a government funded institute for political and economic affairs in Third World nations.

Tasks

1. Who, in the sense of which roles, would you select for this committee, bearing in mind the urgency of the situation for those who are suffering, and the delicacy of the situation from the point of view of all the organisation's staff in the field. Prepare a short paper for the Board announcing the composition of your committee, and justifying your choices.

2. If you were a committee member would you agree to support the appeal or would you suggest an immediate withdrawal until the situation calms down?

Question 23

Consider the five contrasting behaviours for handling conflict shown in Figure 10.6, and in each case give three or four examples of statements that might illustrate the particular form of behaviour. Some examples are suggested to get you started:

Behaviour	Examples of possible statements
Accommodating	*'OK, I'll go along with anything you suggest'*
Competing	*'I'm sorry, but if that idea is not acceptable, too bad!'*
Avoiding	*'I think we should leave things as they are. Let sleeping dogs lie.'*

etc etc

Chapter 11   Leadership and power in organisations

Question 24

State, in relation to the following group tasks and situations, (1) how much authority you would expect the leader to have, and (2) what you would expect to see in terms of (a) leader attributes, (b) individual member characteristics, and (c) team interaction:

1. A simple task with a short time-scale involving a low-cost product,

2. A complex task involving the testing of expensive and complicated equipment within a short time-scale,

3. A demanding task involving group selection of graduate scientists for career posts in a large chemical company.

Set out your results in tabular form, and discuss them with a colleague.

Question 25

a. What are the practical difficulties for managers in changing from an authoritarian to a participative leadership style?

b. In what respects might such a change of style alter the *power* requirements of the manager's job?

Question 26

Henri Fayol's 'Principles of Management' (see Chapter 2 Figure 2.5) were first expounded some 80 years ago. From the point of view of the 1990's, carry out an analysis of Fayol's 'Principles', indicating which of them are now irrelevant, and which are as applicable now as they were in 1916. What does your answer suggest as to the value of the *'reflective practitioner'* in the field of management and organisational behaviour?

Chapter 12   Stress and conflict in organisations

Question 27

List the potential sources of stress for a senior personnel manager in a line-orientated business that has just been taken over by a rival company. Focus your attention particularly on:

1. organisational factors

2. work relationships

3. job factors

and give specific examples of what you would regard as the stress triggers under each heading.

Question 28

One of your organisation's values as set out in its mission statement is *'To care for our employees'*. You have been asked to conduct an organisation-wide welfare/stress audit covering the last twelve months.

1. Where, or how, are you likely to find the information for such an audit?

2. What indicators of stress would you use for each of the following groups of employees:

    a. clerical staff?

    b   skilled maintenance staff?

    c   middle management?

Question 29

Consider (a) how the following types of organisation might approach the subject of conflict, and (b) what preferred methods they might employ to deal with conflict:

1. a paternalistic organisation that has grown out of a family-owned business?

2. a succesful electronics manufacturer determined to achieve 'excellence' in a highly competitive market?

Compare your findings with a colleague and discuss any major dfifferences in your results.

Chapter 13   Organisation culture

Question 30

Whose interests are more likely to be given priority in the organisation culture of the following organisations:

1. A charitable organisation whose charismatic founder, at age 80, is still serving in the role of non-executive Chairman?

2. A Japanese-owned motor-vehicle manufacturer based in Britain and with dealerships at home and overseas?

3. A rapidly-growing company in the fast-food business?

Question 31

Scenario   The artefacts of culture

You have joined a local management group visiting a well-known firm in the area. You have never set foot inside the place until today. All you know is that the company was started over twenty years ago by a woman who by all accounts is a 'bit of a character', and has grown from one shop cum garage to a multi-million pound business with over 1000 retail outlets and its own factory.

Your first port of call is the Factory Shop, where you await your official guide. You are aware of a range of slogans in the shop, pointing out the importance of the natural environment and proclaiming that none of the company's products is tested on animals. When your guide takes you all to the new administrative headquarters, you notice that the building is in the style of a Chinese pagoda. Around the corridors are further slogans about the environment, natural products and the significance of tribal people's and their remedies. There are also numerous notices about staff matters.

In the manufacturing areas, which are scrupulously clean and tidy, visitors' attention is drawn to the range of natural products, such as bananas, brazil nuts and cocoa butter, used in the company's preparations. Hours of work are flexible for individuals, and many work part-time, but every production shift is fully manned when all the lines are operating. All staff at very little cost can make use of the company's well-fitted, professionally-staffed creche for their young children between 0800 - 1800 hours.

In the warehouse goods are stacked according to country of destination, and each area is clearly marked 'Australia, Brazil, Japan, Sweden etc', so that the visitor is struck by the vast number of overseas customers. A wall-mounted graph shows the company's rising production figures over the last five years, and in one corner is a display of South American Indian craftware.

As you leave you are given a brief history of the company on a leaflet that announces that it was 'produced on environmentally-friendly paper from renewable resources'.

Tasks

1. What do you make of the values being expressed at this firm through its various artefacts? Produce a list of values you are aware of.

2. How would you describe the culture of this organisation?

Discuss your results in your tutorial group.

Question 32

1. Give examples of *values, norms, rituals* and *traditions* that you might expect to see in the culture of the following different types of organisation:

    a. A major religious group (select just *one* from Christian, Jewish, Muslim etc)

    b. A world-wide producer of soft drinks

    c. A market-leading hotel chain in a domestic market

Set out your answer in tabular form to show the dimensions and components of each culture, as follows:

Cultural dimension	Cultural components		
	Religious Group	Soft drinks producer	Hotel chain
Values			
Norms			
Rituals			
Traditions			

2. What would you say were the most important components for each organisation, and why?

Chapter 14 Organisational change and development

Question 33

1. What are the main factors affecting an organisation's ability to react successfully to sudden and unplanned change? Give some examples in each case.

2. To what extent can an organisation prepare for unexpected contingencies as part of a planned approach to change?

Question 34

Scenario *Triggering change from the outside*

Your company has established itself over the years as one of the world's most successful airlines. It operates out of Europe, is independent of state funding, and owns a substantial fleet of long and short-haul aircraft, some of which are the latest models of modern jets, and others have been in service for many years. The company operates scheduled flights to every major capital city in the world, and is also licensed to fly to other destinations, mainly holiday centres (eg Florida, the Caribbean, Seychelles etc).

The company's mission statement includes two principal concerns — (1) *total commitment to safety*, and (2) *total commitment to customer service*. To support these key values the company spends a substantial sum on the recruitment of suitably-qualified employees, and their subsequent training and retraining. Flight crew are required to undertake continuing competence tests every six months, cabin crew undertake regular cabin safety exercises, and there are systematic training opportunities for ground crew engineers and check-in staff.

The company operates a principal repair and maintenance facility at its home base, and has substantial smaller facilities at every major capital airport. Elsewhere it employs sub-contractors to undertake routine checks and maintenance.

The company recognises the competitive nature of the business, and employs a busy Marketing Division at headquarters designed to ensure that (a) the company's name, reputation and services are constantly in the public eye, and (b) there is a full flow of relevant market information about customers, competitors, suppliers and government licensing bodies world-wide.

Task

What *external* triggers of change could cause a major effect (good or bad) on this company's business success? Include in your response some reference to the impact of the following:

1. Competitive environment
2. Customer needs (present and future)
3. Suppliers of aircraft
4. Suppliers of maintenance services
5. Suppliers of cabin meals etc
6. Political action by governments overseas
7. Strikes or similar action by local Air Traffic Controllers
8. Campaigning by environmental pressure groups.

Question 35

Scenario *Applying the force-field theory in practice*

A unionised engineering company manufacturing high-quality products for customers at home and overseas is becoming aware that it is losing ground to competitors in both markets. The basic problem appears to be twofold — firstly, productivity is falling behind competitors, who seem to be producing goods more quickly and at lower unit-cost than the company's products. Secondly, there is an inflexibility in the way goods are manufactured, and competitors seem better able to adapt their procedures to produce non-standard items.

The company's senior management have established a small sub-group, consisting of the Production, Marketing and Personnel directors and a few specialist advisers to recommend changes in production processes with a view to moving into more productive and flexible methods. They have had an initial meeting with the senior union representatives in which they proposed a rapid phasing out of the present small batch assembly line system, and its replacement with a Flexible Manufacturing System based on small groups of computer-controlled machine tools. Subject to union agreement in principle to the plan, the company will agree to a no redundancy clause. However, jobs will have to be redesigned along more flexible lines, individuals will have to be trained in the use of new procedures arising from changes in technology, and several existing jobs will disappear. Pay levels will be no less than at present, but bonus arrangements will henceforth be on a group not individual basis.

The union representatives' initial response was to say that they were happy to discuss improvements that they thought could be made to the existing system, but were unhappy with the prospects of wholesale change. They argued that the present workforce was achieving the best productivity since the small batch assembly system had been introduced two years ago, and that people were settled in their jobs.

Tasks

1. Carry out a 'Force-Field Analysis' of the above situation, indicating:

    a. what you think are the most significant forces on each side,

    b. at what points you as senior management would *increase* the pressure for change,

    c. at what points you would seek to *reduce* the resisting forces.

Chapter 15   Designing work and jobs

Question 36

You and a colleague from the Personnel department have been assigned the task of drawing up a 'Code of Good Practice in Job Design' aimed at helping managers in line operations to improve employee motivation and performance. What key messages would you want to put across in this situation? List the points you would include in the code in an appropriate order.

Question 37

Scenario   Creating challenging jobs

The Executive Board of your company (*either* choose (1) a manufacturer of consumer goods *or* (2) a financial service employing mostly clerks and administrative staff) has decided that current approaches to job design are no longer cost-effective. The high degree of specialisation has led to a severe lack of flexibility at the point of manufacture (or customer-interface, in the service industry). A recent audit of employee attitudes carried out by a firm of consultants suggests that many employees find little challenge in their jobs, and are frequently bored. The introduction of technology into the workplace, whilst welcomed initially, has only confirmed the repetitive nature of most jobs at the operating level. Staff turnover has not been a problem due to the unemployment situation in the economy, but staff motivation is low, sickness absence has increased and the number of errors caused by employee mistakes has increased noticeably. The attitude survey also discovered that if one employee made a mistake and another employee noticed it, he (or she) would tend to take no action because *'It isn't in my job description!'*

The Board now wants you to report on the feasibility of introducing at operational levels *either*

1) a job enrichment programme, *or*

2) an autonomous work group approach to organisation.

Tasks

1. Prepare a short paper for the directors explaining what the two alternatives would mean in practice.

2. Recommend *one* of the alternatives, giving your reasons.

3. Give some specific examples of how you would see your chosen system working in practice.

Question 38

1. Examine the following competency requirements for a senior Personnel role reporting to the Director of Personnel in a large public utility, and then suggest two or three possible performance criteria for each:

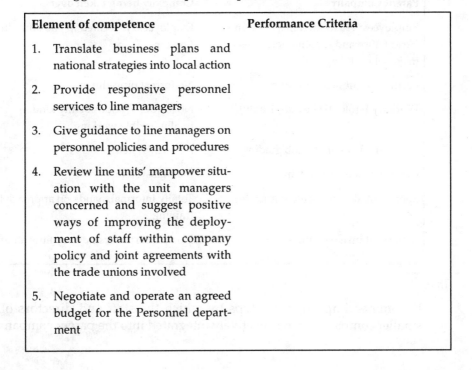

Element of competence	Performance Criteria
1. Translate business plans and national strategies into local action	
2. Provide responsive personnel services to line managers	
3. Give guidance to line managers on personnel policies and procedures	
4. Review line units' manpower situation with the unit managers concerned and suggest positive ways of improving the deployment of staff within company policy and joint agreements with the trade unions involved	
5. Negotiate and operate an agreed budget for the Personnel department	

2. Compare your list of criteria with other members of your tutorial group. What has this exercise demonstrated to you about the task of defining appropriate performance criteria for managerial positions?

Chapter 16 Human resource management, personnel policies & organisational behaviour

Question 39

Scenario *Handling people problems in a takeover*

A medium-sized company operating in the professional training/ publishing business has finally agreed terms for the takeover of a smaller rival in the publishing business. The personnel adviser to the company making the takeover has been asked to examine the personnel implications of the takeover with a view to making recommendations as to how the staff, including directors, of the smaller company can successfully, and fairly, be incorporated into the new parent. There will be no redundancies from the smaller company, which will keep its publishing name and logo, and will retain its two remaining directors on a new Board which will contain two directors from the parent company. Brief details of the two organisations are supplied to enable you as personnel adviser to examine the situation and make your recommendations.

Parent Company	Company being taken over
Employees: 125 located in a London Head Office and six other locations in major cities in England	Employees: 15 located in one office in London
Formal recruitment procedure	No formal procedures
Written job roles (ie key tasks only)	No job descriptions of any kind — totally flexible working
Established system for job grading	No such system
Computerised pay system	Manual system
Some formal training (eg induction)	Totally informal, hands-on approach to training
Some staff turnover and absences	No staff turnover and very little absence

Task

Recommend appropriate steps by which the staff and directors of the smaller company can be effectively integrated into the parent company.

Question 40

With what sort of policies might an influential Personnel department contribute to the development of an organisation culture based on the concept that customer/ client/ patient needs are best met through the efficiency of the organisation's employees led by effective management?

Share your list of policies with a colleague and discuss any differences between you.

Chapter 17   Organisational behaviour and strategic management

Question 41

1. What links are there between organisational behaviour and an organisation's strategic review of its internal environment? Draw up a list of these links, with explanations.

2. What, in your opinion, are the *three* most important aspects of such a review in terms of their impact on individual and group behaviour?

Compare your answers with a colleague and discuss any difference in priorities.

Question 42

1. Select any *five* of the nine units of competence referred to in paragraph 21, and in each case suggest two or three examples of behaviour you would look for in effective senior managers. Set out your results in tabular form and then discuss them with members of your tutorial group

2. What do your answers say about the influence of senior management on organisational behaviour?

Chapter 18   International aspects of organisational behaviour

Question 43

Your company manufactures electronic sub-components for a wide variety of military and civilian applications. Hitherto, mainly because of defence considerations, the company has supplied primarily domestic markets. Now, however, the Board has decided to expand both its customer base and its supplier chain in order to deal on a worldwide basis. What issues will the company have to face in respect of:

(a) potential overseas customers?

(b) potential overseas suppliers of components and raw materials?

Question 44

1. Taking into account, but without following them slavishly, the ideas of Kluckhohn, Strodtbeck and Hofstede, draw up your own list of variables that you would like to see used to test cross-cultural differences and similarities.

2. Compare your list with colleagues and see if any consensus emerges as to the most important issues needing to be addressed by organisations affected by cultural differences.

Part three

Case studies of organisational behaviour

This final part of the book comprises ten case-studies representing a range of issues in organisational behaviour in a cross-section of environments - manufacturing, service industries, retail, and public sector organisations. All the examples are taken directly from, or based on, real situations, drawn in most cases from the public domain. Some material was supplied by particular individuals, whose help is acknowledged.

Each case is followed by three or more suggested questions, but lecturers and tutors are free to pose their own questions if they wish. In order to link the substance of each case with relevant topics discussed earlier in the text, references are given to direct students towards appropriate chapters. This is not to say that they will find the 'answers' there, for there is usually no one correct response to the issues raised, but they should find points of theory and/ or practice which will help in formulating a considered reply to the questions asked.

Case-studies (with chapter references)

1. The Pros and Cons of Devolution — to Divide yet Rule
   Chapters 2, 3 & 13

2. Integrated Patient Care — A New Approach in Hospitals
   Chapters 14 & 15

3. Overcoming the Past at Rolls Royce Motors
   Chapters 3, 11 & 15

4. Communicating with Staff — the John Lewis Approach
   Chapters 7, 10 & 12

5. Focusing on Competence at Royal Mail
   Chapters 2 & 15

6. Creating Integration and Common Purpose in Financial Services
   Chapter 14

7. Sainsbury's — Developing a Company Culture in Retailing
   Chapter 13

8. Handling Stress in the Emergency Services
   Chapters 5, 6 & 12

9. Leadership and Learning — an Individual Case
   Chapters 7, 8, 9 & 11

10. Organisational Behaviour — the Global Dimension
    Chapter 18

Case studies

Case study 1   The pros and cons of devolution — to divide yet rule

The increasing trend towards flatter, devolved organisation structures brings both benefits and disadvantages. On the one hand, profit and cost centres are identified, managers are given greater freedom to manage them,and the net result to the parent organisation is greater profitability or efficiency, certainly over the short term and for some over the long term as well. On the other hand, the new units are frequently given little time in which to demonstrate their effectiveness (commonly a year to 18 months, instead of 2-3 years), and because of the pressures to achieve results in such a short time-span, competition with other units increases. As they begin to work against each other's interests, internal conflict increases and little is attempted by way of training and management development to prepare the organisation's human resources for meeting the longer-term future of the organisation. The key to success seems to have much to do with the strategic direction and vision of the top management, including finding a viable supporting role for a corporate personnel function.

A major British motorists' organisation began a decentralisation process in the early 1990's. The intention was to achieve a greater added value in making its services (breakdown and vehicle recovery services, motor insurance, traffic reports etc) available to the membership, to provide its services more efficiently than its competitors, and as a result to increase its membership base. The organisation is a not-for-profit company with some 8 million motoring members, and more than 3 million other customers (eg for insurance). By 1990 the company had more than 12,000 staff and over 40 different business activities, reflecting the organisation's multifarious efforts to identify and meet its customers' and members' needs. It was decided by the Board of Management that the organisation would have to be streamlined in order to remain competitive. Thus, business activities that contributed little or nothing to added value were disposed of, whilst those that *were* contributing were reorganised into four major groupings around the company's key markets/activities — private motorists in membership, motorists seeking insurance, business and commercial users, and corporate headquarters.

A major decision, perhaps *the* major decision, to be made was what and how much responsibility should be delegated from the centre. It was relatively easy to look at the first three groups' market place and set reasonably demanding targets for financial return, levels of business activity and

355

overall efficiency in the use of resources. It was much less easy to decide how to organise cross-group matters (eg when a member wanted advice on insurance as well as on membership issues) or centrally-provided services (eg personnel, property management etc). For example, a system of inter-group charging was introduced to cater for time 'given' to other groups for services to members/ customers. This has had to be refined to minimise internal conflict. On the provision of central services, it was agreed early on that core terms and conditions of employment (eg job security, pensions and health and safety) would be the same for all staff, but that everything else would be negotiable (ie salaries, holiday entitlements etc). This system eventually caused problems of perceived 'unfair' differentials between staff ostensibly working for the same organisation, but, because they worked for different groups, having different basic terms of employment. This eventually had to be sorted out by corporate personnel who inter-vened with top management support to coordinate pay and conditions, whilst allowing the groups to retain some flexibility.

Competition between groups led to some confusion in the staff concerning whom they worked for — the organisation itself or just their part of it? This required the top management to re-emphasise the corporate mission with its attendant policies, so as to put group activities and priori-ties into a proper organisation-wide perspective. This included a policy on management development to ensure that managers were regarded as a resource for the organisation as a whole, and not just the property of any one group. This policy ensured that managers once again had an incentive to move round the organisation instead of staying in one role in one group, which was a trend that was emerging under the original devolution arrangements. Additionally, in order to encourage collaboration between groups, and between them and the centre, it was decided to amend the management performance pay scheme to reduce the link with *group* results and increase the link with overall *company* results.

The devolution process in the organisation at first began to endanger the essential core of the company. Clearly, the move from central control and direction to decentralis-ation was accompanied by several unexpected and unwanted consequences both between the newly-formed groups, and between them and the centre. However, once the top management began to see where the problems were arising, they were able to take corrective action. Basically this meant making finer distinctions between the respec-tive roles of the centre and each group, and setting standards for the conduct of inter-group relations. The key word being emphasised now at the company is 'partnership', and this important value is perceived as going a long way towards avoiding unhelpful competition internally, whilst still encouraging the separate parts of the organisation to take greater responsibility for their operations, and hence the success of the business as a whole.

Questions

1. What does this case-study tell you about the inherent conflict and tensions that exist in organisations undergoing structural change?

2. (a) How would you split the responsibility for personnel management between the centre and each of the three operating groups?

   (b) What key personnel policies would you advise to embrace centre-group relationships?

3. How important is the company's mission or vision statement to an organisation that is undertaking a process of decentralisation?

Case study 2   Integrated patient care — A new approach to hospital care

Brighton Health Care NHS Trust is one of seven sites selected by the UK Department of Health to test the concept of Integrated Patient Care (IPC). The basis of this concept is to organise care around the needs of the patient rather than around the requirements of medical and nursing procedures. As with flexible manufacturing systems and autonomous work groups in manufacturing industries, the IPC concept is delivered through self-contained work units where the physical layout of the workspace, machines, and materials are planned with the customer, or in this case the patient, in mind.

The implementation of IPC requires a multi-skilled team of carers with specialists brought in as necessary. This implies a more or less continuing process of team-building for all staff involved, extension training for staff who have been trained in more specialist techniques, and similar opportunities for general nurses to obtain experience in more specialised aspects of patient care. A key aspect of the IPC concept is that patients are involved in their own care and play a part, albeit temporarily, in the team's work.

At Brighton the key features of the IPC concept, which is being introduced into the childbirth and maternity wards, include the following:

❏ patients with similar needs are grouped together in the same part of the hospital

❏ an increasing amount of direct care is given to patients

❏ support services are being integrated into the units concerned so as to bring them closer to the patients

❏ multi-skilled and multi-disciplinary teams are being introduced as a central feature of the concept of patient care

An initial attempt to commence the concept in the gastro-enterology department had to be abandoned due to the difficult physical layout of buildings constructed in Victorian times.

The anticipated outcomes for IPC are as follows:

❏ improved patient satisfaction with their care in hospital

❏ better quality of care

❏ proportionately more time spent on patient care

❏ lower costs of providing care

❏ reduction in administration (form-filling etc)

❏ reduced stays in hospital by patients

❏ fewer bed moves by patients

❏ faster turn-round of laboratory and other diagnostic activities

The new approach to patient care will gradually be extended to other pilot areas in the Trust. In the meantime the concept's application in the maternity area will be closely watched and evaluated over the next twelve months.

Questions:

1. What do you think might be the staff training implications of the Integrated Patient Care concept for:

   (a) nursing sisters/ charge nurses?

   (b) other trained nursing staff?

   (c) nurses under training?

   (d) medical staff?

   (e) specialist staff such as physiotherapists, dietitians etc?

2. What are the resource implications for the hospital's senior management of the concept of taking care to the patient?

3. How do you think you might benefit from such an approach if you were a patient in an IPC unit?

Case study 3 Overcoming the past at Rolls Royce Motors

Like most other British car manufacturers Rolls Royce has experienced all the practical difficulties of dealing with craft-based trade unions, each anxious to represent the narrow range of skills of its membership in its relations both with the Company and with other unions. A general agreement with the unions that the *status quo* would be retained until agreement to change were reached successfully ensured that many changes never saw the light of day, whilst others were smothered at birth. Jobs were tightly specified, which meant there was little room for flexibility in work practices. In addition to this extremely mechanistic and essentially fragmented approach to operations, the management structure was highly bureaucratic. It was the effect of the worldwide recession in 1991/2 that brought matters to a head for the Company. Sales had fallen drastically over those two years and the Company had gone into the red. In order to cut costs a number of measures were put into effect including substantial redundancies amongst the employees.

The Managing Director with the support of his board had already in 1991 decided that a massive restructuring of the organisation was necessary. Firstly, a new labour contract was agreed with the unions, and the basis of this was complete labour flexibility within the capability of each individual. No longer were jobs defined narrowly and with an exclusive skill or craft basis. Breadth of skill and flexibility of working became the norm. The employee veto on change contained in the status quo agreement of the past was abandoned.

Secondly, a new management structure was introduced. Some three levels of management in the old hierarchy were swept away, and the first-line supervisory posts were all abolished. In place of the latter work team leaders were introduced, not as a separate layer of management but as leading members of the shop floor work teams. Groups based on ten teams each comprising ten employees were established, with each team leader reporting to a group operations manager. This sizeable span of control (ie 10 team leaders) meant that each operations manager had to work through his team leaders rather than get involved personally in day to day decisions as the old-style foremen would have done. The role of team leader was crucial in this changed structure, but the individuals concerned responded well to the opportunity to exercise their own initiative and to develop their own team using the considerable amount of authority they had been given.

A major change in the way operating teams were serviced was introduced. Instead of calling on remotely-located central services (eg engineering, maintenance, inventory etc), the operations managers (13 in all) were supplied with all the necessary facilities in their work area. The

The benefits of the changes can be summarised as follows:

1. the Company has returned into profit and positive cash flow

2. the time to produce one motorcar has been reduced from 70 days to 28 days

3. little additional capital investment has been required to achieve these improvements

4. on time deliveries to dealers has improved from only 50% to nearly 100%

5. the number of part-built cars in progress has been reduced from 600 to 200 at any one time

6. an overall improvement in labour productivity of 35% has been achieved

Further changes are being introduced, including cross-functional change teams representing different interest groups vertically throughout the structure from director-level to team-worker, and new product development teams. In the space of five years, the production efficiency and capability of Rolls Royce has been transformed from mediocre to outstanding, and worthy of the end-product itself.

Questions:

1. In what ways could *external* circumstances be said to have influenced the nature and speed of change at Roll Royce Motors?

2. What training would you anticipate being needed in order to get the best out of newly-appointed team leaders and operations managers?

3. What does this case history tell you about the nature of work and job design?

Case study 4 Communicating with staff — the John Lewis approach

The flourishing retail business begun by John Lewis in 1864 with one small shop specialising in selling textiles now numbers more than 20 department stores and over 100 supermarkets in locations from Aberdeen to the South Coast of England. Such growth over 130 years is by no means unknown in the British retail trade (eg Marks & Spencer). There is, however, something distinctly unique about the John Lewis Partnership, and it is contained in that word 'Partnership'. John Lewis himself was by all accounts an honest and fair businessman, as well as a prosperous one. It was one of Lewis's sons, Spedan Lewis, who in the early 1900's, aware that the family were drawing more from the business than the whole of the pay-bill of the employees, decided to develop the concept of partnership with the employees. Spedan was not just an armchair philanthropist. He took the view that running a business leaves little room for error, especially against the background of competition *necessary to the general zest of life and to the development and maintenance of ability'.* However, he recognised that in this situation, *'Organisation, no matter how elaborate, comes at last to the point where there has to be trust.'.* Thus was born the John Lewis Partnership, where all the profits of the business, after taking into account the expenses of the business, including the servicing of capital, are payable to the employees. Of course, it is recognised that for future development of the business it is vital to plough back a good proportion of the profits into the business itself. However, to give an example, in 1992 the sum of £34m of taxed profits was retained in the business, whilst over £28m of pre-tax profits were distributed to employees in the form of a cash bonus amounting to 8% of annual pay. In previous years the bonus has varied from a peak of 24% in 1987 to the 8% just mentioned.

It was made clear from the very early days of the business that employees were to be co-owners of the enterprise, and should have an appropriate say in its direction and policies. Lewis also recognised that running a business required expertise and leadership, and established a system which secured a *'degree of democratic influence that is compatible with perceptive and successful management.'* The system effectively ensures that the directors and managers who decide and implement business decisions are accountable to the employees, who are always referred to as 'partners'. The mechanics of the system are as follows:

The management chain from top down consists principally of the following:

❏ Chairman of the Partnership, who appoints the senior management, influences policy and can veto major decisions; he can only be removed from office by the Trustees of the Constitution

❐ Central Board, consisting of the Chairman, Deputy Chairman and ten directors, five appointed by Chairman and five elected by the Central Council (see below)

❐ Directors of the Operating Divisions, who submit their proposals for future trading and resourcing to the Board, and who are accountable for the performance of their divisions

❐ Branch Heads, Principal Buyers and other operational management staff

The partners' chain from the bottom up is structured as follows:

❐ Partners, who make their opinions known through the registrars and councils, and who elect members to the latter

❐ Registrars, senior managers who act as ombudsmen and guardians of the Company's Constitution

❐ Branch Councils, composed mainly of Partners, perform a local role in discussing trading issues as well as pay, staffing levels and other aspects of employment conditions; no changes may be made to employment conditions without the knowledge and consent of the Council.

❐ Central Council, composed of some 130 members, of whom no more than one fifth may be appointed by the management, the others being elected annually by secret ballot of the Partners, is the central forum of the Company; the Chairman is required to give an annual account of his stewardship to this body; the Council appoints three members of the four Trustees of the Constitution, which has the power to remove the Chairman

Not surprisngly, in the light of the participative processes and mechanisms, the Company is able to say

> 'With this extensive provision for the wellbeing of its members, and for their participation in its affairs, the Partnership has little need of traditional trade union procedures.'

Source of quotations: Company brochure 'John Lewis Partnership', November 1993

Questions:

1. Why do you think such a laudable policy as profit-sharing, which appears to have worked well at John Lewis for more than a century has not been taken up by other businesses in (a) retailing, and (b) other industries?

2. What view of organisational behaviour (ie unitary, pluralistic etc) is being taken by the Partnership, and what does this say about the Company's attitude towards internal conflicts and disagreements?

3. What does this case suggest as to the principal motivational techniques adopted by the Company?

Case study 5   Focusing on competence at Royal Mail

Royal Mail with 159,000 employees and a turnover of £4.54bn is by far the largest member of the Post Office Corporation. Like many other public sector organisations in recent years it has been required to adopt an enterprise culture, moving it from a public bureaucracy to a commercially-viable operation. So far there has been considerable success in this transformation. In its Annual Report for 1994-5 the Post Office's Chief Executive was able to announce that the corporation had exceeded its *Group targets, and that 'No other major post office in the world has notched up 19 consecutive years of subsidy-free profit...'* It is recognised that in this electronic age, postal services are in real competition with other forms of communication such as the telephone, fax , E-mail and computerised home shopping. Nevertheless, some 67 million items of mail are posted every working day in Britain. Staying ahead as a business in these circumstances requires Royal Mail not only to provide a speedy and efficient collection and delivery service, but also to devise appropriate strategies to meet customers' communication needs in the light of electronic technology.

In 1992 Royal Mail underwent a major reorganisation from director-level down to postman. The business was given a sharper focus, bureaucracy was cut back, a total quality programme was introduced, and staff numbers were significantly reduced. Culturally, the organisation was moving away from being a relatively efficient business bureaucracy rather absorbed with its internal problems to becoming a lean commercial organisation focusing on the needs of its customers. This cultural change could only take root if the staff at Royal Mail felt able to meet the requirements of the new order, as well as giving their initial assent to the idea. In the past there had been few job descriptions, and those that did exist were expressed in terms of *inputs* rather than on the *outputs* sought by customers. Even less information was available about *performance standards.* Both the expectations of managers and the perceptions of employees were confused. Management styles were authoritarian, and there was an unwillingness to admit what they did not know. Clearly a major rethink on jobs and standards had to be undertaken. A common language had to be developed to enable cross-functional movement between jobs in a flatter organisation whose objectives were primarily customer-orientated.

In 1993 the organisation's senior management decided to introducing a competence-based model of job design and work performance as part of the development of a 'learning organisation' strategy for human resource management. The first step involved piloting the competence approach using Delivery Managers in the North East of England as the spearhead. Initially approaches were made to key managers and staff in the area, their needs and issues were discussed and questions raised. This tactic enabled the commitment of line managers to be obtained, and this was seen as crucial by the headquarters team guiding the competence exercise. Over the course of 18 months, the structure of jobs was mapped out, training implications clarified and coaching skills for managers introduced. Job requirements were expressed originally as needs or requirements, but as the pilot exercise progressed, they were gradually transformed into competency statements arising out of the key accountabilities of each job identified.

A Royal Mail Competence Framework was developed, based on the following critical areas of competence:

1. Communicating for Results — Oral
2. Communicating for Results — Written
3. Improving the Business
4. Making Decisions
5. Managing Change
6. Managing Commercially
7. Managing Resources
8. Managing Yourself
9. Satisfying Customers
10. Working with People

The majority of these ten areas of competence are now applied to every job in the work structure, but with varying degrees of requirement depending on the complexity and responsibility of the job. Each competence is described briefly, for example as in 'Making Decisions':

'To develop and maintain appropriate systems, paper or computer-based, to enable informed decison-making. To ensure that decisions are based on the analysis of relevant information and that the consequences are thought through and communicated appropriately.'

In the case of a junior role (eg Absence Clerk) the requirement is modest:

'Maintains and uses information, checking it for accuracy and completeness. Makes decisions by selecting the best option from a range of possible solutions. Knows when and how to seek guidance.'

Examples of each requirement are given, and in this case include:

'Builds communication channels with line managers to ensure that information is conveyed and recorded accurately.'

In a more senior role (eg Area Personnel Manager) the requirement may be expressed thus: *'Makes sound decisions on issues key to the success of the business unit, translating and making intelligible complex information. Selects and orders that information, forecasting and analysing the options, taking full account of the implications of inaccuracy and error and of any contentiousness and consequences that it might have.'* An example of the application of this competence is as follows:

'Gives guidance on personnel policies and procedures to line managers and team members, often in sensitive situations......Ensures that business policy and employment legislation is interpreted consistently and correctly......'

The framework that has been developed serves as a guide to good practice rather than a blueprint to be followed in every part of the organisation. Royal Mail has nine operating divisions, of 22,000 employees each, as well as nine functional groups, and each division/ group is therefore able to adapt the details of the framework to their own needs, thus gaining 'ownership' of their sets of competences. The system is not linked to job evaluation or pay, but is intended to contribute to staff selection, appraisal, succession planning, job training, career development, and de-selection. It is also intended that the framework will reinforce the success culture of Royal Mail.

Acknowledgement: Based on information supplied by Annette Hutchinson, Employee Development Strategy Manager, Royal Mail Headquarters, London EC1V 9HQ

Questions

1. What is the value to a large organisation of devising a competence framework for its job structure?

2. How far do you think Royal Mail's past bureaucracy was able to facilitate the introduction of the competence framework? In what ways might it have *hindered* the process?

3. What would you think are the major cost elements in devising such a framework, and what benefits would you expect from that investment?

Case study 6   Creating integration and common purpose in financial services

A major building society decided to bring its rather disparate non-retail businesses together in a new division within the overall structure of the business. The five businesses concerned — centralised mortgage provision, investment service for professional investors, commercial lending, postal savings accounts and telephone banking service — were scattered across the UK. Little or no integration of functions took place, there was no shared purpose or goals, and no common culture.

The society decided to invite a small consultancy firm specialising in organisation development to help support the process of change from scattered group with no shared aims to a new division of people able to develop their own aims, culture and ways of collaborating. A key objective was to empower the members of the new division to shape its future direction and increase its strategic capability. It was agreed that the consultant involved should work alongside the division general manager, his direct reports and the top 20 managers in the various businesses to form a lead group for change, using a range of interventions at individual, team and organisation levels. These included personal development planning, management skills development, coaching, process consultation, team development and feedback sessions on operational issues. Numerous individual and team sessions were held by the consultant over a 12 month period, during which assessments were made of how the individual businesses contributed to the goals set for the new division, how well they worked within themselves and across the division, what were the relative strengths and weaknesses of the various teams and functions within and between businesses. The pioneering vision and key values for the new division gradually came to into focus for the lead group, and the managers involved began to share these with their own staff. Whilst the vision was applied commonly throughout the separate businesses, values and subsequent behaviours were adapted to meet the needs of each business, which enhanced the acceptance of certain core divisional values by allowing flexibility in others.

Eventually, in the light of the cultural and attitude changes arising from acceptance of the new vision, a new divisional structure emerged, the separate businesses were brought together under one roof, certain facilities were shared, communication channels between businesses were opened up and collaborative projects became more rather than less usual. With greater confidence in the change process came a greater willingness to explore new ideas on the part of managers at every level. As a result one new business was created, a stagnant one given a new lease of life, and the rest saw consistently improved results over the first year. Even with the creation of new or revised teams as a consequence of the restructuring, the general level of motivation remained high. Members of the division saw themselves as rather special, and this sense of being an elite (a Hawthorne Effect) was recognised by the consultant, who advised the divisional general manager that the process of linking in the new division to the rest of the organisation would require some attention from the division's senior managers. Success in one part of a corporate organisation does not necessarily mean that it can be transferred elsewhere in the structure. Indeed if not handled sensibly, and sensitively, it can cause de-motivation in other divisions. This tranference of learning and success to the other divisions is the next assignment for the consultancy.

Source: This case-study was developed from material supplied by Michael Green, Senior Partner of Transitional Space, Middledown Farm, Middledown Road, Marshfield, Wilts SN14 8HX.

Questions:

1. What expertise can an Organisation Development consultant bring to a situation such as the one just described? As well as knowledge and relevant personal experience, what specific skills would you expect such a consultant to possess?

2. What would you say were the triggers of change in this case-study?

3. What do you think would have been the key change issues in this case for the following internal stakeholders:

   a) Individuals?

   b) Teams?

   c) Each business?

   d) Division?

   e) Corporate organisation?

Case study 7   Sainsbury's — developing a company culture in retailing

J. Sainsbury plc, once a modest string of High Street provision stores in a family business, is now a multi-million pound retail chain with over 300 supermarkets in the UK. It employs more than 120,000 staff of whom over 70,000 are part-time. Two thirds of all staff are women, including some 45% of the management staff. Both in its attitude towards staff and its desire to satisfy customers the Company reflects a developing set of fundamental values in the way it conducts its business — its culture.

In respect of staff, the Company aims to maintain *'a well-trained workforce with a good balance of people of all ages and backgrounds...'.* The Company operates a retail training scheme for junior employees and a retail management training scheme for A-level school-leavers. It also was among the first companies to pilot the employment of older (ie retired) workers in customer service roles, which has been very successful. Such staff are employed on a part-time basis, but on permanent contracts so that they can benefit from profit-sharing and other company benefits. Women's needs for flexible and part-time work in a permanent position with career opportunities have been recognised by the Company, which, acknowledging the unsocial hours in the retail trade, has introduced part-time opportunities for women at supervisory and first-line management levels. All staff vacancies below senior management are advertised internally on a weekly basis, and the Company expects a substantial proportion of jobs to be filled by promotion from within.

In respect of customers, who in a real sense also represent the interests of the local community, the Company selects its sites and stores in accordance with environmental as well as convenience considerations. Store design *'will be appropriate to local building styles and materials....' and 'Comprehensive landscaping schemes are applied to each new site.... Wherever possible existing vegetation is used........In a single year Sainsbury's plants around 50,000 trees and half a million shrubs.'*

In its stores the Company has developed the concept of the 'low energy store', which has reduced the amount of electricity used in store lighting, refrigeration systems, heating and air-conditioning plant and in its in-store bakeries. The Company aims to minimise the packaging content of its products, consistent with hygiene and damage requirements. It uses recycled material for its carrier bags, uses shrinkwrap rather than cardboard boxes where practicable, and uses a thinner plastic film for the packaging of products such as bacon and fresh fruit. In terms of the *contents* of packages, Sainsbury's aims to provide environmentally friendlier products, some produced organically, others with certain chemicals removed (eg phosphates). No cosmetics items are tested on animals, CFC gases are no longer used in aerosol sprays, and most paper products (toilet rolls, kitchen towels etc) are made from high-grade recycled paper. Finally, so as to reassure customers of general hygiene and efficiency, as well as to create an appropriate image of smartness for a food store, the Company has spent considerable time and money in designing, trialling and issuing a new staff uniform.

Source of quotations: Company Information leaflets

Questions:

1. What does the above account tell you about the organisation culture at Sainsbury's?
2. Which stakeholders are especially affected by the actions taken by the Company, and how are they affected?
3. Design a company mission statement on the basis of (a) what you have read in the above account, and (b) your answers to the first two questions.

Case study 8   Handling stress in the emergency services

There are few employees whose jobs are completely stress-free, but there are large numbers whose work regularly brings them into contact with stress in major proportions — these are the front-line police, fire brigade and ambulance personnel who make up the bulk of the emergency services in the UK. In recent years psychologists have come to recognise a condition known as post-traumatic stress syndrome, which is a pattern of behavioural symptoms that develop some time after an event. Typical symptoms include nightmares, sudden recall of the event during waking hours with accompanying emotional reactions, enhanced sense of detachment from others, loss of interest in job, and inattentiveness. In an emergency the individuals helping to rescue injured people or recover dead bodies are all actively engaged in 'doing' activities, often under great time pressures and invariably in collaboration with others. At this stage there is no time for reflection, and little time for feeling, since feelings have to be suppressed during the emergency. The dominant culture on the scene is 'Keep calm, reassure the victim, use your training, do your job quickly and efficiently.' At this point there is no allowance for personal feelings and reflections. They are for later.

Studies into stress in the emergency services, however, have indicated that where individual employees have not had an opportunity to air their feelings after a traumatic event, they tend to suppress them, and over the course of months and years find that they have lost touch with their emotional life. Feelings have been frozen out not just at work, but at home and in people's social life. Individuals in this situation can become cold and heartless, some even becoming brutalised and cynical by what they have experienced. For the worst affected individuals, the body's response to this process is to demand more alcohol and cigarettes or another day off, leading to a range of stress-related sickness absence.

It is unrealistic in the case of the emergency services to expect to be able to reduce stress in the work environment. That just isn't possible. What is possible is to enable the employees concerned to cope with trauma, principally by recognising, and dealing with, the feelings it arouses. People, therefore, are being encouraged to talk about feelings after an emergency. This can be done informally with a colleague over a cup of tea in the canteen or a glass of beer in the local pub. More formally it can be done by having a team briefing after the event, in which feelings are shared openly, or by individual counselling with a trained counsellor. At a Police Staff College in the UK, a stress specialist has developed a debriefing process based on what he calls the 'Three F's' — Facts, Feelings, and Future. The facts of an incident are recalled, people's feelings about them are *shared* (ie not necessarily *discussed*), and the future is discussed in terms of (a) how individuals might cope next time, and (b) what steps team members can take to help one another. Where an individual continues to admit to being stressed, or is identified by senior colleagues as still being traumatised, then one-to-one counselling is advised.

In the work environment of the emergency services, the old culture has been one of machismo — *'tough people keep a stiff upper lip'*; *'tough people keep their feelings to themselves'*; *'tough people don't 'go soft' on themselves.'* This is gradually being replaced by a more honest and open acknowledgement of the deeply unhappy and often quite distressing feelings that are experienced by those working in these services.

Recently, with the celebration of peace following the Second World War fifty years ago, individual soldiers, sailors and airmen of that time are being filmed in tears by the television cameras. We see old men crying over events that took place all those years ago, and many are crying *for the first time*, so long have they suppressed their unhappiness and distress. Avoiding such a denial of feelings in those serving presently in the emergency forces will not only minimise their stress and related illnesses, but will enable the community to be even better served by these individuals in the future.

Questions:

1. Consider a typically traumatic event that might be faced by one of the following, and suggest what feelings might be aroused in the individual concerned:

   a) a policeman called to the scene of a murder of a young child

   b) a fireman recovering the charred bodies of an entire family from the remains of their home

   c) an ambulance driver attending at serious road accident, where the victim is conscious but trapped in the vehicle

2. In the example you have chosen to describe, consider what issues might affect the degree of stress suffered by the individual concerned (eg in terms of their age, experience, sex etc)

3. Why do you think it can be helpful to share feelings as a way of reducing stress in work situations? What advantages are there in sharing in the work-team as opposed to sharing on a one-to-one basis?

Case study 9   Leadership and learning — an individual case

John Burroughs' new job was not turning out as happily as he had hoped after his successful interview nine months earlier. His previous position was as a production controller in a large pharmaceutical company, where he had responsibility for some thirty production staff and four supervisors, all women. Everything then had worked smoothly — staff knew what they had to do, rarely questioned any instructions or changes in routines, respected their supervisors and usually achieved their group production bonuses. His own production manager had been an experienced older man, who put him under no pressure unless production targets were not being achieved. It had all been remarkably easy to manage. In putting himself forward for the new job, Burroughs had wanted to find an extra challenge at work, and to make use of his academic and professional training, which had earned him a very good first degree in chemistry and part-qualification for his professional pharmaceutical qualification.

However, in his new post Burroughs was distinctly uneasy. Although still a young man of barely thirty years of age, he had been promoted to take charge of a product development unit composed mainly of research-orientated chemists and pharmacists. The unit was small comprising ten staff in all, of whom five were considered as very bright research workers with good career prospects in front of them, two were junior researchers just out of university, and three staff were people who had spent some time in either production or sales environments. All in all the company's research director reckoned that he could not have put together such a well-rounded and capable product development group. He had a well-balanced team with a variety of skills and experience, and a team leader who was not only well-qualified academically, and could therefore keep up with the research specialists, but, crucially, was aware of the practical implications of product development's activities for the people working on the production lines.

The reality of the situation, however, was that Burroughs felt considerably less than satisfied with the way his unit was working — there seemed little sense of being a team, people (especially the research-orientated types) kept questioning why they were being asked to do certain tasks, seemed disgruntled at the 'interference' in their work by their new manager, whilst the more broadly-experienced members began to display open exasperation at the research specialists' lack of understanding of the needs of production and marketing. Burroughs' research director had already spoken to him as tactfully as he could about the delay in getting one particular product onto the production line, but at this stage had not offered any form of help.

Burroughs had already held a series of meetings with the team to brief them about targets for product development, links with production and marketing, and health and safety issues. With such a highly-intelligent and well-qualified team he hardly expected to have to do more...........

Questions:

1. What do you think are the primary motivational differences between the employees in Burroughs' earlier production team and those in the present research unit?

2. What differences in Burroughs' management style in the two posts do you sense from this account?

3. What do you think are the main problems facing the present group, and how would you suggest that Burroughs re-thinks his leadership strategy?

4. If you were the research director in this situation, what advice or assistance would you think necessary, and why?

Case study 10   Organisational behaviour — the global dimension

There is a wonderful fable by Aesop about a fox and a stork who befriend each other, and as the friendship develops eventually get around to inviting one another for a meal. As you will no doubt remember the fox as host provides his friend with plates and dishes, which of course the stork cannot cope with, so he goes home hungry. When it is his turn, however, he serves up the food in tall, narrow-necked containers, and this time the *fox* cannot eat any of the food! This complete lack of cultural understanding between the two creatures meant that one or other was always going without. It was a 'win-lose' situation every time. This sort of scenario can take place at the international level of human organisations, where one side makes no effort to understand or accommodate the other.

Firms that are successful in selling and expanding in overseas markets have to be good at cultural relations as well providing quality goods or services. A medium-sized British company manufacturing high-quality safety appliances for the off-shore oil-drilling business decided to investigate the possibility of entering the Far Eastern markets of Japan, Singapore, Malaysia and Sarawak. Its first step was to find out as much as possible about the technical aspects of the market, in economic as well as industrial terms. Its second step was to investigate *how* to do business with people in that part of the world. It discovered that with Japan, in particular, it was necessary to proceed cautiously and courteously. Tentative soundings were made through the good offices of governmental and trade bodies in the two countries. The managing director and his marketing colleague attended selected trade fairs in Japan as well as displaying their products and services at UK events. Gradually a network of contacts began to emerge.

Eventually, after many months of groundwork, the two Britons found themselves in a large Japanese city giving a presentation to a group of oil industry executives. Although they did not realise it at the time, this was more than just a sales pitch to a group of 'interested parties', for the Japanese had already made up their minds that these were products they wanted for their rigs, so long as a satisfactory deal could be reached. For a start the products on offer were exceptionally robust, they were simple to operate and extremely cost-effective given the relative weakness of the pound sterling against the yen. However, sheer technical quality and value-for-money was not enough. The Japanese had been doing their homework too, and concluded that this British company could be trusted. The senior executives were seen as having integrity, and the consistency of their production output more than matched what the former claimed for their company. Japanese companies like to enter business deals on a long-term basis, and therefore need to reassure themselves that their suppliers are not only economically viable but also morally trustworthy.

term basis, and therefore need to reassure themselves that their suppliers are not only economically viable but also morally trustworthy.

Before the first deal was signed, the Japanese requested quite detailed information about the range of products, delivery channels and shipment arrangements, technical advice services and payment procedures. Since many of the safety products were relatively small items, the British company often arranged for small quantities to be flown rather than shipped to their destination. The Japanese were keen to question the two directors on the mechanics of this form of delivery to reassure themselves of its reliability as well as its obvious speed. In their turn the British executives questioned their counterparts about matters of importance to them, and this process itself was seen by the Japanese to be a further indication of this company's suitability — nothing was taken for granted.

On the signing of the first major contract, the British chairman was flown out to Japan to meet his opposite number on the Japanese company's board. This was seen as very important by the Japanese, who like to deal with people at an equivalent level, as appropriate, to the various stages of a negotiation. Thus, when production matters are discussed, they are happy for this to be done by production executives, but when sales and marketing issues are at stake, they field their senior marketing executives and expect their opposite numbers to do the same. In this case, whilst negotiations were moving to a conclusion, they were perfectly comfortable with the British company's chief executive and his marketing director, but once the contract was awarded then it was seen as appropriate that the respective figureheads of each company should be present for the signing and attendant trade and press publicity.

The British company never looked back after the first contract, and is now firmly established not only in Japan, but also in all the other major oil-producers in the Far East — a testament to its initial thoroughness, cultural sensitivity and global perspective.

Questions:

1. What qualities would you look for if you were recruiting an overseas sales manager responsible for maintaining and extending business with existing clients in Japan? Explain why these qualities are important.

2. What features of the negotiations with the Japanese do you think the British executives would have found the most trying given the way business is done in the UK?

3. How different might these negotiations have been if the potential customers had been Americans?

Index

Strategic Management
G A Cole

Contents

Part 1 – Purpose and goals, Assessing the environment, Competitive advantage, Strategy formulation, Business plans, Culture, Managing change, Strategic marketing and Personnel, Measuring strategic performance. **Part 2** – Workbook. **Part 3** – Strategic management in practice – case studies.

It is known to be used on BABS, CMS, HND, BTEC Continuing Education, CIM, NVQ 4/5, IM Postgrad Dip, DMS, IPD.

Review comments

'Another Cole masterpiece!'

'Good insight into strategic management. Case studies realistic and relevant.'

'An excellent analysis of a difficult subject area.'

'The layout and spread of case studies are most pleasing.'

'Very well developed. Explains the requirements of strategic management in practical context.'

'De-mystifies the subject.'   Lecturers

1st edition • 284 pp • 245 x 176 mm • 1994 • ISBN 1 85805 099 5

Tackling Coursework
Projects, Assignments, Reports and Presentations

David Parker

This book provides the student with practical guidance on how to approach the course-work requirement of a typical business studies course, i.e. projects, assignments, reports and presentations. The text makes clear the different approaches needed for the different types of coursework, with examples of each in an Appendix, and there is advice on how to conduct research, collect information and present results, in either written or verbal form. It is expected to be used on the following courses: any business studies course at undergraduate (e.g. BABS) or postgraduate (e.g. MBA) level. It would also be useful as a preparatory text for a research degree.

Contents:

Introduction, Dissertations and projects, Essays and papers, Management reports, Seminars and presentations, Research methods. **Appendices:** *Further reading, Example of a dissertation proposal, Example of citations, Dissertation contents, Example of an essay.*

1st edition • 96 pp • 215 x 135 mm • 1994 • ISBN 1 85805 101 0